KU-212-181

Social analysis

a Marxist critique and alternative

V. L. Allen

Longman

LONDON and NEW YORK

Longman Group Limited
Burnt Mill
Harlow
Essex CM20 2JE

Distributed in the United States of America by
Longman Inc., New York

*Associated companies, branches and representatives
throughout the world*

© V. L. Allen, 1975

All rights reserved. No part of this publication
may be reproduced, stored in a retrieval system,
or transmitted in any form or by any means, electronic,
mechanical, photocopying, recording, or otherwise,
without the prior permission of the Copyright owner.

First published, 1975

ISBN 0 582 48300 X cased
ISBN 0 582 48301 8 paper

Set in IBM Journal, 10 on 12 point

*Printed in Great Britain by
J. W. Arrowsmith Ltd, Bristol*

Contents

Preface

This book is about sociological theory in general. A part of it, however, concerns the analysis of organizations and in the rest most of the empirical data is drawn from organizational activity of one kind or another. This emphasis on organizations occurs for two reasons. Firstly it reflects my own interest in organizational activity. Secondly, as with others, a pre-occupation with trade unions led me to organizational theory and then on to general sociological theory. It was an examination of organization theory which enhanced my understanding of general theory and it became a vehicle through which I saw more clearly the defects of general theory. It is its use in this sense which also accounts for its emphasis here.

The background to the book and some details about changes in my own theoretical position are given in the Introduction. There I name people who influenced me in this respect. There are some, however, who have played a continuing, critical, stimulating and positive part and whose impact has not been through their written work, as was largely the case with Gi Baldamus, but through a close interest and identity with what I was doing. Sheila Allen, my closest companion, has influenced me intellec-tually to an extent which would be embarrassing even to try and evaluate. Her ideas, her arguments, her criticisms and even her phrases which some-how I have made my own, pervade my work. Since the early 1960s our friend Dan Muir, a mathematician whose political and methodological interests coincide almost identically with mine, has discussed with me every theoretical issue of any significance and has brought to bear on them his own outstanding expertise. And then there is Roger Cornu who, though working in Aix-en-Provence, has become an integral part of our intellectual milieu, constantly criticizing and suggesting and agreeing. None of these essential people holds any responsibility for what I have written but they share in whatever contribution towards the elaboration and clarification of Marxism this book may make.

If there is one continuing theme in what I have written it is the unity of theory and practice. It is all too easy for one confined to a university

environment, who regards 'thinking' as his particular expertise, to believe
that what he says and writes is relevant to real life. It is so easy that we
have libraries of irrelevant nonsense purporting to explain ordinary
people's lives. In so far as I have been protected from this gargantuan
mistake it is because of my involvement in the struggles of ordinary men
and women, in particular with British coal-miners during the whole time
spent on this book. With these people I have been constantly reminded not
only of the reality of the everyday lives of most people but that what I
had to say had to be intelligible in essential ways to them. It had to tap
their experiences so that they said 'this makes sense to me'. The miners
who have discussed social issues with me must number thousands and are
scattered over all the coalfields of the country. But I have spent much time
with some of them, Michael McGahey, Lawrence Daly, Dai Francis, Jack
Dunn, Arthur Scargill, Bill McLean, Emlyn Williams and Bill Paynter, in
particular, who have taught me the true meaning of an intellectual by the
width and intensity of their reading and by their grasp of complex social
issues. They have queried concepts, disputed analyses and demanded
clarity. I recommend their company to any social scientists who want the
painful and sometimes embarrassing experience of learning intellectual
humility.

Writing a book, of course, is a tedious undertaking dominated by innumerable boring administrative tasks. During the last two years when
these bore down heavily I have received unstinted help from Mrs Audrey
Speak and I am extremely grateful to her.

V.L.A.

The University,   March 1974
Leeds

Acknowledgements

We are grateful to the following for permission to reproduce copyright material:
Editions Anthropos for an atricle by V. L. Allen from *L'Homme et la Société*, No. 15, 1970, and an article by V. L. Allen from *L'Homme et la Société*, No. 4, 1967; Harvard University Press for extracts from *On Law and Economy in Society* by Max Weber, translated by Edward Shils and Max Rheinstein, Copyright 1954 by the President and Fellows of Harvard College; Macmillan Publishing Company Inc. for extracts from *A Comparative Analysis of Complete Organizations* by Amitai Etzioni, Copyright 1961 by The Free Press; Macmillan Publishing Company Inc. for an extract from *Social Theory and Social Structure* by Robert K. Merton; Prentice-Hall Inc. for extracts from *Modern Organizations* by Amitai Etzioni, Copyright 1964, reprinted by permission of Prentice-Hall Inc., Englewood Cliffs, New Jersey; Rotterdam University Press for an article by V. L. Allen from *Mens en Maatschappij*, No. 1, 1972; the editor of *Sociological Review* for an extract from an article by V. L. Allen from *Sociological Review*, Vol. 10, No. 1, March 1962; the author and University of Chicago Press for a letter by L. Coset from *American Journal of Sociology*, 76, No. 1, July 1970; the author and University of Chicago Press for a letter by W. Breed from *American Journal of Sociology*, 76, No. 1, July 1970; the author and University of Chicago Press for a letter by A. Etzioni from *American Journal of Sociology*, 76, No. 1, July 1970; the author and University of Chicago Press for a letter by R. M. Cook from *American Journal of Sociology*, 76, No. 1, July 1970; the University of Chicago Press for extracts from *American Journal of Sociology*, 76; the author and University of Chicago Press for an extract from a book review by R. M. Cook from *American Journal of Sociology*, 75, January 1970, and John Wiley & Sons Inc. for extracts from *Organizations* by J. G. March and H. A. Simon.

Introduction

During the time I have been writing this book I have been engaged in a process of informal, *ad hoc*, theorizing. It is difficult to say how this process works because for much of the time it consists of a number of separate, seemingly disparate discussions which do not seem to hang together and which do not indicate one is moving in a particular general direction. I began questioning the conventional sociological approach in a variety of small ways and found that a number of other people were asking similar questions at the same time. This led to intensive discussions which were meaningful and fruitful because they arose from common methodological interests. As theorizing is rooted in reality and reality was changing similarly for many people it was only to be expected that similar questions would arise in different places. There was nothing about my own experiences that gave them special relevance for theory construction. In any case I was doing nothing new. I was following a path trodden by many before me and in company with others. Many on the path may not yet have reached my stage of 'temporary conclusiveness', but they will eventually. This is as certain as the fact that society itself will change qualitatively. My transition is part of a collective process. My own biography is significant only in terms of that process. Nor have I written anything that is new. I have simply tried to expose conventional theories and add some substance to the framework of an alternative one. My experiences have no particular relevance for that task. They may have some relevance, however, for explaining why I wrote what I did when I did and for this reason there might be some interest in a brief account of the chronology of my methodological transition. This might also provide some background material for the book as a whole.

I wrote a general framework for the book and the chapters 4, 5 and 6 in 1965. During that year I had much time for the contemplation of theoretical questions for I was in prison, first in Lagos then Jos, Nigeria. The solitude of life in a prison cell, however, whilst it provided a sufficient condition for extensive reading and writing, had nothing to do with the factors which led me to reject conventional social theory. Those factors had been present long before. The process had fairly definite stages. The first stage was a growing awareness of the nature of conventional social theory and a realization of its inadequacies. The second was an ability to articulate criticisms in a consistent methodological manner, while the third was the facility to present an alternative approach. For me, the stages were spread out and involved some years of being in a state of dissatisfaction with conventional explanations without being able to give cogent reasons to account for it.

My first teaching jobs after leaving the London School of Economics were in adult education and took place in the immediate post-Marshall Aid, Cold War period. There were tremendous pressures for consensus in all adult teaching situations. Jobs were insecure. I filled a post at the Oxford University Delegacy for Extra-mural Studies in 1951 not knowing that is was one of a number which had been compulsorily vacated by tutors who were members of the Communist Party. It was a slander to be described as a Communist. There seemed to be no greater qualification for academic promotion than to be a publicly recanted Communist. In that situation I taught what I knew and that was what I had been taught within the highly conventional, in some ways conservative, precincts of the London School of Economics. The only significant nonconformist voice I ever heard raised there was that of Harold Laski. I wrote in the same vein. The situation was not hysterical in the manner of McCarthyism in the USA but the consensus results were similar.

The field in which I worked was industrial relations. There were few reliable texts, most of them were highly descriptive and were out of date so that the task of preparing lectures required thought and initiative. As I was lecturing mainly to active trade unionists my analyses had to match their reality. A number of contradictions began to emerge. They were all related, a part of my totality. There was a contradiction between the popular and academic presentation of industrial relations and its practice as I saw it through my research and teaching. The 1950s saw the heyday of the 'human relations' school in which industrial relations issues were reduced to the level of individual and group psychology. A virtual empire of personnel management was built on the premises of this school. But the 1950s in Britain were characterized by large-scale, bitter unofficial strike activity, then official strikes and growing hostility between unions and the government. Within the social milieux of the students I met at trade union schools, and classes run by the Workers' Education Association and Extra-mural Departments, I detected few of the consensus qualities projected by conventional theorists. There was a contradiction between my own left-wing political position, from which I aimed to alter society, and the methodological stance I was adopting through habit and pressure, and from which I was undoubtedly rationalizing and justifying the existing state of affairs. There was, in other words, a contradiction between my general overall analysis of society, which determined my political attitudes, and my occupational position in society. I was behaving in a schizophrenic manner.

The contradictions clarified and began to be resolved for me during a three year spell as a research fellow at The London School of Economics from 1955 to 1958. The book I wrote then, *Trade Unions and the Government* stood in marked contrast to my earlier ones. Conflict and class figured as permanent, irresolvable phenomena in the society I was examining. Realizing that I was dealing with general methodological issues, but without losing my interest in industrial relations in general and trade unionism in particular, I moved to that part of sociological theory which appeared most relevant, namely the sociology of organizations. This, in turn, led me to sociological theory in general.

I had not done any serious reading in the field of sociological theory before the end of the decade. I regarded myself as an economist who was compelled occasionally to resort to sociological explanations to make sense of my special area, industrial relations. My reading had been highly selective. It continued to be so but with a difference. Whenever I could I sought out nonconformist literature. There was little of it. The work of C. Wright Mills, particularly *The Sociological Imagination*, helped me to articulate my doubts and gave me an insight into conventional sociological theory before I had read much of it. *Fads and Foibles in Modern Sociology* by Pitirim Sorokin, threw additional, different light on the subject. But the contemporary who stimulated me most and had a permanent influence on my work was W. Baldamus, now Professor of Sociology at the University of Birmingham. Baldamus started my transition from the second to the third stage. In the early 1960s I was a political Marxist who did not know how to apply Marxism to his own work. One reason for this was that Marxism had not been developed in a sufficiently sophisticated manner to be applied in the multifarious aspects of social reality. It had been used largely as an indicator of macro-economic trends. There were perfectly good ideological reasons to account for this. Marxism was treated in most Western capitalist societies as a subversive doctrine. It could not develop fully under such conditions for they inhibited the exchange of ideas and free discussion and encouraged its use for political propaganda purposes. The analysis of industrial relations in terms of class conflict was a step in the right direction but it did not constitute a theoretical approach. Seeing society with permanent, irreconcilable class divisions is a consequence of applying a particular analytical method; it is not the method itself.

Efficiency and Effort by W. Baldamus was published in 1961 and I reviewed it in *The Sociological Review* in 1962 as follows:

It is a disturbing fact that the majority of industrial sociologists have barely improved on common-sense interpretations of industrial behaviour. The explanation for this is that they have worked within terms of reference which have handicapped their ability to understand the phenomena they have been examining. They have conducted problem-centred research but their problems, labour turnover, incentives, absenteeism and so on, have not been problems at all to sociologists but merely indices of behaviour; they have worked from the premise that there is an organic unity in industry and this led them to regard conflicts and tensions between employers and employees as mere aberrations from the norm; and they adopted the familiar but undefined terms which were used in industry, such as efficiency, without attempting to isolate the substantial normative elements which are contained in them. The results sometimes have been something less than common-sense value.

It is an event of some importance then when a book appears about industrial administration which is incisively analytical from the valid premise of conflict in industry. Dr Baldamus has written such a book. More than this. The work of Dr Baldamus is undoubtedly the most important of any produced by any industrial sociologist in Britain. Indeed it must rank with the best produced anywhere. The book is closely written, at times difficult to follow due to the author's manner of presentation but it is both exciting and stimulating. It provides an analytical base from which meaningful, as against useful, empirical research should follow.

Dr Baldamus is primarily concerned with the concepts, much used in industry and adopted uncritically by sociologists, of 'efficiency' and 'effort'. He chose to analyse these concepts because their meaning relates to the whole purpose of industrial administration. His intention, he wrote, 'is to show that the organization of industry, with all its complexities and diversities, ultimately revolves on a single process: the administrative process through which the employee's effort is controlled by the employer. This means that the entire system of industrial production will be viewed as a system of administrative controls which regulate quantity, quality, and distribution of human effort . . .' This breakaway from regarding industry as being a process where factors of production are combined to produce commodities and services is a major methodological improvement. [1]

This review was similar to others I was writing in that period except that in most cases I was criticizing conformity to an assumption of consensus rather than praising its rejection. An early and aggressive example of my approach was shown in a review of *The Growth of British Industrial Relations* by E. H. Phelps Brown, published in the first issue of the *New Left Review*, January 1960. I wrote that Phelps Brown's work was a rationalization of and buttress for British capitalist society which added up 'to bad history, and, in consequence, largely worthless analysis'.[2] I had decided that there was nothing to be gained by adopting a compromising attitude towards blatantly conformist texts. As far as possible a policy of exposing conceptual defects and revealing fantasy-like qualities had to be pursued. In general there were virtually unlimited opportunities for this though few subsequently came my way. I had to create my own means through articles such as 'Trade unions in contemporary capitalism' for the 1964 issue of the *Socialist Register*, and through two books, the *International Bibliography of Trade Unionism*, 1968, and *The Sociology of Industrial Relations*, 1971.

The significance of *Efficiency and Effort* for my own work could not, however, be expressed in a review for I was not to feel its full impact for a few years. It started me thinking seriously about the possibility of applying Marxism for micro-analytical uses and it gave me a basis from which to start. Baldamus's book was deceptive because he had deliberately excluded from it any emotive terms which might enable the reader to associate it immediately with Marxism. But in doing this he had taken a positive step towards producing a text which competed point for point with conventional sociology, but which turned that sociology around so that it was firmly based in reality. An ultimate practical consequence for me was that the manner in which Baldamus dealt with effort, which was central to his work, enabled me to understand superstructure and led me to write chapter 9, 'The substance of superstructures'.

Two years passed before I met Baldamus in a seminar at the University of Leeds. In March 1964 he read a paper in which he elaborated about the meaning of effort. I remember walking home from the seminar feeling that Baldamus had explained an issue of some significance to me but without being able to place it in my conceptual scheme. The next month I left Britain for West Africa on study leave. On 16 June 1964 I was arrested in Nigeria and charged with political offences. From then until October I was either in prison on remand or on trial without the conditions or the incentive to think about sociological theory. I was sent to Broad Street Prison, Lagos, in October 1964, and after months of harassment by the Special Branch of the Nigerian police heaved a sigh of relief to be locked away from them. The relief turned out to be illusory because a police informer was one of the cell inmates. But it lasted long enough for me to use sociological theory as a diversion and to get involved again in moving to stage three of my rejection of sociological theory.

The British High Commissioner in Lagos was able to supply me with largely American sociological textbooks so long as they were non-Marxist and did not have 'power' in the title. So for the first time I read the works of Max Weber, Talcott Parsons, R. K. Merton, Philip Selznick, G. C. Homans, H. A. Simon, J. G. March, Reinhard Bendix, Amitai Etzioni and lesser mortals in the American sociology scene. I was able to spend so much unbroken time on them that I felt that I could read some, such as Merton, backwards. This experience confirmed my belief absolutely that conventional sociological theory had virtually no heuristic significance, that its main value was ideological and that it would, for this reason, inevitably be displaced. My reading confirmed the criticisms made by Mills and Sorikin but took me much further in rejecting conventional socio-logical theory in its entirety. I found some of it, particularly the work of Homans, to be more painful than being in prison. It was indeed a maso-chistic exercise. I thought about the Baldamus analysis a lot. Then one day while still in Lagos prison the puzzle fell into place. Baldamus was wrong in treating effort as a major superstructural variable for it was not effort which held the pivotal position. Effort was the way through which skills were transmitted. Effort really had no independent identity. Changes in effort in reality were changes in the rate of applying skills. Once I had started thinking about skills then the other main variables came into play. Power was derived from skills. Both skills and power were in large part perceived and rated through ideology. I saw all three elements as being differentially distributed and causally related so that changes in any one part of any one had repercussive effects upon the others. Skills, however, were predominant and it was through these and not power that economic pressures were transmitted and became a reality in the lives of people. Before I was suddenly transferred from Lagos to Jos, allegedly to stop me discussing politics with my Action Group cell-mates, who were later released to help govern Nigeria, I had started writing the first draft of this book.

I have suppressed many aspects of prison life in Nigeria. Physical depri-vation, violence, rats, bugs, personal degradation in general were daily features of prison life to which one became adjusted. It was not an event to have a grossly overfed rat running around the cell or to hear the cries of prisoners being beaten by other prisoners during the routine of what was termed 'daily beatings' or to be awakened by the nightmares of prisoners condemned to death. One had to accept such features or else go crazy in desperation. Accepting them meant suppressing their significance and once this was achieved it had a permanent effect so that later I was able to re-member them only with great effort. I can, however, vividly remember jump-ing off my bed in excitement on recognizing the substance of superstructures and feeling rather embarrassed because I could not explain to anyone around me what had happened. Following this, my thinking moved on to a new plane and I spent many hours of most days pleasantly involved in what was necessarily an intensely personal affair: working out the methodological significance of seeing superstructures in this way, trying to establish an analytically useful relationship between superstructures and structure and generally within this context clarifying dialectical materialism. After I was transferred to Jos prison in December 1964 I had a cell to myself, a table and chair, plenty of British High Commission writing paper and pens. I was formally in solitary confinement in that other prisoners were not supposed to talk to me, but the prison superintendent was sympathetic and did all he could within the rules to make my life tolerable. Although he had heard rumours that I was writing, even sending out weekly articles, which was untrue, he did not investigate, so that I was able to preserve my precious manuscript under my mattress and eventually smuggle it out to be posted to England. The chapters about Weber's model of bureaucracy and the March and Simon synthesis were actually written in prison and have not been altered since, except for style. Perhaps a spell in solitary confinement is one of the sufficient conditions for theorizing. Whether this is so or not, the progress I made in prison came to a halt when I left. I recommenced my university work in October 1965, under conditions which provided few opportunities for writing. The pressures of university work intensified so that months elapsed in between brief spells on my analytical framework. And years elapsed before I could make significant progress.

It may be that the long haul after 1965 was necessary for clarification and re-equipment. Two important elements were missing from my prison cell. The first was access to the works of Marx and Engels, and the second was discussion with people who started from the same premises as myself. Both elements became important features of my life once I had settled again at the University of Leeds. I read Marx and Engels in a different light from previously, in the manner suggested by Georg Lukács in *History and Class Consciousness* (see the end of chapter 1 for a relevant quotation from Lukács). I was interested in a method and their works were a classic exposition of it. I read them, therefore, for clarification, for new insights and for support. I am still doing this. Concomitant with reading Marx and Engels I became involved in seminar discussions both in England and on the Continent about the development of Marxism as a microtheory. This corresponded with an increase in discussions in general about one interpretation or another of Marxism. It was much easier after 1967 to talk in semipublic and public about Marxism. From 1966 my wife Sheila and I held weekend seminars at our home to discuss nonconformity in sociological theory. Up to twenty-five sociologists attended from different universities, including Gi Baldamus, and from the early meetings I floated my ideas about superstructure. In a paper on 'Notes on organization theory' I outlined a model which expressed my ideas but, so far as I can gather, it made little impression. Baldamus and I conducted a lengthy correspondence from 1966 which consisted mainly of his ideas about my work. We discussed important questions such as the position of values in social theory but never really got to grips with the issue which was of greatest concern to me, namely fitting the Marxist frame of reference to tackle microsituations. There were a number of reasons not only for the inability of Baldamus and myself to communicate on this issue but for my own inability to impress my British colleagues. I was a committed Marxist who was, by this time, equally committed to the idea of a social scientific revolution, as expressed by Thomas Kuhn in *The Structure of Scientific Revolutions*. I could see no alternative to the complete rejection of conventional sociological theory. The case which is presented in this chapter was already in outline. The rejection of the notion of theory building in the pure and natural sciences, as projected by Kuhn, was new and evoked many passions. But for the social sciences it was unthinkable. Even the most nonconformist of my sociology friends was teaching sociology through the works of the great masters, contending that each had made a contribution. They were all either potential synthesizers or, when scratched, Weberians. We were as it turned out a motley crowd of nonconformists, just like the Aldermaston marchers or members of the American Peace Corps, there for a variety of reasons. In this setting I was described as dogmatic and inflexible. Another reason was the crudeness and incompleteness of my ideas at this stage. I had no intention of altering the first reason and only time and application could alter the second.

From 1966 the most useful discussions I had were in Yugoslavia, France, Italy and Germany. Through the medium of our domestic seminar we organized a joint seminar with Yugoslav sociologists at Bohinj, Slovenia, in September 1967. This in itself was not very fruitful. The sociologists were from Slovenia and had a German philosophical background. It was not easy for them to communicate with predominantly British empiricists. The job of translating Hegelian constructs, thought out in German but spoken in Slovene, was virtually impossible. I think we must have been talking nonsense to each other. But the seminar led to useful contacts with the *Praxis* group. American articulated sociology is pervasive in Yugoslavia but there are influential sociologists and philosophers in Zagreb and Belgrade in particular who are most concerned with developing Marxist thought. These people are mainly connected with *Praxis*, the critical philosophy journal. The *Praxis* group organize the annual International Summer School on the island of Korcula, off the coast near Dubrovnik. There, and on other occasions, my wife, who was professionally involved in all of these discussions, and I met Rudi Supek, Vojin Milic, Mihailo Marković, Ivan Kuvacić and other Yugoslavs for wide-ranging discussions about Marxism. Through these people we became acquainted with Lucian Goldman, Serge Mallet, Pierre Naville, Jürgend Habermas, and other members of a European coterie of sociologists and philosophers which collected each year at Korcula.

There is no doubt, in my experience, that France is the most stimulating and rewarding place to discuss developments in Marxism. This was so before Louis Althusser and Roger Garaudy significantly entered the public scene and, in any event, irrespective of them. In Britain it is uncommon to find committed Marxists in prominent academic positions because of its very discreet practice of discrimination. In France, on the other hand, there are a number of such people holding professorial or similar posts and many more approaching them. French outlets for Marxist academic articles and books are more numerous than in Britain. I would not suggest that the pressures for discrimination do not exist in France. Undoubtedly they do. But the power, the influence and the pervasive character of the French Communist Party appear to make it difficult for discrimination to be practised so extensively as in Britain.

My introduction to the French Marxist scene occurred mainly through my friendship with Roger Cornu, a French sociologist, now at the Laboratoire d'Economie et de Sociologie du Travail, in Aix-en-Provence. Through Cornu I met Serge Jonas who is the editor of *l'homme et la société* and director of the publishing house Editions Anthropos. Jonas published chapter 3, which was my first attempt to criticize conventional theory. He continued to publish my articles and invited me to the seminars his journal organized and at which I met many of the people who attended the Korcula Summer Schools. I developed a close working relationship with Cornu, and through him and Jonas found a congenial, stimulating, intellectual milieu which I have never experienced in Britain.

One of the early seminars organized by the journal *l'homme et la société* was held in September 1968 at the Centre Cultural International, Cerisy-La-Salle, in Normandy, in the wake of the May—June strikes and disturbances. I had intended to discuss social change in Nigeria but at an early session I was provoked by some remarks of T. B. Bottomore, Professor of Sociology at the University of Sussex, who was the only other British participant. Bottomore's general approach was that Marxism was adequate for tackling specific problems, say relating to social change, but that in a way a synthesis had taken place in which conventional sociology and Marxism had acted on each other with the greatest pressure being exerted on Marxism. I regarded the notion of a synthesis between qualitatively different conceptual approaches as an intellectual travesty and I said so. Instead of reading my paper I talked about 'Conceptual approaches to dynamic analysis in sociology' and so made public for the first time a generalized version of the case presented here. It was subsequently published by *l'homme et la société* along with other papers presented at the seminar.[3] After that my discussions carried on in France, and Yugoslavia, spread to Italy and, in 1973, took place in Holland and West Germany. All the time I was writing and reformulating what has ended up as the last three chapters of this book. Since about 1968, apart from giving at the most two talks in Britain, I have not exposed myself to a reciprocal exchange of ideas with established British sociologists. My informal theorizing here has been confined to *ad hoc* discussions with my wife and a few friends and to stimulating sessions of my postgraduate seminar in the School of Economics at the University of Leeds. Perhaps I am the better off for this. In general British and American sociologists appear to be willing to take their nonconformity only to the point of criticizing Western sociology and espousing some versions of radical sociology. Beyond that, as I indicate later, seems to lie a forbidden and forbidding land. Only an analysis of the intellectual milieux in capitalist societies can explain this attitude. It is impossible to conduct positive discussions about dialectical materialism in such a situation, as I discovered at a seminar with Alvin Gouldner in Amsterdam in January 1973, for rational attitudes evaporate completely. The state of critical analysis among English and American sociologists is epitomized for me by the announcement, which has just come into my hands, of a new journal, *Theory and Society: renewal and critique in social theory*, edited by Alvin Gouldner and two others, with R. K. Merton as the special advisory editor.[4] The radicals, both old and newly converted, do not envisage a social scientific revolution of the kind presented here. But things are changing fast and rearguard actions, bolstered by what I describe as nonsense arguments against dialectical materialism, will be exposed by the crisis in capitalism itself.

Notes

1. *The Sociological Review*, 10, No. 1, 1962, 100.
2. *The New Left Review*, No. 1 (1960), 61.
3. *L'homme et la société*, No. 10 (Oct.–Dec. 1968), 13–20.
4. *Theory and Society: renewal and critique in social theory*, ed. Alvin Gouldner, Pierre Bourdieu and Randall Collins; special advisory editor, Robert K. Merton; a new periodical published by Elsevier, Amsterdam, 2, 1974.

Part one

The issue

Part one contains only one chapter and it was the last to be written. I have worked on the book intermittently for the last ten years and during that time my thinking about sociological theory has changed, not qualitatively but nonetheless in important details. I am much clearer in my own mind about the nature of conventional sociological theory and my preferred explanation, dialectical materialism. This chapter has therefore been written with the advantage of hindsight, that is, with the advantage of the knowledge of the development of my thoughts, of the difficulties I experienced and how I endeavoured to overcome them. But it is not a conclusion, nor, on the other hand, is it an introduction. It has some qualities of both but it stands in its own right. It differs from the rest of the book in that it is written in the first person: this is because it represents a particular stand in relation to a general methodological position. I am one of those who believes that conventional sociology as taught in Western capitalist countries is exhausting whatever heuristic qualities it has had and is being replaced inexorably by a conceptual approach which more closely explains the reality of most peoples' lives. For many British sociologists with whom I have contact this is an extreme and untenable stand to make. For me it is logical, sensible, and inevitable.

I

The social purpose of social theory

The explanation in this chapter is as I see the methodological situation now. It gives no guide to the development of my thinking since I first tackled the issue and does not, therefore, systematically raise the methodological question which confronted me. I have indicated very briefly in the introduction the nature of some of the questions I felt had to be answered. There are, however, a number of implications arising from my methodological position which need to be explained in order to make it understood and these implications have confronted me at various times during the last decade or so. In part, then, the historical development of my thought is presented here but without any time sequence and in the form of a single, logically consistent argument.

The implications relate, in the first instance to the nature of sociological theory. Some of them are mentioned in subsequent chapters but it is necessary for them to be repeated here for the sake of the general argument.

Theory in practice

The argument concerns the part which social theory plays in society. There are many sociologists, particularly in Britain, who believe that social theory is unimportant and makes no impact on 'real' life. They are empiricists who believe that facts are impartial and as such can tell their own stories undisturbed by theories. If this were so we could draw a neat distinction between theory and practice and leave the theorists to doodle with their models, play with their fantasies and engage in the innocuous and highly complex task of theoretical criticism. However, as I attempt to show in chapter 2, on 'The dogma of empiricism', empiricism has a theoretical position which closely resembles structural functionalism. All empiricists, no matter in which society they reside, make certain assumptions about the nature of the phenomena they analyse and have, therefore, an implicit conceptual approach. A decision not to adopt a monocausal approach, to be open-minded until the situation has been analysed, is derived from a particular theoretical position. It presumes that variables cannot be given an *a priori* ranking, that, therefore, there is no single variable with a dominant causal significance which relates to different phenomena and that, in consequence, there is no common structure which generates movement. Put another way, the approach of empiricists makes an *a priori* stipulation about the nature of movement, and therefore, of change, in social reality. Movement may or may not be present, therefore it is not inevitable. It must, in consequence, be controllable and remedial. It follows that movement must be from a base of no movement, that is from one with organic unity or dominant consensus qualities. Because no common structural determinants of action are permitted it is conceptually possible to separate situations for analysis and to assume that they are causally autonomous, as in systems theory in the social sciences. A system possessing organic unity can be split in parts which themselves possess that quality. This is a rather simple but nonetheless valid statement of the theoretical position of empiricists. It is a static position and can be identified with those explicit theoretical approaches which are also static in conception.

This point is not generally recognized. A common belief is that theory somehow stands apart from real life. The belief is given institutional support by the manner in which the social sciences are taught in schools, colleges and universities. Theory is usually taught as a set of analytical concepts and formalized models which have their own identity, while real life is revealed through descriptive studies compiled from an assemblage of facts. Theory can be taught and examined without any reference to facts, and facts can be presented as 'applied' this or that without any reference to theory. This dichotomy is expressed popularly through the belief that there are theorists who sit in grand ivory-tower isolation thinking, in contrast to those hardheaded practical men who spend their time doing, looking at, and making decisions about real things. Comments such as 'it is all right in theory but not in practice' are heard frequently when the issue of theory is raised. The British Department of Employment's *Annual Report of Research*, 1973, gave an example of the dichotomy when it stated that

Research carried out or commissioned by the Department in the social sciences is almost always of an applied nature. While the Department fully recognizes the importance of more theoretical or basic research in the social sciences, the responsibility for supporting and stimulating such research in areas of interest to the Department lies with the Social Science Research Council.[1]

Many other illustrations could be given of the compartmentalization of theory and practice.

There is, however, no escape from social theory. It is present in all analyses and descriptions of social situations whether it is recognized and admitted or not. This statement raises two questions. First, what is the general significance of theory in real life situations and secondly, in the light of that discussion, why should the dichotomy between them be emphasized so markedly in conventional discussions.

There are two aspects to the first of these questions. The first concerns the need of every individual to be able to simplify complex situations. Social situations of all types and at all levels, are comprised of complex interrelated variables which have to be unravelled, sorted out and put into some order before the situations can be comprehended. An individual has to know how to respond to every situation that confronts him; he has to be able to give it a meaning so that he can react to it. It does not matter at this point whether the meaning is a valid reflection of the situation or not. Any meaning will do so long as it acts as a guide to action. It is impossible to imagine an occasion when this process of simplification and guidance does not take place. Take, for instance, the situation at the point of production where a person sells his labour power. What is his identity? What is his relationship with the person who buys his labour power, with those who supervise him, work alongside him, depend for their subsistence on him? What is it he sells, what is its significance for himself, for his employer and so on? He cannot enter that situation unless he *feels* he can find his way around it. Entering it and giving it a meaning occur simultaneously.

Every individual has to give meanings to his own situation. This cannot be done for him. There is no way in which an individual can attach a meaning to a situation other than through his own ability to see and hear and think. He may repeat the meanings of others but this is a different matter. He repeats them as his own. The second aspect of the question, then, relates to perception. What does he see and what determines how he perceives what he sees? What a person sees, of course, is determined in the first instance by what he is looking at. There are objective differences between situations, between labour markets and kinship relations for example. There are things and events which, though they involve persons, lie outside and apart from each one as an individual. The difficulty is that no one can ever know what these things and events are apart from his own perception of them. Work, strikes, war, famine, trade unions, political parties, monarchies, dictatorships, for example, exist as features of concrete situations. The compulsion to go to work is as much a part of concrete reality as is starvation and exists no matter how individuals perceive it. There are what might be described as 'objective facts' in every situation – the raw material for perception. Every person is presented with something to perceive. However, as no one can see or hear anything except through his powers of perception, social reality consists in every case, on all occasions, at all times, of 'objective facts' which have been interpreted, given meanings and, thereby, transformed into 'social facts'.

Once this is admitted then the possibility for varying degrees of discrepancy between what is objective and what is social has also to be recognized; that is, 'objective' reality might be distorted or presented incompletely through the transition to social reality. The recognition that there is an objective reality is important for understanding the dynamics of perception, the manner in which meanings change, and the extent of the changes. Of course, objective reality for any person comprises the social reality of others and is dialectically related to his own conception of it. It would be a gross distorting simplification to present the 'objective' and the 'social' as two distinctly separate categories. The main point I am making here is that independently of how an individual perceives his situation there are pressures acting on him which emanate from his 'objective reality' with which in some way the meanings he attaches to them have to come to terms and on which the meanings themselves react. This view is consistent with the notion that meanings are pervasive; it is inconsistent with the belief that 'action stems from meanings' as phenomenological sociologists stipulate.

The determinants of meanings

The question 'what determines how a person perceives what he sees' has been answered in a variety of ways. It can usually be agreed that when a person perceives his reality he observes, selects, abstracts and interprets. In other words, he gives a meaning to it. The disagreements occur over the determinants of meanings. The answers range from a stipulation that the mind creates its own meanings because it is autonomous of social forces, to one that the meanings are entirely the product of social forces. The notion that there is 'free will' is rarely defended explicitly in its pure form these days, though there is a reluctance among many sociologists to desert the individual in this way and to assign him as a consequence rather than a cause of social events. This reluctance was aptly expressed by Hans Neisser in his essay *On the Sociology of Knowledge*.

What is immanent in our approach [he wrote] is not the specific development of the human mind which by itself could explain intellectual history, but a certain 'faint urge' of the mind to go ahead. That, by itself, outside of specific historical stages of development, the urge is faint. . . . But although faint, it is never nil; and if under favourable circumstances it grows stronger, it displays peculiar marks which cannot be explained by the circumstances. Intellectual history must, therefore, be conceived as an interpretation of social-historical factors and the autonomy of the human mind. [2]

A version of the notion that the human mind is autonomous, however, gets widespread implicit support through the method of empiricism or what Popper calls the 'bucket theory of the mind'.[3] If a social scientist believes that he gets his facts, in the words of Znaniecki [4], 'without any methodological prepossessions, and gets his explanation entirely *a posteriori* from pure experience', then it follows that he believes that he introduces no meanings to the facts but deals with them as they would have it. The empiricists are at one with the free will advocates in that they all accept that individuals do not inevitably and invariably bring meanings, not of their own making, to the facts they handle. In this respect Popper's ridicule of the empiricists does not free him from association with them. The understanding of social situations must proceed, according to Popper, through the use of the scientific method. This method, namely the process of hypothesizing and testing hypotheses, can and does stand between the individual and his facts, thus preventing the individual from conveying his own meanings to them. In Popper's scheme it is not the mind which is autonomous but the mind's use of a method. Popper then does not have to be concerned about the social construction of reality, except to attack it as a heresy. For him it does not matter what an individual thinks about a situation so long as he is scientific in his appraisal of it. Thus sociology, as indeed all the social sciences, can be value-free. This was the view expounded by Lionel Robbins in his *Essay on the Nature and Significance of Economic Science* [5], published in 1932 and subsequently widely influential. Robbins, understandably, was ecstatic about Popper's arrival at the London School of Economics after the Second World War to give his myth, repeated lecture after lecture, theoretical underpinnings.[6] Sociology had its Robbins. As Alvin Gouldner remarks,

the myth of a value-free sociology has been a conquering one. Today, all the powers of sociology, from Parsons to Lundberg, have entered into a tacit alliance to bind us to the dogma that 'Thou shalt not commit a value judgment', especially as sociologists. Where is the introductory textbook, where the lecture course on principles, that does not affirm or imply this rule? [7]

A concern about the origin and nature of meanings which individuals give to situations has been most marked in the sociology of knowledge generally and in phenomenological sociology in particular. Popper has expressed the position *vis-à-vis* the sociology of knowledge concisely and accurately:

The sociology of knowledge argues that scientific thought, and especially thought on social and political matters, does not proceed in a vacuum, but in a socially conditioned atmosphere. It is influenced largely by unconscious or subconscious elements. These elements remain hidden from the thinker's observing eye because they form, as it were, the very place which he inhabits, his social habitat. *The social habitat of the thinker determines a whole system of opinions and theories which appear to him as unquestionably true or self-evident. They appear to him as if they were logically and trivially true. This is why he is not even aware of having made any assumptions at all. But that he has made assumptions can be seen if we compare him with a thinker who lives in a very different social habitat; for he too will proceed from a system of apparently unquestionable assumptions, but from a very different one; and it may be so different that no intellectual bridge may exist and no compromise be possible between these two systems. Each of these different socially determined systems of assumptions is called by the sociologists of knowledge a* total ideology.[8]

According to phenomenological sociologists

Phenomenological sociologists, such as the advocates of the 'action frame of reference', and ethnomethodologists use the sociology of knowledge as a base but in their use of it they redefine its nature and scope and move it from the periphery to the centre of sociological theory.[9] Berger and Luckmann, relying heavily on Alfred Schutz [10], stated that

the sociology of knowledge must concern itself with whatever passes for 'knowledge' in a society, regardless of the ultimate validity or invalidity (by whatever criteria) of such knowledge. And in so far as all human 'knowledge' is developed, transmitted and maintained in social situations, the sociology of knowledge must seek to understand the processes by which this is done in such a way that a taken-for-granted 'reality' congeals for the man in the street. In other words, we contend that the sociology of knowledge is concerned with the analysis of the social construction of reality.[11]

Thus the central question is how do the subjective meanings of individuals, the commonsense constraints of the man in the street, become reality or 'objective facticities'?

There are a number of branches of phenomenological sociology which attribute different degrees of causal significance to meanings and differentiate between them. Berger and Luckmann, though attaching great

significance to the social construction of reality are relatively cautious in their claims for it:

We would contend that the analysis of the role of knowledge in the dialectic of individual and society, of personal identity and social structure, provides a crucial complementary perspective for all areas of society. This is certainly not to deny that purely structural analyses of social phenomena are fully adequate for wide areas of sociological inquiry, ranging from the study of small groups to that of large institutional complexes, such as the economy or politics. Nothing is further from our intentions than the suggestion that a sociology-of-knowledge 'angle' ought somehow to be injected into all such analyses. [12]

It was clear, however, that the various methodological approaches could not be left in a state of limbo. A relationship between them had to be established and in the process a decision had to be made between the significance of man and his meanings on the one hand, and the structure of his situations on the other. The intention of Berger and Luckmann was to humanize sociology, to project the individual back into the dialogue of sociology and to free him from the prison of social reality by showing that it is of his own making, and therefore in his control. The logical outcome of such an intention was to approach the whole study of sociology from the perspective of the individual, and this was the course taken by the proponents of the action frame of reference and ethnomethodology. The extreme position seems to be a highly subjective preoccupation with subjective meanings such as that of a small but articulate group of sociologists at Goldsmith's College, London. [13] For these people an obsessional involvement with meanings is justified because sociology is deemed to derive its data from the meanings which men attach to social life, and because action stems from those meanings. The significance of phenomenological sociology, however, rests on the fact that many sociologists involved in research in Britain rely for their analyses almost entirely on data drawn from individuals through questionnaires and interviews. Whether by default or through intention they practise phenomenological sociology. It is an easy method to practise, and so long as a few simple statistical rules are followed its validity is unquestioned. All that remains for phenomenologists is for the questionnaires, the interviews and all other methods of recording meanings to be so constructed that the 'structure of everyday life experience and conduct is reflected in them'. [14] It is all a matter of technique.

One would think that the importance attached to meanings would lead sociologists to investigate their source in detail. If commonsense constructs form social reality, what gives rise to the constructs? Why is it that respondents answer questions as they do? But the inquiring mind is not a feature of contemporary sociology. There are some questions which cannot in all seriousness be answered for they might lead to a questioning of the whole conceptual fabric. There are articles of faith in contemporary conventional sociology, like the acceptance of 'common-value patterns', of 'roles and role-sets', of 'commonsense constructs'. I am not saying that in all cases there is no explanation. Frequently, particularly in the case of inadvertent phenomenological sociology, there is not. The point is that what answers are given simply pay lip-service to explanations.

One of the most important works based on the 'action frame of reference' in recent years was the Cambridge study of the affluent worker, published in three monographs in 1968 and 1969.[15] The data for the study was drawn from a sample of 229 industrial workers from three large industrial concerns in Luton, Bedfordshire, England, who were interviewed at work and in their homes. The authors used the meanings which the workers attached to their situations as their main source of data and distributed it between ideal/typical categories which they had formulated. The monographs are largely interpretations of tabulated meanings, concerned with patterns of attitudes and behaviour and the causes of the patterning rather than with the meanings themselves. The authors, of course, had a view about the formulation of meanings but this was not problematical for them. Rather it acted as an assumption on which they based their approach. One of the authors, David Lockwood, spelt out the assumption in an article which preceded the monographs.

For the most part, men visualize the class structure of their society from the vantage points of their own particular milieux, *and their perceptions of the larger society will vary according to their experiences of social inequality in the smaller societies in which they live out their daily lives. This assumption that the individual's social consciousness is to a large extent influenced by his immediate social context has already proved its usefulness in the study of 'images of society' and it has been stated most clearly by Bott, who writes: 'People do have direct experience of distinctions of power and prestige in their places of work, among their colleagues, in schools, and in their relationships with friends, neighbours, and relatives. In other words, the ingredients, the raw materials, of class ideology are located in the individual's various primary social experiences, rather than in his position in a socio-economic category . . .'*[16]

If this statement is seen in relation to the three Cambridge monographs it is clear that it is intended not as an indication of where to look for the determinants of meanings but as a rationale for the teleological approach which concentrates on meanings and neglects their structural causes. In the first two volumes the authors were explicitly empiricist and confined themselves largely to descriptions based on the interview data. The third volume, *The Affluent Worker in the Class Structure*, differed only in the sense that the authors attempted to argue a case from an analysis of the meanings. They gave no indication that they thought it important to spell out the details of workers' 'primary social experiences'. By implication it is possible to eliminate some factors, such as shopfloor work experience, which might reasonably have been included.

Specifically, it may be objected that there is in fact no direct and uniform association between immediate shopfloor experience and employee attitudes, and behaviour that are of wider reference. This is so because the effects of technologically determined conditions of work are always mediated *through the meanings that men give to their work and through their own definitions of their work situation, and because these meanings and definitions in turn* vary *with the particular sets of wants and expectations that men bring to their employment.* [17]

The independent variables here are 'meanings', 'definitions', 'wants' and 'expectations', none of which appears to have a basis in the environment of workers which is sufficiently important to introduce into the analysis. The authors go on to reject what they describe as 'an old philosophical anthropology of production', and call for the 'development of a new empirical sociology of consumption'.[18] This presumably is stated in case the readers have failed to grasp the meaning which the authors themselves so patently attach to sociology.

It may be said that the *Affluent Worker* monographs are not properly representative of the 'action frame of reference' in that they deal with meanings much too superficially, in the manner that data is used by empiricists. This is my view. But the authors do claim a preoccupation with meanings and they take them as given. Indeed meanings take on the qualities of reification in much the same way as goals do in the Parsonsian model. The attitude of the main exponents of the theoretical basis of phenomenological studies is quite different for their preoccupation with meanings has led them away from the empirical relevance of meanings to their identification, measurement and transmission. The ethnomethodologists as represented by the work of Aaron Cicourel are involved in analysing 'meaning collection' techniques on the one hand and linguistics on the other. Cicourel suggests laboratory studies as the most satisfactory way of measuring meanings and utilizes linguistic theory to explain what is being measured. This follows from his belief that 'the ethnomethodologist views meaning as situated, self-organizing and reflexive interaction between the organization of memory, practical reasoning and talk'.[19]

This retreat into the study of language is a retreat from an understanding of the meanings which people assign to the reality of their everyday lives. This is not to say that language is unimportant in a general analysis of meanings. It is obviously one important means of conveying meanings so that its limitations should be analysed in order to discover the extent to which it distorts or prevents expression. Berger and Luckmann stated, for example, that

The common language available is grounded in everyday life and keeps pointing back to it even as I employ it to interpret experiences in finite provinces of meaning. Typically, therefore, I 'distort' the reality of the latter as soon as I begin to use the common language in interpreting them, that is I 'translate' the non-everyday experiences back into the paramount reality of everyday life. [20]

If language is seen to have an ideological content then other more serious limitations might be identified. But the study of language is a long way from the point in question, namely the determinants of meanings. As undertaken by Cicourel it is one of those puzzle-solving activities mentioned by Thomas Kahn, to which social scientists are driven when the heuristic limits of the dominant conceptual approach have been reached. It is an escape from questions which might lead the conceptual approach itself to be questioned.

The question, what is it in the social experiences of people which produce the commonsense constructs of the reality of those experiences? does not appear to have seriously concerned any of the major writers in the field of phenomenological sociology.

Cicourel, now one of the main protagonists of contemporary ethno-methodology, relies heavily on Schutz for guidance in the matter and does not, therefore, give an adequate answer. In his main work on ethno-methodology, *Method and Measurement in Sociology*, Cicourel makes a number of frustrating assertions which state the obvious and little else. 'The actor', he states, '. . . approaches the role-taking situation with a background of conventions of ignorance which precedes his abstractions from the immediate objects and events in his visual field.'[21] Then he adds that 'Operational procedures for measuring meaning must take into account the fact that the actor's awareness and experiences of an object are determined not only by the physical object as it is presented or given but also by imputations he assigns to it.'[22] We are not guided into an understanding and possible identification of the 'background of conventions or ignorance' nor the determinants of 'imputations'.

Schutz, and with approval, Cicourel, regard an analysis of 'knowledge' as important for understanding meanings. Cicourel discusses it in a chapter on 'Theoretical presuppositions', the last in his book *Method and Measurement in Sociology*. At last, I thought, he is going to lay bare his conceptual apparatus and, in the process, take us to a stage where 'knowledge' itself is analysed. But I had no such luck. 'Schutz notes', Cicourel states, 'that the greatest part of the actor's knowledge is socially derived from others. Knowledge is socially distributed and the stock of knowledge at hand differs for different actors.' Which part of the actor's knowledge comes from others and where the rest comes from are unanswered questions. Then in a statement which is intended to clarify he succeeds in reifying the whole issue. 'Socially distributed knowledge taken for granted in everyday communication is exchanged within a context whereby the actor typifies both his own and the other's behaviour. Typical social roles and typical expectations are assumed in the exchange of socially distributed and socially approved knowledge.'[23] If I follow him correctly he is stating that there is a context of typification prior to knowledge which is its environment. It is not a material environment but a system of ordering, putting in slots, pinning labels to, which just exists, like that. But, as if he has not realized the implications of his own analysis, Cicourel adds what is supposed to be a supporting, clarifying quotation from Schutz, rejecting the idea of a context of typification within which knowledge is exchanged and identifying knowledge itself as the source of typification. 'Socially approved knowledge', Cicourel quotes Schutz as stating, 'consists, thus, of a set of recipes designed to help each member of the group to define his situation in the reality of everyday life in a typical way.'[24] All we have to do now is to discover what the recipes are and how they came about, but it is of no use reading ethnomethodologists for that.

Even the most perceptive of phenomenologists, Berger and Luckmann, only approach the question of the source of commonsense constructs indirectly after ruling it out of bounds. 'How', they state, 'commonsense reality may be influenced by the theoretical construction of intellectuals and other merchants of ideas is a further question' (meaning one with which they are not concerned in their book). Then they add that 'within the frame of reference of sociology as an empirical science it is possible to take this reality as given, to take as data particular phenomena arising within it, without further inquiry about the foundations of this reality, which is a philosophical task'.[25] This, of course, is a correct illustration of the state of conventional theory. Conventional theorists in capitalist societies frequently legitimize their inability to do more than describe and categorize by claiming that causal analysis is based on metaphysical or philosophical concepts.

More explicitly, they state: 'The phenomenological analysis of everyday life . . . refrains from any causal or genetic hypotheses, as well as from

assertions about the ortological status of the phenomena analysed.' But, as
Berger and Luckmann should know, a refusal to make an assumption
about causes constitutes an assumption and it is one their readers are entitled to know about without having to read it into their work. There is no
doubt, despite the analytical erudition of *Social Construction of Reality*
and without making any pretence about the separation of theory and
practice, that phenomenological analysis as portrayed by Berger and
Luckmann fits neatly into the conceptual approach of empiricism. 'The
reality of everyday life', they state, 'is taken for granted as reality. It does
not require additional verification over and beyond its simple presence. It
is simply *there*, as self-evident and compelling facticity. I *know* that it is
real', and so on. Despite all this, their analysis leads them willy-nilly to a
clarification, though not specification, of the determinants of the meanings with which they are preoccupied. In their discussion about the 'internalization of reality', and through their categorization of socialization into
primary and secondary elements, Berger and Luckmann reveal insights into
the character of experiences which are valuable contributions for a
structural analysis of meanings.[26]

A primary defect of much of what goes for sociological research is the
creation of categories which break up and apportion social reality as if the
categories themselves were real. This defect obscures both the totality of
situations and their existence as a process. The reality of everyday life is
not compartmentalized with language doing this bit, theory doing that bit
and empirical data doing another bit. Nor is it compartmentalized in the
sense that what goes on at work is separated in the lives of people from
what goes on outside and what goes on today is distinct from what went
on yesterday. Such categories may have an analytical utility but they have
to be removed in the final analysis. The reality of everyday life contains
and compresses all the variables, all the categories, into interlocking experiences, and unless that reality is to be distorted out of recognition, thus
making the analysis as much use as a fantasy, then its totality must be
expressed through the analysis. It is both incongruous and revealing that
phenomenological sociologists who are most concerned with what ordinary men and women think, should recreate for them a reality they never
experience and do so in a manner and language they could never
understand.

An example of a segmented view of reality is provided by Berger and
Luckmann when they describe the function of theory in the reality of
everyday life. In a discussion of 'the institutional world' they state that if

*the integration of an institutional order can be understood only in terms
of the 'knowledge' that its members have of it, it follows that the analysis*

of such 'knowledge' will be essential for an analysis of the institutional order in question. It is important to stress that this does not exclusively or even primarily involve a preoccupation with complex theoretical systems serving as legitimations for the institutional order. Theories also have to be taken into account, of course. But theoretical knowledge is only a small and by no means the most important part of what passes for knowledge in a society. Theoretically, sophisticated legitimations appear at particular moments of an institutional history. The primary knowledge about the institutional order is knowledge on the pre-theoretical level. [27]

This quotation represents a series of implied but categorical statements about the relationship between knowledge and practice, knowledge and theory and, therefore, about theory and practice. It assigns a particular historically limited part to theory in practice. The quotation is so impressive and vague, however, that one has to read between the lines to discover its conceptual details. Theory is a means of legitimation. Having said that, theory can be put into its little box with that function on its label and a timing mechanism afixed to activate it.

Cicourel is even less explicit. When giving advice about how to handle historical materials he states: 'The researcher cannot appraise the conditions that led to the production of the document without some theory which accounts for the commonsense meanings used by the actor and by the social structure within which the material was produced.'[28] This is fair comment but we are left to guess what he thinks about such theories unless we believe that a theory that accounts for meanings amounts to a description of their communication and nothing more which is what Cicourel has produced. It seems clear that one cannot write about the part theory plays in society without first clarifying what is meant by theory.

Conceptual frameworks

A social theory is a means for understanding social reality; to assist understanding it has to clarify and to do this it has to simplify. It has then to be based on a simplification of reality; that is on a notion of reality which contains its basic elements. This notion comprises hypotheses about reality. The starting point for theorizing, then, is the formulation of hypotheses. On the basis of these a logically derived set of generalized analytical tools can be formed which is the theory. The tools we handle may make no reference to the hypotheses, but they are always there. The hypotheses amount to tentative suggestions or presumptions about social reality and therefore involve a conceptualization of reality. In other words, all theorizing starts with ideas about the nature of the subject of the theory, which in the case of sociology is about social relationships. The

ideas themselves must have their origin in the material conditions of existence. It is untenable and fatuous to conceive of ideas about social reality
as autonomous. Even if they are guesses or hunches there must be material
conditions for their existence. It is pure metaphysics to believe that ideas
are free-riding phenomena. They are derived from experiences.

All this may sound rather simple and elementary but it is important to
emphasize the material basis of theorizing for it is this basis which gives a
theory its primary meaning. The assumptions which underlie a theory set
the scope, stipulate its definitions, give meaning to its terms and concepts.
In this way the assumptions influence the collection and collation of data
and enter into the conclusions which are drawn from the analysis. Thus
theorizing is essentially tautological. A social theory which is logically
constructed can only be faulted through its conceptual basis. Because
social theory must relate to reality then it must be based on assumptions
which themselves comprise a valid interpretation of that reality. An explanation which does not relate to reality is not a theory but a fantasy and we
can forget it. An important exercise in understanding the anatomy of
theories, in comparing their utility, is to identify their conceptual bases.

Each individual theorist approaches theorizing through his own experiences which in some ways may be unique to him. However it is not the
uniqueness but the generality of experiences which give rise to assumptions about reality. The theorist may possess an expertise in the collection
and collation of data but in other ways he is the same as other people. He
draws on a common stock of knowledge to which existing theories belong.
He has experiences which are common to other people and to which that
knowledge relates. Theorizing has to concern these common experiences.
It would be of little use theorizing if there had to be a different explanation to account for the behaviour of each individual. There are different
conceptualizations of reality, therefore, but each one has to be a
generalization.

It is possible to be more precise than this. All interpretations of reality
fall within two categories. They assume either that reality is basically a
static phenomenon or that it is a changing one. There are, of course,
different variants within each category but the differences are subordinate
to the qualities which determine the category. A conceptualization of
reality as static implies that it has qualities which make for consensus,
which give it an organic unity, which are prior to any other qualities. A
conceptualization of reality as a changing phenomenon gives priority to
qualities which produce change. I have always found it difficult in discussions with conventional sociologists to convince them of the reality of this
broad categorization of conceptual frameworks. In conventional sociology
the term theory is either loosely defined or not defined at all. Certainly

the term is loosely used in the texts. All manner of explanations are described as theories and different explanations are attributed as different theories. So attached are sociologists to their particular explanations that they refuse to see any conceptual link between them. What they are doing is failing to identify the structure of their explanations and to see, therefore, that many apparently different explanations have a common structure. They are behaving towards explanations as empiricists behave towards empirical data and their conclusions are equally misleading. This inability to identify common conceptual links between theoretical explanations is a protective mechanism for it amounts to an inability to acknowledge the reality of theorizing and to see it as a legitimating process. It thus protects social theorists from seeing the political implications of their activity and enables them to maintain the dichotomy between theory and practice which is seen to be so essential for the maintenance of their status as 'social scientists'. But the conceptual links, like the structures of their observable social situations, are present whether they are recognized or not.

There are a number of ways by which broad conceptual frameworks can be identified. It is possible to see them through the initial assumptions which are made explicitly, through the analytical tools used, through the nature of the data awarded causal priority, by the conclusions which are reached. Indeed, as a conceptual framework determines the form of a theory it must be possible to approach the framework through the theory. This can be illustrated by examples. An explanation is basically static if it is based on an assumption which makes the environment of the subject static. For example, a *ceteris paribus* assumption would do the trick, as would an assumption, such as is used in conventional economics, confining the explanation to a single point of time. Equilibrium analysis falls into this classification since the movement, and hence the possible change which this permits is of a limited remedial character. An explanation which assumes consensus, such as a 'common value system' in structural functionalist analysis, or organic unity assumed in much industrial sociology and industrial relations research, is also primarily static. An explanation is basically static if it uses analytical tools which presuppose consensus qualities. For example, systems analysis, which permits the division and subdivision of social situations into causally autonomous segments, presupposes there are no structural determinants of action which link the systems.

The analytical tools of empiricism have the same implications, for they presuppose that situations are not structurally linked but have each their own meaning, depending on the facts each contains. Both these categories give reality a basically static quality because the movement they permit is of an *ad hoc*, remedial kind which must therefore spring from a base of consensus, of no movement. Analyses which concentrate on individual or small group action and which locate the sources of action in individuals or small groups, or which simply give priority to those sources, are inevitably static in conception for they treat social reality in segmented terms. It is impossible to conceive of a segmented reality having the qualities which give rise to perpetual pressures for movement. A similar situation occurs if the analysis is primarily concerned with the attitudes, goals, values or meanings held by individuals or small groups, such as organizations. In such instances the analysis begins at a point which makes it impossible to give adequate treatment to structural movement creating factors, even though structures be mentioned as having some analytical relevance. All phenomenological analysis, whether it is described as 'action frame of reference' or ethnomethodology, is as static in conception as structural functionalism. Lastly, the static quality of an explanation can be detected if its conclusions illustrate that change is limited in its scope to matters within boundaries, that movement is an aberration and to be resisted, that movement has a controllable, regulable, remedial quality. An analysis, for example, which concludes that strike action or any form of collective action by employees is an aberration and can be remedied is starting from an assumption that the environment of employees is dominated by qualities of organic unity.

The legitimating function of social theory

Even a superficial glance at the complex of sociological explanations in Western capitalist societies shows that each of them falls within one or other of the categories mentioned above and are derived, in consequence, from a common world view which sees reality as having unchanged, unchangeable boundaries with movement, if at all, taking place within them. This is so no matter what the explanations are called and what the claims of the analysts are. There is a fair amount of 'Parsons knocking' taking place these days, coupled with a lot of legitimate criticisms of structural functionalism, but in the vast majority of cases the knockers and critics are unable to reject the basis of the structural functionalist explanations, in part, because they do not recognize it and in part because, even if they do, they do not consider it important. The newer generation of American sociologists now taking over from that of Parsons, Merton and Selznick, and comprising such men as Etzioni, Friedrichs and Gouldner, is as firmly entrenched in the classic static tradition in sociology as its predecessor. I am not going to argue this claim in detail. I go over much of the ground in subsequent chapters, and in any case it is all so obvious. A close examination of the various explanations would show that each one fits more or less into each of the categories: that underneath the verbiage lies a common set of analytical tools producing roughly similar conclusions. This, indeed, is what one would expect from a common conceptualization of the subject matter of research, namely social reality.

Explanations based on a primarily static view of reality do a number of related things which are highly satisfactory for the beneficiaries of the existing state of affairs in the situations under examination. First of all, they are confined to an examination of superstructural factors, for they assume the structures are fixed, immutable. If an explanation concerns a business organization it assumes that the distribution of power in it as indicated by its shape is fixed and beyond the scope of the analysis. If the distribution of power is pyramidal, with control concentrated at the apex in the hands of the owner or his representatives, the explanation will never question this or locate the source of any problem in it. If an explanation is about inflation or unemployment within a capitalist society it will always be couched in terms of an imbalance between variables within the system and never located in the capitalist system itself. If an explanation is about strike action it always relates to factors such as faulty communications, defective leadership, lack of education or political motivation and never to contradictions within capitalism.

A second feature of relatively static explanations is that movement producing change is always an aberration created by a temporary maladjustment of factors. Such movements can never, by assumption, touch and penetrate the structure. The social change which possibly results is of necessity controllable. The maladjustment can be remedied because if it were otherwise the structure of the situation would be threatened and that would jeopardize the conceptual basis of the analysis. This point is raised in later chapters where the purpose of homeostasis mechanisms is outlined.

The third feature concerns their legitimating function. A characteristic of conventional sociological research is that it is invariably problem-centred. There are important reasons for this. When an analysis is based on the assumption that the normal order of things is one of undisturbed consensus it precludes an examination of that order. The question is settled by the assumption. It may, of course, concentrate on a description of the operation of the order, as has been the case with marginal analysis in economic theory, functionalism in anthropology and much of structural functionalism in sociology. The interesting questions, however, are about aberrations from the consensus base — about the problems which arise because the order is not being maintained. Sociological research, in consequence, has been largely about people in marginal situations such as divorce, crime and industrial action. Now when a consensus is assumed infringements of it are not simply issues of interest to sociologists but are defined as problems for the society. Sociologists, therefore, are encouraged to investigation consensus infringements. They are given financial support for such research. It has always been difficult in Britain to get financial support for research into social behaviour unless a problem relating to it has been specified.

The legitimating function of social theory comes in at this point. A theory with a static basis deals with problems in such a way as to exclude specific areas of social activity as being non-problematical. In other words, it precludes structures from analysis and in this way specifies that they do not present problems and need in no way to be altered. A reading of the literature dealing with business organizations in general and business management in particular would lead one to exempt the power relations which create the shape of business organizations from any responsibility for what may be at fault within them. Similarly, sociological literature *in general* depicts capitalist societies beset with problems of youth, of sex, of crime, of sabotage of various kinds, of deprivation, of exploitation, without even alluding to the social relations of production — to the exploitation of resources for private gain. Conventional sociology, because it is static in conception protects structures from criticism through excluding them from analysis. This, however, is a rather negative way of putting the position. If this were all that conventional sociological theory did its part would be limited and much more valuable than it is.

Social theory in general provides the means, the tools, for explaining and justifying. It directs explanations in such a way as to justify. It is through sociological explanations that knowledge about social situations beyond the immediate experiences of individuals is spread. Activity which is excluded because it is deemed to be irrelevant does not enter the body of knowledge, just as social activity in the past which is not recorded does not become a part of history. By its process of data selection, then, social theory determines what people should and should not know about social situations. Statically conceived social theory spreads data about consensus making and breaking factors. By implication, if not openly, it elevates consensus to the status of an ideal and designates infringements of it as being regrettable, undesirable, even dangerous. Knowledge about social situations reveals them to us, then, in a particular, partisan manner. So it is the body of knowledge built up through descriptions of social situations, as well as the analysis which is important in the descriptions, which emphasizes what is problematical and what is not. By its emphasis, its nuances, as well as its specific categorization, the body of knowledge shows what is 'right' and what is 'wrong', what is important and what is unimportant. Knowledge is inevitably concerned with 'justifying'. It never stands aloof from the situations it is about because the means whereby it is obtained are based on views about the nature of the situations.

Conventional social theory articulates values about situations, or rather, gives expression to values ascribed to them. Because the values do not question the structure they assume its continuity. This assumption is confirmation of the desirability or necessity of continuing the structure. Social theory legitimizes through giving what Berger and Luckmann would call a 'normative dignity'[29] to the structure. Sometimes this is done purposely through the translation of what may be attributed as practical imperatives of a situation to laws or principle. We theorize about the laws of supply and demand, the laws of the market and the law of diminishing returns in economic theory, so that the inviolate character of law, *per se*, rubs off on to supply and demand, the market and diminishing returns, and they assume in consequence the same inviolate character. We theorize about the principle of individualism of private profit-making, of competition, and give them the quality of being beyond criticism or reproach, or even of being sacrosanct. Where it is raised at all in theories, inequality is raised to the status of a principle; without it, it is reasoned, there would be no individual motivation, no private accumulation, no private investment and no economic growth. We theorize about the primacy of goals, the principle of shared values, with a similar effect. Most of all, however, the attribute of 'normative dignity' is given inadvertently through the simple act of theorizing. It is relevant at this point to return to a question I raised earlier in the chapter, namely, why should the dichotomy between theory and practice be emphasized so markedly in conventional discussions?

When theory is seen as an inextricable and inevitable part of practice, and practice is seen invariably to involve theorizing, then a theory has no glamour, no special status, no privileged identity. It is simply a tool with the same mundane qualities as practice itself. Conventional social theorists, of course, are prevented from seeing an identity between theory and practice because of conceptual difficulties, but even if this were not so it would be necessary for them to separate the two categories. The process of legitimation depends for its effectiveness on the extent to which conventional theories can be isolated and insulated from an ever changing social reality. If there were a constant analytical relationship between theory and practice, theoretical explanations would constantly be exposed to the glare of concrete reality and would be perpetually subject to scrutiny. In these circumstances the legitimating capabilities of theories would be considerably reduced. No theory would be able to confer 'normative dignity' on any practical imperative. We can see that legitimation is more than a process of explaining and justifying, for under constantly changing conditions it has to maintain a quality of constancy. In other words, a theoretical explanation is only able to fulfil a legitimating function if it is believed despite the facts. The legitimation, remember, is always about the elements of structures. In the case of capitalist societies, a structure which produces conditions favourable for a few, the owners of the means of production, and entails the exploitation of the majority, the non-owners of the means of production, has to be legitimated in the minds of the exploited majority. That is, the exploited majority has to be convinced that the essential elements of the structure such as individualism, profit-making and capital accumulation which so blatantly confer benefits on others are best for their own interests too. Now this can only be achieved if the theoretical explanations involved in the legitimation process are in some way reified. The assumptions, the laws and the principles expounded through the explanations have to be protected from worldly criticism. Competition, for instance, has to be accepted despite the inequalities it produces and despite its own inability to maintain itself as is shown through the growth in the degree of monopoly, the mergers, the takeovers and market manipulation. For this to be possible the theory which contains the explanations has to be safeguarded by being given suprahuman qualities. Theory itself has to be reified and has, therefore, to be separated from practice.

Different types of explanations in the process of legitimation have proceeded along different routes to reification. Economic theory has been elevated as a science with laws, beyond the comprehension of ordinary people, to be believed because it embodies the 'truth' about the economic order, to be accepted because of its irrefutable logic and scientific rigour. So economists have disowned the values implicit in their own theorizing and have taken, as Paul Baran so aptly describes, 'an agnostic view of the ends themselves', believing that they have nothing to do with goals and maintaining a posture of 'ethical neutrality'.[30] Along this course economic theory has become progressively more positivist, and has become obscured from lay scrutiny by the substitution of mathematical symbols for words and mathematical formulations for sentences. Sociology, on the other hand, has proceeded to reification via mystification caused by theoretical confusion. It is extremely difficult to discuss theory construction and model building with many sociologists. They are obscure about conceptualization, vague about assumptions and ill-informed about logic. One has to search for the assumptions in their explanations and to disentangle a mixture of terms, such as stability, progress, dynamic, conflict, harmony, alienation and class, thrown together to add quality, as if they were making a 'Lancashire hot-pot'. They seem to believe that one has only to say the word for the deed to be done. Describe an explanation as dynamic and it is indeed dynamic; introduce the word conflict and conflict is taken care of; throw in the terms alienation and bureaucracy and there we have the best of Marx and Weber, and so on. This confusion has been aided by the use of jargon and unintelligible terminology. It has become increasingly difficult even for sociologists to understand what other sociologists write. Obscurantism in sociology has undoubtedly acted as a substitute for reification where this has failed.

It need hardly be stated that not all theories are involved in the process of legitimation. Only those with static qualities and which describe, explain and justify the *status quo* qualify for this task. So although all theories have necessarily to be separated from practice, and as it would be illogical and untenable to admit that some were and some were not, that they did not all qualify for reification, a distinction has to be made between them. This is usually done by denigrating those which do not support the *status quo* as being 'unscientific', 'dogmatic', 'distortions', 'politically-motivated', 'fantasies' and the like. Alternatively they are regarded as the products of disturbed minds, nurtured in broken homes, criminal backgrounds or some form of depraved environment or simply as consequences of minds afflicted by psychopathic hereditary traits. Those explanations which do support the *status quo* are rewarded with the privilege of entering, through ideology, the thought processes of ordinary people. They comprise the dominant paradigm in society.

Theory in ideology

Every type of society gives rise to, fosters and spreads ideas about itself which protect and help to perpetuate it. These ideas are nobody's brainchild but arise out of the society itself. They are not the only ideas which arise, for the contradictions in a society ensure that there will be alternative, contradictory ideas. But for a large part of the life of a society the protective ideas are the dominant ones. This is so no matter what kind of society it is or in what historical epoch it may fall. Such ideas are dominant because it is in the interests of those who control the power situation that they should be. A society's greatest protection at any time and its only protection in the long-run is a generalized acceptance of what the society stands for. The exceptions are essentially historically short-run ones such as in classical colonialist situations where minorities maintain control over societies through force and irrespective of whether the ideas which represent their interests are generally accepted or not. South Africa is such an exception at the present. In the main, and even in situations where political power is maintained through the use of physical force, those who exercise political power will seek to encourage the formulation and spread of ideas which legitimize their control. They will, on the other hand, be hostile to ideas which challenge and, therefore, threaten that control. What the political power holders try to do, in effect, is to influence and control behaviour in general through the spread of ideas. They endeavour to produce a conformity in attitudes about the basic features of the society. They aim for a blanket acceptance of all that the society stands for. This is done through ideology.

I refer to ideology at some length in chaper 9 and I do not intend to repeat the details here. What I want to state here is that an ideology is the process through which ideas, values and purposes act to influence be-haviour and that, therefore, it is present in all societies at all times. The ideas, values and purposes have to be articulated in a particular way in order to influence behaviour. They have to be presented so as to enter into the thinking of people; to appear through analytical tools which people handle in their everyday lives without really knowing they are doing so; they have to make their impact through the explanations which ordinary people reach about their own and others' situations. They have, therefore, to be embodied in theories. Theories form an integral part of ideologies. Put differently, an ideology is in effect about the dissemination of theories. Because of the identity of theory and practice which I have mentioned earlier, all social activity has a theoretical explanation so that ideology covers every aspect of social activity. Theories enable problems to be solved so that a commonly accepted theory provides uniform answers to common problems. It should be pointed out that ideology is not just a matter of communicating ideas to influence consciousness and, therefore, behaviour. The ideological process involves influencing behaviour through consciousness and the enforced acceptance of ideas embodied in institu-tions. I regard institutionalized ideology as the most effective and perva-sive means of obtaining an acceptance of ideas. Conformity in behaviour, therefore, is produced by a common acceptance of ideas embodied in theories and the institutionalization of the same ideas.

An ideology implies the existence of an institutional framework for the dissemination of theories. The most important aspects of this framework are the family, the educational system and the mass media such as news-papers, radio and television, and, of course, books, pamphlets and leaflets. But ideas are also communicated orally through songs and public speeches, the repetition of folklore, and conversation in ordinary social relation-ships. This institutional framework is not available for the communication of any or all ideas, for significant areas of it are subject to control by those who exercise dominant power in the society. In those areas only the ideas acceptable to the power-holders are usually communicated. In other areas, formal education for instance, there are built-in tendencies to propagate ideas which serve the existing society. All in all, ideas which support the *status quo* get the greater currency.

All this points to the political character of social theories. No matter how detached from sordid reality social theorists may be portrayed, no matter how safely and securely insulated they may be in the panelled studies of ivory towers; no matter what dignity is conferred on them through reification — they all serve one political purpose or another in that they are assisting to preserve a structure or to change it. Alvin Gouldner puts the same point, but more cautiously, when he states:

Rooted in a limited personal reality, resonating some sentiments but not others, and embedded in certain domain assumptions, every social theory facilitates the pursuit of some but not of all courses of action, and thus encourages us to change or to accept the world as it is, to say yea or nay to it. In a way, every theory is a discreet obituary or celebration for some social system. [31]

Social theories service political purposes through entering into ideologies. They do not do this in a dignified manner, in all their glory, but as disembodied statements or slogans. The theories which serve the existing structure are used most extensively in this manner. They are manipulated, abbreviated, sloganized, projected as crude propaganda and submitted as articles of faith, all for political purposes. Political statements such as 'we are one nation', 'we must work together for prosperity', 'we must control wages to defeat inflation', 'we must preserve the value of the pound at all costs', 'we must encourage greater profits to improve efficiency', 'cut public expenditure', 'reduce the tax burden', 'strikes are a threat to democracy', 'let the men run Britain who know how', 'equality would produce drab uniformity', 'high taxes kill incentive', 'leaders are born, not made', and 'keep Britain white' are all supported by elaborate, complex theoretical treatises. It would be virtually impossible to find a political slogan defending the structure which did not have a theoretical counterpart.

It would be wrong to state that all theoretical explanations with a relatively static conceptual basis give a blanket endorsement of the society to which they relate. Many explanations are liberal in character; they enable facets of the system to be attacked and altered; they provide theoretical justification for social change within the society. Through the study of crime, social welfare, community action, race relations and work situations, for example, social scientists have encouraged the development of new attitudes and hence of fresh approaches. Gouldner made the point about American sociology that after the Second World War, American functionalism 'increasingly sought ways to ally itself with and serve the Welfare State'.[32] He stated also that professional sociology tended to drift towards the politics of liberalism.[33] But this does not amount to a criticism of the view that social theory serves the *status quo*. It merely describes the logical outcome of a social systems theory. There are two points to note. First, that a methodology which breaks up reality into autonomous systems or situations will produce innumerable separate explanations; second, that each of these explanations will be about social problems, defined as infringements of norms or consensus or organic unity. In this respect conventional sociology is not tending towards liberalism, it is inherently liberal. The important factor is, however, that in directing attention towards the solution of problems within the super-structure liberal sociology is diverting attention from the structure itself and is thus helping to protect structures from analysis and criticism. The more liberal sociology is, the more subversive it is of attempts to focus interest on structural causes of behaviour.

One of the most impressive examples of the subverting qualities of liberal social science is the theoretical work of John Maynard Keynes. *The General Theory of Employment, Interest and Money* was published in 1935. It was written by Keynes at a time when not only Britain but the whole capitalist world was experiencing large-scale, long-term unemployment. In Britain in the interwar years the rate of unemployment fell below 10 per cent in only one year, 1927, and rose to a rate as high as 22.1 per cent in 1932. Classical economic theory, which was unadulterated equilibrium analysis, explained unemployment as an aberration, a temporary imbalance, in the same way as it explained monopoly practices. The phenomenon of persistent unemployment was so completely at odds with this explanation that the whole body of economic theory was losing credibility. If this situation had persisted much longer even professional economists would have been forced to look for a qualitatively different explanation which perhaps pointed to the structure of capitalism as the major cause of unemployment. But this might have taken some time longer, for classical economics was a highly institutionalized affair. It is pertinent to read what Keynes himself had to say on this matter. The first chapter of *The General Theory* consists of one paragraph on one page. It stated:

I have called this book the General Theory of Employment, Interest and Money, *placing the emphasis on the prefix* general. *The object of such a title is to contrast the character of my arguments and conclusions with those of the* classical *theory of the subject, upon which I was brought up and which dominates the economic thought, both practical and theoretical, of the governing and academic classes of this generation, as it has for a hundred years past. I shall argue that the postulates of the classical theory are applicable to a special case only and not to the general case, the situation which it assumes being a limiting point of the possible positions of equilibrium. Moreover, the characteristics of the special case assumed by the classical theory happen not to be those of the economic society in which we actually live, with the result that its teaching is misleading and disastrous if we attempt to apply it to the facts of experience.* [34]

Keynes's first chapter makes three points which are relevant to this discussion. First, he recognizes the ideological significance of social theory; second, he recognizes that a theory which does not accord with the reality of the 'economic society in which we actually live' may result in 'disastrous' practical consequences, and thirdly, he realizes the necessity of providing a new theoretical formula to take account of that reality the classical theory was incapable of explaining. But he makes clear that his new formula is not conceptually new but an extension of the classical explanation. The classical theory is not seen as incompatible with his but as explaining a special case within a general explanation. Keynes's position on this question is made clear in his *Concluding Notes*. 'Thus', he stated, 'I agree with Gesell that the result of filling in the gaps in the classical theory is not to dispose of the "Manchester System", but to indicate the nature of the environment which the free play of economic forces requires if it is to realize the full potentialities of production.' The classical theory assumed the structure of the society as given and saw no reason to investigate it. Keynes thought likewise and in case anyone misread him he pointed out that 'it is not the ownership of the instruments of production which it is important for the State to assume', and then 'I see no reason to suppose that the existing system seriously misemploys the factors of production which are in use. There are, of course, errors of foresight; but these would not be avoided by centralizing decisions.' [35]

The Keynesian theory, therefore, in no sense threatened the structure of capitalism; rather it was intended to provide a solution to an otherwise intractable problem without questioning its structure at all. In the years which followed politicians eagerly took up the policy implications of Keynesian analysis; indeed the politicians were quicker to accept Keynes than were his fellow economists. The core of the matter is that Keynes successfully analysed short-term fluctuations in the level of employment and produced conclusions which formed the basis for equally successful short-term employment policies. The high level of unemployment ended in the 1940s, not through the application of Keynesian policies but through the impact of war. Thereafter the employment problem was one of regulating short-term fluctuations in a situation of virtual full employment and for this the Keynesian explanation was extremely useful. So John Maynard Keynes, through what might be described as a conceptual adaptation, gave the classical theory a new lease of life by liberalizing it, and in doing so protected the structure of capitalism from a scrutiny and exposure which would have been inevitable if the theory had been unable to break out of its fantasy world.

The rescue operations of liberal social theorists support the protection which conventional theorists give in general to their explanations. They give the dominant conceptual framework a necessary resilience. The general picture is one of a broad conceptual framework, setting limits to explanations, determining their scope, giving meaning to their terms and concepts and generally providing analytical tools. Within the framework, the liberals are perpetually working to remove the more glaring deficiencies of their explanations. They do this in a piecemeal fashion as bits of reality stubbornly persist in spite of what their conventional explanations state. But the whole operation takes place within a protective context which would be incredible if one did not see its political necessity. Conventional theorists tenaciously hang on to their particular explanations no matter how threadbare or discredited they may be. The scientific method which stipulates that a hypothesis which cannot be validated should be rejected is only for the use of others. I remember how Friedrich von Hayek held his head in his hands during tutorials at the London School of Economics, muttering that he could not understand why people did not believe his explanation of the theory of capital. It did not seem to have occurred to him then to reject his theory or even seriously to adapt it. Even the liberals tend to be resisted as saboteurs and it is frequently not until later that they gain conventional respectability. During my time as a student at the London School of Economics, from 1946 to 1949, Keynesian economics was taught diffidently and apprehensively, with an uncomfortable feeling that Keynes might be rocking the boat. The theoretical work of C. Wright Mills, who was a radical rather than a liberal sociologist, was received with some hostility in the USA, even though its main contribution was to reveal deficiencies in structural functionalism in a manner which has subsequently become commonplace.

The sensitivity of sociologists to threats, albeit mild and even ineffectual ones, to their own explanations has been illustrated by Pitirim Sorokin and J. L. Moreno. Sorokin suffered an invasion of his theoretical, and perhaps more unfortunately his actual pitch by Talcott Parsons when Parsons entered the Department of Sociology at Harvard University, where Sorokin had been Chairman since 1930. He reacted by dismissing the claims of Parsons and other 'new' sociologists that they had produced new theories or were covering hitherto neglected areas of sociological behaviour on the grounds that it had all been done before. He described his attitude in a chapter called 'Amnesia and new Columbuses' in *Fads and Foibles in Modern Sociology*.

The germs of amnesia and of the mania of new discoveries have also spread in the field of modern theoretical sociology. T. Parsons and E. Shils can be taken as representative victims of the epidemics discussed. Parsons, in the well-founded words of E. Faris, confidently believes that new knowledge has come into the world (with the publication of Parsons's The Social System*). . . . The proudest boast in Chapter XII is the discovery of the combination of interdependence and independence of personality, culture and system (organization). This claim borders on the incredible.*

Sorokin added that a

Similar criticism of Parsons's and Shils's Towards a General Theory of Action *. . . is made by L. von Wiese. . . . Knowing well that Parsons was an instructor in my courses at Harvard and observing the essential similarity between Parsons's sociological framework and mine. Von Wiese particularly stresses a complete lack of reference to theories of mine published many years before Parsons's work.* [36]

The work and claims of Kingsley Davis and Wilbert Moore, formerly graduate students at Harvard, came in for the same criticism.

J. L. Moreno was much more vituperative about the work of sociologists who followed him in his special field. In the 'Preludes' to *Who Shall Survive?*, a book described by Moreno as 'a new bible, the bible for social conduct, for human societies. It has more ideas packed in one book than a whole generation of books', Moreno is obsessed with establishing himself as an originator of group psychotherapy, as the prime formulator of sociometric theory, and with locating his ideas in the work of others:

Besides the good genies who surrounded every pioneer there is also a class of people who want to steal his ideas and make them their own. It would be harsh to call them intellectual thieves. They are usually honestly affected people. First they become friends and followers because an intellectual commodity cannot be stolen, it has to be absorbed. But once they believe that they master the new skill they prefer that the creator be dead. Indeed, they often deny his existence. [37]

All this is shadow-boxing. The real fighting is reserved for those whose work challenges the basis of existing theory. The main protective characteristic of conventional theory is the manner in which contrary contradictory explanations threatening the credibility of conventional theory can be suppressed by being refused outlets, by being ignored, or by being ridiculed.

It has to be recognized first that conventional social theorists, as a reward for their contribution to the dominant ideology, control most of the publication outlets. They largely edit the academic journals, exercise influence with publishers and generally act as arbiters in the assessment of academic works for research and publication purposes. By and large they can regulate the flow and quality of theoretical work into the ideological process. In this connection they play highly political parts for, in effect, they help to determine which theoretical explanations are to be made available to ordinary people for the analysis of their own situations. Ordinary people may maintain a belief in an explanation simply because there is no alternative at hand. If there is no alternative this may in part be due to the influence of the regulators of academic outlets. I do not want to overstate the influence of these people; they are handmaidens of a political system, but at the stage of articulating ideas in a theoretical form they are important. Nor do I want to personalize the issue by questioning the intellectual integrity of any particular sociologist who may be editors or publishers' readers, or who may advise foundations. This process of control through selection or denigration takes place anyway, no matter who is involved. No insights can be created by scrutinizing the actions of individuals who have rejected this article or ridiculed that or ignored the other. The process, of course, is not a dehumanized one. Decisions to do this or that in relation to non-conventional explanations are made by individuals. Individuals, moreover, project themselves into the process by claiming explanations as their own property and treating criticisms of them as personal attacks. 'It is incredible and unfortunate', Moreno stated, 'that people who steal your ideas become, in addition, also your personal enemies.'[38]

There are difficulties in the way of describing discrimination against explanations which criticize the basis of conventional ones. Firstly, evidence is hard to collect. Articles which do not appear, books which are not published and research projects which are refused financial support, disappear into obscurity so that they can neither be counted nor assessed. Secondly, it is always possible to give legitimate reasons for rejecting work such as 'the book would not sell', 'the article has major defects in its construction', and 'the research project is impracticable, would cost too much or too little' and so on. The intellectual quality of rejected work cannot be assessed because the work is inaccessible. In any case the claims of people who have had work rejected can always be regarded as cases of 'sour grapes'. At the risk of having one or other or all of these accusations made I shall relate the experience of chapters in this book. Three of the chapters have already been published in France, Yugoslavia and Holland where there is a small number of established academic journals which publish nonconformist papers. Each one has been submitted subsequently for publication in a British or American sociology journal, but, has been rejected. In the event it would be invidious to state that they were rejected because they lack quality. Chapter 3, 'The conceptual basis of organization theory', was initially written as an article for *l'homme et la société* in April 1967. The following year it was published in the journal of the Yugoslav Sociological Association, *Sociologija*. Later it became part of the scheme which led to this book. It was, however, rejected by the British journal, *Sociology*, on the grounds that it was too much like a chapter out of a book and too little like an article which stood on its own. Chapter 2, written afterwards, went through a similar experience. After publication in Paris and Belgrade it was rejected by the *Sociological Review* because

any article which sets out to attack a body of material must not only examine that material but also show that its nature is such that it permits statements of a certain kind to be made about it. Our referees felt that you did not, in fact, make this kind of demonstration and that it could not, therefore, be recommended for publication. [39]

The referees, presumably, could not see the common static conceptual framework of the approaches they espoused. I can imagine their comments. The chapter on Etzioni was turned down through, it was stated, lack of space in the American journal *Social Research* but was published in English in the Dutch journal *mens en maatsch appij* in 1972. The articles aroused much interest in continental sociological circles but when the editor of *Gruppendynamik*, the German edition of the *American Journal of Applied Behavioural Science*, endeavoured to publish two of them he was overruled by his editorial board.

I have no doubt that many others have had similar exasperating experiences, particularly during the Cold War phase. Mine, however, occurred during the period when Marx, especially the 'younger' Marx, was being increasingly discovered and talked about, and when literature about Marx was found by publishers to have a lucrative market in the West. In this period, which is still continuing, there has been a distinct attempt to keep Marx's work in its own box, separate from and without relevance to conventional theory. Students have not been encouraged to use Marx's methodology either on practical issues or as a means of assessing conventional theory itself. Conventional theory, despite the tirades against it by people such as Alvin Gouldner, has continued to be protected. Indeed the tirades have turned out to be props for the Gouldners of the sociology world have suddenly had mental blackouts when the question of alternative conceptual approaches has been raised and we have been treated to contortions, like 'reflexive sociology', desperately contrived to remove the defects of conventional theory without rejecting the whole body of theory itself. I shall return to this point later.

A fairly recent attempt to rescue conventional theory was made by Amitai Etzioni through his work *The Active Society: a theory of societal and political processes*.[40] The book was published in 1968 and written, therefore, before the main impact of students' criticism of sociology as a bourgeois discipline. In the words of R. W. Friedrichs:

A more ambitious effort to restructure the controlling paradigm has come most recently from Amitai Etzioni. Both his professional activity and major elements of his theoretical position — his accentuation of power and the political dimension in general, the assumption of social entropy rather than social order as a point of departure, and of 'transformability' rather than homeostatic stability as his goal — have led and promise to continue to lead many of the younger generation within the discipline to perceive him as the rightful heir to C. Wright Mills's mantle at Columbia and within the larger profession. [41]

Friedrichs then went on to spell out the similarity between Etzioni's work and that of Parsons but did not retract from his belief that 'Etzioni's reincarnation of the action frame . . . may have to be taken quite seriously indeed'.

The Active Society was reviewed in the *American Journal of Sociology* early in 1970 by Robert M. Cook in such a manner as to evoke the wrath of 'members of the community of scholars', such as Lewis Coser and Warren Breed. The review and the correspondence form an interesting example of the manner in which the protective mechanism works. Cook questioned the whole conceptual approach of Etzioni by querying the relevance of his book for understanding concrete reality. Then the knives were drawn. The review and the correspondence are reproduced below.

The Active Society: a Theory of Societal and Political Processes *by Amitai Etzioni, New York: Free Press, 1968*

Robert M. Cook
American Independent Movement and Industrial Workers of the World

This is the kind of book that gives sociology a bad name. How easy it makes things for those who argue that sociologists elaborate the obvious — like 'all other things being equal, the larger the number and the greater the diversity of the perspective of a group of units, the more difficult it is to achieve a consensus' *(p. 478, his roman lettering). Over 700 pages of this kind of writing are devoted to justifying Etzioni's grandiose claim to have developed the 'foundations for a theory of macroscopic action' (p. viii). Granted that he modestly uses the word 'foundations' because 'our knowledge is too limited and the task of building a comprehensive theory is too* demanding for any one mason to lay much more than a base' (p. viii) and admits that this new theory is 'at best partly new' (p. x)! His objective, he says, is to explore the conditions under which societies of the 'post-modern' period (since 1945) can exercise the option of becoming masters of themselves, or 'active' (p. vii). The results are literally unbelievable.

Serious analysts of society will find little of value in this compendium of footnotes, jargon and tautologies. The apologists for the rulers of our society will, on the other hand, find a wealth of scientific sounding phrases with which to mask their favourite prejudices. The term 'post-modern', for example, is clearly an ideological cover for those who are afraid or unwilling to deal with capitalism as a major sociohistoric formation. In this book dedicated to the 'active ones, my students at Columbia and at Berkeley', about three paragraphs are devoted to a discussion of capitalism (pp. 519–20). Etzioni's students have long since left him behind. The second major ideological component of this book is Etzioni's idealism, despite his claim to go 'Beyond the Antimony of Idealism and Realism' (p. 21). 'Active societies are engaged in realizing their values, according to Etzioni. What Soviet and American societies 'tend to lack most is effectual commitment' to their values (p. 13). This is an idealist approach, and it is factually wrong. What prevents the realization of some (not all) American values is not a mystical lack of effectual commitment but a concrete social structure based upon the ownership and control of productive resources by a small number of people, and another set of values clustered around private property and profit calculations which they use in their decisions. Etzioni totally ignores the basic socioeconomic principle that 'the rate and direction of economic development in a country at a given time depend on both the size and the mode of utilization of the economic surplus. These in turn are determined by the degree of development of productive forces, the corresponding structure of socioeconomic relations, and the system of appropriation of the economic surplus that those relations entail' (Paul Baran, The Political Economy of Growth, New York, 1957, p. 44).

He has, as a result, almost nothing to say about classes, class struggles or revolution. The major social forces which have shaped modern history, and which will usher in the 'post-modern' period — it did not arrive in 1945 — are nowhere dealt with in serious fashion. Etzioni's own ideological position and the limits of his imagination and vision are made clear by his continual citing of western European countries governed by social demo-cratic parties as approximations of 'the active society'.

For the past five years, I have taught a sociology course on American society and have been heavily involved in what is called the Movement. Recently I have been making a living as a construction worker. The active society has no relevance for the reality of the America that I know. To

*learn about how things really are, sociologists should turn to those who by
and large have been spurned by academics — for example, C. Wright Mills,
Robert Lynd, Paul Baran, Paul Sweezy, or Gabriel Kolko.*

*As Martin Nicolaus said so clearly, sociologists for too long have had
their 'eyes turned downwards, and their palms upwards' ('Remarks at the
A.S.A. Convention, Boston, 1968', Catalyst, Spring 1969). This book does
raise one important question for the profession: Why is it that at this
crucial time in our history an 'important' professor of sociology at a major
American university can produce such nonsense, and worse yet, be taken
seriously by his colleagues?* [42]

Some debate about Robert Cook's review of Etzioni's The Active Society

I should like to strongly protest the review of Amitai Etzioni's The Active
Society *in the current issue of the* American Journal of Sociology. *It seems
to me that a scholarly journal owes to members of the community of
scholars the courtesy of having their books reviewed by other scholars.
The reviewer of this book uses the occasion for an ideological attack and
plainly is actuated by concerns that are far from that of a scholar. I hold
no brief for Etzioni's book; in fact, I happen to disagree rather sharply
with much of what he has to say, but I am outraged at the shabby treatment he has received in your pages. I think that you owe him a public
apology.*

Lewis Coser
State University of New York at Stony Brook

*I would like to protest the treatment given Etzioni's book. It was a non-
review, written by a person who was not equipped and obviously not
prepared to give it a professional and scholarly evaluation. The book is one
of the most difficult and demanding in our field. It may become an
'important' book. Therefore, I would like to see it get an orthodox review
by a trained and experienced sociologist — like the rest of the books you
treat. Whether or not the review turns out pro or con is not the point. The
book should get a thorough and painstaking review in your* Journal.

Warren Breed
Scientific Analysis Corporation, San Francisco

*May I come to the defense of Cook's review of my book? Several col-
leagues wrote to me** expressing their dismay over the political and* ad
hominem *attack the alleged review consists of. Of course, I too would have
preferred a discussion of the book, rather than the author, and an assess-*

* Editor's note: One of those colleagues also wrote to the *Journal* but preferred that
his letter be withheld from publication.

ment of its professional merits in addition to a political evaluation. But as a normative position does run throughout the book, and it is a position old guard Marxists, especially Stalinists, would find deeply offensive, there seems little reason why they should not cuss with all their lungs.

The aspect of the 'review' I do find perturbing is that it is such a poor political commentary. Cook's criteria for radicalism are the number of times one mentions class conflict, capitalism, and Paul Baran. The Active Society challenges the conception that people can be 'socialized' and 'social controlled'; it outlines the reasons societal roles and patterns must be made responsive to the members — rather than the other way around (chap. 21). It characterizes the United States and the Soviet Union as unresponsive societies, although for different reasons (chaps. 16–18). The book defines the conditions under which total transformation of the societal structure of these and other societies may take place and the kind and scope of citizen mobilization needed to transform them (chap. 15 and second part of chap. 21). The Active Society concerns itself less with the fundamental transformation of economic and class relations than a Marxist tract and more with those of social and political relations, but the primacy of politics has been endorsed even by Mao.

Finally the book explores the social conditions the relations between individuals and society will change — in a fundamental and encompassing manner. It is this concern with the societal conditions under which all individuals will find an effective society which is the main basis of the book's 'deviationist' nature. The same may be said about the chapters which deal with cybernetics of society, a science now advanced in Poland and the USSR, at grave risk to its advocates. Cook is quite correct in implying there are strong 'liberal' parts to my theory. Those are most evident in the concern with providing all members of society with an equal access to the guidance mechanisms of society and a study of the institutions which protect civil and human rights. Are these parts so offensive that a radical can completely overlook the commitment of the book to a wholistic transformation of our society? All this is only to say that, if sociological books are to be reviewed exclusively on the basis of their normative message, hopefully political commentators will be found who at least will discharge their responsibilities in the terms of the radical posture they seek to advance. The AJS did not even provide for such a review of my book.

Amitai Etzioni
Columbia University

The reviewer replies

(Robert M. Cook is a construction worker in New Haven, Connecticut.

From 1964 to 1969 he was assistant professor of sociology at Yale University, having received his PhD at Princeton University in 1964. He is co-editor, with Wilbert Moore, of Readings on Social Change, *published in 1967 by Prentice-Hall. In 1966 and again in 1968, Mr Cook was the candidate for US Congress of the American Independent Movement in Connecticut. – Editor.)*

In their hurry to condemn my political views or lack of professionalism, your correspondents missed the main point of my review, namely that The Active Society *(and the school of sociology of which it is a part) is a failure as social thought.*

First, I said that this is the kind of book that gives sociology a bad name because it is filled with pompous italicized elevation of the obvious to 'principles'. Second, I said that it is a compendium of footnotes, jargon, and tautologies which will be of little help to those who want to understand how societies work. Third, I said that the book despite its claim, is marred by philosophical idealism and ignorance of fundamental socio-economic laws. This leads Etzioni to attribute a state of mind (such as 'lack of effectual commitment') to societies, not unlike those who speak of lack of 'faith' or 'moral fiber'. The IWW calls such people 'sky pilots'.

Fourth, I said that the book virtually ignores social classes, class struggle and revolution, and falsely asserts that the 'postmodern' era arrived in 1945. It is true, as one of your readers claims [Editor's note: In a letter not published], that there is considerable talk about stratification. But 'stratification' is one of those terms, so dear to some American sociologists, which obscure rather than illuminate social reality – in this case, the development and existence of social classes.

Finally, I identified Etzioni's political blindness as the source of his intellectual blindness. He does not fail to understand because he is stupid – he fails because he is committed to a set of assumptions which limit his vision. I do not attack his political views because they are different from mine – I attack them because they lead generally to a misunderstanding of social processes and specifically to a gloss over capitalism and the way it works. How little Etzioni can see, even of himself, with these blinders is illustrated by his claim to be interested in the total transformation *(his) of societies while citing, as I said, western European countries governed by social democratic parties as approximations of his ideal.*

Some of your readers seem especially concerned with the professional qualifications of your reviewers. I would think that it might make sense to have more reviews by nonacademics to check the field's headlong slide into scholastic irrelevance. After all, we would hardly expect the emperor's tailors to be the ones to tell him that he has not clothes.

Etzioni's cries of 'old guard Marxist' and 'Stalinist' should be funny to anyone who knows me, but otherwise they are sad. Anti-Stalinism won't be as profitable today as it once was for old dissenters who are now distinguished Professors of Sociology.

I hope that the letters you received are not representative of your readers' views. I doubt they are. More and more younger sociologists, at least, are unwilling to fall into the trap of allowing the limits of rational discourse to be set by a self-perpetuating oligarchy of 'leaders'. The events of the last ten years have created a group of sociologists who refuse to be apologists for capitalism and imperialism. Their voices will be heard in or out of sociology. [43]

Robert M. Cook

The technique of retaliation in this case was to ignore the review and to damn the reviewer. The implications of the correspondence are that academic works should only be criticized on the basis of detailed evidence, that the criticisms should in some way be academic and not ideological and that the critics should be those sociologists defined as sociologists by the conventional theorists. These rules apply, of course, only to the critics of conformity. No holds are barred where criticisms of non-conformity are concerned. Rules are made and legitimated to suit the purpose. One of these is to attempt to damn a book with silence. One of my books, *Militant Trade Unionism*, received not a single notice except in the left-wing Press.

The reverse side of this situation is the manner in which sociologists draw on each other for support and distribute eulogies to each other as a means of enhancing reputations and increasing the prestige of their works. This activity in some form is inevitable. Who else can theorists quote other than those who support their particular view? It is unlikely that Parsons or Merton would draw on Marx for endorsement of structural functionalism though in recent years it has become acceptable to make highly selective references to Marx in order to give the impression that such phenomena as conflict are being taken account of, that the theorists are 'progressive' or that some great synthesizing work is underway. However, it should not be thought that conventional theorists cast around the whole conceptual framework for support. There are, as was indicated earlier, many sharp and bitter divisions between theorists within the same framework. The safest bet for any person in this situation is to quote himself and those of his friends he feels he can trust. In *Social Theory and Social Structure* R. K. Merton quoted his own work more than that of anyone else. He has fifty-six references to himself, thirty-one references to P. E. Lazarsfeld and twenty-two references to Talcott Parsons. A number of the references to

Lazarsfeld and Parsons, both of whom worked closely with Merton, were prefaced by such remarks as 'brilliant insights', 'acute observations' and 'enviable clarity'. There were only four quotations from those whom Merton regarded as critics, one from G. Gurvitch and three from G. Myrdal and in one of these Myrdal is described as 'gratuitous'. G. C. Homans in *The Human Group* also quotes himself more than any other. Sorokin describes this theoretical inbredness as a form of amnesia. Amnestics, he stated, use 'the technique of quoting only each other' and not quoting 'the outsiders to the clique'. He stated that in an analysis of 129 sociology texts it was found that there was a 'mutual back scratching ... in citations'. [44] From the outside it would seem that there was an unscrupulous disregard of scientific rigour. From the inside it all seems so reasonable and necessary. After all if one's own explanation is so precious who else is there to quote anyway?

This rather frantic activity by conventional sociologists is not really necessary for though their works may not be sold in large numbers or read widely, the ideas they contain, the concepts they use and the general conclusions they reach are given exclusive rights by the dominant ideological process. More than this, the theoretical treatises which support the *status quo*, tacitly or otherwise, provide through the institution of ideology, 'instant analyses' for ordinary people. They provide the means whereby reality is interpreted and thereby provide the interpretations too. In other words, commonsense constructs are derived from conventional theoretical explanations.

The dominant paradigm

Since the publication of Thomas Kuhn's *The Structure of Scientific Revolution* in 1962, it has become popular to talk about paradigms. A paradigm, according to Kuhn in the first edition of his book, is a universally recognized scientific achievement that for a time provides model problems and solutions to a community of practitioners.[45] He obviously did not realize the implications of his definition, particularly with regard to theory displacement, and when he was reminded of them he revised his definition in the second edition of his book in 1970.[46] His revised definition was a retreat to a conformist position which added little to our understanding of theory displacement. Kuhn was writing about the physical sciences but his remarks were intended to have a general theoretical relevance and to include historical and social research.[47] It is in relation to social science that Kuhn's initial definition of paradigm was potentially disturbing to conformist social theorists. Karl Popper was one in particular who took up the battle cry, and unfortunately Kuhn himself was quickly shouting with the rest. We do not, however, have to accept Kuhn's revision. We can use his initial draft and be grateful to him for articulating in relation to the physical sciences a situation which is so logically apparent in the social sciences but which is more difficult to make out. Kuhn gave social scientists an indisputable point of reference for understanding the revolutionary implications of theory displacement in the social sciences.

The essence of Kuhn's first edition is that the history of science shows that there is one dominant theory which constitutes the dominant paradigm in each scientific domain; that the dominant paradigm dominates for considerable periods, providing the answer to the main problems; that the dominant theory (paradigm) is based on assumptions which determine its scope and specify its limitations; that once these limitations are reached then theory construction is ended in this case and the heuristic qualities of the theory cannot be developed further; that theorists do not recognize this situation and engage in theoretical exercises which are no more than puzzle-solving; that further theoretical advances are dependent upon the emergence of an alternative conceptual framework on which a new theory will be based; that the new theory will displace the old one in a scientific revolution and that the new theory will constitute the dominant paradigm. A state of crisis arises about the ability of the existing paradigm and ends with its revolutionary overthrow.

This explanation largely fits, as indeed it should, with the situation in the social sciences. The main alterations which have to be made to it concern the extent of social scientific domains and, therefore, the pervasiveness of the dominant paradigm, and the introduction of a dialectical conception of revolutionary change. In the social sciences we are not dealing with specific, demarcated areas of scientific interest for which equally specific theories are applicable. We are dealing with a reality which is at one and the same time an interrelated entity and a process. No areas can be cordoned off or bits broken away as autonomous scientific domains. People's lives cannot be compartmentalized for different theoretical treatments. I deal with this at some length in chapters 9 and 10. In the social sciences the only reasonable domain to work from is that set by the social relations of production. These relations create the conditions which give rise to the ideas lying at the core of conventional social theory and which, in various ways, legitimize and generally support the form of society based on them. The social relations of production do not have geographical or ethnic boundaries, neither does the general theory which arises from them. If it can be stated that there is a general theory reflecting the ideas of capitalism and legitimizing its existence it must equally be said that within capitalism there is a single dominant paradigm.

This raises questions about the nature of a paradigm. In his revised edition, Kuhn attempts to distinguish between two different meanings which could be attributed to the term paradigm. The first refers to 'the entire constellation of beliefs, values, techniques, and so on, shared by members of a given community'. This he calls the sociological meaning. The second meaning denotes 'one sort of element in that constellation, the concrete puzzle-solutions which, employed as models or examples, can replace explicit rules as a basis for the solution of the remaining puzzles of normal science'.[48] The first is described as a 'disciplinary matrix' while the second is identified by the term 'exemplar'. In the social sciences 'disciplinary matrices' refer to consensus systems which neither possess the contradictions which could lead to qualitative change nor confront un-controllable pressures for such change from outside sources. I argue at length in this book that such systems belong to the fantasy world of those who would like to put present structures in cotton wool and preserve them for ever. There are, of course, beliefs which are shared, but invariably they comprise a part of a totality which possesses its own contradictions. If there are situations which are characterized by shared beliefs then they will be sociologically irrelevant. The second type appears to refer to the activities of the different models, such as structural functionalism and ethnomethodology, which operate within the dominant conceptual frame-work and are preoccupied with puzzle-solving. Kuhn, however, regards a puzzle as an issue which places the theorist and not the theory he employs in difficulty. A crisis in such a paradigm can therefore be solved without altering or even questioning its theoretical basis. Kuhn in his second thoughts, does not want his analysis to lead logically to paradigmic up-heavals — and it does not. Neither of Kuhn's categories of paradigm in any way raises any questions for conventional social theory.

This conclusion is doubtless reassuring for conventional social theorists, after the alarm which the first edition of the book had generated. And it accords with the manner in which paradigms have been defined, in sociology in particular, before Kuhn's revisions were published. The ethno-methodologists, through their concern with 'commonsense constructs', have shown most interest in paradigms. David Silverman claimed that Kuhn's argument supported his contention that the 'action frame of reference' was a paradigm replacing the structural functionalist paradigm because of its inability to explain a 'social problem', namely the relation-ship between actors, goals and action.[49] In a later book Silverman implies the existence of many paradigms and makes no reference to a dominant one.[50] In that same book, David Walsh, giving an ethno-methodological interpretation of 'Sociology and the social world', correctly analyses the term paradigm but incorrectly defines an 'organized

conceptual framework' in that he believes that sociological phenomenology has its own framework distinct from that of positivistic sociology,
and, therefore, constitutes a distinct paradigm. Positivist sociology, Walsh
claims, 'attempts to use a natural-science paradigm . . . assuming that social
phenomena possess the same characteristics as natural phenomena'.[51]
Having made this unsubstantiated claim, Walsh then proceeds to demonstrate how natural and social phenomena involve different concepts of
reality and constitute different paradigms. Robert Friedrichs organized his
book *A Sociology of Sociology* (1970) on Thomas Kuhn's general thesis.
The meaning of paradigms, therefore was crucial to Friedrichs. A
paradigm, he stated,

> *communicates the notion expressed by the term 'model' without invoking
> that word's physical imagery. A paradigm is an 'example', but one that is
> typically linguistic in base rather than physical, a conceptual reference
> rather than a perceptual one. But it is a* prime *example that serves as a
> common frame of reference, a 'definition of the situation' that provides a
> basic focus of orientation.* [52]

Friedrichs advances this definition in his first chapter and then proceeds to
give meaning to paradigm by illustrations. It was unlikely, he argued, 'that
there was any broad consensus regarding the fundamental nature of
sociology's subject matter either in Europe or in America during the
period leading up to the Second World War. No single theoretical posture
or piece of research stood as a self-evident key to orthodoxy'. So there was
no paradigm in sociology before 1939. Then came Talcott Parsons and
with him social systems theory and a paradigm. This paradigm lasted until
the 1960s when the conservative equilibrium character of structural
functionalism was challenged by activism. The 'novel problem' which
could not be solved within the paradigm, Friedrichs stated, was '"change"
– fundamental social change'. During the 1960s, the paradigm was criticized and a search for an alternative began around the terms change, action
and conflict. The revolutionary struggle centred around system and
conflict but there were other candidates for paradigmic status, including
the dialectical frame of reference which Friedrichs saw as a synthesizer of
'system and conflict into a single image'.[53] The point is that Friedrichs
likened paradigms to similar models as those suggested by the ethnomethodologists and which concurred with 'exemplars' in Kuhn's second
definition. Neither he nor the other sociologists mentioned give a satisfactory explanation of a change in a paradigm. It is unhelpful to say that the
climax in a crisis is reached when a 'social problem' exists which cannot be
solved within the existing paradigm. What is the problem? How is it
identified? Friedrichs and Silverman identified entirely different issues as

the 'novel problem' structural functionalism could not solve. It is likely that we would have as many examples of 'novel problems' as there are explanations within a common conceptual approach. Nor are we given any guidance as to why or when such problems occur. The approach is essentially an empiricist one.

The main reason why conventional theorists use the term paradigm in such a way lies in their inability to identify the conceptual bases of social theories. This inability is not confined to social scientists. Kuhn states that in the field of physical sciences 'though many scientists talk easily and well about the particular individual hypotheses that underlie a concrete piece of current research, they are little better than laymen at characterizing the established bases of their field, its legitimate problems and methods'.[54] In chapter 2, 'The dogma of empiricism', I show how the theoretical content of empiricism has the same conceptual basis as structural functionalism. In chapter 3, 'The conceptual basis of organization theory', I show how the long line of models from Taylorism to Etzioni's great synthesis, and including structural functionalism, have a common conceptual basis. The conceptualization of social reality in the first instance concerns its state as a static or dialectical phenomenon. Whichever view is taken will provide the essence for the theoretical explanations which follow. There is a qualitative difference between perceiving reality as consisting of systems pervaded by consensus with given structures capable of experiencing only limited changes in their superstructures, on the one hand, and perceiving it as an interrelating entity beset with contradictions which are capable of transforming it. The theoretical implications are enormous and are spelled out later in the book.

All other assumptions which are made, such as that 'action is goal-oriented' or that 'action arises from meanings' are subordinate to the initial one and can only operate within the limits it sets. Indeed if they are logical they confirm and consolidate the initial assumption; if they do not follow logically they are irrelevant. A variety of logical but subordinate assumptions can be made which create an apparent complexity of explanations. If reality is assumed to be dominated by consensus qualities then impediments to it can be treated analytically in a variety of ways short of giving them the ability to penetrate the consensus permanently. The impediments can be treated as peripheral phenomena as in structural functionalism, or assumed away as in classical economic theory, or regarded as permanent but incapable of producing a qualitative change in the situation, as in pluralism. It is logical to assume such conditions as perfect mobility of resources and perfect knowledge of situations, and this leads analysts to be able to attribute the causes of impediments to perverse action by individuals bad communications or superstructural inconsistencies of one kind or another. These subordinate assumptions can have serious practical consequences. If impediments to consensus in business organizations are regarded as remedial, then they must lie within the control of individuals. Employers and their representatives possess the power to make decisions which are binding on employees, and it is consistent with the assumption of consensus to believe that impediments can be removed by these decisions. Hence there is a real belief among management that they can control the distribution and use of resources in their organizations. The enormous educational edifice erected in the Western world to pursue management education rests on this belief. Managers are taught that through the operation of their skills they can determine wage differentials, the relationship between wages and effort, the attitude of workers to their work, the nature and significance of occupational skills and the distribution of power, within their respective firms. In this way the basic assumption about reality penetrates primary social experiences: managers endeavour to act their beliefs out as a means of maintaining their power positions.

It should be emphasized that the complexity of models of behaviour which can be constructed within a single conceptual framework through the formulation of different subordinate assumptions represent analytical differences only, and are not reflected in practical behaviour. They are, in effect, analysed into situations as aids, rightly or wrongly, to assist our understanding of those situations. In the reality of everyday life the whole theoretical construction collapses like a concertina, with the broad conceptual framework having an immediate effect on the way people see themselves and their situations. When people think that they are responsible for their own situations, that it is impossible to change anything, that things would be all right if it were not for this group or the other, that the trouble is caused by 'foreigners' or by a 'tightly-knit' group of politically motivated people, that everything would be improved if only people were reasonable, that education is the answer, that we are all in this together, then they are reflecting a particular conceptualization of reality. In other words, the primary assumptions enter directly into 'commonsense constructs' and give them a widely based logical consistency. In the last analysis all such constructs are about the ability to change situations and the allocation of responsibility for changing them. A basic assumption about reality then enters primary social experiences in two main ways — through the decisions of others and through the manner in which an individual views his own situations and those of others.

We can now return to the question of specifying what is meant by dominant paradigm. As indicated earlier, Kuhn's first definition provides an acceptable basis with amendments. In the social sciences everyone is a practitioner in one way or another, being called on to analyse situations to varying degrees of intensity, so it is not useful to talk about 'a community of practitioners' as Kuhn does. The terms 'scientific domain' and 'scientific communities' also have little use for, in addition to the reason given above, the work of social scientists cannot be isolated and insulated from the social reality of everyday lives. Theoretical work which is not about and transferable to real life situations is fantasy and worthless, and that which is not worthless is generally made available to the general public through the process of ideology to assist its members as practitioners.

The conceptual approach which assumes reality as basically static provides the framework for theoretical explanations which explain and justify the *status quo*. The explanations are necessary in order to legitimize existing power relations and, therefore, become an essential part of the dominant ideology. There is, then, a dominant theory which I have referred to as the conventional theory. This theory comprises many models some of which give different secondary interpretations of the same aspect of reality while others relate to different aspects of reality so that the dominant theory provides analyses to cover every aspect of everyday life. The transmission of the theory through the ideological process provides ordinary people with readymade analytical categories, or what I described earlier as 'instant analyses', which bring to bear on their thinking the influence of the basic assumption. In so far as they use these analyses they are given 'model problems and solutions' which lead them to concentrate on superstructural issues and to neglect structural ones. Their conclusions appear as 'commonsense constructs' which comprise the dominant paradigm. It should be noted that what is commonsense is not simply a statement uttered by ordinary people but one which is consistent with the dominant theory. It would not be considered to be commonsense to say that 'strikes are good for workers' or 'to hell with the national interest'.

The dominant paradigm does not consist of 'the entire constellation of beliefs, values, techniques, and so on shared by the members of a given community',[55] for this implies a consensus society. It consists of the constellation of meanings derived from a particular but dominant conceptualization of social reality. It indicates the pervasiveness of an institutionalized theory and shows how it can be transformed into unsystematized, inarticulate, intuitive type statements. It exposes, but without enhancing our understanding of them, the intricacies of the learning process, for individuals start with analytical tools which they do not know they possess, apply them to situations and derive meanings, believing that these are the result of their own intuitive reasoning. The learning process is even more complex, as a single individual can draw from different paradigms and attribute different meanings to the same phenomena in different situations. This point is raised in chapter 10 where it is shown that an employee can give one meaning to strikes he is involved in and a qualitatively different meaning to strikes involving others. The dominant paradigm shows, but again does not clarify, how an institutionalized theory can provide accepted meanings which contradict concrete reality. There are many examples of this, such as the legitimation of poverty and gross inequalities, and the acceptance by the poorest members of a society of responsibilities for conditions which blatantly belong elsewhere. To my mind the acceptance by wage-earners of the subordination, indignities, humiliation and material discomfort of wage-earning is a classic example of the mysterious ways in which the learning process works.

An examination of the dominant paradigm reveals the slow and tortuous process of theory displacement in the social sciences. It also shows the inevitable and inexorable displacement of one dominant paradigm by another. Alan Musgrave, when reviewing Thomas Kuhn's change of heart stated:

Some of Kuhn's critics took him to be claiming that the victory of one theory over another in a scientific revolution is not brought about by rational argument. Rational standards can play no role in theory — choice, since each theory itself sets different standards for science. The victory of the new theory is accomplished partly by irrational propaganda, which prods a few scientists into making the necessary 'leap of faith', and partly by the demise through natural causes of the old-guard. Revolutionary change substitutes one way of viewing the world and of practising science in it for another one, incommensurable and not merely incompatible with the first. [56]

In so far as the social sciences are concerned Kuhn's critics were correct in interpreting him thus and, in the main, Kuhn was correct in providing the basis for the interpretation. Two points need to be made here. First, there is the issue of theory-building and second that of theory displacement.

Theory-building

It is a belief common among conventional social theorists that scientific progress occurs through the gradual process of theory-building. This is reflected in their research activities where they are forever trying to find neglected patches for which they could claim some academic glory. Chapter 3, 'The conceptual basis of organization theory', shows how a succession of sociologists attempted to build on structural functionalism with each one adding new concepts or reinterpreting old ones. In a special edition of *The Sociological Review* devoted to 'New approaches in sociology' in 1973 two articles aim to add new dimensions to existing conventional explanations. Alan Dawe attempts to add experience as the title of his article 'The role of experience in the construction of social theory' suggests. He endeavours to show that 'elements of personal experience and self-expression in sociology have a direct and demonstrable impact on the discipline' and that 'what a sociologist writes must be grounded, not only in his own experience, but also in the experience of those for and about whom he writes'.[57] In an article on 'Social reality and social stratification' Peter Hiller concludes that 'Phenomenologically-informed sociological theory has been related to the field of social stratification and several hitherto neglected dimensions of analysis have been explicated.'[58] Such examples are legion. He would be a very diffident sociologist indeed who refused to try and add his mark to the scriptures.

The notion of theory-building is essential for those who refuse to believe that their theoretical explanations have an ideological basis. It would be going a very long way towards destroying the sanctity of conventional explanations if it was admitted not only that they have a conceptual basis which gives them their meaning but that there is a choice of conceptual bases and the one selected has the possibility of being heuristically inferior to the others. So the notion that there are social theories which develop over the ages persists. Kuhn's evidence from the physical sciences sharply contradicted this notion. It made matters worse that Kuhn was able to write so authoritatively. After all, data from the physical sciences is so precise in its meaning and is not so readily manipulable. But while it is obviously useful to have Kuhn's support for an understanding of social theories it is not essential. The explanation of the character of social theory given below indicates the impossibility of an evolutionary construction of theory.

A theory is not necessarily constructed at the outset to utilize the full scope of its conceptual possibilities so that a limited form of genuine theory-building may take place. The classical economics of the Manchester School persisted from the last quarter of the nineteenth century until the 1930s, without reaching its capacity. Gaps in it were filled by *The Theory of Monopolistic Competition* by E. H. Chamberlin in 1932 and *Economics of Imperfect Competition* by Joan Robinson in 1933. Then came Keynes's *General Theory*. It was made more comprehensive after the Second World War with the addition of intensive studies of particular areas of economic activity and its heuristic utility was enhanced by the application of mathematical techniques. Sociology has gone through a similar though less rigorous development. Structural functionalism has been the sociological equivalent of classic economic theory and it has been extended by the works of R. K. Merton, Ralf Dahrendorf and Amitai Etzioni, in particular. Gaps have been filled much less spectacularly than in economic theory and it has been much less amenable to quantification and, therefore, the use of mathematics.

The social sciences have experienced what I described earlier as 'conceptual adaptations'. I use this term because it is essential to make a distinction between adaptation and innovation. I regard a conceptual innovation as an alteration in the conceptual basis itself while an adaptation simply makes it more efficient. The conventional social sciences have experienced only adaptations for an innovation would not alter them but would stand as an alternative conceptual approach to them. The works by Chamberlin and Robinson I regard as conceptual adaptations. An earlier work of a similar calibre was the famous article by Piero Sraffa, 'The laws of returns under competitive conditions'.[59] J. K. Galbraith stated that Sraffa attacked the assumption that the frictions (diverting resources from equilibrium positions) were 'a secondary and fugitive phenomenon. He argued that they were stable and indeed cumulative and yielded a solution consistent not with a competitive but a monopolistic equilibrium.'[60] Commenting on the work of Chamberlin and Robinson, Galbraith stated that:

For years there had been marked discontent with the accustomed assumptions and the standard analysis of competitive and monopolised markets. Discussion and teaching had too long centred on what, too obviously, were limiting cases. . . . The new works had the great advantage, from the viewpoint of marketability of adding something new to something old. . . . Both books were solidly in the tradition of Marshallian partial equilibrium analysis; and in the United States, and the United Kingdom this had become not only an utterly respectable but an all but impregnable tradition in economic thought. . . . In retrospect the most important contribution of Professor Chamberlin and Mrs Robinson was to emancipate the analysis of markets from the inadequate categories of competition (impaired by sundry frictions) and single firm monopoly. [61]

This statement by Galbraith correctly describes the manner in which a conceptual adaptation operates.

Conceptual adaptation in sociology, as I indicated above when referring to the development of sociological theory, has been less marked and dramatic. But it has taken place. I regard the introduction of dysfunctions as a conceptual adaptation to enable functionalism to account logically for movement within systems. Anthropologists had used the concept of dysfunction but it was mainly R. K. Merton who fitted it into conventional sociological theory so that it could give some account of social tensions

and problems.[62] About this Gouldner stated that 'Although Functionalists have added a concept of the "dysfunctional" to their inventory of
concepts, it is difficult to avoid the impression that this was done in part
for the sake of formal completeness.'[63] But this is precisely what a conceptual adaptation is. It helps to take an explanation to the stage of logical
completeness. The use of homeostasis mechanisms is also a conceptual
adaptation but of an inferior kind, for once the existence of movement
with dysfunctional qualities had been recognized it was imperative that
something should be assumed about systems which protected them from a
possible transformation. The next adaptation, I suppose, was to move
away from seeing movement as destructive to the position where it could
have positive as well as negative qualities — where it could be functional as
well as dysfunctional. That position was reached by Lewis Coser in *The
Functions of Social Conflict* in 1956. In the preface to his book, Coser
stated: 'Our concern is mainly with the functions rather than the dysfunctions, of social conflict, that is to say, with those consequences of social
conflicts which make for an increase rather than a decrease in the adaptation or adjustment of particular social relationships or groups.'[64] He
explained that he viewed this concern as a conceptual adaptation.

*This book [he stated] is an effort to clarify the concept of social conflict
and in so doing to examine the use of this concept in empirical sociological
research. Concepts may be thought of as being neither true nor false; they
are apt or inapt, clear or vague, fruitful or useless. They are tools designed
to capture relevant aspects of reality. . . . Before the 'facts' can speak, they
have to be arranged through some conceptual scheme. The divorce
between research, conceived as a quest for 'facts', and theories which too
often soar beyond the reach of facts, is responsible for many of the shortcomings of American sociology. And this divorce is responsible as well for
the lack of cumulation and continuity in American sociology. Periodic
conceptual analysis, in our view, serves to mitigate these two kinds of
shortcomings. This study seeks to clarify and to consolidate conceptual
schemes which are pertinent to data of social conflict.* [65]

Coser's contribution was received with gratification by some sociologists.
David Silverman considered that it made it clear 'that functionalism could
handle social conflict', and contributed towards grinding the conflict/
consensus debate slowly but surely to a halt.[66]

It might be said that the conceptual adaptation to which Coser contributed was the introduction of conflict into the system frame of reference. This was the view of R. W. Friedrichs who described C. Wright Mills as
'the prime catalytic agent' in the matter.[67] But Mills did not consciously conceive of providing a category for conflict in the conventional
theory. He attacked American sociology in the late 1950s for neglecting

conflict and adopted an antagonistic posture so far as it was concerned but without proposing conceptual alterations of any kind.[68] Ralf Dahrendorf behaved differently. Plausibly and in some ways deceptively he did in his book *Class and Class Conflict in Industrial Society* [69], what others had been unable to do previously because of the politically oppressive nature of the acute cold war period in Western capitalist countries. He devised a conflict model to take account of conflict situations and drew on Marx's works and terminology as aids. The frequent references to Marx made Dahrendorf plausible to many of those who had criticized conventional theory for its static, consensus qualities. It seemed that he had synthesized relevant bits of Marxism with relevant bits of conventional theory and for the radicals this was indeed an achievement. He laid a foundation for what has since become an industry, introducing into conventional theoretical discussions words such as class struggle, conflict, power and class consciousness which have a Marxist connotation. But because he used a conventional theoretical approach the liberalizing words derived their meanings from it, making them tools of conventional analysis. In this respect Dahrendorf's work was deceptive. But he did contribute a conceptual adaptation which enabled conflict to be treated systematically as a permanent feature of reality rather than as a minor remedial friction. He did this by introducing assumptions about the character of industrial society which enabled him to analyse conflict as a consequence of authority relations rather than as the result of the social relations of production on the one hand or disturbed equilibrium on the other. He assumed that there had been a divorce of ownership from control in industry and that the controlling managerial class possessed its own values, but that these did not place employees and their unions in implacable opposition to management. Authority-derived conflict, therefore, was not seen as a disintegrating force, dividing classes and providing the stimulus for structural change but as an adapting one which through institutionalization and democratization contributed towards the achievement of equilibrium within the existing social relations of production.

The work of Ralf Dahrendorf was of most significance in the sociology of industry and was a great encouragement to the synthesizers and the pluralists in that field. I shall return to the question of synthesizing below. Here I want to mention pluralism as a conceptual adaptation. Conceptual adaptations are rarely comprised of new ideas. Merton was preceded by anthropologists in the use of dysfunction, Coser relied heavily on Georg Simmel. Usually old ideas are employed in new contexts and for new purposes. This was certainly the case with pluralism. Once the image of society as a consensus system was seriously questioned and sociologists felt impelled to write conflict into their explanations the logical procession was to the point where conflict could be treated as a permanent feature within the limits imposed by the conceptual framework. Conflict had to be defined and analysed in such a way as to prevent it from altering structures. Dahrendorf showed one way of tackling the issue by locating permanent conflict in superstructural phenomena and making it general for all types of societies. Another way was that provided by pluralism. Ideas which had been expounded by J. S. Furnivall, in particular, about colonial societies before the Second World War were developed to meet a postwar need.

Pluralism assumes permanent diversity of interests, objectives and power within groups, organizations and societies, and between them. Thus every conceivable tension, friction or conflict can be acknowledged. All situations are diffused, fragmented and competitive. There are rival sources of power, of leadership and attachment. The diversity, however, is reconcilable by assumption. The different interests are assumed to comprise coalitions or viable collaborative structures in which the diversity can be maintained, freedom of action can be provided, consistent with the preservation of the system or society under consideration — in which, in other words balance can be achieved.[70] Pluralism is a particular expression of equilibrium analysis; it represents permanent aberrations from equilibrium positions in which the possibility of achieving them is always present.

Pluralism and consensus or unitary systems were posed as alternative conceptual approaches by Alan Fox in 1966 but he retracted from this position in his article on 'Industrial relations', published in 1973, and recognized pluralism as a conceptual adaptation of conventional sociological theory:

The pluralist ideology would be the choice of a structural — functionalist seeking to identify the appropriate integrative mechanisms for industrial relations systems in Western capitalist societies — appropriate, that is, whatever its professed intentions, in maintaining the status quo *of highly unequal power, wealth, and privilege.*[71]

He added that 'the idea that the functionalist approach could not deal with conflict had to be laid to rest', and pluralism was a means used for this purpose. Sheila Allen argued that 'the attempt to develop pluralism as a theory of social relations is a response to the inadequacies of much macro-sociological theory'.[72] The point was put more strongly by Ralph Miliband:

Notwithstanding elaboration of various elite theories of power, by far the most important alternative to the pluralist-democratic view of power remains the Marxist one. Indeed, it could well be argued that the rapid development of pluralist-democratic political ideology after 1945, particularly in the United States, was largely inspired by the need to meet the 'challenge of Marxism' in this field more plausibly than conventional political science appeared able to do. [73]

The theoretical activities which take place within a conceptual framework in addition to conceptual adaptations, can be described in Kuhn's terms as 'puzzle-solving'.

We have already seen [Kuhn stated] . . . that one of the things a scientific community acquires with a paradigm is a criterion for choosing problems that, while the paradigm is taken for granted, can be assumed to have solutions. To a great extent these are the only problems that the community will admit as scientific or encourage its members to undertake. Other problems, including many that had previously been standard are rejected as metaphysical, as the concern of another discipline, or sometimes as just too problematical to be worth the time. A paradigm can, for that matter, even insulate the community from those socially important problems that are not reducible to the puzzle form, because they cannot be stated in terms of the conceptual and instrumental tools the paradigm supplies. [74]

This is a succinct and accurate description of the position in the social sciences. Kuhn has been taken to task for his definition of puzzle-solving and advised by Alan E. Musgrave to drop it and use 'problem-solving' instead. [75]

From our point of view there are puzzles and problems and both are covered by Kuhn's description. Within the dominant paradigm time is taken up in abstract model building, the use of abstruse concepts, the invention of terms and mystification. Quantophrenia and the use of complex mathematical models have made this activity more likely and more rewarding for a puzzle-solver. But it is an activity which rewards only the puzzle-solvers. It poses no problems for theory, nor does it reap any positive results for it. Economics has been strongly affected by puzzle-solving of this kind, as has American sociology. The problem-solving activity concerns virtually the whole range of empirical research. The extent and nature of problem-solving in British sociology is noted in a later chapter. It simply needs to be emphasized here first that the scope of problem-solving is set by the conceptual approach. In the sociology of industry anything which adversely affects production, such as strikes, labour turnover, absenteeism, is regarded as a problem. The analysis of organizations, and of management in particular, presents problems because it concerns the maintenance of power. Behaviour concerning sex, suicide, drug-taking, alcoholism and the like, constitutes problems when it deviates from conventionally accepted norms. And so one could go on. The definition of what is a social problem is fixed for the researcher. Questions concerned with changing structures are not problems; activities such as strikes which query the validity of structures are problematical only from the point of view of interests that wish to maintain unchanged structures. Morale is a problem only as it concerns production and not as a determinant of the outcome of a strike. Theoretical issues like dialectics relating to methodology to analyse changing structures are treated as metaphysical. Kuhn's general point could be catalogued with illustrations.

Secondly, the problem-solving activities have little, if any, relevance for theory-building. They present us with a seemingly endless series of descriptions of social minutiae which at the most relate to a particular point of time but may even be a distortion of that, and which do not add up to provide a totality. Those problem-centred works which make claims to theoretical finesse and construction, such as the *Affluent Worker* monographs (see note 15), are generally pretentious and mundane. In fact research work within the dominant paradigm is part of a great pretence at showing reality as highly complex, making it appear incomprehensible to the ordinary people who daily live it out, producing new insights into it and highlighting the causally irrelevant. That, indeed, is its social purpose. If it were otherwise far less of it would be permitted for a start.

Theory displacement

This section could equally well be entitled 'paradigm displacement', for to displace a social theory involves displacing a paradigm and this, in turn, depends on overturning one ideology in favour of another. Those individual theorists who make claims for themselves or others that they are putting a new social theory in place of the old should be reminded of the gloom and despondency of Herbert Marcuse when he looked at the issue of theory displacement in the USA. Marcuse saw 'one-dimensional thought' in a 'one-dimensional society' and could detect nothing which would destroy its predominance. 'One-dimensional theory', he stated, 'is systematically promoted by the makers of politics and their purveyors of mass information. Their universe of discourse is populated by self-validating hypotheses which, incessantly and monopolistically repeated, become hypnotic definitions or dictations.' He concluded his study by stating: 'If the established society manages all normal communications, validating or invalidating it in accordance with social requirements, then the values alien to these requirements may perhaps have no other medium of communication than the abnormal one of fiction.'[76] Even for someone much less despondent than Marcuse the destruction of 'one-dimensional thought' is an historic occasion and must be sought for in historical changes. It is something of an understatement and an anticlimax to state that theory displacement is not something which occurs within the panelled walls of the study of a great thinker or even in the reading room of the British Museum.

The issue can be put quite simply, for it is essentially simple. I have gone into greater detail in chapter 10 for those who like their explanations to be complex if they are to be serious. The main points have been made already. Ideas reflect social reality and relate to it. Theories embody ideas about social reality and provide means of simplifying and understanding it through them. The two major ideas about social reality concern its character as either a basically unchanging phenomenon or a basically changing one. These ideas represent conceptualizations which are frameworks for theoretical explanations. All such explanations fall within one or the other and none, therefore, can be neutral. Nor can any explanation operate within both; an idea which represented social reality as being both predominantly static and constantly changing would be absurd; an explanation based on both would be equally absurd.

The dominant idea, therefore the dominant theory, is that which represents social reality as basically unchanging. This theory purports to explain societies as they are, assumes their structures as given, and in doing so justifies and legitimizes them. Explanations drawn from this theory are welcomed by those who own the means of production and therefore exercise political control in the societies, and are disseminated through all of the main means of communication. In this way they provide 'instant' analyses which create commonsense constructs and become the dominant paradigm. All the time, however, the dominant theory is confronted by concrete reality. It is always being tested in that commonsense interpretations of social situations have to be squared with the reality of those situations. People are always having to make their own assessments and how they respond depends in part on them.

The ability of the dominant theory to explain social reality is determined in the first and major instance by the ideas or assumptions about social reality on which it is based. Here comes the crunch. The theory assumes a relatively static reality with at the most pluralist characteristics, but these assumptions are a distortion; the real thing is under constant pressure to change, does not possess the mechanisms to protect itself permanently, and does change qualitatively. The history of any aspect of social behaviour is dominated by changing circumstances and changes in itself. This is a penetratingly obvious characteristic which even conventional theorists cannot ignore, hence their preoccupation with equipping their explanations to cope with movement. Capitalist societies are characterized by the private ownership of the means of production and the exploitation of those means for private gain through the market mechanism. These characteristics constitute the structure of the societies, create class divisions between owners and non-owners of property, give rise to a contradiction between the relations of production and the forces of production, and shape and mould the superstructures of societies. Capitalist societies are neither unitary nor pluralist but divide in the first instance into two major irreconcilable economic classes, and this is reflected in their power relations. They do not possess unitary, consensus or equilibrating qualities; their contradictions create never-ending pressures with repercussions throughout societies, producing movement which can be temporarily obstructed but never wholly suppressed, and which can and does produce qualitative changes in structures.

The tools of the dominant theory, then, are shaped by an assumption of an unreal distorted reality with the consequence that they contribute to the distortion. They direct attention to peripheral variables, limit the scope of inquiries and generally lead to perception of particular situations or relationships which are consistent with the initial assumption of consensus. When the tools become the instruments of ideology they act to generate what Marcuse has aptly called 'The Happy Consciousness', 'the belief that the real is rational and that the established system, in spite of everything, delivers the goods'.[77] Agents in this generation are beliefs in individualism, in the necessity of inequality, in compromise, in partnerships between employers and employed, in the virtue of harmony and stability, in the undesirability of changing to the unknown and so on. These beliefs are reinforced by the application of the tools of 'instant' analysis. There is nothing mechanical about the relationships between the variables in this situation. The end result is that people categorize themselves and their relationships in particular ways which embody these beliefs.

The theory displacement process begins when these ways and, hence, beliefs, blatantly appear to be misconstructions and false. In other words it begins when the dominant ideology begins to be questioned and this occurs as the contradictions in society intensify to make the experiences of people, the reality of everyday lives, a refutation of commonsense constructs. The displacement occurs where the contradictions act first, namely at the point of production, so it is in the sphere of their own industrial work activities that people first begin to question the parts cast for them by the dominant ideology. The displacement is reflected in the rejection of those parts. When people who sell their labour power see themselves as employees in a conflict situation with employers and not as partners in a joint enterprise, and act collectively themselves, they are in effect rejecting their pre-cast parts in a limited way. As they begin to locate their problems in the structure of society and question its ability to provide acceptable solutions, the rejection is extended. The process of rejection of the dominant social theory occurs through crises in the capitalist system itself. A complete rejection of the theory can only happen through a rejection of the capitalist system; that is, through its revolutionary overthrow. Here we see the complete identity of theory and practice.

The contradictions which create the conditions for the rejection of the dominant paradigm also give rise to its alternative. There is never a situation where explanations are absent. As some become inappropriate others become appropriate. A worker who rejects the explanation of himself as a partner of his employer is *ipso facto* defining himself as in a conflict situation. The process of rejection is historically slow and uncommon and for long periods imperceptible. For this reason people in favour of change, such as Marcuse, spread their gloom and others who want to maintain the *status quo* sit back in contentment. But it is taking place as inevitably as societies themselves are changing. And with it occurs the spread of the alternative paradigm.

An alternative and conceptually different explanation does not wait on the rejection of the dominant theory for its development only for its acceptance. I attempt to show in chapter 10 how the alternative conceptualization of reality has been articulated in a theoretical form. It has had its most impressive expression in the works of Karl Marx and Friedrich Engels and in consequence is generally described as Marxism. Its precise designation is dialectical materialism. Because it is based on the view that reality is a changing phenomenon it coincides with concrete reality and is able to explain it in a much superior manner than conventional theory. It locates causes in structures; it can cope with qualitative change. It provides 'instant analyses' which facilitate perception without distortion. On heuristic grounds it should always take precedence over conventional theory. The heuristic ability of a theory, however, is only of serious account in crises involving alterations in power relations. Such crises are occurring now in Western capitalist societies. From the middle of the 1960s the crises have become more frequent and intense, and more pervasive. Few sections of capitalist societies have been protected from them.

Dialectical materialism represents a wholly different concept of reality from conventional social theory and, therefore, is not merely incompatible but is incommensurable with it. The concepts, the definitions, the categories of one cannot be compared with those of the other. The ascendancy of dialectical materialism can only occur through the complete rejection of conventional social theory. There is no way in which the two, or parts of the two can be synthesized for all that they can have in common are symbols of communication in abstraction. Once the symbols are used they are given meanings. The same symbols have different meanings depending on which conceptual approach is used. A word, such as alienation or class taken from a Marxist frame of reference must take on the meaning of the conceptual approach of the analyst. It cannot take its meaning with it. I endeavour to illustrate this in chapter 7 with a few examples relating to movement and change, but it would be possible to construct a complete glossary of terms with alternative meanings.

Theory displacement does not occur through rational argument; nor, as Musgrave suggests, is it accomplished 'partly by irrational propaganda, which prods a few scientists into making the necessary "leap of faith", and partly by the demise through natural causes of the old-guard'.[78] There is nothing fortuitous about it. It occurs as changes in the material conditions of life make commonsense constructs appear false and is therefore part of a dialectical process involving tools of explanation and concrete reality. Although the displacement is a process it is so only in a dialectical sense. It is not a gradual encroachment by one theory on another; its progress depends on the frequency and intensity of crises. Individuals as individuals and as parts of collectivities become aware of the distorting characteristics of the dominant ideology at different times and in different circumstances. They may be aware of the distorting characteristics in respect of only part of their own activities or in respect of the whole operation of society. Although there is not an evolutionary change there are undoubtedly jumps as crises alter consciousness. And once a jump has been made and there has been an increase in the use of alternative explanations their ideological context will be reinforced and it is unlikely, after the crisis has subsided, that there will be a complete retreat to conventional explanations again.

The real test of theory displacement lies in action which can take various forms depending on the character of the social situations of individuals. For social theorists, action may involve critiques of conventional explanations and a formulation of alternative ones; for students it may involve the rejection of explanations because of their irrelevance in their own cases. These forms of action are, however, as related to crises in capitalist society as is collective working-class action. The action of social theorists and students has a particular relevance for they influence the quality of the alternative explanations and, therefore, the precision of the alternative ideology. During the period of continuing crises, since the middle 1960s, there has been a wave of academic criticism of conventional social theory, a search by academics for alternative explanations and a

growing interest in Marxism as a source of such explanations. It is important to note this growth but its importance should not be exaggerated.
Conventional theory is much too institutionalized to be easily displaced
within the curricula of universities, colleges and schools. Still, books about
Marx and Marxism appear in a manner and abundance nowadays which
would have been treated as subversive of national security in the 1950s.
Marxism has become a bandwagon on which an increasing number of
social theorists have jumped. Many of them have not been at all clear
about the nature of their newly espoused theory so we have been treated
to a variety of interpretations, many of which have mystified it. For this
reason I want to conclude this chapter by examining the meaning of
Marxism.

The meaning of Marxism

A fairly common conventional reaction to my position was expressed by
Alan Dawe when he wrote about 'that variety of mindless Marxism which
leads to the dismissal of the entire discipline, in all its complexity and
contradiction, as being merely "bourgeois" '.[79] Conventional theory
serves 'bourgeois' interests, of course, in that it legitimizes a society which
does them well, but its rejection is due to the fact that it misrepresents
non-bourgeois interests which happen to concern the majority of the
inhabitants of capitalist societies. Its rejection, therefore, is essentially for
methodological reasons. It is a faulty theory and as its faults are discovered
in bits and pieces so it is thrown out.

The question here is what is it that takes its place? The answer should
clearly be a theory, fully articulated, based on a view of reality which
recognizes its dynamic quality. In other words, the answer should be
dialectical materialism. Unfortunately in many cases it is not. There is, it
seems, something politically sinister about dialectical materialism which
frightens social scientists off; it invokes emotions about bloody revolution,
Communism, the Soviet Union, Stalin and the Chinese Cultural Revolution. It involves a commitment to a particular view of totality which for so
long has been subversive in capitalist societies. So when sociologists are
faced with the question of choosing a replacement after having rejected
conventional analysis they stop abruptly and search either for some ingenious synthesis such as reflexive sociology which will let them out, or
for a definition of Marxism which will avoid dialectical materialism.
Perhaps I am being unkind. In the main, because they have rejected the
analysis but retained its conceptual framework they do not have to search
for a way out; it comes naturally to them and dialectical materialism is not
in the running. I should emphasize that their freedom to look round for
suitable alternative explanations is fictitious. Dialectical materialism is

located in the conditions of capitalist societies in precisely the same way as conventional analysis is. To reject it is to ignore the reality of reality and to maintain the illusion of consensus. Social scientists, however, engage in the pretence of having a genuine choice so that they can perpetuate the charade of impartiality, of being above it all.

Another factor which has to be taken into account is that Marxism, whatever its meaning, has always been an industry of detraction and denigration. The non-Marxists have always claimed to know better than the Marxists what Marxism means. Z. A. Jordan, for instance, wrote a book called *The Evolution of Dialectical Materialism* in order to reveal a misconception of dialectical materialism which 'originated in the Soviet Union but has also been accepted by Western exponents of dialectical materialism, as well as by the majority of students of the "Marxist theory"'. He goes on to state that:

'Marxism' is the name customarily *given to the tradition of orthodoxy* allegedly *first established by Marx and Engels, preserved and protected from distortions by Plekhanov and Kautsky, and held to have been codified in its pristine purity by Lenin and Stalin. . . . Marxism is not a name with proper credentials. It is an ambiguous term. . . . It is also a vague term. . . . What it is presumed to designate is merely a figment of the imagination and what it does denote is a wide and vaguely circumscribed collection of views, often incompatible with each other.* [80]

And what is the figment of the imagination? It is that Marxism is 'a single, continuous, and uniform doctrine, conforming to one set of fundamental principles and methodological rules' described in other words as dialectical materialism.

Much has been written about dialectical materialism. Mostly it is examined as a product of and in the context of the works of Karl Marx and Friedrich Engels and this is basically correct. A discussion about dialectical materialism at some point has to draw on the works of Marx and Engels. Credit, moreover, for the origin of dialectical materialism lies unquestionably with Karl Marx. However, Marxism is used frequently by social scientists to cover very much more than dialectical materialism and in some instances to cover other things exclusively. Often the usefulness or otherwise of Marxism as an analytical method is determined solely by an assessment of these other things. This can mean that dialectical materialism is rejected, wrongly assessed, or simply ignored, because Marxism is measured by some arbitrarily chosen criterion which has little or no bearing on it.

It is difficult in works on Marxism by social scientists who do not claim to be Marxists to discover just what they mean by Marxism. Writers sympathetic to Marxism tend to be obscure while those who claim to have been Marxists once upon a time but to have rejected the designation tend to distort its meaning. Marxism can mean the whole of Marx's writing, his theses and forecasts; it can mean the works of Marx and Friedrich Engels; it can mean these plus the work of Lenin; it can mean an ideology, a political movement or the Soviet political system. The meaning attributed to Marxism depends in part at least on the motives of the writer. The intending denigrator of Marxism, for example, has simply to say that Marxism consists of Marx's forecasts, choose one particular forecast, say, that the working class in capitalist societies would experience increasing misery, show that this has not happened, and claim conclusively that Marxism has no relevance for contemporary society anywhere. This has been the commonest and crudest approach. Some established sociologists have tried to be more sophisticated.

A recent illustration of a non-Marxist interpretation of Marxism was provided by J. A. Banks in his book *Marxist Sociology in Action*, subtitled *A sociological critique of the Marxist approach to industrial relations.* [81] Banks claimed to test Marxism 'by scientific procedure'. He identified a set of hypotheses which he regarded as constituting Marx's thinking and then specified the consequences which followed from them. This method, Banks claimed, led to a scrutiny of 'Marx's speculations on class consciousness, collective bargaining and revolutionary politics'. [82] As would be expected, a question was raised about the usefulness of Marxism as an analytical method whenever one of the speculations was not in accord with the 'data which have been systematically accumulated and analysed by sociologists and others over many years'. Frequently throughout his book Banks referred to 'the Marxist set of hypotheses', the 'Marxist system of ideas', the 'Marxist framework'. At one point he explicitly stated that 'the Marxist approach to industrial relations, as it has been outlined here, consists of a set of hypothesis intended to explain the behaviour of capitalist and proletarians within their organizations in the industrial context'. [83] In order to elaborate these Banks had to refer continually to Marx's work. Nowhere did he recognize that the hypotheses he was dealing with must have been derived from a method, so there is barely any mention in the book of the method which Marx himself used. There are a few references to materialism of one kind or another but nothing is stated which implied that dialectical materialism may have had some relevance for what Marx wrote.

Both C. Wright Mills and Norman Birnbaum have shown a sympathy towards those whom they regard as Marxists. But each has been obscure and confused about the meaning of Marxism. At no point in *The Marxists* [84] did C. Wright Mills give Marxism a clear and specific meaning. He posed Marxism as an alternative political philosophy to that of Liberalism. 'Liberalism and Marxism,' he stated, 'have also each provided grand views of the nature of the social world, designated the agencies of historic change, and suggested programmes for achieving these goals.' But Marxism was 'an insurgent creed'; the 'ideas of Marx and the slogans made up from them'. Classical Marxism consists of the work of Marx and Engels, while vulgar Marxism is Soviet Marxism or the 'ideology of the Soviet bloc'.[85] Despite these sweeping definitions Mills lists the qualities of Marxism in methodological terms:

Many of those who reject (or more accurately, ignore) Marxist ways of thinking about human affairs are actually rejecting the classic tradition of their own disciplines. The 'social science' in the name of which Marxism is ignored or rejected is more often than not a social science having little or no concern with the pivotal events and the historic acceleration character-istic of our immediate times. It is a social science of the narrow focus, the trivial detail, the abstracted almighty unimportant fact.[86]

This is a pungent indictment of conventional sociology.

Norman Birnbaum did not define Marxism in his perceptive essay on 'The crisis in Marxist sociology',[87] but he indicated that for him it is a 'mode of liberation' or a method with a 'critical and interpretive character' in which the dialectics may or may not be used. He implied that this character could be present in a non-dialectical method, but he did not spell out its details. For Birnbaum, Marxism was a type of nonconformity.

In Alvin Gouldner's *The Coming Crisis of Western Sociology* items in the index under the heading of Marxism rank third in number, next to Parsonsian functionalism and functionalism. Yet none of these items leads to a clear unambiguous definition of the term in the text. This long book is about methodology, the deficiencies in Parsonsian functionalism and the challenge of Marxism. Yet Marxism is not seen as a method. It is many things. For one thing, it is what Marx wrote. It is also the effect of what Marx wrote. Gouldner detected two sociologies in Western sociology. One was Academic Sociology while the 'other was the sociology of Karl Marx, or Marxism, the party sociology of intellectuals oriented towards the proletariat, which achieved its greatest success in Eastern Europe'. On the next page Marxism becomes a one-sided political philosophy which 'sought both to understand and to produce social change. Instead of being in love with order and stability, Marxism − at least in its early, prerevisionist stages − had an amplified sensitivity to the sounds of street fighting'.[88] Marxism and 'what Marx saw' are frequently interchanged in the text. Still without giving even an implied definition, Gouldner wrote of the con-tinuously growing crisis in Marxism because of its lack of radicalism. 'The search for the young Marx', he stated, 'suggests that Marxism in some of its dominant historical embodiments, is no longer felt to be radical, and thus no longer sufficiently different from forms of contemporary conservatism.' Marxism, then, is or should be a 'radical ideology'. Towards the end of the book, where Gouldner had apparently forgotten how he used Marxism earlier, he wrote about 'historical materialism or Marxism—Leninism'.[89]

Amitai Etzioni, in his almost 700-page long analysis of the active society, 'one that is a master of itself ... an option the post-modern period holds', contained in *The Active Society*,[90] barely discusses Marxism, but it is quite clear that to him it means the analysis of Marx as expressed in his writings. Etzioni's rejection of Marxism, whatever its meaning, contrasts sharply with T. B. Bottomore's utilization of it in his sociology textbook, *Sociology*.[91] Frequently Bottomore presents his sociological theory through contrasting different interpretations of aspects of social behaviour and almost invariably one of the interpretations goes under the heading of Marxism. Bottomore is an authority on Marx's writings and has a reputation as a translator of some of them. Yet it is difficult to find a single, coherent meaning for Marxism in Bottomore's own work. Marxism, Marxist ideas, Marxist thought, orthodox Marxist view, popular Marxist doctrine, varieties of intellectual Marxism and the Marxist method are terms used by Bottomore to describe different phenomena. He wrote about Marxism as a general theory of society, as a theory of social development, as a doctrine of social evolution, as not only "a sociological theory but a philosophical world view and a revolutionary doctrine", as a Western doctrine for refashioning social structure, as a theory which treats "revolution as a basic phenomenon of social life", as something along with socialism, which inspired revolution in predominantly peasant societies, as the dominant creed of the working class in France and as a "sociological system" '. In most cases, the examples which Bottomore used to portray Marxism are drawn from Marx's work giving the impression that he considers that Marxism is what Marx wrote. In one statement Bottomore implied that Marxism was a nineteenth-century European phenomenon by fitting it into the context in which Marx lived. He wrote that 'whereas the Marxist theory unmistakably reflects the character of social and political conflicts in nineteenth-century Europe, the functionalist theory reflects equally the social situation in the USA, where neither a working class political movement nor a working class ideology has ever become established'.[92]

The above illustrations are drawn from major writers in the field of sociology. Many more, confirming the general impression of confusion, could be added from the works of other writers. The confusion, as I indicated earlier, has a purpose. It is both an escape mechanism for those sociologists who find themselves in a tight methodological spot and a means of obscuring the question of an alternative conceptual approach. I accept that the term Marxism can have different connotations for people in different social milieux but underlying these connotations is the common strand of method. Eric Hobsbawm put the point clearly when he wrote that 'the strength of the Marxist belief in the triumph of the free development of all men, depends not on the strength of Marx's hope for it, but on the assumed correctness of the analysis that this is indeed where historical development eventually leads mankind'. [93]

Marxism is essentially a method. This was pointed out shortly after the First World War by Georg Lukács:

Let us assume for the sake of argument, that recent research had dis-
proved once and for all every one of Marx's individual theses. Even if this
were to be proved, every serious 'orthodox' Marxist would still be able to
accept all such modern findings without reservation and hence dismiss all
of Marx's theses in toto — *without having to renounce his orthodoxy for a*
single moment. Orthodox Marxism, therefore, does not imply the un-
critical acceptance of the results of Marx's investigations. It is not the
'belief' in this or that thesis, nor the exegesis of a 'sacred' book. On the
contrary, orthodoxy refers exclusively to method. *It is the scientific con-*
viction that dialectical materialism is the road to truth and that its method
can be developed, expanded and deepened only along the lines laid down
by its founders. [94]

This statement by and large conveys the meaning of Marxism which is employed in this book.

Notes

1. Department of Employment, *Annual Report of Research*, 1973, HMSO, 1974, p. 3.
2. Hans Neisser, *On the Sociology of Knowledge*, Heinemann, 1952, p. 33.
3. K. B. Popper, *The Open Society and Its Enemies*, Routledge & Kegan Paul, 1952, ii, 213—14.
4. Florian Znaniecki, *On Humanistic Sociology*, University of Chicago Press, 1969, p. 83.
5. Lionel Robbins, *Essay on the Nature and Significance of Economic Science*, Macmillan, 1932.
6. I was a student at the London School of Economics at the time and attended the lectures of both Robbins and Popper, and those of their close ally, F. A. von Hayek, who was for a time my tutor.

7. Alvin Gouldner, *For Sociology. Renewal and Critique in Sociology Today*, Allen Lane, The Penguin Press, 1973, p. 3.
8. Popper, *The Open Society*, p. 213.
9. Peter L. Berger and Thomas Luckmann, *The Social Construction of Reality*, Allen Lane, The Penguin Press, 1967, p. 29.
10. Alfred Schutz, *The Phenomenology of the Social World*, Heinemann, 1972.
11. Berger and Luckmann, *op. cit.*, p. 15.
12. *Ibid.*, p. 208.
13. See Paul Filmer, Michael Phillipson, David Silverman and David Walsh, *New Directions in Sociological Theory*, Collier Macmillan, 1972; and D. Silverman, *The Theory of Organizations*, Heinemann, 1970. There are of course others, such as A. V. Cicourel, *Method and Measurement in Sociology*, The Free Press, New York, 1964; and Harold Garfinkel, *Studies in Ethnomethodology*, Prentice-Hall, New Jersey, 1967, who take a similar stance.
14. Quoted from Cicourel by Silverman, *The Theory of Organizations*, p. 227.
15. J. H. Goldthorpe, David Lockwood, Frank Bechhofer and Jennifer Platt, *The Affluent Worker: industrial attitudes and behaviour; The Affluent Worker: political attitudes and behaviour*; and *The Affluent Worker in the Class Structure*, Cambridge University Press, 1968, 1969, 1969.
16. David Lockwood, 'Sources of variation in working-class images of society, *Sociological Review*, **14** (1966), p. 249.
17. Goldthorpe *et al.*, *The Affluent Worker in the Class Structure*, p. 181.
18. *Ibid.*, p. 183.
19. A. V. Cicourel, *Cognitive Sociology*, Penguin Books, 1973, p. 100.
20. Berger and Luckmann, *op. cit.*, pp. 39—40.
21. Cicourel, *Method and Measurement in Sociology*, p. 213.
22. *Ibid.*, p. 220.
23. *Ibid.*, p. 216.
24. *Ibid.*
25. Berger and Luckmann, *op. cit.*, p. 33.
26. *Ibid.*, pp. 34, 37, 149ff.
27. *Ibid.*, pp. 82—3.
28. Cicourel, *op. cit.*, p. 154.
29. Berger and Luckmann, *op. cit.*, p. 111.
30. Paul Baran, *The Longer View*, Monthly Review Press, New York, 1969, pp. 9—10.

31. Alvin W. Gouldner, *The Coming Crisis of Western Sociology*, Heinemann, 1971, p. 47.

32. Gouldner, *For Sociology*, p. 144.

33. Gouldner, *The Coming Crisis of Western Sociology*, p. 59.

34. J. M. Keynes, *The General Theory of Employment, Interest and Money*, Macmillan, 1947, p. 3.

35. *Ibid.*, pp. 379, 378–9.

36. Pitirim Sorokin, *Fads and Foibles in Modern Sociology*, Henry Regnery Co., Chicago, 1965, pp. 13–14.

37. J. L. Moreno, *Who Shall Survive?*, Beacon House Inc., New York, 1953, p. lxvi.

38. *Ibid.*, p. lxii.

39. Letter from the Editor, *Sociological Review*, 7 August 1969.

40. Amitai Etzioni, *The Active Society: a theory of societal and political processes*, The Free Press, New York, 1968.

41. R. W. Friedrichs, *A Sociology of Sociology*, The Free Press, New York, 1970, p. 38.

42. Robert M. Cook, review of Amitai Etzioni, *The Active Society*, in *American Journal of Sociology*, **75** (1970), 564–5.

43. Correspondence relating to above, *American Journal of Sociology*, **76**, No. 1 (1970), 155–8.

44. Robert K. Merton, *Social Theory and Social Structure*, The Free Press, Illinois, 1957; G. C. Homans, *The Human Group*, Routledge, 1951; Sorokin, *Fads and Foibles*, p. 19.

45. Thomas Kuhn, *The Structure of Scientific Revolutions*, University of Chicago Press, 1962, p. x.

46. *Ibid.*, second edition, 1970, pp. 174–210; see also Imre Lakatos and Alan Musgrave, ed., *Criticism and the Growth of Knowledge*, Cambridge University Press, 1970, and Alan Musgrave, 'Kuhn's second thoughts', *British Journal of the Philosophy of Science*, **22** (1971), 287–306.

47. *The Structure of Scientific Revolutions*, 1970, p. ix.

48. *Ibid.*, p. 175.

49. David Silverman, *The Theory of Organizations*, Heinemann, 1970, pp. 5–6.

50. Paul Filmer, Michael Phillipson, David Silverman and David Walsh, *New Directions in Sociological Theory*, Collier Macmillan, 1972, 169.

51. *Ibid.*, p. 16.

52. Friedrichs, *op. cit.*, p. 4.

53. *Ibid.*, pp. 11, 25, 51.

54. Kuhn, *The Structure of Scientific Revolution*, University of Chicago Press, 1970, p. 47.

55. *Ibid.*, p. 175.

56. Musgrave, 'Kuhn's second thoughts', *loc. cit.*, p. 294.

57. Alan Dawe, 'The role of experience in the construction of social theory', *Sociological Review*, **21**, No. 1, new series (1973), 34.

58. Peter Hiller, 'Social reality and social stratification', *Sociological Review*, **21**, No. 1, new series (1973), 34, 94.

59. Piero Sraffa, 'The laws of returns under competitive conditions', *Economic Journal*, Macmillan, **36** (Dec. 1926), 535–50.

60. J. K. Galbraith, 'Monopoly and concentration of economic power', in H. S. Ellis, ed., *A Survey of Contemporary Economics*, American Economic Association, 1948, p. 100.

61. *Ibid.*, pp. 100–1.

62. Merton, *Social Theory and Social Structure*, ch. 1.

63. Alvin Gouldner, *The Coming Crisis of Western Sociology*, p. 336.

64. Lewis Coser, *The Functions of Social Conflict*, Routledge & Kegan Paul, 1956, p. 8.

65. *Ibid.*, p. 7.

66. Silverman, *The Theory of Organizations*, p. 5.

67. Friedrichs, *A Sociology of Sociology*, p. 48.

68. C. Wright Mills, *The Sociological Imagination*, Oxford University Press Inc., New York, 1959.

69. Ralf Dahrendorf, *Class and Class Conflict in Industrial Society*, Routledge, 1959.

70. See Alan Fox, *Industrial Sociology and Industrial Relations*, Royal Commission on Trade Unions and Employers' Associations, Paper No. 3, 1966, p. 4; also Alan Fox, 'Industrial relations: a social critique of pluralist ideology', in John Child, ed., *Man and Organization*, Allen & Unwin, 1973, pp. 198–9; Ralph Miliband, *The State in Capitalist Society*, Weidenfeld & Nicolson, 1969, pp. 2–5; and Sheila Allen, 'Plural society and conflict', *New Community*, **1**, No. 5 (1972), 389–92.

71. Fox, in *Man and Organization*.

72. Allen, *op. cit.*, p. 391.

73. Miliband, *The State in Capitalist Society*, p. 5.

74. Kuhn, *The Structure of Scientific Revolutions*, 1963, p. 37.

75. Musgrave, *op. cit.*, p. 293.

76. Herbert Marcuse, *One-dimensional Man*, Routledge & Kegan Paul, 1964, pp. 14, 247.

77. *Ibid.*, p. 79.

78. Musgrave, *op. cit.*, p. 294.

79. Alan Dawe, 'The role of experience in the construction of social theory', *loc. cit.*, p. 30.

80. Z. A. Jordan, *The Evolution of Dialectical Materialism*, Macmillan, 1967, p. ix.

81. J. A. Banks, *Marxist Sociology in Action*, Faber, 1971.

82. *Ibid.*, dust cover blurb.

83. *Ibid.*, p. 119.

84. C. Wright Mills, *The Marxists*, Penguin Books (Pelican), 1963.

85. *Ibid.*, pp. 15–16, 21, 28, 22.

86. *Ibid.*, p. 12.

87. Norman Birnbaum, 'The crisis in Marxist sociology', *Social Research*, **35** (1968).

88. Alvin Gouldner, *The Coming Crisis of Western Sociology*, pp. 111, 112.

89. *Ibid.*, pp. 335, 473.

90. Amitai Etzioni, *The Active Society: a theory of societal and political processes*, New York, The Free Press, 1968.

91. T. B. Bottomore, *Sociology*, rev. edn., Allen & Unwin, 1971.

92. *Ibid.*, pp. 24, 35, 53, 79, 132, 222, 225, 244, 289, 202.

93. Karl Marx, *Introduction to Pre-capitalist Economic Formations*, p. 12.

94. Georg Lukács, *History and Class Consciousness*, London, Merlin Press, 1971, p. 1.

Part two

Static sociology

The five chapters in this part of the book deal primarily with the attempts of some of the most prominent conventional sociological theorists to analyse organizations. The first two concern general issues while the remaining three concentrate on specific writers in the field. The purpose of this part is not to provide a comprehensive picture of the work on the sociology of organizations, though it does deal in one way or another with the most important of them. Its purpose is to use work in a particular sphere of sociology to illuminate methodology in conventional sociology in general. What is written in chapter 2 about empiricism is valid for empiricism as a method; the conceptual links between what are described as models in chapter 3 can be identified in other areas of sociology. Chapter 3 is in effect about those conceptual adaptations which have already been described in the first chapter. I believe that the works of any and every writer in the social sciences, irrespective of whether it is conformist or nonconformist, can be taken and stripped down to its conceptual basis, as has been attempted in chapters 4, 5 and 6. The exercise has its usefulness in exposing those writers who claim to be conceptually different from others, who claim to break new ground, who claim to synthesize this and that work. As I suggest later there is a tendency among sociologists to know little about theory construction and, therefore, not only to hide their basic assumptions but also to be illogical in their use of concepts. A concentration on particular works is specially relevant for sociology because of the emphasis sociologists place on great names, on founding fathers, and because of their inclination to teach general sociological theory through a time series of specific writers. An exposure of the anatomy of the works of other writers than those mentioned here would, I believe, have a healthy impact on those students who have drearily to wade their way from Comte to Etzioni.

2

The dogma of empiricism

The purpose of this chapter is to start the discussion about the conceptual basis of conventional sociological theory through an examination of empiricism as a method for studying organizations. At the same time the points already raised in relation to empiricism in chapter 1 are examined in greater detail. Put differently, the intention is to reveal the theoretical basis of empiricism and to show its similarity with conventional sociological theory. This is attempted in two sections. The first section deals with the use of empiricism as a method by sociologists who study organizations. This method is posed as a preferable alternative to theoretical analysis as if it had no theoretical basis itself. The section shows, however, that the very denial of the use of theory is itself a theoretical position. The second section shows that there is a trend towards empiricism by the acknowledged theoreticians of organizational behaviour and that eventually both the empiricists and the theoreticians will be locked together by the dogma of empiricism, searching for data to satisfy their commonly held, though not commonly acknowledged, conceptual framework.

The extent of empiricism in Britain
The main research activity of British analysts of organizations is concerned with problem-centred empirical studies. By and large they are preoccupied with what are termed managerial problems such as leadership issues, decision-making, lines of communication, production control and the like, though in recent years some attention has been focused on such matters as workers' consciousness. Only rarely are there incursions into theoretical questions. In so far as organization theory is discussed it is normally through the medium of reviews of German and American theoretical models. Very occasionally these models have been used as means of explaining organizational behaviour. The contribution to theory in one of the few books by a British author to deal with organization theory, Joan Woodward's *Industrial Organization, Theory and Practice*, consists, in the

main, of a review of American theory. *Organization and Bureaucracy* by
Nicos P. Mouzelis, a Greek sociologist writing in Britain under British
influences is about the theoretical contributions of others and makes no
pretence about its purpose. The brief chapter on 'Sociological approaches
to organizations' by M. A. Smith in the symposium *The Sociology of
Industry*, by S. R. Parker and others, consists of a simple structural functionalist view of a very limited range of contributions. The nearest to
theoretical originality comes from the research team which was located at
the University of Aston. This team, led mainly by D. S. Pugh and including
D. J. Hickson, has produced conceptual suggestions from an empirical
study of bureaucratic organizations.[1] The team has broken up now but
the various individuals at different universities still largely pursue themes
established at Aston; in essence these are variants of the dominant
American articulated structural functionalist approach to organizations
and are in no real sense original.

An exception on the British scene has been the work of David Silverman
who, in articles and in his book *The Theory of Organizations* (1970), has
analysed contributions to the theory of organizations through the 'action
frame of reference'. In his book he also projected an 'action' approach to
organizations. This approach undoubtedly influenced the construction of
the Open University reader *People and Organizations* by Graeme Salaman
and Kenneth Thompson (1973). But whereas Silverman's enunciation of
the 'action framework of reference' was primarily theoretical the application of the approach falls within the empiricist tradition, as an examination of some of the articles reprinted in *People and Organizations* shows.
The main difference between the classical empiricist, antitheory, approach
and the 'action framework of reference' is that the latter is not antitheory.
The 'action framework of reference' relies on commonsense meanings
which are obtained from questionnaires and interviews as its primary
source of data. This source has become a paramount one for empiricists.
Moreover the insistence by empiricists that the facts must tell their own
story has become an article of faith among the 'action' approach theorists
who claim to leave the meanings of the actors unsullied by the meanings of
the analysts so that they can project the social reality of everyday life.

It remains correct to state that the most marginal phenomenon of all in
British sociology is a contribution towards a theoretical understanding of
organizational behaviour. In so far as there is an identifiable British contribution to the subject it stems from the use of empiricism as a method of
analysis and is based on a number of seemingly disparate, data-packed,
problem-centred studies.

The reasons why organization analysts preoccupied with empiricism are
to a large extent similar to those which account for the prevalence in

general of empiricism in British sociology. These are in part historical.
Sociology, according to Morris Ginsberg,

has had a fourfold origin in political philosophy, the philosophy of history, biological theories of evolution and the movements for social and political reform which found it necessary to undertake surveys of social conditions. The different current conceptions of sociology and the unequal development of its branches appear to be due to the fact that one or other of these aspects of social problems has received particular emphasis in different countries and at different times. [2]

In Britain an important base has been social reform, leading to systematic collection of data about living conditions. Various people in Britain in the eighteenth and nineteenth centuries became involved in social investigations which were either privately organized or stimulated by government action, as was the case with parliamentary inquiries into the working conditions of women and children in the mid-nineteenth century, or were simply social reporting of the kind undertaken by Charles Dickens. [3] This reformist approach to social issues was supported and therefore encouraged by the theoretical works of J. S. Mill which endeavoured to blend utilitarianism with social reform. The first organized empirical investigation of any note was that conducted by Charles Booth into the life and labour of London people in 1886. Booth's subject matter and methods of analysis set a pattern which was frequently copied in succeeding years. On it was built the study of social administration and social work which preceded the development of sociology in most British universities. As D. G. MacRae has written: 'Given such a background it will readily be seen why sociology in Britain cannot be treated separately from the practice and study of social administration and social work.' [4] Social anthropology too was oriented towards practical policy issues because of Britain's commitment as a colonial power and the interest shown by the British Colonial Office in social research after the beginning of the Second World War. It also developed a marked administration and, therefore empirical bias.

The current preoccupation with empirical studies is also attributed to the influence of the biological theories which directed attention to genetic factors in the life of social groups, [5] and which led, in consequence, to attempts at experimental sociology of the kind practised in biology. The adoption of biological methods and terms has been seen as an endeavour to treat social phenomena scientifically.

These two explanations have, in a sense, been complementary. The desire to emulate the methodology of the physical and natural sciences could not compensate for the difficulties involved in manipulating social phenomena for experimental purposes. It is known that controlled experiments are virtually impossible in the social sciences unless abstractions are introduced of such a quality as to render the experiments virtually irrelevant. However, the practice of social investigation has given rise to a belief that simple involvement with actual situations in itself has some scientific validity, that a collection of facts will in some way produce their own satisfactory explanations. The best combination, in consequence, has been regarded as that where experiments have been made in actual situations. In some odd way the fact of handling concrete data has been treated as compensation for the inability to manipulate the data in an experimental fashion.

The historical explanation of the development and use of a particular analytical method should explain not only why that method is dominant in, say, Britain, but why it is not dominant elsewhere. It should give reasons not only for the absence of any serious theoretical contributions from British organization analysts but also for the prevalence of theoretical analysis in the USA and for important theoretical contributions in Germany and France. In most countries empiricism is prevalent and popular, usually for the same reasons as in Britain, but in few places where sociology is a developed discipline is it without any theoretical accompaniments, as it is in Britain. This kind of explanation is difficult to give briefly for it requires not only a comparison between countries but also between disciplines. Britain has been the scene for the most important theoretical contributions in economics. An explanation about sociology has to be consistent with this fact. It is, perhaps, in the relationships between the disciplines in different countries and their environmental contexts that an answer must be sought.

Breakthroughs in social science theory have generally occurred in times of crisis either for the subject or the social system it supported. The work of Edmund Burke came in response to a challenge for democratic tendencies; Adam Smith's theorizing was a necessary prop for the powerfully developing economic system of *laissez-faire*; Marxism arose from the inadequacy of existing explanations to account for the socially disastrous dynamics of capitalism; marginal analysis in economics was a counterblast to Marxism; Weber's theory of bureaucracy was a rationalization, and, therefore, a theoretical justification of large-scale German monopolies in an environment dominated by *laissez-faire* thought and sentiments; structural functionalism was the sociological equivalent of marginal analysis and developed in response to the challenge of Marxism; Keynesian economics was a product of the crisis of mass unemployment and the inability of conventional economics to explain its cause; the resurgence of Marxist explanations, this time in sociology, is caused by the failure of conventional sociological theory to account for the dynamics of capitalism and its social consequences. Now where any of these crisis conditions are common to one or more countries the theoretical breakthrough will depend on (i) the existence of developed social science disciplines and (ii) the relative states of development of the disciplines. Where social science disciplines are relatively developed then whether or not the breakthroughs are in economics or sociology or psychology will depend upon their relationships. In Britain economics has consistently been the dominant discipline, permitting sociology to encroach only at the margins of its sphere of interest. In other words, institutionalized economics was in a position to dictate the allocation of spheres of interest and the allocation of research resources. It allowed sociology the periphery which was social pathology and precluded it, therefore, from making theoretical generalizations. The dominance of economics has, however, itself created a crisis in theoretical explanation which eventually will have to be met by sociologists. Empiricism in Britain will give way to explicit theorizing. This account of the relative absence of theorizing in British sociology is only a rough one but it indicates how an explanation of the issue should be sought.

The meaning of empiricism

The dogma of empiricism emphasizes either the importance or the exclusive importance of experience. As a scientific method it may mean either that 'whilst theory is essential and desirable, it ultimately depends for its validity on observation and experiment' or it may assert or recommend the absence of theory altogether.[6] In any case empiricism draws a distinction between theory and experience or practice and opposes one to the other. The implication is that there can be practice without theory and vice versa, or that there can be practice with degrees of theory, noting that theory, in so far as it exists at all, is always subordinate to practice. Those who use this method rarely state its meaning and implications; these are implied and unless they are identified empiricism might have the appearance of possessing qualities which it does not have. For instance it might be thought that empiricism has no theoretical basis and is, therefore, value-free and devoid of bias. This is what many empirical sociologists like others too think. It might be thought, too, that empirical and theoretical approaches are qualitatively different and alternative. An examination of empiricism as a scientific method, however, shows that it not only has a theoretical basis but constitutes a particular theoretical approach. It is an emphasis within the general framework of systems analysis, called in sociology, functionalism or structural-functionalism and contains the major defect of systems analysis, which is an inability to explain social change. Empiricism serves the dominant ideology; it is a *status quo* analysis.

Before proceeding with the main argument one point needs to be clarified. The use of empiricism should not be confused with the empirical validation of hypotheses. All theoretical propositions must at some point be verified or be capable of verification by empirical tests, otherwise they constitute fantasies. Indeed, by definition a theoretical proposition must be capable of verification. A theoretical proposition is a conceptual category of, in this case, social phenomena. It is, in other words, a form of the categorization of practice. It is possible to construct unreal categories which, in consequence, do not aid understanding or categories which are less useful than others but both kinds would be uncovered in the empirical testing process and be either rejected or modified. All theoretical propositions are abstractions of reality to one degree or another for otherwise they would have little or no general use. They are also interpretations of reality and so the possibility of misinterpretation and of different interpretations exists. Empirical testing enables both the degree of abstraction to be assessed and the relevance of the interpretations to reality to be examined. Although all theoretical propositions or analytical categories have no meaning and usefulness apart from the reality they present in abstraction, it does not automatically follow that every such proposition or category has to be examined in the light of empirical findings or that nothing theoretical can be said until the situation to which it refers has been investigated. Where a sociologist stands on this issue depends upon his conception of causality. This matter is discussed below.

The forms of empiricism

Empirical studies are largely problem-centred. The core of practical experience on which they are based is usually a problem requiring solution by employers, administrators, politicians or other policy makers. In the main a social problem is identified when difficulties occur in the operation in reality of the dominant ideology. In a capitalist society individualism is the ideal motivation. In practical terms for a person who has nothing to sell but his labour power this means offering labour power in such a way and in such quantities as will maximize his financial returns. Ideally, then, an employee should take work whenever and wherever it is available and should respond to the offer of higher incentives by working harder. When this ideal situation does not prevail or is contravened problems are said to exist. And as the ideal situation does not prevail there are many problems, for example, relating to absenteeism, labour turnover, productivity and financial incentives. As major contraveners of the ideal society, defined in terms of the dominant ideology, trade unions raise problems within the capitalist system which sociologists are encouraged to investigate. It is not coincidental that the behaviour of employers in relation to employees is rarely investigated while the behaviour of employees is a permanent attraction for sociologists. Problems are identified wherever the norms of social behaviour associated with the dominant ideology are violated and these too have a greater or less significance depending on the intensity of their impact on the *status quo*. Lastly, problems are identified for examination whenever fresh needs for the operation of the system occur which are not readily met from the existing distribution of resources. The relatively rapid expansion of industry after the Second World War gave rise to shortages of particular skilled personnel, including managers. This drew attention to many facets of organizational activity and stimulated sociological interest in management education.

It should be emphasized that while British organization analysts may choose to do problem-centred research for ideological reasons they are encouraged in this activity by the grant-giving agencies. Since the Second World War the Department of Scientific and Industrial Research and its successor in the field of social research, the Social Science Research Council, with the Medical Research Council, external agencies such as the European Productivity Agency, the Organization for Economic Cooperation and Development, and various foundations and large industrial benefactors, have all, either explicitly or implicitly, encouraged problem-centred research, mainly in industry. From 1948 until 1957 the American Government Conditional Aid Funds substantially supplemented the finance from other sources which was directed at solutions to practical social problems. Because of their substantial size and because they were often used in conjunction with finance from other quarters, the manner in which Conditional Aid Funds were distributed influenced research policy in general.

The most important government agency for financing social research in Britain from 1953, when it was formed, until 1965, was the Human Sciences Committee of the Department of Scientific and Industrial Research. In 1957 this Committee spelled out its policy. It stated that throughout it was concerned with immediate problems and the 'purely scientific exploration of a new field of knowledge', but its development

was dominated by the Conditional Aid Scheme, through which a large sum of money became available within a short period. Two essential features of the research financed under the Conditional Aid Scheme were that it should promise results by the end of the three years and that these results should be relevant to the broad problems of increasing industrial productivity. The research was concentrated, therefore, on the study of problems arising out of practical situations. . . . As far as our own research programme is concerned, we accept the view that work in industry should satisfy other than purely economic needs, and that human relations are important in their own right. . . . But since improved industrial efficiency is a widely accepted social objective, we consider it desirable that productivity should be an important object of study, and that the results of human relations research should be applied to that end. [7]

The Committee frequently made reference to the wider, long-term implications of research but it did little subsequently to alter its policy to make these attainable. In 1961, for instance, the Committee was sponsoring forty-four research projects. Almost all these projects fell within the scope of the sociology and psychology of industry and covered such matters as the development of teaching techniques for scientific and industrial use, the principles of batch production, subjective judgment in inspection and quality control, the education and employment of professional mechanical engineers, the role of the Youth Employment Officer, the training of skilled operatives and plant operator skills and automation.[8] In effect the offer of grants was and still is conditional on research being problem-centred. This methodological emphasis can be seen most markedly by the difficulties in getting finance which confront sociologists who do not conform and who reject the problem-centred method. Such sociologists have difficulty in convincing grant-giving agencies that their purpose is serious and of utility to the society. They are accused of being biased and ideological, and even of not being intellectual. Moreover, even if the finance problem can be overcome, the collaboration of organization executives is not easily obtained unless it can be proved that the research activities are going to be directed towards the solution of conventionally accepted problems.

The problems which have been presented for solution have been invariably aberrations, deviations, maladjustments, frictions and the like. They have been issues involving adjustments here and there. This is understandable because a problem, as was shown above, is by definition a difficulty which arises in operating society as it is. Problems are difficulties encountered in maintaining the *status quo*. In the main they are numerous and small. Problem-centred research, then, has concerned the behaviour of small groups. It has been concentrated where the problems exist, that is in particular restricted situations; and when they existed, that is at single points of time. Each situation which contained a problem was, therefore, a case to be studied.

Sociologists have tackled the problems in two main ways. They have either made their own diagnoses, taking into account all the factors they considered to be relevant, or they have focused their attention on the problem as defined for them by those for whom the problem was a reality, that is by administrators and employers. These two ways have been described by A. W. Gouldner as 'clinical' and 'engineering' sociology to emphasize the problem-solving qualities of problem-centred research.[9] The 'engineering' approach is more narrowly problem-centred than the 'clinical' one in that it does not question the definition of the problem which is given to the sociologist. On this matter A. W. Gouldner wrote:

From an engineering standpoint the problems as formulated by the client are usually taken at face value; the engineer tends to assume that his client is willing to reveal the problems which actually beset him. The clinical sociologist, however . . . assumes that the problems as formulated by the client may often have a defensive significance and may obscure, rather than reveal, the client's tensions. [10]

The 'clinical' method introduced the techniques of psychoanalysis into sociological investigation and made it interdisciplinary. It has been extensively used by the Tavistock Institute of Human Relations in its capacity as a consultant in industry. This Institute has used the case histories it has constructed from its consultancy work for research purposes.[11]

The 'engineering' method is used usually by those who reject the need for an interdisciplinary approach and concentrate on what they define as a sociological one. There are many such sociologists in Britain. Perhaps because sociology is a relatively newly established discipline they cling to it tenaciously and emphasize its virtues beyond proportion. Members of this group possess the methodologically defective trait of accepting for their own analyses the problems of others as defined by others. This has meant two things. First, it has meant that certain organization problems have been treated as sociological when they have not been so at all. A problem to an employer or an administrator may involve social behaviour but it does not necessarily constitute a sociological category from which analytical sense can be drawn. The labour turnover rate in a factory which rises to such a level that it increases production costs does not constitute a sociologically meaningful category. Such a rate is only of interest to a sociologist as an index of behaviour which can be related to other indices, such as absentee and accident rates, in an endeavour to understand organizational behaviour in industry. If industrial behaviour is understood then some sense can be made of turnover rates. The reverse order is impossible. For a sociologist it is as important to ask why workers stay in their jobs as to inquire why they leave them. The organization executives may think differently, but this should be of no intellectual consequence for sociologists. The second result of accepting the problems of others as defined by others has been that definitions of terms connected with them have also been accepted. Scientists are usually scrupulously careful about their definition of terms because the manner in which a term is defined can profoundly influence the subsequent analysis. The very act of defining carries with it conceptual implications, for at the very least it sets limits to the analysis. But with an abandon which befitted adolescence rather than scientific maturity some sociologists have accepted terms without questioning their relevance, let alone their usefulness. They have made inexcusable breaches of scientific practice. In practice, the *industry* they investigated was a technological phenomenon not a set of social relationships; *efficiency* was inseparably associated with productivity so that anything which adversely affected productivity could not be efficient; *productivity* referred to the physical output of industry; *morale* was related to efficiency so that in some situations and for some types of behaviour it could not be used. They accepted work categories such as skilled, unskilled, manual, non-manual, professional and non-professional which had no sociological justification and simply mystified behaviour and confounded analysis. They accepted management as an entity which could be usefully analysed because management was said to present problems to employers without questioning whether management was a sociological category or not.

The use of both the 'clinical' and 'engineering' approaches implies the existence of clients whom sociologists are serving. In so far as the practitioners of either method are actually employed to solve problems, the existence and identity of clients are not doubted. Many of the sociologists, however, who get grants for their problem-centred research projects would consider it an affront if they were described as serving the interests of clients. They would protest in the name of academic freedom and assert their precious intellectual integrity. The protests would be hollow because the existence of a client, of someone whose interests are directly served by the research, is implicit in problem-centred research. The research is always concerned with the problems of others for apart from matters of methodology there is no such thing as a sociology problem in itself. There is simply social behaviour of different types. The problems for sociologists do not arise out of organization behaviour itself but out of difficulties in analysing it.

The underlying notion of causality

It may be said that 'clinical' problem-solving sociologists overcome some of the deficiencies involved in the 'engineering' approach by defining the problem, and therefore its setting, in their own terms. They can include all the factors they themselves consider relevant. This is a significant improvement but unfortunately it is overshadowed by the major deficiency of *all* problem-centred research. An examination of this deficiency reveals the notion of causality which underlies such research and identifies the conceptual framework within which it takes place. In this chapter the examination is confined, to case studies, but this is not unduly restrictive for such studies are representative of the kind of work done by empiricists and, therefore, present representative conceptual limitations.

The case study method focuses attention on the internal relationships involved in the problem under investigation and precludes any comparative analysis. It is thus assumed that it is meaningful to study those relationships in isolation. In other words, it is as if a boundary isolates and insulates those relationships from any causal link with others. Empiricists tackle many organization problems so that if each problem has its own analytical existence it follows that the social relationships involved in them can be divided into problem areas, each of which can be treated as an independent system. Now there is no logic in the location of the dividing lines in so far as sociologists are concerned. Indeed the divisions are made by others according to their own criteria. Nor does an area have to be of a particular size or scope. A problem can be broken down into a number of lesser problems, each of which can be analysed separately, according to the whims of the investigator. Thus in a single industrial organization there might be a number of problems all related to an overall factory one of low productivity. The grades below management level might be showing a relatively high level of labour turnover; the manual workers might be strike prone; a particular department might have a high rate of absenteeism; the women workers might be difficult to recruit; coloured employees might suffer from discrimination and managers might be lacking in commitment to the firm. Empirical sociologists could tackle each of these problems in isolation. They might, of course, detect and acknowledge a causal relationship between factors involved in the different problems but this detection would depend entirely upon the empirical investigation; it would not be given *a priori*.

The first conceptual point which emerges is that the case study method is based on the assumption that there are no *given* causal relationships for only if this assumption is made can the study of social relations as if they constitute an indeterminate number of separate and relatively independent systems be justified. The second point is that, as no causal relationships are given *a priori*, no order of priority between different determining factors is given either. Empirical sociologists do not say what the causal relationships in any given situation are until they have investigated the situation. One situation might produce a different order of relationships from another so that there is no generalized order. The case study method then is based on the belief in a plurality of causes, and as this belief guides the research conduct of the empirical sociologist his subsequent studies show a plurality of causes. A conceptual framework, whether implicit or explicit, is like a self-fulfilling prophecy in that it ensures the empirical endorsement of the assumptions on which the study is initially based. It is sometimes stated, though in the case of British sociologists usually implied, that a refusal to give factors an *a priori* causal rank gives them a manoeuvreability which, say, economic determinists do not have. These sociologists act as if they are escaping from the defects of dogmatism. But by refusing to give an *a priori* causal rank to factors they are taking a theoretical stand which is as dogmatic as any other course of action. It acts as a fixed, unalterable determinant of the form of empirical studies.

The assumption of multicausality about organization behaviour has led to an interesting theoretical consequence. A sociologist acting on the assumption that nothing can be said about the causal relevance of anything until after it has been investigated has to face a daunting mass of data without any conceptual guides. His assumption inhibits him from reaching any conclusion which attributes a dominant significance to any one factor even in a single situation he may be examining, and this is reinforced by the daunting mass of data. In order to cope with his task he tends to break down the issue, to narrow its scope, to simplify his questions. He tends to categorize rather than explain, and as a consequence to talk of categorization as being a preferable alternative to explanation. Attempts at explanation he finds leads him into the trap of determinism. A belief in the plurality of causes leads to a retreat from causal analysis, to simple descriptive studies. We are given fact upon fact, classification after classification, but no attempt to analyse causes or identify effects. Hans Neisser calls this an incomplete model.[12] But to accept Neisser's position involves accepting the premises on which the model is based and simply criticizing its construction. This is an untenable position to hold for the premises determine the construction. The retreat from causal explanations is not a fortuitous happening but a direct consequence of the theoretical basis of empiricism.

The theoretical points identified so far can only be sustained if the view is taken of society that it contains no structural contradictions which influence behaviour. It is only possible to justify the separate analytical treatment of segments of society without reference to the whole if the structure of the whole is assumed to be irrelevant for the behaviour of its parts. Thus the view of society is that it possesses a basic organic unity. From another aspect this view is necessary to support the 'engineering' and 'clinical' approaches, for both are undertaken in the belief that action on an individual or small group scale can rectify whatever is wrong, and that can only happen if society is assumed to have no structural determinants of action. The case study method rests on the assumption that the societies for the analysis of which it is used contain no class conflict and are harmonious systems with common internalized values and generally accepted aims. If it were assumed otherwise the method would be a futile exercise.

Another theoretical point can be made now about the case study method: the method is static in conception. Any conceptual framework which presupposes the existence of social relationships within boundaries and does not permit scope for changes in the boundaries provides only for static analysis, or, at the most, changes within those boundaries. Case studies concern groups of little problems, each with an assumed sociological identity and protected in some way from its environment. The integrity of the identity of each problem can only be protected if it is assumed that there is no change, or that the change is never sufficient to penetrate the boundaries, or that each little system of social relationships possesses some kind of internal mechanism which continually restores the *status quo*. Empiricists who deny the usefulness of sociological theory refuse to admit that such damning theoretical constrictions act on their work. In so far as the problems about which case studies are made are sociological their examination reveals only the operation of special circumstances at a particular point in time. Move from the circumstances or the point in time and the research has little if any relevance. In so far as the problems are not even sociological, the heuristic limitations of the research are greater still.

Enough has been stated so far to show that the American articulated systems analysis expresses exactly and succinctly the theoretical basis of empiricism. Case studies involve systems analysis in which the questions of change, of boundaries, of the ranking of causal factors are dealt with in a given logical manner. British empiricists can confidently handle the texts of Talcott Parsons, R. K. Merton, Philip Selznick, Amitai Etzioni and many others, knowing that they open no avenues to questions liable to disturb the *status quo*, or to reveal the serious limitations of their method.

The theoretical trend towards empiricism

The most prominent theoretical analysts of organizations possess a common conceptual framework in systems analysis so that there is a close theoretical link between them and empiricists. In so far as there are differences they concern matters of detail which have no general significance. Among theoreticians, however, matters of detail are important, for they distinguish one model from another and signify the extent of theoretical progress. In some cases the models represent alternative explanations of the same organizational phenomena. Max Weber's theory of bureaucracy, for instance, is an alternative way of presenting the formal system of organizational authority as described by the classical administrative school which used diagrams to show lines of authority, chains of command and so on. In other cases, the models are elaborations and modifications of earlier ones. These cases have occurred largely through the entry of sociologists *per se* into the field of organizational analysis and have been stimulated by the need to construct models which more closely represent reality than do others. The normative functionalist model of Talcott Parsons as a device for explaining organizational behaviour has been modified first by R. K. Merton, then by J. G. March and H. A. Simon, Amitai Etzioni and A. W. Gouldner.[13] The modifications have constituted a movement towards theoretical complexity and have resulted in a significant methodological consequence.

The organization theorists who have used the tools of systems analysis have been attempting the impossible task of explaining the reality of change with static concepts. In their frustration they have sought dynamic explanations through their material rather than their analytical tools. By a twist of reasoning they believed that in order to explain reality they had to make continual reference to it. The more they referred to the facts of situations the more closely relevant for reality they considered their analyses to be. The consequence for organization theory was a shift from the deductive reasoning of Talcott Parsons to the inductive reasoning of subsequent structural functionalists. The shift represented a development from normative to structural functionalism. Areas of organizational activity which were initially resolved by theoretical exposition became problematical until contemporary analysts reached the stage where virtually nothing could be stated prior to empirical investigation, except, of course, the theoretical contention that nothing could be stated prior to empirical investigation. The transcendental importance of facts has become a dogma even with the theoretical analysts of organizations. This development can be seen from a brief glance at the works of J. G. March and H. A. Simon, Amitai Etzioni and A. W. Gouldner.

The early organization theory, described as 'classical administrative science', was criticized by March and Simon because it did 'not confront theory with evidence'.[14] They talked about 'empirically vacuous' contributions to organization theory and added that 'in the case of classical administrative science, the problems of making operational the key definitions of variables and of providing empirical verification for those propositions that can be made operational seem particularly pressing.[15] March and Simon set about the task of identifying the variables which needed to be tested empirically and altogether accounted for 206 which are listed in an appendix to their book. The authors recognized that some of the variables were substantially under-identified but believed that all appeared to be reasonable and worthy, therefore, of empirical testing. As an indication of their concern for accounting for reality, March and Simon concluded their work thus: 'We hope . . . that we have pointed to a hundred opportunities for using human behaviour in organizations as an empirical testing ground for some of the central generalizations and major methodological innovations of the behavioural sciences.'[16] The reliance of this particular analytical base on empirical research data captured the imagination, it was stated, 'of a rather elite *avant garde*'.[17]

Amitai Etzioni did not belong to this *avant garde*. He claimed to take account of factors which March and Simon had 'largely neglected' and moved into the methodological position mentioned above, where virtually nothing could be asserted without prior empirical investigation. This position was reflected by the 'system model' which Etzioni used for analysis and which he contrasted with the 'goal model' of the structural functionalists. 'The "goal model", Etzioni stated, focuses attention on "the study of goals and of organizations as their servants, obedient or otherwise.'[18] The analyst has to define the goals the organization is pursuing and then, by empirical research, discover the extent to which these goals are realized. The 'system model' on the other hand does not entail comparisons between practice and an ideal set of goals but between practice and the actual goals in the organizations concerned. This model, Etzioni claimed,

is more exacting and expensive when used for research. . . . Real goals, those the organization actually pursues, are more difficult to establish. To find out the organization's real orientation, it is sometimes necessary not only to gain the confidence of its elite but also to analyse much of the organization structure. . . . The system model requires that the analyst determine what he considers a highly effective allocation of means. This often requires considerable knowledge of the way an organization of the type studied functions. [19]

Etzioni took it as given that organizations tend to be oligarchic but considered it necessary to engage in empirical investigations to discover which were more oligarchic than others. In the same way he accepted that conflict is perpetually present in organizations but believed that it comes in different forms so that 'questions as to whether high or low-level conflict settlement is more desirable, and under what conditions one is better than the other, are matters for empirical research'.[20] Other sociologists believe that nothing specific can be said about even the existence of conflict until after a situation has been investigated.

It is unnecessary to elaborate at length about the tendency towards empiricism by organization theorists. A brief description of the tendency in A. W. Gouldner's work on organizations [21] will suffice to complete the case that such a tendency exists. In any event the tendency is not a development about which conventional sociologists are secretive or ashamed. On the contrary they point to it as a methodological advance of some magnitude. Just as some areas of activity which were theoretically resolvable for Talcott Parsons became problematical for R. K. Merton, so some areas which were not problematical for Merton became so for Gouldner. For instance, Gouldner took the notion of the interdependence of parts of a system as problematical rather than given. The identification of the parts of a system was also a matter for inquiry. Gouldner did not go so far as to state that analysis about functional reciprocity must cease until it has been established empirically. He simply stated that there is not an unqualified principle of reciprocity, that the interdependence of parts depends on the existence of reciprocal relationships *or* a compensating mechanism, and that whether it is one or the other has to be determined empirically. In effect what Gouldner did was to identify possible variables and postulate possible relationships and cross relationships between them. The actual existence of the variables and the nature of their relationships had to be empirically determined. There is little doubt that Gouldner's postulates will become problematical as the futility of their use becomes obvious. The frustration with intellectual gymnastics will push theoretical systems analysts into the position where they become crude empiricists, unless, of course, they are forced by environmental pressures to recognize the complete futility of their static conceptual framework as a means of explaining dynamic reality. Such a recognition in general would be dependent on an alternation in the whole ideological basis of sociological research.

The trend in empirical analysis

Empiricism has its contradictions as well as its limitations, and the resolution of them is shaping empirical studies into an even more heuristically unhelpful mould. Empiricists above all need data which is amenable to scientific manipulation. The data has to be capable of being used in a logical and testable manner, otherwise even the façade of empirical plausibility would disintegrate. The problem for empiricists has been well stated by Sherman Krupp:

In the social sciences practical application of strong verification principles may be possible for a very few hypotheses. The more urgent and significant problems frequently must be solved from observations that are few and indirect. But 'generalizations with only a limited number of instances . . . are of little interest in science'. Consequently, there is a tendency in the social sciences, particularly among those who seek to imitate the natural sciences, to turn to fields of observation where many instances are to be observed, and to impose the natural science rules upon the game . . . and as a result, hypotheses frequently merely reflect those fields of observations where numerous instance can be observed, even though in science 'no hypothesis is a mere enumerative generalization'. The fewness of instances in important matters of human concern in part necessitates a liberal intertwining of causal empiricism, reason, and value judgement in the development of propositions. Action typically cannot be postponed until vigorous rules of inference are met. The requirement that large numbers of instances are necessary for significant scientific results, when applied to the subject matter of the social sciences, readily confines research (and theorizing) to trivial matters.[22]

The fields mentioned by Krupp, where many instances can be observed and the internal science rules can be imposed, are those in which behaviour can be quantified and is therefore amenable to treatment by mathematical techniques. Empiricists above all like to think of themselves as scientists. As C. Wright Mills has written 'their most cherished professional self-image is that of the natural scientist. . . . In the discourse of the more sophisticated, or in the presence of some smiling and exalted physicist, the self-image is more likely to be shortened to merely "scientist".'[23] The more mathematical they can become, the more precise and complex their models are, the more closely they think they resemble natural scientists; and the more they justify the utility of their method.

This need for precision has had a number of consequences. First, it has led to a situation where the techniques are given precedence over the material treated. The fact that mathematical techniques can be used or that the material can be fed into a computer is given as sufficient evidence of the scientific nature of the analysis. This, of course, is rarely overtly stated, but it can be inferred from the increasing use of mathematical techniques and computers in aspects of organizational behaviour which are subjective and highly non-measurable. It is not being suggested that mathematical techniques should not be used. On the contrary where precise calculations and categorization can be done there is every reason to do it. All that is being argued is that mathematical techniques cannot improve the quality of the material; that an analysis can be no more accurate than its data will permit. It might be an interesting mathematical exercise to analyse quantitatively the process of making a decision in an organization, as I. J. Good has done in a paper on 'Measurement of decisions',[24] but the task involves making so many assumptions about the nature of decision-making that the work degenerates into an abstraction without relation to reality. In Good's paper, for instance, a decision is defined mathematically in terms of utility; this is a concept of proved uselessness in economics. Utility crops up frequently in decision-making analyses as a device for measuring the non-measurable. Indeed much of the language of mathematically orientated empiricists closely resembles that of largely discredited welfare economics, couched in a certain amount of sociological jargon. Henry Allen Latari, in a paper on 'Criteria for choice among risky ventures',[25] combines the conventional economist's use of a utility function with a form of normative functionalism in order to analyse a problem of 'portfolio management'. This amounts to abstracted empiricism run riot. Latari writes:

Where there is no strategy superior to all the rest in all possible future occurrences, the decision-maker needs some other guide for making decisions, since the goal itself does not enable him to make his choice. This guide is here called the 'subgoal'. The need for a subgoal exists because the outcome of specific strategies is subject to probabilistic uncertainty. In utility theory the payout matrix is expressed in terms of some measure of subjective utility, say, utiles. Choice of the strategy that will give the maximum payout in utiles is the goal, and choice of the strategy with the maximum expected utility is taken as the subgoal ... the subgoal of maximization of the expected value of the pay-outs expressed in utiles is logically related to the goal of maximization of the forthcoming payout also expressed in utiles. [26]

And all this is expressed neatly, concisely, in mathematical terms.

Sociologists in general had an early and timely warning about the dangers of attributing to quantification qualities of perfection which it does not possess in two delightfully written articles on 'Quantiphrenia' by Pitirim Sorokin.[27] The empiricist brand of organizational analyst could well take note of the warning. If the present trend towards quantification continues, with an increasing dependence upon abstraction in order to make social facts amenable to mathematical techniques, then empiricists will destroy their main claim to be taken seriously, namely that their analyses represent reality. At the most their studies of organizations will apply to measurable, controllable, inanimate aspects but will have no bearing on social relationships. At the worst their studies will be wholly irrelevent exercises in mathematical methods.

Notes

1. Joan Woodward, *Industrial Organization, Theory and Practice*, Oxford University Press, 1965; Nicos P. Mouzelis, *Organization and Bureaucracy*, Routledge, 1967; S. R. Parker, R. K. Brown, J. Child and M. A. Smith, *The Sociology of Industry*, Allen & Unwin, 1967;

D. S. Pugh *et al.*, 'A conceptual scheme for organizational analysis', *Administrative Science Quarterly*, March 1963, pp. 289–315; see also D. J. Hickson, 'A convergence in organization theory', *Administrative Science Quarterly*, September 1966, pp. 224–37.

2. Morris Ginsberg, *Reason and Unreason in Society*, Longmans, Green, 1947, p. 2.

3. See D. G. MacRae, *Ideology and Society*, chapter 2, for a description of the development of sociology in Britain, MacRae omits mention of the government reports which provided much evidence for the economic histories of Britain in the nineteenth century, such as J. L. and Barbara Hammond, *The Town Labourer, 1760–1832*, Longmans, Green, 1920.

4. MacRae, *op. cit.*, p. 18.

5. Ginsberg, *op. cit.*, p. 2.

6. See Julius Gould and W. L. Kolb, eds., *A Dictionary of the Social Sciences*, Tavistock Publications, 1964, p. 238 for a definition by E. A. Gellner of the term 'empiricism'.

7. DSIR, *Final Report of the Joint Committee on Human Relations in Industry, 1954–1957*, HMSO, 1958, p. 2–5.

8. DSIR, *Investigations Supported by the Human Sciences Committee*, No. 3, November 1961.

9. A. W. Gouldner, 'Explorations in applied social science', in A. W. Gouldner and S. M. Miller, eds., *Applied Sociology*, The Free Press, New York, 1965, pp. 5–22.

10. *Ibid.*, p. 19.

11. See Richard K. Brown, 'Research and consultancy in industrial enterprises, *Sociology*, 1, No. 1 (1967) for an account of the work of the Tavistock Institute of Human Relations.

12. Hans Neisser, *On the Sociology of Knowledge: an essay*, James H. Heinemann, New York, 1965, p. 95.

13. Talcott Parsons dealt specifically with organizations in his articles 'Suggestions for a sociological approach to the theory of organizations', *Administrative Science Quarterly*, 1, Nos. 1 and 2 (1956). For the use of the Parsonsian model in general for explaining organizations see Max Black, ed., *The Social Theories of Talcott Parsons*, Prentice-Hall, New Jersey, 1961, pp. 214–67. R. K. Merton explained his contribution in *Social Theory and Social Structure*, The Free Press, Illinois, 1957. See also J. G. March and H. A. Simon, *Organizations*, Wiley, 1958; Amitai Etzioni, *A Comparative Analysis of Complex Organizations*, The Free Press, New York, 1961, and *Modern Organizations*, Prentice-Hall, 1963; and A. W. Gouldner, 'Reciprocity and autonomy in functional theory', in Llewellyn

Gross, ed., *Symposium on Sociological Theory*, Row, Peterson & Co., New York, 1959.

14. J. G. March and H. A. Simon, *Organizations*, p. 32.
15. *Ibid.*, pp. 30, 33.
16. *Ibid.*, p. 212.
17. William G. Scott, 'Organization theory: an overview and an appraisal', in J. A. Litterer, ed., *Organizations: structure and behaviour*, Wiley, 1969, p. 16.
18. Etzioni, *Modern Organizations*, p. 16.
19. *Ibid.*, pp. 17–18.
20. *Ibid.*, p. 27.
21. Gouldner, 'Reciprocity and autonomy in functional theory', *loc. cit.*
22. Sherman Krupp, *Pattern in Organization Analysis: a critical examination*, Holt, Rinehart & Winston, 1961, pp. 71–2.
23. Wright Mills, *The Sociological Imagination*, p. 56.
24. I. J. Good, 'Measurement of decisions', in *New Perspectives in Organization Research*, ed., W. W. Cooper, H. J. Leavitt and M. W. Shelly II, Wiley (1964), pp. 391–404.
25. Henry Allen Latari, 'Criteria for choice among risky ventures', in W. J. Gore and J. W. Dyson eds. *The Making of Decisions: a reader in administration behaviour*, The Free Press of Glencoe, 1964, pp. 128–40.
26. *Ibid.*, p. 129.
27. Sorokin, *Fads and Foibles in Modern Sociology*.

3

The conceptual basis of organization theory

The purpose of this chapter is to examine the nature and significance of changes in the theoretical approach to organizations and in doing so it extends the argument of chapter 2 in showing that all the main approaches represent different models within a single analytical framework and not distinct theories. A theory is defined here as a logically consistent, deductively derived set of generalized analytical tools based on a simplified version of reality. A model on the other hand, is a strictly formalized body of propositions which may refer to a particular aspect of a theory and is just one interpretation of it.[1] A model is a heuristic device constructed to give a particular explanation of a theory. There may be many models, then, of a theory referring either to its entirety, to different aspects or the same aspect. Each model would differ from the others in its formal construction but all would have the same theoretical basis. Theories differ as the versions of reality on which they are based differ. Thus two explanations of the same aspect of reality would have to represent entirely different versions of it in order to qualify for the description of theories. In the field of organizational activity an explanation of behaviour based on a static version of reality would constitute a different theoretical approach from one based on a dynamic version.

The version of reality which underpins the models of organization theory described here is a static one. The aspect of reality in question, namely organization activity, can, in consequence, be analysed without reference to any factor external to it. Indeed any segment of activity can be isolated as an autonomous system. Since the Second World War there has been a growing awareness, even amongst the most insular and conservative sociologists, that some provision had to be made in their models to account for social change. There has been, in consequence, a switch from the static models of the 1920s and 1930s to the equilibrium models of the post 1940 years. Terms such as dysfunction, tension, friction, strain and, of late, even conflict, have become commonplace in the vocabulary of Talcott Parsons, R. K. Merton, P. Selznick, Amitai Etzioni and others.

The attempts to take account of social change, however, have not produced new theories, only new models with mechanisms to take account of limited movements. Nothing was done to disturb the autonomy of organizations so that they could still be analysed independently of external environmental factors. Changes within organizations were permitted but to prevent them getting out of hand and making qualitative differences it was assumed that organizations possessed automatic self-equilibrating mechanisms which made change a deviant quality and ensured a return to the *status quo*. In other words the possibility of a limited, arrested movement of change was introduced into an unaltered analytical framework by the use of an ingenious assumption. The preferred simplified version of reality did not have to be altered.

Organization theory has gone through a process of conceptual adaptation and has become more complex as a consequence. Apart from the re-emergence of variants of phenomenology, such as 'action frame of reference' and ethnomethodology, the most significant developments in recent years have been syntheses of earlier approaches. The syntheses have brought no new evidence to bear on the analysis nor have they introduced new analytical tools. They have simply drawn together and synthesized what is known. The most significant of these have been *Organizations* (1958) by J. G. March and H. A. Simon, and *Complex Organizations* (1961) by Amitai Etzioni. This chapter is not concerned with the details of these particular works for they are dealt with later but it is concerned with the elements which they have attempted to synthesize, for it is through these that syntheses must be judged. The chapter is also not concerned with *all* contributions to organization theory; it deals only with those which are credited as significant modifications of previous explanations and it ends with the predominance of structural functionalism.

It might be said, of course, that such an ending dates the analysis and renders it incomplete on the grounds that structural functionalism is no longer at issue and that to argue against it is to carry on a struggle five years too late. This view is based on four misconceptions. First it fails to recognize structural functionalism as a model in a long line of others and as a not very distinctive expression of a particular general conceptual approach. Second, it mistakenly identifies a model which satisfied the ideological needs of an historical period with the academic influence of one person, namely Talcott Parsons. It suggests that with the academic demise of Parsons went structural functionalism. Third, by implication it attributes to current fashions such as ethnomethodology and reflexive sociology conceptual qualities they do not possess, and fails to recognize their conceptual kinship with static models within the social systems theory. Lastly, such a view can only be held by those who are so divorced and insulated from reality that they believe that the tiny worlds of make-believe struggle between variants of phenomenology for fashionable pre-dominance in the sociology departments of universities reflect the reality of applied sociology in management schools and departments of all kinds in Britain and other capitalist countries.

The classical theory

The earliest attempts to explain organizational activity arose directly from a desire to improve managerial efficiency. They emphasized management needs and used management terminology. There was no ambiguity about this approach. It spoke the language of employers and management, did not confuse with jargon and made no pretence about impartiality. It is generally described as 'scientific management', but in descriptions of types of organization theory it is listed as 'classical' theory. This approach had two distinct parts. The first dealt with technical control and efficiency through the coordination of men with machines and was based on the work of Frederick W. Taylor.

The main work of Taylor was contained in his book, *Scientific Management* (1911).[2] In it he attempted to show how the physical output of a firm could be increased by analysing, measuring and manipulating the physical activities involved in production. Taylor was not concerned with the whole range of physical activities in a firm but only with simple, repetitive jobs. His work was criticized for its incompleteness. The tasks which Taylor and his followers examined did not, according to March and Simon,

require complex problem-solving activity by the worker who handles them. . . . Because they are relatively routine, the tasks with which the theory has been concerned can be described fairly completely in terms of overt behaviour, without explicit reference to the mental processes of the worker. . . . Traditional time and methods study has avoided problem-solving tasks, and thus has not dealt with the aspects of human behaviour that will concern us throughout most of this volume. [3]

The work was also criticized because of its prescriptive character.

Scientific management cannot be fully understood, nor can its contribution towards explaining organizational behaviour be assessed, without first constructing the analytical framework which contained it. The organization (the firm) was identified by its legal status. It was a bounded entity, isolated and insulated from other entities and from its environment. The firm was not only in an environment it could ignore but was also a static entity itself: it contained no divisions which could not be reconciled or forces which could not be controlled by the application of science and rational action within it. It was assumed that there was complete economic motivation and that conditions, unspecified, existed which made rational responses possible. It was also assumed that each firm had a single goal, namely the maximization of profits through the maximization of physical output from given combinations of factors of production. Everything, including the work force which was regarded as an appendage to machines, was subordinated to this goal and to the rules of the firm which were designed to fulfil it. It follows that the authority structure in support of the rules was a given, unquestioned factor and so, of course, was the distribution of the means of production determining its form. The question of the legitimation of authority never arose.

The second part of the classical theory took Taylor's approach a stage nearer to what recent organization theorists would call completion by placing it in a formal administrative framework. It was called the 'administrative management' theory or the 'classical administration' theory or just simply 'organization' theory. March and Simon describe it as follows:

The general problem to which the formal theory addresses itself is the following: Given a general purpose for an organization, we can identify the unit tasks necessary to achieve that purpose. These tasks will normally include basic productive activities, service activities, coordination activities, supervisory activities, etc. The problem is to group these tasks into individual jobs, to group the jobs into administrative units, to group the units into larger units, and finally to establish the top level departments — and to make these groupings in such a way as to minimize the total cost of carrying out all the activities. In the organizing process each department is viewed as a definite collection of tasks to be allocated among, and performed by, the employees of the department. To understand the formal theory, it is important to recognize that the total set of tasks is regarded as given in advance. [4]

This approach gave rise to formal models showing the division of labour in terms of function and authority. It attempted to show growth through increasing functional specialization, causing a regrouping of parts, and through extensions in the chain of command, changes in the delegation of authority and responsibility. The static model of scientific management was thus slightly modified. Structure referred to line and staff management, committee and liaison activities, and the span of control which described the extent of the overall authority of the senior management. It did not relate to anything outside the firm. There was a hierarchical authority system within a pyramid of control, after the manner described by Weber. But Weber, although he preceded the 'administrative management' theorists in time, had no influence over them. They, like Weber, merely described in formal terms what they considered to be the correct structure of the administrations they saw. But unlike Weber, they had no concern for the legitimation of the authority they so precisely outlined in their diagrams. The employee was regarded as 'an inert instrument performing the tasks assigned to him'.[5] This approach depicted rational decision-making processes with communications systems containing lines of authority, staff-line relations, twoway channels and the like and was, in some cases, supported by contrived principles of action.

The most pervasive attempts to enunciate the principles of action or 'management philosophy' for scientific management were made by Mary Parker Follett and James D. Mooney.[6] Both writers theorized about the firm strictly within the analytical context of scientific management. They made the same basic assumptions about behaviour. They saw activity as taking place within organic systems so that it was integrative, collaborative, unified in a common purpose. They used a concept of a whole which was an integrated unity and which, therefore indicated the unifying tendency of the behaviour of its parts. Miss Follett wrote at various times of the unity of interests in society at large and organizations in particular. She identified the same common underlying principles in every form of activity.

It seems to me [she wrote] that the first test of business administration, of industrial organization, should be whether you have a business with all its parts so coordinated, so moving together in their closely knit and adjusting activities, so linking, interlocking, interrelating, that they make a working unit — that is, not a congeries of separate pieces, but what I have called a functional whole or integrative unity. [7]

And in another paper:

Every social process has three aspects: the interacting, the unifying, and the emerging. But our consideration of the interacting has shown us that the interacting and unifying are one ... the emerging also is part of the same process. . . . There is one simultaneous process, and these three are aspects of that process. [8]

James D. Mooney expressed the same notion:

Community of interest *is the legitimate basis of every organization. In searching for its psychic fundaments we find that it can mean only* mutuality of interest. *This in turn implies mutual duties, which means the obligation to* mutual service. *This obligation is universal, transcending, therefore, the sphere of organization ... it is the moral phase of the principle of coordination. . . . A true coordination must be based on a real community of interest in the attainment of the desired object.* [9]

Both Follett and Mooney logically rejected the idea that there could be real, permanent differences within organizations which could result in changed organizational forms. Follett regarded conflict as 'a moment in the interacting of desires' which could be resolved constructively through integration. Conflict 'as continued unintegrated differences', she stated, 'is pathological, but the difference itself is not'.[10] Mooney barely discussed any degree of difference within organizations because he saw them as coordinated, functionally correlated organisms. Differences, in any case, he regarded as remedial. 'The industrial organizer', he wrote, 'is faced with the proposition of determining how a common understanding, a full loyalty and a clear discharge of duty and responsibility can be achieved. He must study human friction as well as the mechanical variety, and find out how to reduce it.'[11]

It can well be understood why only the most marginal and transient differences were considered by the 'classical' organization theorists. Power had no place in their models. Its existence as a causal factor was assumed away through the emphasis on integration and functional correlation in organizations and through the implicit acceptance of mechanistic responses. The exercise of power over others was regarded by Follett as being incompatible with the principle of integration for it resulted in domination — that is in only one side getting what it wanted — and this created a false unity rather than an effective solution.[12] In an examination of power Follett made the distinction between *power-over* which represented domination and *power-with* which was consistent with integration.[13] The issue, as she saw it, was to reduce the *power-over* or domination element. This, she stated, could be done:

(1) through integration, (2) through recognizing that all should submit to what I have called the law of the situation, and (3) through making our business more and more of a functional unity. In a functional unity, each has his function — and that should correspond as exactly as possible with his capacity — and then he should have the authority and the responsibility which go with that function.[14]

Integration, in contrast to domination, was seen as a stabilizing phenomenon. Action, therefore, which was integrative could not be motivated by power which was disintegrative. Such power had to be excluded from the analysis. This treatment of power is implicit in the analysis of later organization theorists. Thus it can be seen that Follett and her conceptual kin did not illogically ignore the issue of power because it raised awkward questions. The issue was ignored because its treatment as a causal factor was inconsistent with the analytical base on which the organization models rested.

Follett differed from subsequent organization theorists in two main ways. First, she was explicit about the normative element in her analysis. Secondly, she made general statements and did not attempt to relate principles directly to detailed formal organizational activities. She did not, in consequence, disguise normative elements with empiricism as later writers did.[15] Mooney's work had a much more empirical orientation. He described the coordinative principle as the basis of organization; the scaler principle as that on which the hierarchical distribution of authority was based; and functionalism as the explanation of line and staff divisions. E. F. L. Brech went further still and inserted theoretical matters into an immensely detailed empirical structure in such a way as to give the general impression that his work was value-free and empirically based. The jargon of science has been used extensively to cover over and disguise substantial normative elements.

The human relations approach

The range of classical theory from the general to the empirical approaches did not attract criticism for its static and thereby descriptive nature, but for its neglect of day-to-day administrative matters and what have been termed 'informal' activities. In other words scientific management was regarded in the main as useful but incomplete. Amitai Etzioni, for instance, stated that its neglect of many factors 'should not mislead us. A full half of what organizational analysis is all about — namely, the formal organization — is covered by the Classical and the Neo-Classical approach'.[16] March and Simon gave a fuller though essentially similar opinion.[17]

While the 'administrative management' aspect of the classical theory was evolving, the detail which Etzioni and others considered was necessary to achieve a complete coverage was actually being collected. The collection started really with the studies by Elton Mayo and his research team at the Western Electricity Company's Hawthorne Works from 1927 to 1932.[18] Independently of Mayo's team and influence, Kurt Lewin, J. L. Moreno and other social psychologists began studies of the structure of groups of various kinds in the 1930s and 1940s, dealing in their own way with questions of leadership, participation and interaction. Problems of human relations involving individual personality, 'informal' groups, intra-organizational conflict and decision-making were approached socio-logically through Mayo and psychologically through Lewin and Moreno, and they converged in industrial sociology. Thus began small-group, problem-centred research, first as a trickle in the 1930s and early 1940s and then, after the Second World War, as a flood. Various approaches were used such as *group dynamics* as devised by Lewin and described by him in his *Field Theory in Social Science* (1951), *psychodrama* from J. L. Moreno's *Psychodrama* (1946) and the *small-group interaction process* as used by G. C. Homans in *The Human Group* (1950).[19] The emphasis was on field work and by and large all that was necessary was a problem which management wanted to solve and the belief that it could be solved within the context and terms of reference stipulated by employers. In the period following the Second World War, with a high level of employment in all industrial societies but particularly in the USA, where a sociological and psychological interest in industry was keenest, there was an abundance of such labour problems, such as incentives, labour turnover, absenteeism, accidents, morale and discipline in general. It became the fashion to study the manner in which individuals and small groups fitted or did not fit into existing institutional structures: to concentrate on human relations. The Human Relations School, as the fashion was called, performed an ideological function by keeping problems on the level of individual and small group interaction and thus diverting attention away from the needs for institutional change. It assisted in protecting the integrity of existing organizational forms. As one American sociologist wrote:

Bureaucracy . . . with its monistic system of rights, needs an ideology which denies the validity of intra-organizational conflict. 'Managerial sociology' supplies this need. Whereas leadership studies have sought to . . . legitimize the hierarchical positions and roles, 'managerial sociology' has supplied legitimacy to the whole institutional structure.[20]

Such strictures, it should be noted have been rare. Although occasional sociologists such as C. Wright Mills in *The Sociological Imagination* and P. A. Sorokin discussing 'The wonderland of social atoms and small groups' criticized small group research during the time of its ascendancy, the majority of sociologists who called themselves 'functionalists', 'structural functionalists' or 'structuralists'[21] either accepted fully the analytical and ideological implications of the human relations approach, or ignored them or played down their defects. Another American sociologist, William G. Scott, provides a good illustration of the playing down process. He, calling small group research the neoclassical school of organization, wrote:

The neo-classical school of organization has been called bankrupt. Criticisms range from 'human relations is a tool for cynical puppeteering of people' to 'human relations is nothing more than a trifling body of empirical and descriptive information'. There is a good deal of truth in both criticisms, but another appraisal of the neo-classical school of organization theory is offered here. The neo-classical approach has provided valuable contributions to the lore of organization. But, like the classical theory, the neo-classical doctrine suffers from incompleteness, a short-sighted perspective, and lack of integration among the many facets of human behaviour studied by it. [22]

March and Simon criticize small group research simply because it neglected formal organizations. Etzioni was critical mainly because the research was based on the assumption of harmony in organizations but he was also lyrical in praise of some of its achievements:

Following . . . experiments, and the writings of Mayo and Lewin, the Human Relations approach came to emphasize the importance of communication between the ranks, *of explaining to the lower participants the reasons why a particular course of action is taken; the importance of* participation in decision-making *in which lower ranks share in the decisions made by higher ranks, in particular in matters that affect them directly; and the virtues of* democratic leadership *which not only is highly communicative and encourages participation but also is just, non-arbitrary and concerned with the problems of workers, not just those of work. There are few social science studies and insights that have received more attention or were more widely reported in popular literature and in the trade manuals than these experiments and the conclusions Human Relations drew from them.* [23]

In Etzioni's view human relations research revealed informal activities in organizations which needed only to be synthesized with the formal, classical, theory in order to present a complete organization theory. Neither Etzioni nor any other 'modern' organization theorist saw any marked inconsistency between the approaches. Nor was there one.

Individual and small group research is based on certain implicit assumptions about causality. It has to be assumed that it is possible to take any segment of activity, say fourteen workers in a bank wiring room as in the Hawthorne studies, and find the main determinants of action within it. If, for instance, there is a problem of absenteeism in a clerical department of a firm it has to be assumed that it is possible to effect a solution to the problem by studying that department alone. In other words, it has to be believed that the prime responsibility for action lies with individuals or small groups of individuals. Now this belief can only be held if an assumption of organic unity is made about society so that nothing exists to disrupt seriously or permanently the unity of purpose or harmony of interests of the whole. Society then has to be seen as a static unified system containing no serious contradictions and, therefore, no disintegrative forces which cannot be corrected without structural changes. This means that it is believed that corrections can be made without disturbing the *status quo* — without having to cause shifts in the ownership of the means of production, the distribution of income and of property. This assumption represents the ideological base to human relations studies. The same assumption, as the discussion about Mary Parker Follett and James D. Mooney made clear, lay at the basis of scientific management. There could, therefore, be no theoretical inconsistencies between the two approaches. Within the same analytical framework there were merely differences of emphasis. The formal theorists neglected interpersonal relationships while the human relations school just took it for granted that their studies were taking place within formal organizations. The two approaches were also similar in that they were both concerned with employers' problems and used terms such as efficiency, morale and industry as they were presented to them by employers.

The theory of bureaucracy

While the Human Relations School was becoming established a third model appeared and marked the entrance of sociological theorists *per se* into the field of organization theory. This model, described as a theory of bureaucracy, was based on the analysis of bureaucracy by Max Weber which had been largely unnoticed except by German sociologists. Weber's work was not translated into English until 1947 but one of his translators, Talcott Parsons, had summarized Weber's analysis in his book, *The Structure of Social Action* in 1937. From 1940 Weber's analysis of bureaucracy became an integral part of the prevailing sociological theory and it has remained so, though with certain modifications. An influential integrator was R. K. Merton, with an article on 'Bureaucratic structure and person-ality' (1940); Philip Selznick followed with a basically similar bureaucratic model, described in his articles 'An approach to a theory of bureaucracy' (1943) and 'Foundations of the theory of organization' (1948).[24] Others followed Selznick. Etzioni, the most recent, claims Weber directly, not through Parsons, Merton and Selznick, as a founding father of his school of thought.

The prevailing sociological method which was used to analyse bureauc-racies was structural functionalism. This approach was developed by Parsons, Merton and Selznick.[25] Functionalism and structural func-tionalism can be criticized for being both teleological and tautological, but it is not intended to cover that ground here. The present intention is briefly to describe how these approaches have been developed in their application to organizational behaviour and to show their continuity with earlier methods.

Functional analysis in its pure form is a theory of an organic system, borrowed from the biological sciences and adapted via anthropology for use in sociology. It is based on the postulate of the functional unity of society, called by functional sociologists a social system. Each social system is assumed to have a paramount goal, towards the attainment of which all action is orientated. There are subgoals and sub-subgoals, forming a common integrated value pattern. All activities then are functional in that they contribute to the achievement of the goals in the system. While activities have functions the participants or actors have roles which are also consistent with each other. Looked at in another way a social system is a system of differentiated statuses ranked in a stratified form according to the common integrated value pattern. Each position in the system has a social status which in turn consists of a role set. Merton has defined a role set as a 'complement of role relationships which persons have by virtue of occupying a particular social status'.[26] This social system is static. Functionalism was regarded by its protagonists as pertinent for the analysis of the parts of a social system which are themselves subsocial systems.

A common identity

The functionally unified social system is the sociological equivalent of the perfectly competitive economy. The subsocial systems are equivalent to economic segments of the economy. In other words functionalism and conventional economic analysis are alternative ways of examining the same phenomena. They are both static and both involve the same assumptions about society. The classical organization theory is an extension of conventional economic analysis to explain the organization of economic activities. This extension has been transposed into sociological terms through functional analysis. So, in effect, the classical organization theory and the functional analysis of organizations represent alternative ways of examining the same phenomena. The formal industrial organization in the classical theory is regarded as a social system in functional analysis; its profit-making purpose is the paramount goal; its division of labour and authority structure ensuring that productivity is maximized is equivalent to the orientation of all action to the fulfilment of the goal; the hierarchical distribution of occupations corresponds to the distribution of statuses and the collection of tasks which each occupation involves are, in sociological terms, described as roles. In neither case is any obstacle recognized in the way of achieving the primary objective. The use of functional analysis instead of classical organization theory is nothing more than a transposition of terms. It has the disadvantage of eliminating clarity, for diagrams are much simpler to understand than the language of Parsons, Merton and Selznick. But it reopened the field of organization theory to sociologists and most sociologists since the 1940s have passed through the same opening.

Contemporary sociological analysis of organizations started from a base constructed by functional sociologists from the analysis of bureaucracy by Max Weber. There was no problem of synthesis here. In the first place Weber's analysis had much in common with the classical organization theorists. Even March and Simon supported this view for they wrote that Weber wished to show 'to what extent bureaucratic organization is a rational solution to the complexities of modern problems . . . [and he] appears to have more in common with Urwick, Gulick, and others than he does with those who regard themselves as his successors'.[27] So, as the classical organization model was a wholly consistent alternative way of describing what functional organization model describes, it is not surprising that Weber's analysis was acceptable to the functional sociologists.

Weber's analysis, based on the assumption of perfect competition, fitted neatly into a functional model and gave it the detail it needed. His conformist approach, particularly his treatment of the question of the distribution of authority, strongly supported those who used the functional or organic unity postulate and assumed the *status quo* thereby as given. His emphasis on the administration of control was consistent with the ideological commitment of both the classical organization theorists and the functional sociologists. Once the Weber source was tapped by Parsons and Merton it was used with undying gratification by a succession of sociologists.

The Weber source was used by R. K. Merton in 1940 for an article on 'Bureaucratic structure and personality' in a manner which both set the pattern for subsequent sociologists and became a stereotype explanation of organizations.[28] Merton wrote:

A formal, rationally organized social structure involves clearly defined patterns of activity in which, ideally, every series of actions is functionally related to the purposes of the organization. In such an organization there is integrated a series of offices, of hierarchized statuses, in which inhere a number of obligations and privileges closely defined by limited and specific rules. Each of these offices contains an area of imputed competence and responsibility. Authority, the power of control which derives from an acknowledged status, inheres in the office and not in the particular person who performs the official role. Official action ordinarily occurs within the framework of pre-existing rules of the organization. The system of prescribed relations between the various offices involves a considerable degree of formality and clearly defined social distance between the occupants of these positions. Formality is manifested by means of a more or less complicated social ritual which symbolizes and supports the pecking order of the various offices. Such formality, which is integrated with the distribution of authority within the system, serves to minimize friction by largely restricting (official) contact to modes which are previously defined by the rules of the organization. Ready calculability of others behaviour and a stable set of mutual expectations is thus built up. Moreover, formality facilitates the interaction of the occupants of offices despite their (possibly hostile) private attitudes toward one another. In this way, the subordinate is protected from the arbitrary action of his superior, since the actions of both are constrained by a mutually recognized set of rules. . . . The ideal type of such formal organization is bureaucracy and, in many respects, the classical analysis of bureaucracy is that by Max Weber.

He added, without a glimmer of intellectual caution, that:

The chief merit of bureaucracy is its technical efficiency, with a premium placed on precision, speed, expert control, continuity, discretion, and optimal returns on input. The structure is one which approaches the complete elimination of personalized relationships and non-rational considerations.[29]

In this quotation can be seen the essential ingredients of the earlier models. There is the conceptual framework of functional analysis within which Weber's analysis and that of the classical theorists are combined and fitted. It shows organizations as abstractions from their general environment; reveals them as being conceived almost entirely as control mechanisms; emphasizes formal activities, that is, rules, regulations, designated positions; assumes mechanistic responses from participants, given and consistent goals, and rational action; and assesses the end results in terms of technical efficiency as defined by employers. Unlike Weber and the classical organization theorists, however, Merton used the concept of equilibrium for his model in an attempt to account for social change. In using this device he made an analogy between the physical and biological sciences on the one hand and the social sciences on the other and was following a practice well established by economists and sociologists.[30] Its introduction caused an improvement to static models and, from the point of view of conventional theorists, it had the advantage of not requiring any alteration in their conceptual framework. In so far as their conceptual framework precluded a dynamic analysis of social change then equilibrium analysis was no more than a means of paying lip-service to reality.

The concept of equilibrium
The term equilibrium does not have the same meaning as stability, for

stability is a distinct quality which an equilibrium position may or may not have. An equilibrium may be stable, unstable or neutral depending on the relationship between the elements which are defined as constituting equilibrium. To quote Sherman Krupp:

When a slight change in condition creates a movement that feeds on its own relationships, thereby creating further change, equilibrium is said to be unstable. It is spoken of as stable if it returns to the original position after having been disturbed. . . . If the system moves but stays in this new position, equilibrium is neutral. . . . Neutral equilibrium describes a system that may come to rest anywhere within some broad but designated range. [31]

Nonetheless, equilibrium analysis, as it has been used by organization theorists, has a stability bias. The equilibrium position is seen to be the stable and, therefore, the desired one. This has resulted because equilibrium relates to the behaviour of the main properties or variables assigned to the organization or whatever is under investigation. One has to talk about the equilibrium of related variables such as supply and demand, goals, social control, or sentiments and interests, or whatever are regarded as the prime determinants of behaviour. It would make nonsense of the concept to do otherwise. The very choice of the variables carried with it a stability bias. When the variables are in harmony, or consistent, or integrated then they are in equilibrium and there is stability. Disequilibrium, on the other hand, is equated with disharmony or conflict or disintegration or any movement away from a consistent relationship between the chosen variables and represents instability. A consequence of the use of equilibrium analysis has been to emphasize that a change away from any given equilibrium position must have negative or derogatory effects. It is but one logical step away to claim that change itself is undesirable. Thus equilibrium is equivalent to *status quo* analysis.

The concept of the equilibrium position was introduced into organizational analysis explicitly by Elton Mayo and members of the Hawthorne study group. In their work stability was given an efficiency significance. Mayo believed that workers could only function efficiently when they were in equilibrium with their surroundings. [32] He stated that 'the psychologists have found that work can continue to be performed only in a "steady state",' in other words, 'only for so long as an inner equilibrium is maintained between a large number of mutually dependent variables'. [33] A 'steady state' was a situation of social equilibrium within an organization. If anything happened to disturb the equilibrium then forces came into operation to restore it. Roethlisberger and Dickson wrote that:

We are, intentionally referring to the social organization as a social equilibrium in order to emphasize what we conceive the chief character of a social organization to be: an interaction of sentiments and interests in a relation of mutual dependence, resulting in a state of equilibrium such that if that state is altered, forces tending to re-establish it come into play. [34]

This quality of equilibrium maintenance is an essential element in all organic models. It is implicit in the very notion of systems analysis which rests on the belief that systems can and do maintain their boundaries. Equilibrium maintenance in analytical practice means system maintenance which is what structural functionalism is all about. It is the central part of the theory of social action as constructed by Talcott Parsons. Organizational equilibrium, in Parsonsian terms, is the maintenance of certain stable patterns of activity and interaction in relation to the pursuit of goals and it is maintained all organizations have a tendency towards this state.

Conceptual adaptations

Because this tendency was regarded as characteristic of systems, no special mechanisms to maintain a stable interaction had to be spelled out. Problems only arose in connection with deviance from the stable patterns and these were settled by defence and adjustments.[35] Deviant action was that which was contrary to or inconsistent with the pursuit of the goals of the system. But, in order to be consistent with the motivational predominance of goals in the model, deviant action itself had to be in pursuit of goals. The question was, if systems consisted of stable patterns of activity, which goals? R. K. Merton came to the rescue with the concept 'dysfunction', which explained how activities calculated to achieve ends can become ends themselves causing a displacement of goals. This displacement, Merton wrote, 'of sentiments from goals on to means is fostered by the tremendous symbolic significance of the means (rules)'.[36] The reliance on rules in a bureaucracy caused rigidities which prevented it from adjusting readily to changed circumstances. Activities became dysfunctional through overconformity to rules. Whether activities were functional or dysfunctional was a matter for empirical investigation.

The structural functionalist model was amended by Philip Selznick in his article 'An approach to a theory of bureaucracy' in 1943. Selznick, drawing his evidence largely from the bank wiring room experiment in the Hawthorne studies, concluded that every organization creates an informal structure, that in every organization the goals of the organization are modified, abandoned, deflected or elaborated — by processes within it and that the process of modification is effected through the informal structure. Two elements are present in Selznick's analysis: these are goal-oriented activity and a structural element which consists of the day-to-day activity of men which 'is ordered by those specific problems which have a direct relevance to the materials with which they have to deal', and which, since they 'consume an increasing proportion of the time and thoughts of the participants . . . are — from the point of view of actual behaviour — *substituted* for the professed goals'.[37] These two elements, show clearly one interpretation at least of the meaning of structure in the analytical method called structural functionalism.

The purpose of structural functionalism was to explain why and how it was that non-rational elements disturbed the rational, calculable, manipulable action of bureaucratic organizations. In this conceptual framework the functional unity postulate was modified to take account of dysfunctions or unintended consequences of rationally intended acts. There may or may not be functional unity at any one time but there *will be* functional unity if dysfunctional elements are not present. The organizational goals were still given and organizational activity was orientated towards their fulfilment. The recognition that an informal, or substitute, pattern of goal-oriented activity might exist meant that the mechanistic view of motivation had to be altered. Control in pursuit of the formal goals could not be assumed to be applied unequivocally in every case because it could be frustrated by informal activities. This meant, in turn, that control and consent had to be regarded as being indivisible; in consequence a wider view had to be taken of an organization than as a system in which resources were manipulated. The organization had to be seen, Selznick maintained in 1947, as a *cooperative* system.[38] The assumption that organizations were cooperative systems allowed participants to be accounted for within the formal system of control as individuals or members of small groups and permitted the introduction into the analysis of personal goals which participants hoped to achieve within the organization. These personal goals might be consistent or inconsistent with the formal organizational goal. But the assumption that action was cooperative meant that the organization had the qualities to survive a predominance of multiple personal goals which conflicted with the formal organizational one. Thus this new concept was another rescue operation. Whenever the attempts to explain the reality of social change led logically to a questioning of the analytical usefulness of structural functionalism a fresh assumption, supposedly a clarifying one, was introduced which had the effect of removing the difficulties. There was much scope in this connection for the sort of intellectual imagination which in another context would be called guile.

Whenever attempts were made to adapt the structural functional or systems analysis to account for social change, questions arose on which depended the very usefulness of the model. That is, once some change within a system was acknowledged its potentiality and its sources had to be explained. How dysfunctional, for instance, could dysfunctional activities be? Could they alter an organization qualitatively? If dysfunctional activities could be persistently and consistently disruptive of stable patterns then the concept of the social system, and hence the whole approach of structural functionalism, would have to be reconsidered. If the nature of the change was such that the system could not contain it, then the relationship between the system and its environment had to be explained. These questions directed attention to the meaning of the term structure. Did it refer to elements of the system alone or to elements external to it as well? The integrity of the system, so essential for equilibrium analysis and the core of structural functionalism, depended upon the answer.

The structural functionalist masters were not caught out. Both Parsons and Merton, as shown above, and others who followed them, in effect answered both questions by assuming that mechanisms or qualities existed in organizations which limited the scope of change and enabled organizations to maintain themselves. Philip Selznick stated that 'a given empirical system is deemed to have basic needs, essentially related to self maintenance: the system develops repetitive means of self-defence. . . .'[39] He added: 'It is a basic postulate of the structural-functional approach that the basic need of all empirical systems is the maintenance of the integrity and continuity of the system itself.' Another sociologist, William G. Scott, explained that 'It is impossible to conceive of an ordered relationship among the parts of a system without also introducing the idea of a stabilizing or an adapting mechanism.'[40] A. W. Gouldner, in a very sophisticated and plausible article, 'Reciprocity and autonomy in functional theory' started his analysis of social change from the assumption that systems 'should be expected to maintain their boundaries'.[41] This point does not need elaboration. If there are systems it *must* be assumed that in some way they can maintain their identities, otherwise system is not a workable concept.

Once this assumption was introduced the mechanics of limitation, of self-preservation, had to be explained. There was scope for imagination and disagreement here and it is indeed the area of analysis where disagreement has centred. The differences have centred on dissatisfaction with the mechanistic integrative processes in functionalist theory. Change was assumed to be derived from conflict. The conflict which was explained by normative functionalism, as expressed by both Merton and Selznick, was considered to be inadequate because it neglected what in reality seemed to be non-normative sources of conflict.[42] So attempts were made to *introduce* into their analytical framework the consideration of changes resulting from institutional sources — from the existence of 'power-over' as Follett would have described it. The contributors were not specifically concerned with organization theory, but their analyses related to organizational change. Plausible disarming tactics were used. The contributors tended to acknowledge merits in what A. W. Gouldner called 'factor theories', derived from an historical materialist frame of reference and drew on the works of Karl Marx for analytical support. Gouldner went further in claiming to fuse the system and factor analysis. This exercise however, merely introduced inconsistencies into the tightly consistent models of Parsons and Merton. The fusion did not, and could not, make sense.

The question of theoretical convergence

Two prominent contributions in this attempt to explain social change were *Class and Class Conflict in an Industrial Society* by Ralf Dahrendorf, and an article called 'Reciprocity and Autonomy in Functional Theory' by A. W. Gouldner.[43] Dahrendorf believed that social structure has two faces — an integrative one and a conflict one and that separate theories were necessary to explain each one. In other words, that systems and factor analytical models were complementary and not alternatives. 'Strictly speaking,' he stated, 'both models are . . . useful and necessary for sociological analysis.' But he did not think that the construction of a coercion model required 'a complete, or even partial, revision of the conceptual apparatus that by now has become more or less generally accepted by sociologists in all countries. Categories like role, institution, norm, structure, even function are as useful in terms of the coercion model as they are for the analysis of social integration.'[44] So Dahrendorf introduced the categories of role and power into a modified version of structural functionalism and used the notion of relations of authority to give them meaning. Superimposed on the normative system, coterminous with it, was an authority system. 'In conflict analysis', Dahrendorf stated, 'we are concerned *inter alia* with the generation of conflict groups by the authority relations obtaining in imperitively coordinated associations.' He maintained that the differential distribution of authority becomes 'productive of clashes of role interest which under certain conditions lead to the formation of organized antagonistic groups within limited social organizations as well as within total societies'.[45] The question at issue here is not whether or not a differential distribution of authority gives rise to conflict or tension. It can be shown empirically that it does. The question first is whether Dahrendorf's coercion model belongs to the same analytical framework as the structural functional one. If it does then it must possess similar heuristic limitations. It seems that Dahrendorf believes that analytical terms are there for the taking, irrespective of their conceptual origins. It is quite clear, however, that this is not the case. Terms such as role, norm and structure take their meaning from the conceptual framework to which they belong, unless they are redefined they carry meanings with strict conceptual implications to them. The meanings Dahrendorf gives to his terms belong unequivocally to a structural functionalist model. Their use is limited to movements within an organic system which, by definition, are aberrations from some standard or norm and which are remedial. Talcott Parsons, indeed, defined social change to mean just this. 'From a dynamic or performance point of view,' he stated, 'social interaction is a continual back-and-forth alternation between performance and "sanctions".'[46] Dahrendorf's model as he conceives it, has no such consistency for the change he is concerned with arises from 'group conflicts of the class type, class being understood in the traditional sense'.[47] By traditional he means Marxist. Thus he is using an organic model in which action is mainly integrative to explain a conflict which is permanent, inexorable and insoluable within its existing context. This inconsistency, however, rests in Dahrendorf's claims, not in his actual model, for his prime variable, the authority relations is almost as teleological as the norms which comprise the main variable in the functionalist model. The classical organization theory model represented an essentially coercive system — the prime variable was authority — though mechanical responses were assumed so that coercion was not seen to apply and the responses to which it gave rise were not recognized. When the assumption of mechanical responses were removed, as it was by the introduction of informal activities into the classical model, the existence of conflict out of authority relations was made possible and the main lines of Dahrendorf's model were laid.[48]

A. W. Gouldner gave a different and logically more consistent explanation of the operation of the mechanisms of systems and therefore of social change. He postulated that the ability of a system to maintain its boundaries would depend upon its engagement in reciprocally functional interchanges with others, or on the presence of 'compensatory mechanisms'. It must be assumed, Gouldner added,

that parts with some degree of functional autonomy will resist full or complete integration into the larger system. Conversely, the system itself, straining towards integration, can be expected to seek submission of the parts to the requirements of the position they occupy. Consequently, there may be some tension between the part's tendency to maintain an existent degree of functional autonomy and the system's pressure to

*control the part. . . . Organization is seen then as shaped by conflict,
particularly by the tensions between centripetal and centrifugal pressures,
as limiting control over parts as well as imposing it, as establishing a
balance between their dependence and independence and as separating as
well as connecting the parts.* [49]

Gouldner accounts for the possibility of change as a result of such tension
by postulating 'different strategies with which this situation can be played
from the standpoint of the part'. A functionally autonomous part, an
organization, may insulate itself, expand, or reorganize internally in some
way in response to tensions. These strategies may correspond to what is
empirically evident as Gouldner claims, but their analytical possibilities are
confined by the limitations imposed by the framework. In so far as
Gouldner was attempting to develop Merton's functional analysis he was
on relatively safe methodological ground. But he did not let his claims rest
there. He contended that by emphasizing '*degrees* of functional autonomy
and *degrees* of system interdependence' he was partly resolving 'the
classical tension between two lines of sociological theory, one of which
stemmed from Comte and Durkheim to Parsons and the other from
Marx'.[50] This was an extravagant claim to make. The functionalist
model, in its purest form, because it was fully integrated, could admit of
change being derived only from forces external to the system while the
Marxist model stressed that the system could change due to its internal
contradictions. So Gouldner stated. His own model took account of forces
internal and external to the system and consequently joined the two lines
of thought. On a later occasion, Gouldner stated that he believed reciprocity to be 'one of the major but overlooked convergencies in the history of
sociological theory'.[51] In his eyes the difference between the Parsonsian
and Marxist models was quantitative and not qualitative.

The justification for Gouldner's claim rests on his interpretation of what
he calls the Marxist tradition. It does not require a lengthy dissertation
about 'what Marx really meant' to show that Gouldner's interpretation is
inaccurate because it was tailored and distorted by his own conceptual
limitations. In the functionalist model, equilibrium theory is both logically
and strategically anterior to a theory of change.[52] The explanation of
change is reached, therefore, through adapting the explanation of equilibrium. The definition of change is derived from the conception of equilibrium and stability. If this is the analytical starting point, as it was with
Gouldner, then it is conceivable to see only quantitative differences
between explanations of social change. But if a starting point is used which
makes a theory of change, both logically and strategically anterior to static
or equilibrium theory, then there must be a qualitative difference in the

explanations for every term and concept will be qualitatively different. Marxism, as it was defined by Lukacs and how it is used in this book, gives a theory of change that superiority. Its dialectical basis is dynamic in conception, capable of dealing with a continuously evolving subject matter through the identification and analysis of contradictions. These contradictions are not, as Gouldner suggested, the core of an internal mechanism in systems. They are the product of historically determined environmental forces. Given this, there can be no equilibrium; stability is a state of obstructed change, as transient and peripheral as change is itself in the structural-functionalist model; and change is capable of having uncontrollable, boundary-destroying qualities. This issue is explored in much greater detail in Part three of this book but even on the basis of this brief introduction it can be seen that Marxism and structural-functionalism rest on qualitatively different versions of social reality and, therefore, constitute entirely different theories. It is methodologically impossible to converge these theories and it is nonsense to try.

Notes

1.   Cf. Sherman Krupp, *Pattern in Organization Analysis: a critical examination*, Holt Rinehart & Winston, 1961, pp. 52ff.
2.   There have been many descriptions and interpretations of Taylor's work. The only relevant ones for our purpose are those by organization theorists, and of these three are of particular significance: March and Simon, *Organizations*, chapter 2; Etzioni, *Modern Organizations*, chapter 3; and Krupp, *Pattern in Organization Analysis*, chapter 2.
3.   March and Simon, *Organizations*, p. 14.
4.   *Ibid.*, pp. 22–3.
5.   *Ibid.*, p. 29.
6.   Mary Parker Follett, *Dynamic Administration: the collected papers of Mary Parker Follett*, ed., H. C. Metcalfe and L. Urwick, London, The Camelot Press, 1941; Miss Parker wrote these papers during the 1920s and early 1930s; she also wrote other works. James D. Mooney, *The Principles of Organization*, rev. edn, Harper, 1947 (first published under the title *Onward Industry*, in collaboration with A. C. Reiley, 1931).
7.   Follett, *Dynamic Administration*, p. 71.
8.   *Ibid.*, p. 198.
9.   Mooney, *op. cit.*, pp. 8–9.
10.   Follett, *op. cit.*, pp. 34–5.
11.   Mooney, *op. cit.*, p. 173.
12.   Cf. Krupp, *op. cit.*, p. 89; Follett, *op. cit.*, pp. 35, 213.

13. Follett, *op. cit.*, ch. 4.
14. *Ibid.*, pp. 106–7.
15. There have been innumerable contributors in the field of organizational analysis — too many to list here. Most of them represent organizations as charts with arrows pointing in different directions to indicate lines of authority and the like. Of the many contributors see particularly L. Gulick and L. Urwick, eds., *Papers on the Science of Administration*, Institute of Public Administration, New York, 1937, L. Urwick, *The Elements of Administration*, Pitmans, 1947; and E. F. L. Brech, *Organization*, Longmans, 1957.
16. Etzioni, *Modern Organizations*, p. 31.
17. March and Simon, *op. cit.*, p. 33.
18. Apart from Elton Mayo's book, *The Human Problems of an Industrial Civilization*, Harvard University Press, 1933, the most influential works to result from the research were F. J. Roethlisberger and W. S. Dickson, *Management and the Worker*, Harvard University Press, 1939, and F. J. Roethlisberger, *Management and Morale*, Harvard University Press, 1941.
19. Kurt Lewin, *Field Theory in Social Science*, Tavistock, 1951; J. L. Moreno, *Psychodrama*, vol. 1, Beacon House, 1946; G. C. Homans, *The Human Group*, Routledge, 1950.
20. Victor A. Thompson, *Modern Organization*, Knopf, 1961, p. 123.
21. This is the name given by Etzioni to his approach to organization theory.
22. William G. Scott, 'Organization theory: an overview and appraisal', in J. A. Litterer, ed., *Organizations: structure and behaviour*, Wiley, 1969, p. 21.
23. Etzioni, *Modern Organizations*, p. 38.
24. Max Weber, *The Structure of Social Action*, trans. Talcott Parsons, Allen & Unwin, 1937; R. K. Merton, 'Bureaucratic structure and personality', *Social Forces*, **18** (1940); Philip Selznick, 'An approach to a theory of bureaucracy', *American Sociological Review*, **8** (1943), and 'Foundations of the theory of organization', *ibid.*, **13** (1948).
25. Talcott Parsons, 'The present position and prospects of systematic theory in sociology', in G. Gurvitch and W. E. Moore, eds., *Twentieth-century Sociology*, Philosophical Library, 1945; R. K. Merton, 'Sociological theory', *American Journal of Sociology*, **50**, (1945), reprinted in *Social Theory and Social Structure*, The Free Press, Illinois, 1963; Selznick, *op. cit.*
26. R. K. Merton, *Social Theory and Social Structure*, rev. edn, New York, Free Press, 1957, p. 369.

27. March and Simon, *op. cit.*, p. 36.
28. R. K. Merton, 'Bureaucratic structure and personality', *Social Forces*, **18** (1940).
29. *Ibid.*, reprinted in *Social Theory and Social Structure*, pp. 195–6.
30. See C. E. Russett, *The Concept of Equilibrium in American Social Thought*, Yale University Press, 1966, for an account of the general development of the concept.
31. Krupp, *op. cit.*, p. 36.
32. Mayo, *The Concept of Equilibrium in American Social Thought*, p. 143.
33. Mayo, *The Human Problems of an Industrial Civilization*, p. 27.
34. F. J. Roethlisberger and W. G. Dickson, *Management and the Worker*, Harvard University Press, 1939, p. 365.
35. See Russett, *op. cit.*, p. 144, for a comment on the Parsonian model in this connection.
36. Merton, *Social Theory and Social Structure*, p. 201.
37. Philip Selznick, 'An approach to the theory of bureaucracy', *American Sociological Review*, **8** (1943), 48.
38. Philip Selznick, 'Foundations of the theory of organization', *American Sociological Review*, **13** (1948), 25–35.
39. *Ibid.*
40. 'Organization theory', *loc. cit.*, p. 23.
41. A. W. Gouldner, 'Reciprocity and autonomy in functional theory', in Llewellyn Gross, ed., *Symposium on Sociological Theory*, Row, Peterson & Co., New York, p. 255.
42. Selznick's view was: 'Cooperation systems are constituted of individuals interacting as wholes in relation to a formal system of co-ordination. The concrete function is, therefore, a resultant of the reciprocal influences of the formal and informal aspects of organization. Furthermore, this structure is itself a totality, an adaptive "organism" reacting to influences upon it from an external environment' ('Foundations of the theory of organization', *loc. cit.*).
43. Dahrendorf, *Class and Class Conflict*; A. W. Gouldner, 'Reciprocity and autonomy in functional theory', in Gross, ed., *op. cit.*
44. Dahrendorf, *Class and Class Conflict*, p. 163.
45. *Ibid.*, p. 165.
46. Talcott Parsons, 'Revised analytical approach to the theory of social stratification', in R. Bendix and S. M. Lipset, eds., *Class Status and Power: a reader in social stratification*, The Free Press of Glencoe, 1960, p. 99.
47. Dahrendorf, *Class and Class Conflict*, p. 165n.
48. David Lockwood has also identified Dahrendorf's coercion model

with that of the normative functional one ('Social integration and system integration', in G. K. Zollschan and W. Hirsch, eds., *Explorations in Social Change*, Routledge & Kegan Paul, 1964, pp. 244—57). He linked the 'conflict analysis as stated by John Rex (*Key Problems of Sociological Theory*, Routledge & Kegan Paul, 1969), with that of Dahrendorf, and stated that the 'themes of norms — consensus — order, and power-aberration-conflict are not regarded as viable sociological alternatives. It is, therefore, a little surprising to find that both Dahrendorf and Rex consider it necessary to develop their antitheses to normative functionalism in a *systematic* form' (p. 247).

49. Gouldner, 'Reciprocity and autonomy in functional theory', *loc. cit.*, pp. 255, 257.

50. *Ibid.*, p. 264.

51. A. W. Gouldner, 'The norm of reciprocity: a preliminary statement', *American Sociological Review*, **25**, No. 2 (1960), 167.

52. Cf. Russett, *The Concept of Equilibrium in American Social Thought*, p. 145.

4

Max Weber's model of bureaucracy

Contemporary organization theory springs from various sources which have made impressions of varying degrees of permanence and intensity. In some instances the effect has been made but the imprint has disappeared. Only the historian is interested in those whose contributions have been absorbed without trace of their origin. But there have been contributions which have had a continuing effect and which, therefore, require analysis in order to illuminate contemporary theory. There is little doubt that the most prominent of such contributions is that made by Max Weber through his analysis of bureaucracy. His model of bureaucracy has been used as a base for theorizing by some sociologists, such as Etzioni, or has become an integral part of a more general approach, as with the work of Merton. Terminology from the model has drifted into everyday usage so that what are described as commonsense interpretations of organizational behaviour are in reality interpretations through Weber's analysis. Organizations are seen as Weber described them and not necessarily as they are. This is a sign of the extent of his influence. Bureaucracy as defined by Weber has become synonymous with organization. The qualities he attributed to bureaucracies have been largely accepted by subsequent sociologists. No other single contributor has had such an impact. He has evoked so little criticism, even of the mildest kind, that in any analysis of his model the question of the continued relevance of his explanations must be raised. No explanations persist for half a century unless they retain a utility of some kind. What utility exists in Weber's model of bureaucracy for present-day organizations? Or, in other words, what in the determining environment of Max Weber in Germany before the First World War is still relevant today not only in Germany but in other industrial countries?

The answer to these questions can only be obtained by looking at Weber's analysis in its historical context. The model of bureaucracy is not the product of a mind in a vacuum but of a mind in a particular set of circumstances and itself a product of those circumstances. In order to understand the model of bureaucracy a series of further questions relating to the objective conditions surrounding the model has to be asked. In particular it is necessary to know about the industrial, political and social environment of Weber, the kinds of analytical tools and methods on hand for his use, and the intellectual milieu in which he operated. The analysis can never be dissociated from the analyst, who in turn is inextricably associated with his environment. In this chapter we are examining not a model of bureaucracy but a model of bureaucracy constructed by Max Weber in Germany before the First World War.

Weber's work on the theory of social and economic organization was written largely between the years 1911 and 1913 though it was not published until after his death in 1920 and was not translated into English until 1947.[1] The aspect of his work which became particularly relevant for the analysis of organizations was his study of bureaucracy. At the time Weber worked on his study the question of the distribution of power within organizations was a topical one arousing interest in alternative power structures to the one that prevailed. In the decade preceding the First World War the democratization of control in industry through workers' participation under forms of collective ownership of the means of production was widely propagated. Democratic ideas were a part of Weber's intellectual environment, as a study of his works indicates. Interest in them stimulated Roberto Michels to examine their impact in his work *Political Parties* published in 1911. Weber was an acquaintance of Michels and embodied the latter's conclusions in his own work. It is not possible to state that Weber was stimulated to repudiate the notion of industrial democracy, or that he did anything other than attempt to examine problems of power in organizations as dispassionately as he could, but in every sense he was a strict conformist to the social values closely derived from the dominant legitimate value of a capitalist Germany.[2] His father was a wealthy lawyer and National-Liberal parliamentarian at the time of Bismarck, belonging to a family of textile manufacturers. Weber had the conventional education of this social group; its values influenced his attitude to nonconformist ideas and therefore his academic work. Indeed Weber provides a case study of the conformist academic. In saying this one is not unduly detracting from his pioneering sociological work. Given the set of values within which he worked he most probably could only have done better if he had recognized the limits these imposed on his intellectual capacity. But if he had done this, of course, his analysis would have been different. He challenged no established theories but simply added a new dimension to existing ones. And he did so with a firmness which in itself should have aroused intellectual suspicion.

The dominance of economics in Weber's milieu

When Max Weber became interested in the study of organizations economics was the dominant, only firmly established social science discipline. Other disciplines arose to answer the questions with which economists were not concerned. They were initially marginal and subordinate to economics. Seen another way, the questions deemed by economists to fall within the scope of economics were taken as given by psychologists and sociologists and formed a starting point for further analysis. This factor had a profound effect on the study of organizations. More than this, the manner in which the economists' questions were tackled, the methodology which was used, strongly influenced subsequent analyses, particularly in sociology. The study of economics was a part of the structure of the intellectual milieu of Max Weber.

Economic phenomena were treated to rigorous, static analysis based on value dominated but simplifying assumptions. In order to construct a linear system at all it was necessary to make assumptions about motivation, individual rationality and utility or satisfaction. The assumptions made related to the prevailing free private enterprise industrial system. Private ownership of the means of production and the existing distribution of property and income were taken as given. Individuals were assumed to be motivated by the desire to maximize their own economic interests and to be wholly rational in doing this. Rational in this context meant that if an individual preferred A to B and B to C then he would prefer A to C. Economic models based on these assumptions showed the free market mechanism, without interruption or obstruction, distributing and combining resources in uses and at places at prices which provided the maximum satisfaction to all involved in the system. The freely competitive system which the models depicted was described as perfectly competitive, which in fact meant the perfect or ideal system.

In order for the models to work, some secondary assumptions had to be made. It was assumed that no buyer or seller in any market was large enough to influence the market transactions, so that each market consisted wholly of a large number of units. Any difficulties, therefore, which might have been created by acknowledging the existence of monopolies or economic transactions by governments were safely assumed away. It was also assumed that there was complete mobility of labour and capital within and between each market so that whenever and wherever new opportunities for maximizing profits or incomes arose the factors of production could move freely to exploit them. In order to make this assumption workable in the model it had also to be assumed that every buyer and seller and consumer in every market possessed a perfect knowledge of the market so that everyone knew just what rates of profit and income prevailed and what the commodities and their prices were which were being offered for sale. Nothing was allowed to impede the rational pursuit of the assumed purpose of economic activity, namely the maximization of satisfaction measured in money terms.

The market mechanism which performed this function of distributing, allocating and combining operated mechanistically and impersonally. There was no scope for personal intervention, for altering the market way of doing things. The owners of labour power provided labour power while entrepreneurs who controlled capital performed the function of combining labour power and capital in order to produce goods and services. Having done this, that is having provided what was euphemistically called enterprise, entrepreneurs were assumed to act as the agents through which the market mechanism worked. If they did as the market dictated all was well for them; if they did not then their profit fell and eventually they went out of business. In all this some important questions were not asked because they fell outside the scope of economics. But in any event, they were covered, in part at least, by assumptions governing motivation and rationality.

Implicit in the task of combining labour power and capital was the need to control and regulate this relationship in such a way as to determine the pace of work and the quality of production. In other words, the entrepreneurial function was to establish authority structures within which production could take place. The classical and neoclassical economists provided answers to the problems of production, distribution and exchange but not to those concerning the establishment and administration of means of supervision. So long as rational responses were assumed, of course, there was no problem of control, but this device simply removed the issue, it did not resolve it. When a sociological interest was first taken in organizations between the approximate years of 1900 and 1914 it was understandably and inevitably concerned with control. The distribution of factors of production within organizations was explained by external market conditions, and sociologists had no alternative but to examine what was left, namely the control of the pace and quality of work.

Thus an early and effective dichotomy between economics and sociology was created in the field or organization theory. It set the scope for Max Weber's analysis of organizations, stipulating the questions which could legitimately be asked by a non-economist. The study of economics also provided the analytical base for Weber's approach to organizations for his work fell strictly and logically within its ambit. He was concerned with one form of social relationship within a perfectly competitive sphere of economic activity. Assumptions about the nature of that activity inevitably intruded into his own analysis.

In this chapter three consequences of Max Weber's work on organizations will be examined. The first concerns the question of the distribution of power; the second relates to his emphasis on administration and the third is about the meaning of the term 'rational'.

The distribution of power

The attention of Max Weber was concentrated on the large-scale capitalist organizations which dominated the pre-1914 German industrial scene. He defined an organization aiming at capitalist profit as one in which purposes are relatively fixed, membership is generally closed and management is carried on bureaucratically 'with some influence, however, of an assembly of the members, in which they participate either themselves or through proxies, which is *de jure* organized democratically, but plutocratically *de facto*'. [3] He regarded an organization as a way of distributing the powers of command and these powers as being derived from a type of domination which expresses itself and functions through an administration. The powers of command in an administration must be in the hands of somebody and in one aiming at capitalist profit they must ultimately rest with the members or shareholders who are the owners of the means of production and the buyers of labour power. In Weber's words they are 'based upon influence derived exclusively from the possession of goods or marketable skills guaranteed in some way and acting upon the conduct of those dominated, who remain, however, formally free and are motivated simply by the pursuit of their own interests'. The powers in this type of domination obtain their validity or are legitimized and become authority first through

a system of consciously made rational *rules (which may be either agreed upon or imposed from above), which meet with obedience as generally binding norms whenever such obedience is claimed by him whom the rule designates. In that case every single bearer of powers of command is legitimated by that system of rational norms, and his power is legitimate in so far as it corresponds with the norms. Obedience is thus given to the norms rather than to the person.* [4]

But obedience is also obtained, Weber considered, because the ruled are accustomed to obedience and have 'a personal interest in the continuation of the domination by virtue of their own participation in, and the benefits derived for them from, the domination'. The upshot of this is that the authority in an industrial organization is exercised by employers through their representatives or directly through rules and, according to Weber, is accepted because employees accept the validity of the rules, are accustomed to obedience and, in any case, have no other alternative because their personal welfare depends upon participating in the organization. The pure form of this type of domination, Weber stated, was in a bureaucracy, which he considered to be the most efficient method of management in an industrial organization.[5]

The shape and form of the dominational structure of a bureaucracy, according to Weber, were immutable. Reinhard Bendix interpreted Weber by stating that 'a fully developed bureaucracy implements a system of authority relationships that is practically indestructible' and added that 'Weber emphasized that the bureaucratic form of administration is both permanent and indispensible, contrary to the arguments of anarchists and socialists who believe that administration can be done away with in an ideal society or that it can be used to implement a freer and more equitable social order.'[6] These unequivocal conclusions were reached by Weber in the following way. He believed that industrial organizations or, as he called them, bureaucracies, were rationally based entities. I shall not examine the meaning of rational here because that is done later. For the present it will be accepted that Weber believed a rational method to be the most technically efficient one possible. To achieve this degree of efficiency, Weber considered it was necessary, among other things, that there should be a hierarchy of authority with each layer responsible to the one immediately above it. Within this hierarchy, control would rest, inevitably, with a single head or an oligarchy thus resulting in a pyramidal shape. Weber set out to prove this but, of course, it needed no proof in a private enterprise economy where industrial organizations were by definition monocratic. Nonetheless the proof is important because it is used to justify the claim that whatever the motivation, the structure of domination will remain the same; that is it will be a hierarchical pyramidal structure.

There are two aspects to Weber's case. The first is that those in the organization with the most effective education and training will become more influential than others; that, in other words, where there are functional distinctions demanding different degrees of education and skill there will be a power differentiation as well. Indeed Weber believed that the authority of the bureaucrat was based on his knowledge and training. 'The growing complexity of the administration tasks,' he stated, 'and the sheer expansion of their scope increasingly result in the technical superiority of those who have had training and experience'.[7] His attitude to democratic control follows logically from the above belief.

Democracy becomes alienated from its priority where the group grows beyond a certain size or where the administration function becomes too difficult to be satisfactorily taken care of by anyone whom rotation, the lot, or election may happen to designate. . . . As soon as mass administration is involved, the meaning of democracy changes so radically that it no longer makes sense for the sociologist to ascribe to the term (its pure

meaning). There always thus exists the probability of the rise of a special,
perennial structure for administrative purposes, which of necessity, means
for the exercise of domination. [8]
The clinching part of the argument rests on the second aspect, however,
which is the use of the 'iron law of oligarchy' expounded by Roberto
Michels in *Political Parties* which stipulated unequivocally that minorities
will invariably control organizations. Michels' 'iron law' appeared in
Weber's work as 'the so-called "law of the small number" '. [9] A ruling
minority possesses, he claimed, many advantages over the majority. It can
reach understanding quickly among its members; it can quickly initiate
rationally organized action necessary to preserve its power and it can
establish secret rule so essential for the preservation of domination.

   All this amounted to a theoretical justification of the free private enterprise power distribution which prevailed in Weber's environment. There
could be no greater vindication of the then existing type of domination
than to say it was not only the most technically efficient, but was so
efficient that it was permanent and inevitable. His work in this respect
followed in the classic tradition of academic conformity. Subsequent
organization theory has been virtually dominated by Weber's dogmatic
assertion about the power shape of organizations; up to now he has been
allowed formidably and conclusively to answer the question for sociologists. The issues he raised in his discussion of 'the law of the small number'
were settled so conclusively that they never really appeared on the research agendas of sociologists. It is, of course, not unrelated to the substantial contribution he made to academic conformity with the dominant
power structure that subsequent sociologists have taken the distribution of
power as given. On this matter the attitude of sociologists can only be
described as obscurantist.

   With the question of the distribution of power settled all that remained
for sociologists to study was the administration of power. This emphasis
was evident in Weber's own work. The possession of power, he stated, had
to be legitimated; once it had been, that power became authority. Weber
introduced into the mechanistic models of authority the question of the
acceptance or legitimation of power and then went on to detail the
administration of authority. Organization theorists since Weber have
almost without exception been preoccupied with the issue of administration of authority and questions related to it. In a recent major work by
Amitai Etzioni, for instance, compliance was used as a base for a comparative study of organizations 'because it is a central element of organizational structure'. [10] There has been no deviation from either Etzioni's
view or the one that assumes away a problem of compliance and concentrates on relating the most efficient way of exercising authority.

Sociologists, then, not only undertook organizational analysis on the terms stipulated by economists but narrowed the terms down to exclude the possibility of being confronted by issues which might question the rights of dominant power holders.

A preoccupation with administration

The second factor concerns Weber's emphasis on one aspect of administration as if this embodied all that was necessary for organization theory. The acceptance by Weber of the restrictions which conventional economic analysis placed on the study of organizations resulted in the exclusion from his analysis of the production aspects of organizations, for these were determined by impersonal market forces. Furthermore the restrictions also excluded the economic aspects of administration such as the distribution of administrative labour and its relative payment, for these were determined by the same forces. Weber was left, therefore, with the segment of organizational activity relating to administrative decision-making and his work on bureaucracy was mainly about the conditions which were necessary to make a rational form of that kind of activity possible. Thus the administration of authority was only analysed in so far as it concerned the decision-making of administrators.

The following principles were stipulated by Weber as being necessary for bureaucratic administration:

1. that official business is conducted on a continuous basis;
2. that it is conducted in accordance with stipulated rules in an administrative agency characterized by three interrelated attributes: (a) the duty of each official to do certain types of work is listed in terms of impersonal criteria; (b) the official is given the authority necessary to carry out his assigned functions; (c) the means of compulsion at his disposal are strictly limited and the conditions under which their employment is legitimate are clearly defined;
3. that every official's responsibilities and authority are part of a hierarchy of authority; higher offices are assigned the duty of supervision, lower offices the right of appeal, though the extent of supervision and the conditions of legitimate appeal may vary;
4. that officials and other administrative employees do not own the resources necessary for the performance of their assigned functions but that they are accountable for their use of these resources: official business and private affairs, official revenue and private income are strictly separated;
5. that offices cannot be appropriated by their encumbents in the sense of private property that can be sold and inherited;

6. that official business is conducted on the basis of written documents. [11]

There are two points to be noted here. The first is that the impression is created by Weber's analysis that administrative activities take place for their own sake. Yet this never happens. The activities which Weber's principles are supposed to govern may take place within an industrial organization engaged in manufacturing commodities or otherwise directly concerned with production activities, or they may take place in an industrial organization providing services of an administrative kind, such as banks and insurance companies. But wherever and however they occur they comprise an integral part of the industrial process and have always done so. In even the simplest form of industrial activity with one employer and one employee their relationship and its production consequences have to be administered. All the various administrative services provided have always been dependent services arising out of production needs. Of course Weber was interested only in large-scale administration. But this was not new either. The only novelty about what Weber called bureaucracy was its sociological treatment. Large-scale administration was no more independent of production activities than at any other scale. Indeed the scale of administration is a function of the scale of production. As production activities expand then so do administrative requirements increase. There will be more employees to recruit, to pay, to supervise; more raw materials to purchase and more finished goods to dispose of. A general expansion of industrial production will cause an increase in the demand for money, for credit facilities, for insurance cover and the like. The separation of administration from production can be identified in visible social relations, but its presence does not make it a sociologically useful category. It constitutes one of many illustrations where definitions and problems are accepted by sociologists without asking whether or not they carry any sociological significance.

The second point to be noted is that the principles governing bureaucracies as enunciated by Weber are not specific to administration but are generally applicable to the whole industrial process. This indeed is what should be found if the contention that administration and production are inseparable parts of the same industrial process is correct. A brief look at Weber's principles confirms this contention.

First, it is a characteristic of all industrial activity that it is conducted on a continuous basis. This is not simply a condition for efficient operation but a consequence of the dependence of participants on it for their complete subsistence. In so far as administration is concerned, as a dependent activity it relies on continuity of production for its own continuity;

therefore the latter is not, an independent determinant of efficiency. Commenting on this point of Weber's, Etzioni states that 'rational organization is the antithesis of *ad hoc*, temporary, unstable relations; hence the stress on continuity'.[12] Of course it is! It is equivalent to saying that continuity is the antonym of discontinuity.

Secondly, stipulated rules have always regulated industrial activities in its production and administrative aspects, and one would expect this to be so. Even relatively simple industrial organizations in the British textile industry in the late eighteenth and early nineteenth centuries had rigid rules governing the behaviour of employees in terms of their duties and authorized powers. Organized activity is activity governed by rules. Weber's statement that a bureaucracy is conducted in accordance with stipulated rules is tautological and adds nothing to the understanding of organizations. The three attributes which characterize activity governed by rules describe functional differentiation within administrations governed by rules and determined by perfect market forces, and they apply to both production and administrative activity, given those conditions. The reference to perfect market forces will be made clear below when the term 'rational' is examined.

Thirdly, given the private ownership of the means of production, there must be a hierarchy of authority, even if only one employer and two employees are involved. But it is a hierarchy which encompasses the whole process within the area of activities bounded by rules. The existence of layers of authority depends, as does so much of Weber's analysis, on the scale of operation. The larger the organization the more likely it is that there will be vertical differentiation which will correspond with authority differentiation. The bigger an organization gets the more an entrepreneur has to delegate authority and administrative functions. As the organization continues to grow the process of delegation continues because the burden of work, including supervision, becomes too great for positions which previously carried it to continue doing so. This is mere empirical observation.

The fourth point, that official and other administrative employees do not own the resources necessary for the performance of their assigned functions, etc., is an unnecessarily complicated way of saying that these people sell their labour power and do not own the means of production, as was the case with employees in the kind of industrial society with which Weber was concerned. Indeed as this point is a basic distinguishing mark of the whole society it is bound to characterize industrial activities. The fifth point follows from the fourth. People who sell their labour power do not own or control the offices in which their labour power is used, whether the offices involve filling in accounts or digging trenches, giving orders or executing them. This also is descriptive of the society and not a peculiar characteristic of bureaucracies.

It should be clear that administration is an industrial activity just as production; it subdivides tasks and simplifies them and as the scale of similar work situations and are subjected to similar pressures; that these employees have relationships, depending upon the nature and intensity of the pressures on them, which influence their respective behaviour. The application of the division of labour affects administration as it affects production, it subdivides tasks and simplifies them and as the scale of operation increases it routinizes them. With advances in mechanization in both spheres it is not unrealistic to imagine a work situation in which administration and production are technically similar. Until that happens it may be justifiable to describe the manner of doing administration as bureaucratic and the manner of doing production as technocratic.

Rationality

The last factor to be examined here under the heading of Weber's analysis of bureaucracy is the meaning of 'rational'. This is a key term in Weber's analysis and an understanding of it reveals the normative, unstated, element in that analysis. In his examination of domination Weber listed three 'pure' types:

1. *The* charismatic *structure of domination rests upon that authority of a* concrete individual *which is based neither upon rational rules nor upon tradition.*
2. *Social conduct bound in relationships of* traditional *authority is typically represented by patriarchalism.*
3. Rationally *consociated conduct of a dominational structure finds its typical expression in* bureaucracy. [13]

He added that the 'forms of domination occurring in historical reality constitute combinations, mixtures, adaptations, or modification of these "pure" types'. A 'pure' type, however, was not an abstract form used for analytical purposes but one which, so long as it was unaffected by either of the other 'pure' types, could exist in historically reality, alongside 'combinations, mixtures, adaptations, or modifications' of the 'pure' types. An organization which satisfied the conditions for a bureaucracy, as laid down by Weber, would be a practical illustration of a 'pure' type, and it would be distinguished from the others by its 'rationally consociated conduct'. The point is that when Weber was referring to 'rationally con-sociated conduct' he was referring to a practical form of social conduct, perfect in conception but attainable nonetheless. Likewise 'rational rules', 'rational law' and 'rationally organized large-scale enterprises' indicate perfect but practical types. It is clear that in order to understand the qualities Weber had in mind for bureaucracies it is necessary to go beyond a mere examination of his enunciated principles and discover his meaning of rational; it is this which distinguishes bureaucracies from the other types of domination. In the process Weber's conception of the mechanism of an industrial society will be revealed, as will the extent to which he was influenced by conventional economic theory without feeling obliged to reveal its conceptual limitations.

A rational act, according to Weber, is one which results from the application of reason, is controlled by the intellect and is achieved through a consistently impersonal motivation. It is devoid of traditional and charismatic elements. Thus he was able to write about 'a purely rational law . . . free from all historical "prejudices" '.[14] It is an act oriented to an end. He described purpose-rational conduct as being determined by the expectation that objects in the world outside or other human beings will behave in a certain way, and by the use of such expectations as conditions of, or as means towards, the achievement of the actor's own, rationally desired and considered, aims.[15] This is the nearest Weber got towards outlining the assumptions on which his conception of rationality rested.

This conception of rationality has to be put into its context. In his discussion of bureaucracy Weber was concerned with acts motivated by economic interests and therefore rational acts were those which were determined solely by the pursuit of those interests. It should not be surprising to learn then that Weber regarded 'the archetype of all rational social action [to be] the consociation through exchange in the *market*'.[16] The market, from a sociological point of view, represented a 'coexistence and sequence of rational consociations'. It existed wherever there was competition. He throws further light on the 'archetype of all rational social action' in the following quotations:

Formally the market community does not recognize formal coercion on the basis of personal authority. It produces in its stead a special kind of coercive situation which, as a general principle, applies without any discrimination to workers, enterprisers, producers and consumers, viz., in the impersonal form of the inevitability of adaptation to the purely economic 'laws' of the market. The sanctions consist in the loss or decrease of economic power and, under certain conditions, in the very loss of one's economic existence. The private enterprise system transforms into objects of 'labour market transactions' even those personal and authoritarian—hierarchical relations which actually exist in the capitalistic enterprise . . . authoritarian relationships are thus drained of all normal sentimental content. Within the market community every act of exchange . . . is not directed, in isolation, by the action of the individual partner to the particular trans-

action, but the more rationally it is considered, the more it is directed by the actions of all parties potentially interested in the exchange. The market community as such is the most impersonal relationship of practical life into which humans can enter with one another. . . . The reason for the impersonality of the market is its matter-of-factness, its orientation to the commodity and only to that. Where the market is allowed to follow its own autonomous tendencies, its participants do not look toward the persons of each other but only toward the commodity; there are no obligations of brotherliness or reference, and none of those spontaneous human relations that grow out of intimate personal community. . . . Market behaviour is influenced by rational, purposeful pursuit of interests. [17]

There is no doubt that Weber was referring to perfect competition when he wrote about market transactions and stated that he regarded the qualities of perfect competition to be embodied in rational action. It is possible now to define some of the qualities of the term rational. The conditions necessary for the existence of perfect competition have already been mentioned. They are that there should be economic motivation, many buyers and sellers in each market so that no one of them could influence the transactions of the market, perfect mobility of resources, and perfect knowledge of the market by all buyers and sellers. A further condition can be added, that individuals should be consistent and predictable in their behaviour. The first condition can be taken as given as some assumption has to be made about motivation while the last condition, mentioned by Weber in his description of purpose-rational conduct, is necessary for the purpose of analysis, so that too can be taken as given. The essential meaning of 'rational' in the context of Weber's analysis of organizations is contained in the remaining three conditions.

The condition of many buyers and many sellers is necessary in order to achieve the quality in economic transactions of 'impersonality' and 'application without discrimination'. If any market units were large enough to influence market transactions then the possibility of non-economic, personal factors would arise and the laws of the market would be obstructed. Unless this condition prevails and buyers and sellers are strictly helpless in the face of market operations one cannot talk, as Weber did, about 'the impersonal form of the inevitability of adaptation to the purely economic "laws" of the market'. But Weber could never have explicitly accepted this condition, for his whole analysis is about large-scale organizations. How then did he reconcile his belief in the existence of impersonal market forces with his recognition of the existence of large-scale organizations? No economist could have reconciled the two. Consequently economists ignored the existence of large-scale organizations until the 1930s, when tentative attempts were made to take account of them but not in the perfect competition model. Large-scale organizations had to have models to themselves.

Weber did not explain his way out of this analytical anomaly. It does not seem that he even recognized it; he simply made a few bald statements about the characteristics of large-scale industrial organizations as if one should take his word for it and leave it at that. His implicit use of the assumptions of perfect competition is more difficult to explain because he believed in the inevitability of monopoly in a free private enterprise economy and was at pains to describe how the transition from competition to monopoly production occurred:

> *In . . . an emerging capitalistic economy, the stronger it becomes, the greater will be its efforts to obtain the means of production and labour services in the market without limitations by sacred or corporate-status bonds, and to emancipate the opportunities to sell its products from the restrictions imposed by the sales monopolies of corporate-status organizations.*

[These are such organizations as guilds which have the monopoly to sell certain goods within a city or legal associations which have the monopoly to give legal advice.]

> *Capitalistic interests thus favour the continuous extension of the free market, but only up to the point at which some of them succeed, through the purchase of privileges from the political authority or simply through the power of capital, in obtaining for themselves a monopoly for the sale of their products or the acquisition of their means of production, and in thus closing the market on their own part.*
>
> *The breakup of the monopolies of the corporate-status organizations is thus the typical immediate sequence to the full appropriation of all the material means of production. . . . Another consequence is that the scope of those rights which are guaranteed as acquired or acquirable by the coercive apparatus of the property-regulating community becomes limited to rights in material goods and to contractual claims, including claims to contractual labour. All other appropriations, especially estatist appropriations of opportunities of sale or purchase, are destroyed. This state of affairs, which we call free competition, lasts until it is replaced by new, this time capitalistic monopolies which are acquired in the market through the power of property. These capitalistic monopolies differ from monopolies of corporate-status organizations by their purely economic and rational character. By restricting either the scope of possible sales or the permissible terms the monopolies of corporate-status organizations excluded from their field of action the mechanism of the market with its dickering and rational calculation. Those monopolies, on the other hand,*

which are based solely upon the power of property, rest, on the contrary, upon an entirely rationally calculated mastery of market conditions which may, however, remain formally as free as ever. The sacred, corporate-status, and merely traditional bonds, which have gradually come to be eliminated, constituted restrictions on the formation of rational market prices; the purely economically conditioned monopolies are, on the other hand, their ultimate consequence. The beneficiary of a corporate-status monopoly restricts, and maintains his power against, the market, while the rational-economic monopolist rules through the market. . . . [18]

It is not necessary to read more to see that Weber believed that the rational character of the market was not destroyed by the growth of monopolies, because those monopolies took on the characteristics of the rational market and therefore became rational themselves. Now this may be a neat way of getting out of a difficulty but it is completely untenable analytically unless it can be assumed, as Weber implicitly assumed, that the educated and trained hands of the bureaucrats can act in precisely the same impersonal way as the unseen hands of the market mechanism, so that by decision-making they can allocate factors of production to various uses, price them and control them in their performances in such a manner as to maximize the input—output ratio in production terms. But even if it is granted that bureaucrats can make rational decisions, the conditions of perfect mobility and perfect knowledge still have to be present if the decisions are to have the consequences Weber claims for them. And these conditions have to be present both inside and outside the monopolies.

The picture which emerges of Weber's economy is one which consists of factors of production moving freely from small-scale to large-scale organizations and from one large-scale organization to another and, where the organization is large enough to influence market transactions, of the factors being intercepted by educated and trained bureaucrats who allocate them in the functions to which they would have been allocated if the market mechanism had been permitted to operate unhampered. So even if it is granted that there could be perfect mobility in the market as a whole the same condition would have to exist within each organization. This means that there would have to be no impediments of any kind in the way of the movement of factors to their most efficient uses and this in turn would involve no differentiation according to wealth or social background, only ability. Any sociologists who knows of the manner in which traditions, conventions, and non-economic factors generally influence economically motivated acts should realize the unreality of a perfect mobility assumption, the main purpose of which in economics is to enable a linear model to be set up. All sociologists, however, who describe organizations or bureaucracies as rational are implying that there are no obstructions to mobility within them. Etzioni seems to interpret Weber to mean this:

Underlying the whole analysis is a set of principles that follows from the central organizational problem as Weber saw it. The high rationality of the bureaucratic structure is fragile; it needs to be constantly protected against external pressures to safeguard the autonomy required if it is to be kept closely geared to its goal and not others. [19]

If this interpretation is so then it means that bureaucracies are pockets of rational behaviour resisting potential imperfections in the markets around them. By and large, however, Max Weber believed that market transactions were rational and provided the basis for rationality in capitalistic monopolies.

Everything which can be said about the perfect mobility of resources applies to the other condition, perfect knowledge of the market for the two are complementary. It is of no use having perfectly mobile resources if it is not known where they can be most effectively used and it is of no use knowing where they should be used if they cannot get there. Again it seems that Weber considered that perfect knowledge existed in each market as a whole, that is in the economy, and was also possessed by bureaucrats by virtue of their education and training. This meant two things; first that everyone involved in a market knew of the qualifications required for work in bureaucracies, of the prevailing rates of pay, conditions of work and of the nature of the work. With this knowledge and no obstacles in their way, sellers of labour power moved to the jobs which maximized their returns. But where they moved towards bureaucracies they were intercepted by functionaries of one kind or another, and *selected* for posts they would have occupied if the selection had been done by impersonal market forces. In this way the bureaucracies maximized the physical output from their resources.

Above all, bureaucratization offers the optional possibility for the realization of the principle of division of labour in administration according to purely technical considerations, allocating individual tasks to functionaries who are trained as specialists and who continuously add to their experience by constant practice. 'Professional' execution in this case means primarily execution 'without regard to person' in accordance with calculable rules.

Then to emphasize that he considered there were no obstacles such as tradition or social background to prevent bureaucrats from applying their knowledge, Weber went on to say:

The consistent carrying through of bureaucratic authority produces a levelling of differences in social 'honour' or status, and, consequently, unless the principle of freedom in the market is simultaneously restricted, the universal sway of economic 'class position'... for modern bureaucracy, the element of calculability of its rules 'has really been of decisive significance'. [20]

Weber clearly believed that the selection of personnel in bureaucracies and their movement between tasks or positions was done 'without regard to person'. As selection was done primarily by written examination, if the principles enunciated by Weber were adopted, it must be assumed that he believed that all subjective elements could be eliminated from the tests. This all amounts to the fact that he believed bureaucrats knew exactly the qualities required for each administrative task, knew how to identify the qualities, knew how to combine the qualities of different factors in the correct proportions and knew many other things too. As the labour demands of large-scale organizations are such as to interfere with the market determination of incomes one must presume that bureaucrats knew about these too. This, of course, is only one area in the field of knowledge necessary for the rational operation of large-scale organizations.

There remains one more point relating to the meaning Weber gave to the term 'rational'. So far it has been seen that he believed that rationality was achieved through organizational means. That is, given the motivation and the correct bureaucratic apparatus, certain results would be obtainable. These results were of the highest technical order.

The decisive reason for the success of bureaucratic organization has always been its purely technical superiority over every other form. A fully developed bureaucratic administration stands in the same relationship to non-bureaucratic forms as machinery to non-mechanised modes of production. Precision, speed, consistency, availability of records, continuity, possibility of secrecy, unity, rigorous coordination, and minimization of friction and of expense for materials and personnel are achieved in a strictly bureaucratized, especially in a monocratically organized administration conducted by trained officials to an extent incomparably greater than in any collegial form of administration or in any conducted by honoratiores *or part-time administrators.* [21]

This was high praise indeed. Weber re-emphasized the point when he stated:

The utmost possible speed, precision, definiteness, and continuity in the execution of official business are demanded of the administration particularly in the modern capitalistic economy. The great modern capitalistic enterprises are themselves normally unrivalled models of thoroughgoing bureaucratic organization. Their handling of business rests entirely on increasing precision, continuity, and especially speed of operation. [22]

Despite occasional words of warning such as 'the bureaucratic system can, and often does, produce obstacles to the appropriate handling of certain situations'[23] it is difficult not to be impressed. It is important to note that, provided the bureaucratic apparatus is present, these results will be achieved, for it is assumed that the decisions taken in a bureaucracy are always on matters which consistently permit of rational consequences. In other words provided the motivation is correct and the sustaining apparatus is present everything else will follow. For instance, if a patrimonial administrator, who by definition allows his decisions to be influenced by traditions and personal preferences, is replaced by a bureaucratic apparatus then, though the same matters for decision-making remain, rational consequences will follow. To confirm the contention that he believed that all administration matters were amenable to rational decision-making, Weber wrote: 'Behind every act of purely bureaucratic administration there stands a system of rationally discussable "grounds", i.e. either subsumption under forms or calculation of means and ends.'[24] It seems odd that a sociologist who so methodically made distinctions between different types of values and who emphasized the influence on social behaviour which traditional values, for instance, could have, should permit his enthusiasm for bureaucracy to prevent him from examining the objects of bureaucratic action for their value content. Yet this is clearly what he did.

Such then was the conceptual framework within which Max Weber constructed his model of bureaucracy. And such was the model on which a succession of sociologists unquestioningly built their complicated analyses, often for practical prescriptive purposes.

Notes

1. Max Weber, *The Theory of Social and Economic Organizations*, trans. A. M. Henderson and Talcott Parsons, The Free Press, New York, 1947.

2. See the introduction to C. Wright Mills and H. H. Gerth, trans., *From Max Weber: essays in sociology*, Routledge, 1961; also Reinhard Bendix, *Max Weber: an intellectual portrait* (ch. 1, Career and personal orientation), Heinemann, 1960, for details of Weber's social background.

3. Max Weber, *Law in Economy and Society*, Cambridge, Mass., 1954, pp. 174—5.

4. *Ibid.*, pp. 324, 336.

5. *Ibid.*, pp. 335, 337.
6. Bendix, *op. cit.*, pp. 424–5.
7. Weber, *Law in Economy and Society*, p. 334.
8. *Ibid.*
9. *Ibid.*
10. Etzioni, *A Comparative Analysis of Complex Organizations*, p. 3.
11. Summarized by Bendix, *op. cit.*, pp. 418–19. See also Etzioni, *Modern Organizations*, pp. 53–4; and Weber, *The Theory of Social and Economic Organization*, pp. 324–36.
12. Etzioni, *Modern Organizations*, p. 53.
13. Weber, *Law in Economy and Society*, p. 337.
14. *Ibid.*, p. 286.
15. *Ibid.*, p. 1.
16. *Ibid.*, p. 191.
17. *Ibid.*, pp. 190, 192.
18. Weber, *Law in Economy and Society*, pp. 195–6.
19. Etzioni, *Modern Organizations*, p. 54.
20. Weber, *Law and Economy in Society*, p. 350.
21. *Ibid.*, p. 329.
22. *Ibid*, p. 350.
23. *Ibid.*
24. *Ibid.*, p. 355.

5

The March & Simon synthesis of organization theory

Periodically in the development of organization theory, as with all theory, someone has attempted to act as the synthesizer of the threads and the trends, the motley of information and the bits and pieces of theory, only to be superseded later on by another synthesizer. In a way both James Mooney and R. K. Merton were synthesizers. But the most systematic and influential synthesis until quite recently was that by J. G. March and H. A. Simon in *Organizations*, 1958.[1] The March and Simon book ranks as a treatise of considerable importance because it is widely and intensively quoted and because it really does attempt to draw together all the loose ends of organization theory. The work, moreover, has played a significant part in the development of operational research and mathematical programming in that parts of it relating to rationality and decision-making were derived from those areas and through a process of clarification have subsequently contributed to them.

This is how the authors view their task as synthesizers:

In this book we shall review in a systematic way some of the important things that have been said about organizations by those who have studied them and written about them. We have already observed that the effort devoted by social scientists to understanding organizations has not been large. Nevertheless, organizations impinge on so many aspects of our society that pieces, bits, and snatches of organization theory and empirical data can be assembled from a wide range of sources.

1. Many executives and administrators have recorded their organizational experiences in biographical or systematic form in books and articles.

2. The scientific management movement has been concerned with organization theory, and almost every standard textbook in management devotes a chapter or two to a statement of principles of good organization.

3. Some sociologists, most of them influenced by Max Weber's analysis of 'bureaucracy', have theorized about organizations and carried out some systematic observations.

4. Social psychologists have shown particular interest in two aspects of organization behaviour: in leadership and supervision on the one hand, and in morale and employee attitudes on the other. More recently, they have undertaken some studies of the effects of communication patterns upon organizational behaviour.
5. Political scientists have been concerned with problems parallel to those of the scientific management group — the efficient operation of governmental organizations — and also with the problem of securing external (democratic) control over governmental administration.
6. Economists have theorized about the business firm as a building block for their broader concern with the operation of markets and the pricing and allocative mechanisms in the economy. Moreover, organizational considerations have played an important, if unsystematic, role in the debate over planning versus 'laissez-faire' (pp. 4–5).

At first sight March and Simon have undertaken a formidable task of synthesis. But it is bigger than even the above quotation suggests, for, they state, 'in organizing our material, we wished to impose order without imposing a parochial point of view stemming from a particular or special conception of organization theory. We have tried to steer a middle course between eclecticism and provincialism. We shall let the reader judge how far we have succeeded' (p. 6).

The task here is not to reproduce details or even all the arguments. After all the authors list 206 variables and combine them freely. The number of hypotheses, postulates or predicates made have not been counted but they are numerous. The task is the modest one of discovering whether or not there is a theoretical continuity running through previous works into this and in doing so to disclose the conceptual framework within which the analysis is made. Thus it might be possible to reveal the limitations of the analysis which might be obscured by the variables, the predicates, the apparent tightness of thought, the mathematical symbols and the jargon which invariably creeps into sociological analysis.

Theoretical continuity

The first point is easily answered. There is a theoretical continuity running through from Weber, the classical theorists and the functional sociologists into March and Simon's synthesis. This is revealed through the method March and Simon use. They take as a model the formal organization as constructed by the classical theorists, in which there is a rationally determined division of labour and allocation of resources within a rigid hierarchical authority structure. This model assumed mechanical responses from the participants. The authors wrote that traditional organization theory views the human organism as a simple machine.

*In this model, leaders are limited in their achievement of organization
goals only by the constraints imposed by the capacities, speeds, durabili-
ties, and costs of these simple 'machines'. The postulates of the traditional
theory, explicit and implicit, amount to rather severe assumptions about
the environment of an individual in an organization, the impact of that
environment on him, and his response to it. The environment is viewed as
a well-defined stimulus or system of stimuli. Each such stimulus (e.g. an
administrative order) evokes in the individual to whom it is directed, a
well-defined and predictable psychological set* (p. 34).

The authors aimed to *amend* the conception of an employee as an
'instrument' by eliminating, one by one, the artificialities of this description; and 'to replace this abstraction with a new one that recognizes that
members of organizations have wants, motives, and drives, and are limited
in their knowledge and in their capacities to learn and to solve problems'
(p. 136). The amendments amounted to a re-examination of how motiva-
tions and goals affect human behaviour in organizations and of the
characteristics of a rational man. Thus from the beginning the other postulates of the classical theory and, to a large extent of Weber, which refer to
the organic unity of the environment in which organizations operate, the
conception of an organization as an authority structure, and the emphasis
on the administration of control and therefore decision-making are
accepted without question. The position is fairly clear from the outset. In
making their criticisms, the authors state, they do 'not mean that the
"classical" theory is totally wrong or needs to be totally displaced' (p. 35).

In order to amend the classical model March and Simon used existing
analytical tools. They devised no new ones. Their tools came from two
main sources. First, they depended heavily on functional and structural
functional analysis. Indeed it will be shown below that if they are to be
labelled at all they should be called structural functionalists. Although
none of Talcott Parsons's work is listed in the book's bibliography his
theoretical influence is obvious, as is that of Merton, Homans and Selznick
who have each added or refined particular analytical concepts. But if
March and Simon owe an intellectual debt to any one sociologist then it
must be to Selznick, whose analytical scheme for the study of organization
they appear to have drawn on heavily. Like Selznick, March and Simon
attempt to fit individuals as separate and whole personalities into the
formal organization. This emphasis on individuals led them to seek the
analytical tools of social psychologists. This was their second source. Here
the influence of Kurt Lewin's group dynamic approach can be clearly seen.
The synthesis of March and Simon, then, is the application of structural
functional analysis with a psychological bent to the facets of organiza-

tional behaviour which were deemed to have been neglected by the classical theorists. This had not been attempted before in such a detailed manner, so to that extent, but to that extent only, the work was new.

An organization, according to March and Simon, is an assemblage of interacting human beings whose actions are oriented towards the attainment of goals in a structured and highly coordinated manner. They emphasize the precision and specificity of organizational action by using the concept 'roles'.

Roles in organizations as contrasted with many of the other roles that individuals fill, tend to be highly elaborated, relatively stable, and defined to a considerable extent in explicit and even written terms. Not only is the role defined for the individual who occupies it, but it is known in considerable detail to others in the organization who have occasion to deal with him. Hence, the environment of other persons that surrounds each member of an organization tends to become a highly stable and predictable one. It is this predictability, together with certain related structural features of organization . . . that accounts for the ability of organizations to deal in a coordinated way with their environments (p. 14).

It should be noted that the organization deals with its environment and not vice versa, so it should be no surprise to read that organizations are considered to be adaptive, for it is only if organizations are attributed with at least semi-automatic equilibrating mechanisms that they can deal with their environments. The equilibrating mechanism insulates them from environmental pressures. So far this is consistent with a sociologically oriented version of the classical theory. They go on, however, to amend the manner in which it deals with motivation.

Motivation

Although March and Simon consider that the interaction of the needs of individuals, primary workgroups and the larger organizations must be examined they are primarily concerned with the interaction between the needs of individuals and organizations. They pay, therefore, particular attention to the psychology of individuals in much the same way as Selznick did in his article, 'Foundations of the theory of organization'.[2] Selznick went so far as to talk of a 'Freudian' model for organizational analysis. The view March and Simon have of the attributes of individuals in relation to their environments corresponds with that of group dynamic theorists who believe that individuals can markedly influence their environments through reason. In emphasizing the relative independence of individuals March and Simon are making a *major* postulate about social behaviour. But there is no intimation in *Organizations* that the postulate might be open to question.

The qualities which March and Simon ascribe to individuals rate as the core of their approach for they lead to whatever analytical distinction can be claimed for the approach. The authors make the following psychological postulates: that the behaviour of a human organism through a short interval of time is determined by the simultaneous influence of nature and environment; that most of the internal state of the organism is contained in the memory; that the memory has passive and active elements; that memory content

includes: (a) values of goals: criteria that are applied to determine which courses of action are preferred among those considered; (b) relations between actions and their outcomes: i.e. beliefs, perceptions, and expectations as to the consequences that will follow from one course of action or another; and (c) alternatives: possible courses of action (p. 11).

The general picture of the human organism is one of

a choosing, decision-making, problem-solving organism that can do only one or a few things at a time, and that can attend to only a small part of the information recorded in its memory and presented by the environment (p. 11).

This is an amendment to the mechanistic individual in the classical model and to Weber's rational man. The March and Simon individual can be a passive instrument, one who takes attitudes, values and goals into the organization and one who is a decision-maker and problem-solver. Their definition, therefore, includes propositions about motivation from the classical theory, structural functionalism and rational and statistical decision-making theory.

In line with the emphasis of the classical theorists, March and Simon give their attention to the analysis of decision-making. The question now is, how do the individuals with the characteristics described above interfere with the rational decision-making process within a formal structure? Because the individual enters an organization as a whole personality his response to stimuli from within the organization cannot be taken for granted. In order to exercise control over him, therefore, his consent has to be obtained. The organization is seen as a cooperative system in which individuals have to make decisions to participate, that is to stay or to leave, and to produce. Consideration of these two main decisions enable March and Simon to examine within their theoretical framework practical issues such as morale, productivity and labour turnover, and to this extent the scope of their analysis is wider than that of other formal theorists.

The decision to produce is examined first because this relates directly to the question of motivation. It is examined with the use of analytical tools from functional sociology. Individuals participating with whole personalities are not predictable; they may respond to stimuli more than anticipated or less than anticipated. There may exist other unanticipated consequences which are latent as against manifest functions. The internal state of the individual, that is his memory which includes values, goals, expectations, will determine his responses. As each individual has his own internal state which is taken into the organization there must be (*a*) a differentiation of goals within the organization and (*b*) the possibility that the individual goals will diverge from the stated organizational goals. The extent of the divergence is explained largely through reference group theory which involves a major, though unstated, postulate about value formation.

Humans in contrast to machines, evaluate their own positions in relation to the value of others and come to accept others' goals as their own. In addition, individual members of an organization come to it with a prior structure of preferences – a personality, if you like – on the basis of which they make decisions while in the organization. Thus, individual goals are not 'given' for the organization but can be varied both through recruitment procedures and through organizational practices (p. 65).

At this point March and Simon make a concession to 'small group' sociology by accepting that individual goals might be shared. Goal-sharing is analysed through a combination of Homan's human group analysis and reference group theory. The significance, however, which they attach to informal groups is not very great and this has led to criticisms that they are much too concerned with formal factors. They make the point that the divergence between individual and organization goals can be narrowed or eliminated by organizational controls consisting of reward systems and supervisory practices. This point is taken up again in the discussion of rationality, as is the question of the differentiation of goals.

The element of consent in organizational decision-making is further examined through an analysis of the decision to participate in the organization. Participation means not to join but to stay and produce once having joined. This decision is not seen as a function of the control mechanism but of what we might call conditions of employment opportunities. Whether or not a participant will stay in an organization will depend on whether or not he is satisfied, and this will be measured by what March and Simon call the 'inducements-contributions utility balance' where, if the participant is an employee, 'inducements' are income and 'contributions' are labour power. The authors in this section display a naive propensity to transpose simple economic terms into organizational theory jargon. Thus they state that 'to estimate the inducement-contribution utility balance directly, the most logical type of measure is some variant of individual satisfaction' (p. 85). Individual satisfaction or dissatisfaction can be observed by discovering whether participants desire to stay or leave the organization, which, of course, depends on their inducement-contribution utility balance. Whether they actually leave if they desire to do so is determined by the existence of opportunities to leave. This analysis involves a different set of factors from that dealing with the decision to produce and does not fit at all into the structural functional model. Indeed, shed of its jargon, it resembles the opportunity cost analysis of economics which rests on highly restrictive simplifying assumptions. The decision to stay in an organization, however, is as much a part of the question of motivation as the decision to produce and March and Simon are justified in dealing with it in so far as they consider, as they do, that motivation is more complex than the classical theory would indicate.

Rationality

After motivation comes rationality. In the discussion of Max Weber's model of bureaucracy rationality was dealt with at some length. The meaning given to it there is that attached to it in the classical theory. March and Simon's amendment is based on their interpretation of the human organism and the structural adjustments which individuals bring about in order to cope with their limitations:

Our treatment of rational behaviour rests on the proposition that the 'real' situation is almost always far too complex to be handled in detail. As we move upwards in the supervisory and executive hierarchy, the range of interrelated matters over which an individual has purview becomes larger and larger, more and more complex (p. 150).

The decision-making problems created by the limited ability of an individual to know and tackle a real organizational situation are resolved in various ways.

A decision-maker with finite powers, operates within an environment which sets the frame of reference for his decisions by determining 'what consequences he will anticipate, and what ones he will not; what alternatives he will consider, what ones he will ignore' (p. 139). There are then subjective and objective aspects to rationality. This consideration led March and Simon to conclude that a decision-maker will always operate within a 'limited, approximate, simplified "model" of the real situation' (p. 139). An activity which initiates a problem-solving process will involve a *search* for alternatives and evaluated consequences of action. The search may be random and dependent on memory, or, if the experience has been repeated, systematic. Because of the above-mentioned limiting factors they maintain that the search will be for 'satisfactory' standards and not 'optimal' ones: 'most human decision-making, whether individual or organizational, is concerned with the discovery and selection of satisfactory alternatives; only in exceptional cases is it concerned with the discovery and selection of optimal alternatives' (p. 141).

The difference between 'satisfactory' and 'optimal' will depend on the validity of the postulates relating to the ability of a human organism to handle a real situation. In most instances of behaviour in organizations, March and Simon state, the interval for search is virtually eliminated and decision-making action involves a straight-forward choice between alternatives. Where the 'choice has been simplified by the development of a fixed response to a defined stimuli' the activities involved are regarded as being routinized. Also where an environmental stimulus evokes an immediate organized set of responses they are called a 'performance programme'. Decision-makers embark on performance programmes.

So far March and Simon have provided a number of hypotheses which set the stage for the completion of their model for the analysis of organizational behaviour. In some instances the hypotheses are supported by references but these are usually works of others who have hypothesized. The uncertain nature of the foundations on which the model is built should be noted. As the analysis has proceeded the number of explicit and implicit assumptions has increased. Nonetheless March and Simon can be granted their assumptions in order to see what becomes of their model.

Problem-solving processes

Activities in organizations are all subject to problem-solving processes which are created specifically to take account of the inability of individuals to cope with real situations. What March and Simon mean by this is that for individuals there are two situations; one, complex and beyond their comprehension and one, a simplified model of the first which they can manage. The problem-solving processes have the following components:

1. The activities in industrial organizations are systematized so that search is largely eliminated and choice is restricted to fixed responses. Each of these responses consists of a performance programme. 'The whole pattern of programmed activity in an organization', the authors write, 'is a complicated mosaic of programme executions, each initiated by its appropriate programme-evoking step' (p. 149). Each organization has a repertory of programmes 'that, collectively, can deal in a goal-oriented way with a

range of situations' so that decision-making can be simplified by recombining existing performance programmes to meet new situations instead of having to devise fresh ones.

2. The second component is the factorization of the general goal into subgoals, sub-subgoals and so on. The subgoals and sub-subgoals are allocated to units of the organization in hierarchical fashion and become the goals of the individuals concerned. This means that individuals do not have to evaluate their actions in terms of the general goal of the organization. The purpose of the factorization is to simplify each situation to which a goal is attached sufficiently to bring it within the capacity of the human mind as defined by March and Simon. The principal way to factor a (problem) is to construct a means—end analysis. The means specified in this way become subgoals which may be assigned to individual organizational units. This kind of jurisdictional assignment is often called 'organization by purpose' or 'departmentalization by purpose' (p. 152). The subgoals become incorporated in the task assignments. March and Simon consider that it is the tendency of members of an organizational unit to evaluate action only in terms of subgoals, even when these are in conflict with the goals of the larger organization, but of course if the factoring is accurate there will be little possibility of conflict — what is rational for each unit will be rational for the organization of a whole. It should be readily discernible that the factorization of goals is another way of describing the differentiation of functions or specialization.

As individuals bring goals with them into an organization, and as goals may be shared within informal groups, there is a possibility of conflict between these goals and those which are the result of factorization. March and Simon consider that the factorized goals will dominate because of the influence of reward systems and supervisory practices. There will not, therefore, be any inconsistency between different goals held by individuals or groups of individuals which will have operational consequences. But there may be operational consequences when individuals or groups participating in the same decision-making process (*a*) share the same goals but differ about action to be taken to fulfil them; or (*b*) do not share the same goals. These two possibilities constitute conflict for March and Simon. Conflict, they write is a term 'applied to a breakdown in the standard mechanisms of decision-making so that an individual or group experiences difficulty in selecting an action alternative' (p. 112). Where the conflict arises from shared goal differences over courses of action it will be resolved analytically through the problem-solving mechanism. Where the goals are not shared agreement is reached through bargaining which can be identified 'by its paraphernalia of acknowledged conflict of interests, threats, falsification of position, and (in general) gamesmanship' (p. 130).

Goal conflict which is resolved through bargaining weakens the control mechanism because it legitimizes heterogeneity of goals in the organization. Because of this, March and Simon state that the organizational hierarchy will attempt to treat all conflict as if it were individual conflict which can be treated analytically.

3. The last component in the problem-solving process is a communications system. Given March and Simon's approach to rational action it can be seen that communications are bound to be important as an aid to memory, as a means of conveying information about alternatives and, in general, decreasing the need for search when matters are unsatisfactory. But communications figured prominently in the classical model and in Weber's analysis. In each case organizational problems were largely assumed to be the creation of faulty communications. Rational action depended on the possession of perfect knowledge, and this was a function of communications. So March and Simon started with a model containing lines of communication as vital to it as the nervous system is to the human body. And they introduced few alterations. The performance programmes and factorization of goals are both dependent on the effectiveness of a communications system in the March and Simon model so that communications play a vital part in its decision-making, problem-solving process.

The concept of *perception* is used frequently by March and Simon to convey their contention that what individuals see is not necessarily what exists but is usually a simplified form of what exists. This simplification lies at the basis of the formation by individuals of expectations of the consequences of actions. March and Simon talk of perceived expectations, perceived consequences, perceived alternatives, individual perceptions, differentiation of perceptions, all of which fall under the heading of reality perception. Perceptions are built up from information from various sources so that the manner and effectiveness with which information is conveyed affects perception and therefore action, for action is assumed to be based on perception. The differentiation of perception may result in differences between individuals or groups over means when goals are shared, or in a differentiation of goals themselves. The communication system, therefore, in so far as it determines perception also determines conflict. In other words conflict is seen as some function of the communications system. This is not very far removed from the classical view of frictions, tensions, organizational difficulties. An effective communications system in the March and Simon's model would work towards a common reality perception. If conflict is taken to mean a breakdown in decision-making, then it follows that 'The capacity of an organization to maintain a complex, highly interdependent pattern of activity is limited in part by its capacity to handle the communication required for coordination. The greater the *efficiency of communication* within the organization, the greater the tolerance for interdependence' (p. 162). There is then a correlation between the capacity of a communications system and the ability of an organization to integrate its activities and, presumably, to survive. A breakdown in coordination, caused by ineffective decision-making through communication defects, is equivalent to an outbreak of conflict.

The description which is given of the communications mechanism is that of one developed to simplify complex problems. March and Simon write that the 'adaptive problem of organizational design is one of balance. If its model of reality is not to be so complex as to paralyse it, the organization must develop radical simplifications of its responses' (p. 164). There are various simplifying devices. First, there is a tendency to use existing information for new situations as they arise, and to cover them by standard operating procedures. This, it is contended, will reduce the volume of communication required from day to day. Secondly, information may be communicated through the use of shorthand methods such as symbols, blueprints, accounting definitions and technical language. Thirdly, information may be classified, thus facilitating uniform dissemination. This method is related to the creation of a repertory of performance programmes so that any new contingency can be met immediately. Lastly, inferences rather than the evidence may be communicated. This last method, it is stated, makes verification difficult and affects 'the influence structure of the organization' by placing discretion and influence in the hands of those who handle the evidence. Communication control over inferences, however, will legitimize them and assist coordination.

March and Simon recognize that there may tend to be informal communications, particularly between members of a common profession and between those who possess common social characteristics. But they hold that these will usually pass through the formal channels.

Formal hierarchical channels tend to become general-purpose channels to be used whenever no special-purpose channels or informal channels exists or is known to the communicator. The self-reinforcing character of channel usage is particularly strong if it brings individuals into face-to-face contact. In this case . . . informal communication, much of it social in character, develops side-by-side with task-oriented formal communication (p. 168).

The adaptive social system
This postulate, as was shown in an earlier chapter is essential to the structural-functionalist approach. In much of the literature some reference

is made to the equilibrating mechanism necessary to make a system adaptive, but there is no general agreement about its detailed operation. Indeed, organizational theorists appear to claim distinction for their own theoretical contributions by presenting their own versions of the mechanism. March and Simon are not exceptions to this tendency.

An organization is in a state of equilibrium, it is stated, when, taking the organization as a whole, there is an inducements-contributions balance. This balance concept was used by March and Simon in relation to the analysis of a decision to participate but they also use it to describe organizational equilibrium. It is derived, they say, from the Barnard–Simon theory of organizational equilibrium which describes the conditions under which an organization can induce its members to continue their participation (p. 84). According to this theory:

At any time in the life of an organization when a change is made that (a) *explicitly alters the inducements offered to any group of participants;* (b) *explicitly alters the contributions demanded from them; or* (c) *alters the organizational activity in any way that will affect inducements or contributions — on any of these occasions, a prediction can be made as to the effect of the change on participation. The effects may be measurable in terms of turnover rates of employees, sales, etc., as appropriate* (p. 88).

When a change occurs in its environment, then, an organization has to adapt itself to preserve this balance. Ordinarily the adaptation will be initiated by management. In general,

there is not a single, unique set of conditions for organizational survival . . . but various sets of alternative conditions that would produce a favourable inducements-contributions balance. Adaptation of the organization for survival may move it in the direction of any one of these alternatives (p. 109).

The nature of an organizational response to an environmental change will depend on whether it is of short- or long-term significance. Adaptiveness is said to be achieved through altering performance programmes and there will be procedures 'for developing, elaborating, instituting, and revising' these (p. 170). If the change has a short run significance then the procedures for selecting a programme from an existing repertory will be used.

The process used to select an appropriate programme is the 'fulcrum' on which short-run adaptiveness rests. If, now, the organization has processes for adding to its repertory of programmes or for modifying programmes in the repertory, these processes become still more basic fulcra for accomplishing longer-run adaptiveness. Short-run adaptiveness corresponds to what we ordinarily call problem-solving long-run adaptiveness to learning (p. 170).

To cope with long-run changes there have to be processes for bringing new performance programmes into existence and for modifying them.

The treatment of that aspect of adaptiveness which involves organizational change, or rather the introduction of new performance programmes, is, as logically it should be, consistent with the postulates of the model as a whole. The treatment as we see it has the following analytical sequences. An environmental stimulus will involve first a choice between inaction and action — that is, between persisting with existing programmes or introducing new ones. The choice will be determined ultimately by the nature and intensity of the stimulus but within the organization it will depend upon whether or not existing programmes are considered to be satisfactory.

Individuals and organizations give preferred treatment to alternatives that represent continuation of present programmes over those that represent change. But this preference is not derived by calculating explicitly the costs of innovation or weighing these costs. Instead, persistence comes about primarily because the individual or organization does not search for or consider alternatives to the present course of action unless that present course is in some sense 'unsatisfactory' (p. 173).

March and Simon add, however, that inaction does not absorb resources. They pose this choice problem not as one caused by a resistance to change within the organization but as one involving alternative policies.

Assuming that the decision is in favour of action a search for innovations will begin and alternatives will be evaluated. Even so the search will not be for innovations which are markedly different from prevailing programmes because of the postulate that an organization will attempt to 'satisfice' rather than optimize. And what is satisfactory is closely related to what is achieved.

The most important proposition is that, over time, the aspiration level tends to adjust to the level of achievement. That is to say, the level of satisfactory performance is likely to be very close to the actually achieved level of recent performance (pp. 182–3).

Thus, in line with the postulate of limited human cognitive powers, the search for innovation will be simplified to fall within the limits, as defined by March and Simon, of rational action.

The search is made easier because the criteria of satisfaction, in so far as they depart from the *status quo*, are said to be influenced by the norms of the reference groups of the individuals concerned or by the standards of achievement of other organizations.

In general, awareness of a definite course of action that will yield substantially better results than the present programme, or awareness that some other person or organization is achieving better results — even if the exact method is not known — will lead to revision of the standards of satisfaction (p. 183).

The search is confined within the area of what is known. More than this, March and Simon contend

that most innovations in an organization are a result of borrowing rather than invention. The borrowing may take the form of more or less direct imitation or it may be accomplished by importing new persons into the organization. In either case borrowing saves an organization many of the costs associated with innovation such as: (a) the costs of actual invention, (b) the costs of testing, (c) the risks of error in evaluation (p. 188).

Where innovations are borrowed their type and rate of introduction are said to be a function of the communications system in the organization. Innovation activity in general, however, will be largely influenced by the freedom which innovators have from day-to-day routine tasks. Its introduction, therefore, may be slowed down by the need to free individuals or groups of heavy operating responsibilities or to create a new organizational unit specifically charged to introduce a new performance programme.

Lastly in this section on organizational adaptiveness we come to the manner of analysing a problem which can only be resolved by innovation. Again March and Simon introduce the assumption of limited human cognitive powers and on this basis assert that a problem will never be treated as a whole but always in stages. The introduction of new performance programmes, called non-programmed decision-making, is undertaken through the use of means—end analysis which were referred to in the discussion of goal differentiation. This analysis involves the technique of successive approximations or alternatively the factorization of a goal or problem. The general goal is identified first, then the means of achieving it are specified and are designated as subgoals; the subgoals are factorized in the same way as the general goals and this process goes on until the detailed means reach the level of existing programmes. The analysis will have a hierarchical shape so that each problem treated in this way will resemble a hierarchy of goals consistent with the goals hierarchy of the organization itself. Underlying the March and Simon use of means—end analysis is a psychological interpretation of problem-solving processes adapted, where necessary, to group problem-solving. This is consistent with their general approach.

This is a very bare presentation of the March and Simon model but enough has been stated to reveal its conceptual framework and to show it as a synthesis of prevailing theoretical notions. But there is one way in which it differs significantly from most work before it. The classical model of organization was constructed along ideal lines on the basis of what were called principles of organization, and was intended as a guide for management practice. No part of it was problematical so that it did not depend on empirical verification. Weber's analysis of bureaucracy was an ideal type which equally did not depend on empirical verification. The functional theory of organization or bureaucracy was an analytical construction on given assumptions. Its ability depended on the correspondence of its hypotheses to reality but it did not depend on its construction on empirical data. Every element in it was consistent and predictable because of its base assumption. The recognition, however, that variable and unpredictable structural elements might influence the operation of the formal functional model made prediction dependent upon obtaining empirical verification of hypotheses at several points in the construction and tended to confine the predictions to particular situations. This gave rise to a modified functionalist theory which was called structural functionalism. The term structure in structural functionalism refers to that element of action which is determined by the environment of an organization or, to use Selznick's meaning, the conditions of interaction within an adaptive social system. There is nothing within the structural functionalist model to indicate what the mix of functional and structural determinism should be. But it is clear that the less the reliance on the functionalist approach the greater the need for supporting empirical data of interaction. The line from functionalism to this version of structuralism leads to empiricism as a method of analysis, hence different mixtures of functionalism and structuralism produce different emphases on the need for empirical verification. A structuralist approach in which structure refers to the whole environment in which organizations operate is a different approach and is examined in Part three.

The model of March and Simon is different from most which went before it because of the manner in which it introduces structural determinants into a functional framework. The authors continually refer to the need for evidence about the structure and for verification of the postulates they frequently make at many stages of the analysis. Thus while the general goal of an organization may be given, the goal structure of the participants in a decision-making process may have to 'be determined by observation of their interaction or by interviewing or opinion-polling techniques' (pp. 156–7). The criteria for satisfaction need also to be revealed through empirical investigation for they have no given or *a priori* meaning. The very emphasis of March and Simon on psychological factors is an admission that they believe individual differences exist. The perception of individuals, then, of alternative courses of action, of consequences, etc., requires verification. The unanticipated consequences of action which March and Simon recognize might occur, can, by definition, only be discovered by investigation. It is possible to go on with illustrations of the built-in concern of March and Simon for empirical verification. So while they used a formal model as an analytical base, March and Simon moved appreciably towards empiricism. This meant, too, that they moved away from the ideal type, prescriptive analysis, though in fact many of their predictions were markedly like prescriptions for good management.

It can be seen that the March and Simon model constituted a conceptual adaptation of the conventional theoretical approach to the study of organizations. It remained strictly within a static conceptual framework and retained, therefore, its defects. March and Simon made no claims to do otherwise and what they did was logically consistent with the primary assumption which underlies that framework. In this sense its main fault lay in the extent to which that assumption distorted concrete reality. But this is not how some contemporary conventional sociological theorists saw the situation. They accepted the structure of the explanation and complained about its superstructure. This inevitably led to attempts at syntheses to supersede the March and Simon one. The most ambitious of these is examined in the next chapter.

Notes

1. J. G. March and H. A. Simon, *Organizations*, 1950. All March and Simon extracts in this chapter are from this source.
2. Selznick, *loc. cit.* (see ch. 3, n. 38).

6

'The great synthesis' of Amitai Etzioni

Sociological theory has not yet been subjected to the rigorous analytical treatment which has stripped economic theory of much of its logical inconsistencies and many of its vague, unsubstantiated generalizations. This is due in part to the fact that there is not yet a tradition in sociology of analytical rigour. But whatever the full reason it is clear that progress in the formulation of sociological theories depends upon the introduction of tools which will expose bare the framework of analysis, the assumptions about social behaviour on which it is based and the logic of its construction.

In this chapter an attempt is made to examine the construction of one organization theory for logical consistency. The exercise is a case study of what is called the structuralist theory of organization contained in two books by Amitai Etzioni: *A Comparative Analysis of Complex Organizations*, 1961, and a shorter and more general book, *Modern Organizations*, 1963.[1] The first describes the tools Etzioni uses while the second identifies more clearly the conceptual framework within which the tools are used.

There are obvious reasons for selecting Etzioni's work for scrutiny. His writings contain an ambitious attempt to reach a theoretical understanding of organizational behaviour. They are widely acknowledged as an advance on earlier theories of organization. Moreover Etzioni himself makes such substantial claims for his theory that he invites attempts at validation. He is not the sole advocate of a structuralist approach to organization theory but he is the acknowledged spokesman of a particular version and it is this version with which this chapter is concerned.

Claims made for the theory
The claims are extensive and fundamental. First, the theory is described as the 'great synthesis', a synthesis of what Etzioni calls the 'Classical' and Human Relations approaches representing studies of formal and informal

organizations with Max Weber's theory of bureaucracy and one of Karl
Marx's analytical tools (*MO*, pp. 48, 41).

*It remained the task of a third tradition in organizational thinking to relate
the two concepts of the formal and informal organization and to provide a
more complete and integrated picture of the organization. This convergence of organizational theory, the* Structuralist approach, *was made
considerably more sophisticated through comparative analysis* (*MO*,
pp. 20–1).

The third tradition is not yet, according to Etzioni, universally accepted,
despite its claimed superior analytical qualities:

*The application of the Classical approach with its concern for formal
organizational structure has by no means died out. Some continue to
apply it as if it had never been criticized. Some new and fruitful developments, however, have arisen out of the Classical tradition, especially
efforts to find an empirical basis for studying administration* (*MO*, p. 25).

The new developments, described as Neo-Classical, are represented by the
work of March and Simon. Nor, he adds, has the purely informal approach
been discarded for there 'are still Human Relations training manuals whose
authors have learned little and forgotten little since Mayo wrote his first
books'. But 'generally . . . those who still identify themselves with one or
the other of these earlier schools have come to broaden their theoretical
approach, and are moving in the general direction of the synthesis
suggested' (*MO*, p. 48).

Etzioni is exuberant about the theoretical potential of his great
synthesis. It can enable comparative studies to be undertaken thus
broadening considerably the scope of organizational theory. In justification of his approach, he wrote in the introduction to *Complex Organizations* that

*Organizational analysis has reached the stage where it becomes crucial to
study systematic differences among the various social units classed as
organizations. . . . The comparative analysis of organizations will lead to a
richer and more precise organizational theory* (*CO*, p. 12).

And he claimed that:

Eventually, the comparative study of organizations will:

1. Establish the truly universal propositions of organizational theory.
*2. Reduce overgeneralized propositions to middle-range (specific) state-
ments, specifying the categories of organizations for which they hold.*
3. Develop new middle-range propositions, so that knowledge of

universals will be supplemented with statements about analytical types of organization (CO, p. 14).

More specifically, Etzioni claimed that his organizational theory had been broadened to include:

1. both formal and informal elements of the organization and their articulation;
2. the scope of informal groups and the relations between such groups inside and outside the organization;
3. both lower and higher ranks;
4. both social and material rewards and their effects on each other;
5. the interaction between the organization and its environment;
6. both work and non-work organizations (MO, p. 49).

Within its scope are fitted factories, banks, insurance companies and a 'large variety of organizations from the Communist Party to the Catholic Church, and from a maximum-security prison to a small residential college' (*MO*, p. 48). But as well as this all-embracing scope, the synthesis purportedly enables its users to perform the exceptional feat of extricating themselves from the constraints of the value-judgments admittedly contained in the approaches which make up the synthesis: 'The Classical approach . . . viewed the organization from a highly managerial standpoint', whereas the 'Human Relations approach . . . favours management and misleads the workers' (*MO*, pp. 21, 41). On the other hand, the great synthesis which has a

more encompassing and balanced perspective not only encourages the growth of a value-free, neither pro-management nor pro-worker, approach to organizational analysis and the expansion of its scope to include all types of organizations and all the elements of organization, but it enriches the study of any single element by providing a context within which to place it, and points of reference for judging its importance to the organization (MO, p. 49).

Etzioni held that

It remained . . . for the Structuralists to . . . emphasize that social science is not a vehicle to serve the needs of either worker or organization. It is no more concerned to improve the organization of management than it is to improve organization of the employees (MO, p. 40).

Whether Etzioni successfully freed his analysis of value-judgments can be seen as soon as the conceptual framework within which he operates is identified.

Compliance as a prime variable

Firstly the whole of Etzioni's work is concerned with the exercise, the administration of power within organizations defined, after Parsons, as social units oriented to the realization of specific goals. An organization is seen as a large, complex social unit in which many social groups interact. It involves the coordination of a large number of human actions and 'combines its personnel with its resources, weaving together leaders, experts, workers, machines, and raw materials. At the same time it continually evaluates how well it is performing and tries to adjust itself accordingly in order to achieve its goals' (*MO*, p. 1). Within this complexity, the prime variable is power. Indeed it is because Etzioni is concerned with the 'kinds and distribution of power in organizations' that he calls his study a structural one. He follows, therefore, in the tradition of Weber. His model is an elaboration of Weber's, employing more sophisticated analytical tools and using a more complex set of assumptions. Weber is accorded the status of a founding father of the Structuralist school. After Weber, Etzioni accepts the pyramidal, hierarchical shape of organizations as given and concentrates on the administration of control in pursuit of goals which may or may not be those stated. He extended Weber's analysis of authority, including its legitimation, to cover non-legitimate power so as 'to give full status to both legitimate and non-legitimate sources' (*CO*, p. 15). Etzioni, concentrating on the phenomenon of legitimation in Weber's analysis, identified 'compliance' as the 'central element of organizational structure' and chose it as the basis for the classification of organizations. 'Compliance,' he wrote, 'is a relationship consisting of the power employed by superiors to control subordinates and the orientation of the subordinates to this power' (*CO*, p. 15). In other words, after examining legitimation, he asked,

To what extent can the organization expect its participants to accept its rulings because 'they always were so', to what extent because the rulings agree with a law the participants acknowledge, and to what degree must the person who issues an order be highly persuasive (*MO*, p. 50).

Compliance is undoubtedly a more analytically useful concept than legitimation. Compliance then was chosen by Etzioni as the main variable and was related in the analysis to certain other variables which were not examined in relation to each other. There are two parties to a compliance relationship: one which exercises power and one which is subjected to it. But in any one organization compliance relationships are likely to be complex so, in order to simplify the analysis, Etzioni dealt only with what he called 'higher participants' and 'lower participants'.

Control by higher participants

The next stage in the analysis was to categorize the means of control at the disposal of the higher participants and to distinguish between the kinds of responses of the lower participants. After that the types of means of control and the kinds of responses were related, constituting compliance relationships, and acted as a basis for the classification of organizations.

Etzioni identified three means of control, or means whereby higher participants exercised power over lower participants. They were physical, material or symbolic. The physical means he describes as *coercive*, resting on the

application, or threat of application, of physical sanctions such as inflic-
tion of pain, deformity, or death; generation of frustration through restric-
tion of movement; or controlling through force the satisfaction of needs
such as those for food, sex, comfort, and the like.

The material means constitute *remunerative* power and are based on the

control over material resources and rewards through allocation of salaries
and wages, commissions and contributions, 'fringe benefits', services and
commodities.

Lastly symbolic means entail the

allocation and manipulation of symbolic rewards and deprivations through
employment of leaders, manipulation of mass media, allocation of esteem
and prestige symbols, administration of ritual, and influence over the dis-
tribution of 'acceptance' and 'positive response',

and are based, in short, on *normative* power (*CO*, p. 5).

So far coercive power, remunerative power and normative power are analytical categories which assist towards understanding how control in organizations is exercised. When, however, organizations have to be classified according to these categories the assistance is seriously weakened. It is pertinent to say that 'most organizations employ all three kinds of power, but the degree to which they rely on each differs from organization to organization' (*CO*, p. 6). It is difficult to say which organizations obtain compliance mainly through which type of power and in what proportions the types are combined. Yet as a first step towards an understanding of the actual situation different organizations have to be put into precise categories. What is more important, however, is that the three types of force are given equal weight by Etzioni as determinants of compliance, and therefore of behaviour. The three major sources of control, Etzioni states,

whose allocation and manipulation account to a great extent for the
foundations of social order . . . are coercion, economic assets, and norma-

tive values. Social relationships differ in the relative predominance of this or that kind of control; but none has an a priori superiority, nor is there one which, as a rule, is the most powerful. . . . All three enjoy equal status. No assumption is made that force is necessarily disruptive, or that economic factors ultimately determine the distribution and dynamics of the others, or that an organization is one integrated collectivity (CO, pp. 16—17).

Etzioni uses, then, a multicausal analysis in which nothing can be said for certain until it has been empirically determined.

This is the first significant insight into Etzioni's conceptual framework. With the assumption that no source of power has priority over any other, then a causal explanation depends on the way in which Etzioni, or anyone else who uses his models, classifies organizations according to their dominant means of control. If, for instance, so-called professional organizations are described as normative controlled, then it is equivalent to saying that behaviour in those organizations is largely value-determined. The all important thing is the classification and this is beset with difficulties, particularly as on Etzioni's own admission most organizations employ all three kinds. The question concerning the causal relationships between the three types of power is not even posed, let alone answered, in Etzioni's model. It was not necessary for him to engage in the long-standing controversy about the merits of economic as against normative determinism but as he introduced physical power, coercion, as an independent variable and claimed this addition as an improvement on Weber's model the reader is surely entitled to a comment (CO, p. 17). It is misleading to contract out of making a causal explanation without some comment because this position in itself constitutes a causal explanation. The only assistance Etzioni gave in this direction was to say that:

Organizations can be ordered according to their power structure, taking into account which power is predominant, how strongly it is stressed compared with other organizations in which the same power is predominant, and which power constitutes the secondary source of control. . . . Most organizations tend to emphasize only one means of power, relying less on the other two. . . . The major reason for power specialization seems to be that when two kinds of power are emphasized at the same time, over the same subject group, they tend to neutralize each other (CO, pp. 6—7).

And with that it is possible to move on to another part of the model.

Responses of lower participants

This section distinguishes between the kinds of responses of the lower participants. 'Organizations,' Etzioni asserts, 'must continually recruit means if they are to realize their goals. One of the most important of these means is the positive orientation of the participants to the organizational power' or, in other words, the intensity of involvement (*CO*, p. 10). The participants can be placed along an involvement continuum where at one extreme there is positive involvement or commitment and at the other extreme negative involvement or alienation. 'Actors can accordingly be placed on an involvement continuum which ranges from a highly intense negative zone through mild negative and mild positive zones to a highly positive zone' (*CO*, p. 9). Etzioni found it convenient to name three zones on the involvement continuum: *alienative* involvement where lower participants tend to be alienated from their respective organizations as prisoners or enlisted men are; *calculative* involvement, a low intensity phenomenon characteristic of economic relationships; and *moral* involvement designating a positive orientation of high intensity and found among church parishioners or devoted members of political parties.

Compliance relationships

There are then three kinds of power and three zones of involvement and the relationships between them constitute compliance relationships. In Etzioni's typology there are nine types of compliance grouped into what he calls *congruent* and *incongruent* types. A congruent type is one where

the kind of involvement that lower participants have because of other factors . . . (such as personality structure, secondary socialization and membership in other collectivities) . . . and the kind of involvement that tends to be generated by the predominant form of organizational power are the same (*CO*, p. 12).

It follows that congruence is more effective than incongruence and because organizations are under external and internal pressure to be effective, congruent types are more frequent than incongruent ones. Thus the more frequent cases are where normative powers are applied on highly committed participants, remunerative power is applied on participants in the calculative involvement zone and coercive power operates on highly alienated participants. Since organizations are under pressure to be effective, Etzioni adds,

organizations tend to shift their compliance structure from incongruent to congruent types *and* organizations which have congruent compliance structure tend to resist factors pushing them towards incongruent compliance structures (*CO*, p. 14).

This is presented as a dynamic hypothesis. The dynamic determinants are environmental factors which have to be empirically determined and can, because of Etzioni's assumption about causality, be almost anything. The congruent types are referred to as coercive compliance, utilitarian compliance and normative compliance.

The three kinds of power and the three zones of involvement are basic but bare hypotheses of a general nature. In order to take the matter further and to make sense of the concept of 'compliance relationships', it is necessary to identify the lower participants. Only then will it be possible to decide about the distribution of lower participants into the three zones of involvement and to understand the determinants of involvement. Answers to these questions explain much about the subjective content of the analysis.

The identification of lower participants

Etzioni defines lower participants in terms of the intensity of their involvement and describes them in concrete terms as employees, rank and file, members, clients, customers and inmates. The lower participants in industrial organizations are employees, those in churches are members and those in prisons are inmates. Customers and clients figure as lower participants if they satisfy specified criteria for participation. These criteria are involvement, subordination and performance. Before deciding on who would rank as participants Etzioni would want to know the nature of involvement, its direction and intensity; the degree of subordination and the amount of performance. He does not rate the criteria in any order of importance so that the evaluation is left largely to the discretion of the analyst. A participant, however, must rank high on at least one of the three dimensions (*CO*, p. 21). As an illustration of how the ranking operates Etzioni states that inmates are more subordinated than employees, employees more than members and members more than clients, but against this one must evaluate the amount of performance which is high for employees, low for inmates and lowest for clients and customers. Soldiers in combat are high on all three dimensions; inmates are high on involvement and subordination but low on performance; while employees are medium in involvement and subordination but high on performance. Customers and clients usually score low on the three dimensions but not necessarily in every case, so they may or may not figure as lower participants.

The consequence of applying the three criteria is that participants are included who may not usually be identified with organizations sufficiently closely to warrant their inclusion as participants. Etzioni is aware of this for he says that his manner of delineating organizations 'draws the line much lower than most studies of bureaucracies, which tend to include only persons who are part of a formal hierarchy: priests but not parishioners; stewards but not union members; guards but not inmates;

nurses but not patients'. But to exclude the parishioners, union members and patients, he claims would 'be like studying colonial structures without the natives, stratification without the lower classes, or a political regime without the citizens or voters' (*CO*, p. 21). To this comparison Etzioni adds that if priests were regarded as the privates of the church or school-teachers as the lowest ranking participants of a school the analysis would ignore 'the psychological import of having "subordinates" '.

The identification of lower participants raises questions of much greater analytical significance than Etzioni's comments would indicate. It was necessary that Etzioni *should* define lower participants as he did in order to complete his model and not because an analysis would be defective if they were defined in any other way. Having assumed the existence of three kinds of power it was necessary that there should be related kinds of involvement so that compliance relationships could be constructed. If, for instance, only the members of formal organizations had been included in the analysis then all the lower participants would have been in some way employees, with a largely dominant calculative involvement. There would then have been only one congruent type, namely where remunerative power was used. The coercive category would have to disappear altogether for it is impossible to conceive of an organization based on coercion if there are no recipients of the coercion. There would remain then the normative category in which the only clear indication of the normative element would be in the stated goals of the organizations. The exercise of normative controls where the involvement was largely of an economic nature would pose analytical difficulties for in this as in other analyses there must be comparable elements or categories so that correlations can be established as Etzioni himself indicates. When faced with defining lower participants Etzioni has *either* to include among them actors who were patently not motivated by remuneration and who appeared to be moti-vated by the use of force or the influence of values *or* alter his initial hypothesis, which stipulated three kinds of power systems.

The difficulty Etzioni would have faced if he had defined lower partici-pants as employees is illustrated by his treatment of higher participants or elites.

The compliance structure of elites or higher participants varies much less from one type of organization to another than the compliance structure of lower participants. The basic differences between the compliance of higher and lower participants are as follows: Coercive power is rarely applied to higher participants; their involvement is usually moral or calculative, and only rarely alienative. Second, pure moral involvement is relatively rare because higher participants are more likely than lower participants to have career or economic interests in the organization. This means that the higher ranks exhibit a more limited range of compliance patterns than lower ranks do. The compliance structure of guards in a prison is quite similar to that of foremen in a factory, and, since the clergy too is a vocation, with income, promotions, and prestige differentials, the compliance structure of ministers does not differ as much from the foremen's pattern as his parishioners differ from workers in compliance (CO, p. 202).

If he had not been able to stretch his definition of lower participants as he did it is likely that he would not have been able to maintain his analytical power categories. The importance of this can be seen from the fact that his three categories, equal in causal weight, constitute the assumption about causal explanation on which his whole analysis rests. Faced with a single compliance relationship with a utilitarian basis Etzioni would have had to assume, explicitly or implicitly, a variant of economic determinism. His subsequent analysis would have been qualitatively different.

So far the analytical importance of the definition of lower participants has been emphasized without any objections being raised to it. All the organizations with which Etzioni is concerned have goals by definition. In every case the fulfilment of the goals results in the provision of a service or the production of a commodity. This is so whether, to use the concrete terms employed by Etzioni, the analysis includes hospitals, prisons, schools, churches, industrial organizations, the Communist Party, the Mapai or any other type. The point at which the service or commodity enters its market marks the end of formal organizational responsibility. It does not end, of course, the interest of the organization, as a relationship exists between the organization and the consumer and the significance of this relationship for organizational behaviour depends upon the nature of the market. Put another way, every organization works within a market of one kind or another, whether it be for religious beliefs, medical care, coercive detention or manufactured goods, but the market, no matter how much its characteristics react on the organization, is not a part of the organization. There is no essential sociological difference between the service a hospital provides and the commodities many industrial organizations produce. The patient is no less the consumer of a service than the person who buys a motor car is a consumer of a commodity. If there is a difference between the two it will depend on the characteristics of the market; on the extent to which the providing organization has control over the amount and quality of the service or commodity and, relatedly, on the value attached to the service or commodity by the consumer. It is clear that there is a serious inconsistency in Etzioni's manner of defining lower participants. This does not mean that the warder—prisoner, nurse—patient relationships which concern Etzioni so much are being neglected or underestimated, but simply that they should be regarded for analysis as market phenomena. There is no doubt that similar relationships exist between producers and consumers in commodity markets depending upon the degree of monopoly which exists in them. There is no doubt also that lower participants must belong to formal organizations.

The determinants of involvement

The next question concerns the determinants of involvement; this means the orientation of lower participants to the organization as a power system. Why is it that there is, in terms of Etzioni's analysis, this continuum of involvement ranging from intensive commitment to intensive alienation? First, lower participants are influenced in their attitudes to the elements comprising a power system, such as the directives the organization issues, the sanctions by which it supports its directives, and the persons in power positions, by external environmental factors. Etzioni describes these factors as membership in other organizations such as labour unions, basic value commitments obtained from, say, Catholic as against Protestant religious commitments, and the personality structure of the participants, which may, for instance, be authoritarian (*CO*, p. 13). Second, lower participants are influenced by organizational power. Indeed he insists that organizational powers *generate* involvement, that is, either commitment or alienation.

He gives some guidance about the generation process. He says that

involvement . . . is affected both by the legitimacy of a directive and by the degree to which it frustrates the subordinates' need-dispositions. Alienation is produced not only by illegitimate exercise of power, but also by power which frustrates needs, wishes, desires. Commitment is generated not merely by directives which are considered legitimate but also by those which are in line with internalized needs of the subordinate. Involvement is positive if the line of action directed is conceived by the subordinate as both legitimate and gratifying. It is negative when the power is not granted legitimacy and when it frustrates the subordinate (*CO*, pp. 15–16).

Coercive power is regarded as illegitimate by subordinates, therefore it is alienative. It is for this reason that inmates are said to be alienated from prisons and that some degree of alienation exists among students and pupils: 'Levels of alienation are closely associated with the degree of coercion applied' (*CO*, p. 49).

Normative power, on the other hand, is generally regarded as legitimate and therefore generates commitment. This process occurs through the internalization of normative directives and is seen in its extreme form in churches. Where norms are internalized there is presumably no conflict between directives and the need-dispositions of participants. Where they are not internalized, as in prisons, the need-dispositions of participants are frustrated. In between the extreme cases where there are degrees of legitimacy and illegitimacy it is necessary to make more detailed correlations between elements of power systems and the frustration of need-dispositions. Thus Etzioni states that factors which allow for the greater application of normative controls increase commitment; he lists higher rewards, closer and more personal contact with management and deference from clients as such factors. Presumably lower wages, less contact with management and little or no deference from clients lead to increasing alienation. The need-dispositions of participants involve other factors than those just mentioned; they involve anything which goes towards determining satisfaction with work. In so far as any meaning can be given to the term 'satisfaction', it too operates on a continuum coincident with involvement. Etzioni wrote that high intrinsic satisfaction from work is positively associated with involvement and so presumably the reverse must also hold (*CO*, p. 53). It should be noted that the area on the continuum between the extremes is largely occupied by work organizations which he describes as blue-collar, white-collar and professional organizations, where compliance is a mixture of three sorts but is primarily utilitarian, and where the lower participants are employees. He divides the blue-collar, white-collar and professional organizations into normative influenced categories with the normative element increasing with the movement away from manual work. Alienation, therefore, is greatest in blue-collar organizations and least in professional organizations. But there is more to it than this. There are alienating creating factors which are common to work organizations and which, depending upon the intensity with which they are present, can cause different degrees of alienation to occur even between organizations in the same category. The factors are described in *Modern Organizations*. Their operation poses what is to Etzioni the main organizational dilemma.

The use of human resources by organizations to achieve their goals creates, Etzioni believes, a central dilemma which previous theorists did not recognize: 'The problem of modern organizations is . . . how to construct human groupings that are as rational as possible, and at the same time produce a minimum of undesirable side effects and a maximum of satisfaction' (*MO*, p. 2); or, rephrased in a manner which illuminates his approach more clearly, the problem is 'how to control the participants so as to maximize effectiveness and efficiency and minimize the unhappiness this very need to control produces' (*MO*, p. 50). The undesirable side-effects stem to a significant extent from the increasing rationality of organizational action. Etzioni does not believe, as did the classical theorists, that rational behaviour through increasing productivity and therefore incomes leads to greater worker satisfaction; or that there is a positive correlation between productivity and worker satisfaction, as do the members of the Human Relations school.

Modern civilization depends largely on organizations as the most rational and efficient form of social grouping known [but the] increase in the scope and rationality of organizations has not come without social and human cost. Many people who work for organizations are deeply frustrated and alienated from their work. . . . At this point we must confront a major misunderstanding. Not all that enhances rationality reduces happiness, and not all that increases happiness reduces efficiency. . . . Generally the less the organization alienates its personnel, the more efficient it is. Satisfied workers usually work harder and better than frustrated ones. Within limits, happiness heightens efficiency in organizations and, conversely, without efficient organizations much of our happiness is unthinkable. . . . Thus, to a degree, organizational rationality and human happiness go hand in hand. *But a point is reached in every organization where happiness and efficiency cease to support each other. Not all work can be well-paid or gratifying, and not all regulations and orders can be made acceptable. Here we face a true dilemma* (MO, p. 2).

Efficiency results from rational action through increasing specialization. Alienation results from increasing specialization.

At this point instead of seeing alienation simply as negative involvement it can be recognized as a term borrowed from Karl Marx and referring to the attitude of work caused by the inability to become identified with the whole of a particular work process, including the disposal of the product. The point is, however, that the term is borrowed from Marx and not from the conceptual framework of which it is a part and it therefore has a somewhat different meaning in the hands of Etzioni. This is how he sees the connection between specialization and alienation:

Specialization has fragmented production so that each worker's labour has become repetitious, monotonous, and lacks opportunity for creativity and self-expression. The worker has little conception of the whole work process or of his contribution to it; his work is meaningless. He has little control over the time at which his work starts and stops or over the pace at which it is carried out. To this Marxian analysis, Weber added that this basic estrangement exists not only between the worker and the means of production, but also between the soldier and the means of warfare, the scientist and the means of inquiry, etc. This is not just a legal question of ownership . . . but rather that with ownership goes the right to control, and that those that provide the means also define their use; thus the worker, soldier, and researcher — and by implication all employees of all organizations — are frustrated, unhappy since they cannot determine what use their efforts will be put to since they do not own the instrument necessary to carry out independently the work that needs to be done. When asked, 'all said and done, how satisfied are you with your work?' about 80 per cent of American blue-collar workers answered 'not satisfied'. Alienation is a concept that stands for this sentiment and the analysis of its source in the Marxian—Weberian terms (MO, p. 42).

Thus the movement towards large-scale production with its base of specialization is seen as the source of alienation. But not all work is alienating and not all alienation-creating work affects workers to the same extent; only 'after a point' does the organization of work create unhappy, frustrated workers. Once alienation exists then workers become uncooperative and come into conflict with management. Industrial conflict, then, is seen as a product of alienation.

Etzioni's interpretation of the alienation generating process involves a number of propositions about organizational behaviour which need to be made explicit. They must perforce be stated barely though some are highly controversial and lie at the root of major methodological differences in industrial sociology.

1. First is the proposition that the subdivision and simplification of work caused by specialization creates dissatisfaction with work. If this is valid then the converse should hold good that the less the specialization the more employees are satisfied with their work. An historical analysis of organizational change should reveal increasing unhappiness among employees.

2. If the first proposition is valid then, although all workers who are in any way affected by specialization will experience some dissatisfaction with their work, there will be sharp differences in the incidence of dissatisfaction both within organizations and between them as the degree of specialization varies. The greatest dissatisfaction will be experienced by those performing the simplest and most mechanical tasks. There should be some empirical evidence concerning this proposition.

3. If alienation causes conflict between management and workers and alienation is defined as a form of dissatisfaction, then industrial conflict must be a function of dissatisfaction.

4. As dissatisfaction is created by specialization and itself creates conflict there must be a positive correlation between specialization and industrial conflict. The more specialized work is the more intense should conflict be. It should be possible to validate this proposition.

5. It follows that as specialization is the result of rational action and

rational action is positively associated with efficiency, the more efficient production is the more likely there will be conflict between managers and workers. This proposition too can be tested empirically.

6. If dissatisfaction becomes more intense as tasks become subdivided and dissatisfaction creates conflict, then the sharpest conflict in any organization should involve management and the least skilled workers. Lowly skilled workers on mechanical tasks and clerical workers on routinized tasks should be in a deeper conflict with management than, say, apprentice-skilled workers. More specifically, low-skilled surface workers in the coal-mines should be more militant than coalface workers. All the evidence is to the contrary.

7. If rational action based on specialization increases both productivity and dissatisfaction, then there must be a positive correlation between productivity and dissatisfaction and an inverse correlation between productivity and satisfaction. This is completely contrary to the proposition on which the Human Relations school is based and although Etzioni criticizes that school he does so for its incompleteness rather than for its use of false assumptions about industrial behaviour.

8. It follows from the above propositions that the Structuralists correlate the physical work environment or organization of work (an independent variable) with satisfaction from work (a dependent variable) and conflict between management and workers (a dependent variable). If, therefore, the physical work environment is varied to make work less repetitive and monotonous and more autonomous and creative, employees will adopt a more cooperative attitude towards management. In other words the intensity of conflict can be varied by adjustments within organizations. In this sense they are working from the same basic assumption as the Human Relations school, that conflict is a dependent variable. They differ only in the kind of adjustment they think necessary to produce any given conflict situation.

The above propositions, though they may read like a skit on a serious academic work, follow logically from Etzioni's analysis. They suggest the ludicrous conclusion that rational action results in both efficiency and inefficiency in such a way that the more efficient an organization becomes the less efficient it is.

Apart from revealing that Etzioni has not examined the logic of his analysis, the propositions indicate an approach to conflict which is basic to his analysis. This approach is implicit in the whole of his work.

Conflict

First, Etzioni recognizes that conflict, tensions or frictions do exist in an organization. His whole work deals with the question of power and its acceptance: his prime variable is compliance. Throughout his model he is concerned with obstructions to positive involvement, with the sources of alienation and with the realignment of the beliefs, norms and perspectives of participants with those of the organization. In other words he is constantly concerned about what he would describe as the sources of conflict. He goes out of his way to dissociate himself from those who deny the existence of conflict. He rejected, he stated, the 'harmony' assumption of the Human Relations school and mentioned that it was

in exploring the harmony view . . . that the Structuralist writers first recognize(d) fully the organizational dilemma: the inevitable strains which can be reduced but not eliminated — between organizational needs and personal needs; between rationality and non-rationality; between discipline and autonomy; between formal and informal relations; between management and workers, or, more generally, between ranks and divisions (MO, p. 41).

More than this, he considered that conflict could be functional.

Industrial conflict is viewed by many social scientists of the older generation and by most Human Relations writers as basically undesirable. . . . The Structuralists, however, point to the many important social functions of conflict, including its positive contributions for the organizational system itself, and object to any artificial smothering of conflict. The expression of conflict allows genuine differences of interests and beliefs to emerge, whose confrontation may lead to a test of power and adjustment of the organizational system to the real situation, and ultimately to organizational peace. If glossed over, conflict and its concomitant latent alienation will seek other outlets such as withdrawal or increase in accidents which in the end are disadvantageous to both worker and organization (MO, p. 44).

It is not necessary to dispute this interpretation of conflict in order to illustrate the analytical irrelevance of the distinction Etzioni has made. The distinction is that Human Relations writers on the one hand see conflict as being analogous to pain in the human body in that they believe that by correct action conflict can be resolved completely whenever it occurs, while on the other hand the Structuralists regard conflict both as something which can be prophylactically treated and as a phenomenon which itself has prophylactic qualities. The distinction relates to different views about the sources of conflict within the organization. In the one case conflict is wholly the product of maladjustment between parts whereas in the other case it may be this but it may also result from internal structural factors and not be amenable to remedial treatment. Now it is not suggested that such a distinction is worthless. The interpretation of Etzioni does, in fact, constitute a modification of equilibrium analysis in that it takes it closer to reality. But it is a modification of equilibrium analysis and not an alternative. It is of the same order as the move to pluralism in general within conventional social theory.

The existence of conflict as seen by Etzioni no more disturbs the insularity of the organization as a social system than does that of the Human Relations school. The types of conflict are not differentiated; no distinction is made between primary and secondary conflicts and the primary conflict is not located in contradictions involving structural factors which inevitably and invariably belong to organizations and are determined by environmental forces. There is not even a hint of the possibility that organizations might become transformed through the intensity and pervasiveness of irremedial structural conflict. Etzioni, as is the case with structural functionalists, pays only lip-service to the existence of an environment. For instance, he stated that

> *both the initial involvement of lower participants and the involvement they develop while in the organization are determined in part by the organization's environment. The kinds of power an organization applies are affected by its 'social license' to use coercion, by its market position and by its social status. The goals an organization serves are formulated in part to maximize its input—output exchange with the environment. The legal system of the external collectivities in which organizations operate imposes constraints on recruitment and control methods; so does the political power exercised by lower participants in external systems. Recruitment, scope, and pervasiveness are all directly concerned with 'boundary' processes or relationships (CO, p. 310).*

But he gave environment no causal part to play in his analysis and the relationships he mentions do not appear anywhere in his elaborate model.

The crux of this matter is that if an organization is regarded as a social system with some means of insulating itself from environmental pressures, possessing, therefore, elements specific to itself, it is this which is the major analytical distinguishing feature, because such an organization can consistently be abstracted from its environment for analytical purposes and be attributed with the qualities which determine its own behaviour. There can be, and are, differences of opinion about the internal nature of the system, but these are not conceptual differences. A conceptual difference arises when contrary views are put about the insularity or autonomy of the system. An important clue to conceptual differences is contained in the approach to conflict, and on this score there is no doubt where Etzioni and the Structuralists stand. They may argue with the classical theorists, the human relations school, and the structural functionalists about the extent, the intensity and the function of conflict, but their analysis of conflict stands fairly and squarely within a common conceptual framework.

Notes

1. Amitai Etzioni, *A Comparative Analysis of Complex Organizations*, The Free Press, New York, 1961; and *Modern Organizations*, Prentice-Hall Inc., N.J., 1963. In this chapter page references are given as *CO* and *MO* respectively.

Part three

Dynamic sociology

The task I set myself in Part three is the most formidable one in the whole book. During the early stages I was often reproached by sociologists for emphasizing the shortcomings of conventional sociology without suggesting an alternative approach. The point was not that I did not know of an alternative approach but that the existing alternative was not equipped to deal with the same range of issues as conventional sociology and could not be presented without a great deal of qualification. I have tried in Part three to equip the alternative approach, dialectical materialism, with the tools which I believe enable it to tackle micro as well as macro situations. I am convinced that methodologically dialectical materialism is superior to conventional sociology in every aspect of its application. I am equally convinced that because dialectical materialism is grounded in concrete reality and reflects the contradictions in that reality it is not a preferred alternative but an inevitable one.

In order to fulfil my task I have had to do a great deal of explanation and clarification. As I suggest in chapter 1 there is much confusion about the meaning of Marxism and this does not altogether disappear once the meaning has been established. Indeed the matter then takes on a new dimension through fear and prejudice. So, in chapters 8, 9 and 10, I have gone into some detail to explain in basic terms what dialectical materialism is. Chapter 7 is, in effect, a statement of the major problem confronting sociologists, namely the analysis of movement. The three last chapters point to its solution. Chapters 8 and 9 deal with structure and super-structure as analytical tools. They comprise an elaboration of the meaning of materialism. Chapter 10 introduces the dialectic to materialism and confronts both the fear and the prejudice. It provides static materialism with the facility to analyse qualitative change and, in consequence, to be a truly dynamic theory.

7

The analysis of movement [1]

The most important issue confronting organization theorists is the analysis of movement, the location of its source and the identification of its transmitting mechanism. The significance of the issue is not always recognized by sociologists because some do not see the limitations of their models. Others are strangely satisfied with their static categorizations of a moving reality. But, as the preceding chapters show quite clearly, the prime defect of conventional explanations is their inability to go beyond static categorizations and the most prominent theorists are conscious of this defect. The issue is sometimes put differently. It is seen as the need to explain organizational growth for the practical benefit of employers and managers. The recently published volume of readings on *Organizational Growth and Development*, for instance, was intended 'to help managers towards that objective view of their organizations which is such a basic requirement for an accurate prediction of the consequences of their policies'.[2] Its task was defined as providing answers to such questions as 'Why do organizations grow? How do they change with size and age?' It attempted to identify and illustrate 'Four main areas of interest — Motives for Growth, Adaptation and Growth, Models of Growth and Administrative Structure and Growth'. Other works concentrate on attempting to explain the process whereby organizations experience social change without explicitly relating their explanations to management needs.

The question of movement may arise in a different way. Most conventional works deal mainly with the ability of organizations to preserve themselves, to maintain effective functioning. The issue in these cases is about resistance to movement and in order to tackle it some assumptions have to be made about the source of movement and its transmitting mechanism. Works which are preoccupied with stability are as concerned with movement as those which claim to treat dynamics. Only the approach differs. All works which claim predictive qualities must make provision for movement of some sort. This is so even if the treatment is wholly static.

Although all organization theorists have to say something about movement their main concern is about that which is pervasive and against which homeostasis qualities are ineffectual. They are concerned, that is, with movement which can alter social relationships. This has arisen from the inability of conventional explanations to take account of movement in reality. Chapter 3, dealing with the conceptual basis of organization theory, illustrates how successive adaptations to models have been made to help remove this defect, but without effect. The reason for this is clear. All the preceding chapters show that given a logically consistent treatment of the data, the limitations of any theoretical explanation stem from its conceptual basis or framework. If the models described in chapter 3 are defective then, assuming they are not illogical, it must be because they have a defective conceptual basis. The point is that if the conceptual basis of a model is static the explanation will be in static terms, and it is this fact which should be the object of criticism. All the explanations which have been described are of a static or relative static nature. They analyse changes in social relationships not as they are seen in concrete situations but as they are defined by the limitations of their common conceptual basis. Now if concrete reality is static it is logical to use a static model to analyse it. If concrete reality is not static it is illogical and inconsistent with reality to use a static model. As there is abundant empirical evidence that neither concrete reality in general nor that for organizations is static it is necessary to formulate a conceptual framework which takes account of this fact.

Conceptual frameworks and concrete reality

It is important that the relationship between a conceptual framework and concrete reality should be recognized. A conceptual framework is a conceptualized version of reality. All the tools, concepts and propositions which comprise the framework relate to that reality. The framework does not have an existence independent of practice or experience; it is an explanation of that practice or experience and can only be useful if it assists an understanding of it. It is possible to categorize practice in an unreal way, but this would confuse rather than assist an understanding of it. It is possible to formulate conceptual categories which have no bearing on practice at all, but this would be a fantasy not a theory. It is also possible to construct some categories which are more or less reflections of reality than others and which, therefore, are more or less useful as means to understand that reality. The degree of usefulness of one conceptual approach rather than another is discovered in the empirical testing process, but in the social sciences validation is a difficult, sometimes an impossible task. It may even be hard to detect misinterpretations which can so easily appear. A conceptual category is really an abstraction of reality and, therefore, an interpretation of it. Misinterpretations, even distortions, are likely consequences, but they are not always avoidable analytical defects. Whenever a complex situation is simplified some distortion takes place and as simplification is a necessary step in the process of analysis the distortion which goes with it must be accepted. What is clear is that in the last analysis, and in the social sciences this is often coincident with the first, conceptual categories have to add to an understanding of reality and if they cannot do this because they consistently ignore essential features of reality or consistently distort it in some way, they should be reconstituted or displaced altogether. There can be no permanent dichotomy between theory and practice.

A conceptual framework is derived from the theorists' simplified version of reality. There is not a single, generally accepted version which could give rise to a single commonly accepted general theory because reality is not an objective phenomenon but is subjectively perceived. The social scientist sees largely what he assumes to exist. It is therefore important to know what these assumptions are. They comprise a simplified version of reality. The assumptions can act as blinkers on a social analyst: they direct his attention to particular data, thereby stipulating what is relevant and what is not, and they give meanings to concepts and terms, thereby setting the scope of the analysis.

It is not sufficiently recognized in the social sciences how important the question of definitions is for analysis. Certainly it is not a matter which seems to have bothered many theorists of organizations who have taken over terms from technical or popular usage without even asking whether they possessed any sociological significance. Some of the consequences which flow from a defective theory have their origin in the use of inappropriately or loosely defined terms. Once a term has been defined then its use in the analysis is limited to the scope stipulated in the definition. Once a matter under investigation has been defined then the limits of the analysis are stipulated. For instance, if an organization is defined in terms of authority, as was done by Weber, or in terms of compliance, as was done by Etzioni, then it is equivalent to stating that the prime variable in organizations is authority or compliance and that, in other words, organizations consist primarily of authority or compliance relationships. If an organization is defined as a social system which can be analysed independently of other social phenomena then the definition carries with it the limitations of systems analysis. A definition which involves the recognition of boundaries which isolate and insulate social relationships from each other in some way is also making a distinction between cause and effect, between entity and process, with serious analytical consequences.

Is is through this influence on definitions that sociological research tends to be tautological in that it ends up by proving what has already been assumed to exist. Thus if a sociologist assumes that social reality or any part of it is static he will end up by showing that it is static. If he assumes not only that it is static but that its static form is ideal, his analysis will confirm that any deviation from the static form is also a deviation from the ideal and in this respect is undesirable. If he assumes that the ideal state is a condition of equilibrium his analysis will confirm this by showing that deviations from the equilibrium position are temporary and remedial. There can be no doubt about the importance of the initial assumptions about reality on which theoretical superstructures rest. When comparing different theoretical explanations, given that they have no logical inconsistencies, the difference or sameness will be determined by the correspondence or lack of it between the versions of reality on which they rest.

The importance of the initial assumptions about reality can be emphasized further by looking more closely at their influence on the ability of analyses to cope with changes. It was stated at the beginning of this chapter that all the explanations of organizational behaviour described above were of a static or relative static nature. It was added that the extent to which they could account for change was determined by this fact. Now if the explanations had not been of a static nature their ability to account for change would have been different.

The assumption of organic unity
The assumption about reality underlying all the theoretical explanations so far described here is that societies no matter how they are defined, have an organic unity. It is assumed, that is, that there is nothing within the structure of any society which will inevitably, inexorably, give rise to divisions.[3] Left to themselves, societies will function in a coordinated and harmonious fashion. It follows that if there is a lack of coordination, an absence of harmony in social relationships, then it must be due to external interference. Now what is assumed for the entity applies also for the parts. It is logical to assume that any segment or system within a society possesses organic unity. So organizations are seen as basically harmonious entities; this means that if they are left alone by external influences they will function smoothly in perfect coordination. There is nothing within them which has a disruptive nature with the strength to effect qualitative changes.

If the assumption that there is organic unity is made it is equivalent to assuming that the structure of the phenomena under examination is immutable: that it cannot and will not alter. If there is any change, therefore, it must take place within a given structural context and must be incapable of altering that context. The structure of an organization defined in terms of authority relationships will give rise to the shape of the distribution of authority. Thus if authority is distributed hierarchically with a single apex of control giving it a pyramidal shape it will be assumed that nothing can significantly alter that shape. All movement will take place within the pyramid. All this is equivalent to saying that every system of social relationships has fixed boundaries around it.

We can see now how an assumption of organic unity determines the analysis of change within organizations. If the boundaries of an organization are fixed the possibility of alterations in them is excluded from the analysis. Change cannot involve a movement of factors or elements which is of sufficient pressure to make a qualitative impact on the organization as a whole. This means firstly that the causes of movement must be of a secondary order. They must either be so weak that they are unable to make a serious impact or be sufficiently weak to be resisted by change resisting mechanisms. Secondly, it means that the movement is not and cannot be cumulative because a cumulative effect on boundaries cannot be tolerated.

An analytical model based on the assumption of organic unity has to contain supporting assumptions which are logically consistent with the base assumption. In other words, the possibility of change occurring which could disrupt the organic unity has to be excluded from the outset. To achieve this end the models assume on the one hand that change is temporary, or remedial, or is a backward and forward movement; or they assume, on the other hand, that organizations have homeostatic qualities. Homeostasis has been defined by Mason Haire as

a mechanism for sensing the level of a particular variable and especially deviation from an appropriate level, a self-correcting mechanism for initiating an adjustmental process to return the level to its proper state and finally, the means for shutting off the correcting process. [4]

Others have called the same process self-regulating or equilibrating mechanisms. As each system has organic unity it does not contain any sources of change within itself. If change occurs at all it must originate from sources external to the system. All that is necessary in order to protect the integrity of the system is to assume that some kind of self-regulating mechanism exists.

Equilibrium analysis, involving movement along a succession of points of equilibrium, is consistent with the assumption of organic unity. The difference between static and equilibrium models is that the latter express the conditions for stability or a static state, say in terms of the relationship between goals and action, and make detailed provision for maintaining balance between them. An equilibrium model must possess homeostasis qualities so that disequilibrium can be removed. A movement from one position of equilibrium to another does not entail a qualitative change in the system concerned but simply a shift of a basically undisturbed system to another level. In conventional economic theory equilibrium is defined in terms of the relationship between supply and demand and occurs where the two intersect. A movement from an equilibrium position occurs through alterations in amounts demanded and supplied. Changes in any other variable such as time, the nature of commodities or tastes cause a movement to a new situation and, therefore, a fresh position of equilibrium. This process can be repeated indefinitely but it all takes place within an unaltered system of free market distribution.

The functionalist and structural functionalist version of systems analysis, as was mentioned earlier, is the sociological equivalent of equilibrium analysis in economics. An alteration in the pattern of goals is equivalent to a change in the nature of demand; it creates a new situation and, therefore, the need for a new position of equilibrium. A business organization could experience moving equilibria through changes in production methods, a switch in the type of commodity produced, or anything which makes it necessary to recalculate the relationship between goals and action. Disequilibrium would occur when the goals of the organization were not consistent with its action, as, for example, when its employees go on strike. A new position of equilibrium exists when the goals of the organization are altered in some way so that for consistency a different level of action is necessary and is achieved. It should be pointed out, however, that although a moving equilibria analytical model can be based on the assumption of organic unity it has not yet been rigorously developed in the sphere of organization analysis.

The meaning of terms
At this point the manner in which the initial prime assumption sets the scope of the analysis can be seen more clearly. Once the assumption of organic unity is made, whether explicitly or implicitly, then the analytical starting point will be either a static state, a condition of stability or a position of equilibrium. The examination of change will be derived from and subordinated to this point. The terms static, stability and equilibrium get their meaning from the initial assumption. The term static in this conceptual framework means a state involving no movement at all because of the absence of both internal inconsistencies and external pressures. A static organization can be conceived of as a consensus system in a vacuum. It is a theoretical abstraction and is a simplifying device for analysis. Stability and equilibrium, as was suggested in chapter 3, do not possess the

same meaning, but they are closely related. The term stability indicates a condition of settled, consistent relationships and therefore involves a quality of equilibrium. Stability in this context has a positive preferred quality which is always to be sought after. It is a state of no movement where movement is possible but is undesirable because it is disruptive. The ideal situation, when organic unity is assumed, is when the unity is preserved. Any movement at all must result from aberrations from the norm of unity. Movement, therefore, is seen to be a negative phenomenon, to be avoided or eliminated or corrected. Stability is a state of unspecified equilibrium. Equilibrium, on the other hand may or may not be stable. This was pointed out in chapter 3. The term equilibrium is a specified relationship between particular variables. It involves the possibility of movement, but this is always limited and remedial.

There is no doubt that the type of movement permitted in models based on the assumption of organic unity can be said to produce social change only in so far as this term is so defined as to bring it within the scope of the models. Social change is clearly not synonymous with progress, evolution or development.[5] It involves an alteration in social relationships on a scale sufficient to produce different patterns of behaviour and therefore implies the existence of pressures from one source or another. But the fact that pressures exist, that there is movement involving one or more variables, does not mean that there will be social change, for the movement may either be too weak to effect changes in behaviour or it may be temporary, rectifiable or containable. Movement which is unable or incapable of effecting permanent alterations in social relationships should be described in terms of *social adjustment* rather than social change. Social adjustment involves the kind of movement which has no effect on the structure of the organization and can be seen to be the consequence of such matters as alterations in the communications system, modifications in the lines of authority and interferences in the achievement of prescribed organizational goals. Any reallocation of resources in an organization which has neither an immediate nor an accumulating effect upon the form of the organization can result in social adjustment. In so far as the models described in this book are capable of analysing movement it is of the social adjustment type. Most of the analysis however, is of a situation at a single point of time. It tends to be descriptive, a compilation of categories and correlations between variables.

Unfortunately the inability of organization theorists to analyse social change has not prevented or even inhibited them from using the terms 'change' and 'dynamic'. This practice has added to the definitional confusion which exists in sociology. When Peter M. Blau analysed the dynamics of bureaucracy, for instance, he treated the term 'adjustive development' as a dynamic phenomenon,[6] while Amitai Etzioni used the term 'dynamic' to describe the very limited type of movement his model was able to analyse.[7] There is no doubt that conventional organization theorists have been conscious of the need to give a theoretical explanation of change. The only serious adaptations of their models have been towards that end. But the adaptations have always been within the limitations of their unchanged conceptional framework. In these circumstances the use of the terms 'change' and 'dynamic' is inexplicable unless they believed that the terms brought their own meanings with them so that a frequent use of them would convert a static analysis into a dynamic one.[8] In the main, terms have been used in a decorative manner without their meanings being made clear. The result has been to give them an imprecise and insipid quality which has considerably reduced their analytical utility.

Types of movement

An important step towards extending our understanding of social situations must be to distinguish between the different types of movement which can influence them. It is necessary here to attempt to see movement as it affects or could affect social situations rather than to impose on them a concept of movement derived from an ideal-type analytical model. The important distinction, which has already been made, is between movement which does not alter social relationships and that which does. Only movement which alters social relationships can be said to produce social change. The distinction is therefore an important one. On the side of no social change there are two possible categories. There is the situation *displaying* no movement at all. The conventional sociological equivalent is the static situation in which all relationships are ordered and balanced, showing no signs even of potential disorder or imbalance. As the analysis here assumes continuous movement as a starting point, the concept static has no part to play unless it is so rigorously redefined as to make it unrecognizable and therefore confusing. The equivalent of a static situation is one where all movement is frustrated by institutional obstacles of one kind or another. The absence of apparent movement may persist over a long period of time so that this analysis is not inevitably concerned with activities at a single point of time, as is static analysis.

The second category involving no social change is where there is movement which cannot wholly be frustrated but which is reversible so that its effects are remedial. Such movement adjusts rather than alters social relationships. The conventional sociological equivalent of this category is the equilibrium situation, the situation with homeostatic qualities where the *status quo ante* would be restored or where a new equilibrium position was reached. The concept of equilibrium is as untenable as that of static for there can never be a settled position in a situation where pressures for movement are unbroken. Social adjustment, then, is a feature of situations with controllable remedial movement.

There are also two categories on the side of social change. On this side there are no conventional sociological equivalents for social change has a meaning which lifts it right out of the capabilities of such explanations. Social change means a qualitative change in social relationships. The question of social change is examined in detail later. At this point it is simply intended to categorize types of movement. The first category here concerns situations where there is continual, irremedial movement which alters social relationships within given structures. In other words the changes are at the level of superstructures. The second category relates to qualitative changes in structures. In both instances unremitting pressures have transforming qualities. Transformations may result whatever the intensity of the pressures. It is generally the case in the pure and applied sciences that variables have a definite, unambiguous meaning only within a certain range of movement. Beyond that range they take on different identities. This means that continuous adding may introduce a qualitative difference in the nature of that being added. For this reason it is a generally accepted scientific precaution in the pure and applied sciences to take this possibility into account and to refrain from extrapolating dogmatically. It seems sensible to assume a similar attitude of caution, of scientific humility, in the social sciences.

The methods of the pure and applied sciences cannot, of course, be transferred without modification to the social sciences. This is partly because of the much greater degree of subjectivity in the collection and use of data and partly because of the immense difficulties in conducting controlled experiments for purposes of validation. This is so in all the social sciences but it is greatest in what is usually known as sociology. In sociology there is great preponderance of unassessable elements and great ignorance about their formation and reformation. This is all the more reason for proceeding with scientific caution and admitting the possibility of qualitative change occurring. All the categories of movement may be present simultaneously in social situations and to varying extents. An adequate social analysis must therefore be capable of taking them all into account.

In summary the following points can be made:

1. Social movement of some kind is an empirically verifiable fact.
2. Given the existence of movement of any kind then the possibility must be considered that it will change social relationships qualitatively.

3. The possibility of qualitative change can only be considered within a framework which gives it analytical recognition.

4. An analysis based on the assumption of organic unity precludes itself from consideration because by definition, it can permit no movement which can disrupt, distort and unalterably change the unity.

5. This means that systems analysis in all of its forms is incapable of coping with social change and that no manner of adaptation will equip it to be otherwise.

6. It is not permissible to contract out of the difficulties of analysing social change by using organic concepts such as homeostasis because this would involve simplifying reality to the point of perversion.

7. It is a legitimate methodological practice to assume away peripheral difficulties in order to isolate the core of an issue for analysis but it is quite a different matter to assume away the core of the issue itself.

8. There is a case for using a dynamic interpretation of reality as a basis for analysis which rests both on its positive attributes and on the clearly pronounced deficiencies of a static or equilibrium basis.

The prevalence of movement

It is not the intention of this chapter to argue in detail and at length the reasons for assuming that societies are dynamic rather than static. Most conventional sociologists assume that societies possess an organic unity and leave it at that. Some do not even trouble to mention their assumption but start with their theoretical superstructures as if they have no conceptual basis. It is not possible here to be as confident and nonchalant as that for a variety of reasons. The confidence of conventional theorists has elements of arrogance and indifference and comes more from being in the majority, on the side of authority, in support of the *status quo*, than from the explanatory usefulness of their theories. They see little need to give reasons for their assumptions. The nonconformists are in a wholly different position. They must explain; their explanations have to meet the highest standards of precision set by the conformists. They have to set out to convince by reason and argument, for they can offer none of the rewards which conformity brings. Moreover, as a part of the case against conventional explanations is that they do not sufficiently relate to reality, the alternative explanation has to show that it does not have a similar defect. This can only be done by illustration. Something, therefore, has to be said about the alternative assumption to organic unity. But it will be said briefly because the main purpose of this section is to discuss the consequences of making such an assumption.

The existence of movement in societies which results in social change is an empirically and historically verifiable fact. All societies analysed through the various disciplines which constitute the social sciences have shown evidence of movement. There is historical evidence of qualitative changes in the nature of societies. There has been a movement from feudal to industrial societies, from slave societies to feudal societies, from subsistence societies to industrial societies and from semi-feudal to socialist societies. This is so well known that it is unnecessary to document it here. The transition from subsistence tribal activities to industrial activities in tropical Africa has been observed and recorded during the last twenty or so years. Virtually every book about tropical Africa deals with movement in one form or another. Indeed the transition there is so compressed in terms of time and so intense in its impact that it is virtually visible. Within industry in general and organizations in particular movement has been recorded in a variety of dimensions: in size, measured by numbers employed, output per man hour, aggregate output, profitability and total assets; in methods of production; in methods of administration and in the nature and spread of ownership. Organizations have grown larger, more administratively complex, more technological. The occupational composition of work forces has altered; hand skills have either been displaced by machine skills or so diluted by them that old skills are disappearing and new ones are emerging. No matter what aspect is observed or from what occupational position the observations are made, the existence of movement cannot be denied. It takes place between employers, between employers and employees, between employees of different skills and grades, between employees and machines. Moreover it can be seen that movement in all these spheres is not an isolated, discontinuous phenomenon, peripheral to the main activities but is central and pervasive in the short as well as the long run. There can be no doubt that the static society, involving no movement at all, is at the best an ideal type analytical category and at the worst a fantasy.

The interpretation of movement

However, while the existence of movement is fairly generally recognized, it is not interpreted in the same general manner. The conceptual approach of conventional sociologists does not prevent them from seeing movement but it does determine their perception of it as was shown earlier in this chapter. In so far as qualitative change is concerned, the perception of conventional sociologists is oddly inconsistent. It can be recognized that societies changed qualitatively in the past and that underdeveloped societies are changing qualitatively during the present. It is safe, involving no cost, to admit that societies and institutions possessed transient forms in the past, while it is reassuring for Western sociologists to note that the changes in underdeveloped countries are largely towards Western capitalist forms. It is quite a different matter when contemporary capitalist forms are being considered. Then change is viewed within its strict conceptual limits as the result of an interplay of forces within systems. The possibility of contemporary capitalism changing qualitatively as a result of the movement of its constituent elements is never considered.

The inconsistency, perhaps, is more apparent than real because where qualitative change is admitted it is usually viewed as an *ad hoc* phenomenon, as a once for all process, as an 'historical accident' or a 'fortuitous happening'. And where the changes are from the form of capitalist societies they are usually regarded as uncertain, unstable and likely to revert back to their previous capitalist form. In other words, an empiricist approach to qualitative change is adopted which gives it a quite specific meaning. Such situations are perceived as basically relatively static phenomena in the same way as are other situations. Even revolution is seen in this way. The sociologists look for observable evidence to provide explanations for qualitative change and they find it often in the form of unique personalities like Lenin, Mao Tse Tung and Fidel Castro, or Henry Ford, Lord Nuffield and other successful entrepreneurs.

It should be clear that the treatment of movement in an empiricist fashion is illogical. Once movement is recognized the possibility of it producing consequences which lead to further movement must be admitted. Once the existence of continuous movement, or causally related movements, is entertained it would be rashly unscientific not to admit the possibility of qualitative change. Even, as was stated earlier, where movement is seen as a series of additions it would be incautious not to consider that the variables might alter their form in the process. In the interests of scientific analysis, therefore, all social situations should be treated as temporary phenomena, as stages in a never-ending process. This very simple precautionary measure, however, would involve the complete rejection of the systems analysis approach in the social sciences.

Qualitative change, to be consistent with observable reality, must entail a transformation process, something which in systems analysis terms involves the destruction of boundaries. It means an alteration in the essential qualities and primary preconditions for a social phenomenon. It is frequently described as a structural change, but this is only correct if one of two meanings is given to structure. As the place for a discussion of structure is in the next chapter, an elaboration of the meaning of qualitative change must wait till then. It is sufficient to note here that a qualitative change cannot be analysed unless it is assumed that systems do not have qualities of self-preservation and that the source of movement comes from within as well as without the systems; in other words, unless the basis of systems analysis is removed.

Once it is accepted that there is continuous movement in reality it is logical to talk of historical process. If movement in an organization is continuous its state at any one time must have a causal connection with its preceding states. Even if the movement is broken or interrupted, it is inconceivable to imagine it as having risen from completely different and new conditions each time, with no relationship with previous sources. Continuous movement is an historical process. Looking at situations historically, however, does not imply continuous movement. It is not the recognition of the value of historical data which is important but the interpretation of contemporary reality. There can be, and have been, many static histories written, where no continuously operating causal elements have been recognized. The views of history as a compilation of facts, as a series of fortuitous happenings, or as the acts of great men, are static in conception.[9]

Necessary and sufficient conditions
There is, moreover, a causal relationship between levels of social activity. This is implied in the use of necessary and sufficient conditions as analytical tools. The direction of movement is not simply horizontally through time-related stages. It would be impossible to conceive of this in real terms. Movement is a pervasive factor which may be contained but not on predetermined courses. It can go in all directions. For the purpose of causal analysis its most significant direction is a vertical one stemming from the necessary conditions of whatever phenomenon is under examination. A business organization arises because certain conditions exist which make it possible that it will. Given the private ownership of the means of production; given the free combination of these means for production purposes; given the stimulus for production both from subsistence needs and the desire to accumulate, then some organization of production is inevitable. The necessary conditions, however, give no idea about the forms of organizational activity, about the timing of their occurrence, or about their rate of development. All these factors are determined by what are described as sufficient conditions, that is, conditions which are sufficient to cause organizations to be as they are. These conditions are not hidden from view; they can be identified and assessed in the environments of organizations. They comprise anything which activates and guides the necessary conditions. The necessary condition for trade union organizations is the buying and selling of labour power on the open market. But this does not cause unions to be formed. Employees may be prevented from organizing for political reasons as they have been under dictatorships or colonial regimes. They may be persuaded not to organize because they do not recognize the need to do so. There may be a number of other

factors preventing organization. All the factors account for the precise forms, shapes and sizes of union organizations and exist in the immediate environments of unions.

What is being said, in effect, is that organizations are causally related to their previous states and both to hidden and observable features of their environments. They are causally related to their past states; they arise from common necessary conditions and are, therefore, related to each other; and they are causally related to their immediate observable environments for it is there that the sufficient conditions for organizations exist. Once organizations arise and take shape they do not sever themselves from their bases, for an alteration in their necessary conditions will produce a qualitative change in their form; equally, organizations remain causally related to their immediate environments and respond to changes in it. In other words, organizations are never protected from the forces which give rise to them and determine their actual shape and methods.

The question of autonomy and systems analysis

This raises an immediate question concerning the autonomy of organizations. How autonomous are organizations? Systems analysis provides for the complete autonomy of any system or subsystem. Clearly it would be untenable to presume complete autonomy. If it is accepted that social forces in some way effect qualitative changes then there cannot be boundaries around systems which isolate and insulate them. There may be boundaries of kinds but none which cannot be penetrated or permeated. Organizations cannot preserve themselves against all odds. But once the ability of an organization to maintain itself is questioned the possibility of it having no sociologically significant boundaries must be considered. An organization which has complete autonomy is a system, but what is it if it has less than complete autonomy? Is it three-quarters of a system or half a system or no system at all? What kind of system is less than a complete one? It is possible to postulate the existence of systems *a priori* as Talcott Parsons does but systems with degrees of autonomy cannot be postulated because there are an infinite number. It would be of no analytical value to assume systems with variations ranging from zero to infinity and it would be nonsense to construct an analysis on the assumption of a given degree of autonomy of an organization in its environment. The proof of degrees of autonomy must be a matter for empirical investigation, for it will depend on the relationship between the pressures for movement and the institutionalized resistance to movement and this cannot be stipulated *a priori*. The point is then that once it is accepted that organizations do not have immutable forms the concept of systems ceases to be of analytical use, for the nature of their existence, even their existence itself, becomes a matter for empirical investigation. A concept which is central to a theory must be completely unambiguous in its meaning. It was for this reason that Parsons, Merton and Selznick went to such lengths to ensure that the integrity of systems was preserved. The concept of system is not un-ambiguous; it is indeterminate and should therefore be dropped from the vocabulary of sociologists. It would, of course, take with it the battery of analytical tools which are based on it.

The question of autonomy can be put differently: to what extent is an organization a part of its environment, or to what extent are the properties of an environment present in an organization in that environment? Clearly, when the concept of system is discarded the relationship between an organization and its environment, or thing and process, ceases to be clear-cut. If it is assumed that pressures from environments can penetrate organizations it is possible that the essential qualities in each will be similar. If it is accepted that the shapes or forms of organizations can be altered it follows that there must be a sufficiently close similarity between organizations and their environments to permit an overlapping or absorp-tion of one by the other. The point has to be considered that while organizations are observably different from other social relationships the difference is not of vital sociological significance but represents a par-ticular arrangement of elements which are common to them all — which are common to organizations and their environments.

To pose the issue as one where organizations are reacting to and on their environments is a simplification of social reality. The environments of organizations consist of a variety of social relationships which have observably distinct characteristics. These relationships have causal relations with their environments, of which organizations are a part. They therefore react on and to organizational pressures. They have, moreover, basic qualities in common with organizations because they all bear the same relationship to a common environment. The total environment, that is one comprising organizations, appears as a network of social relationships in which there is a perpetual process of interaction involving encroachment and absorption. It is an environment with no definable limits and no rigid internal demarcations. This conception of the reality of environment follows logically from the generalized view that social reality is pervaded by movement.

The issue which is raised involves creating an analytical distinction between entity and process. If the entity and the situation in which it operates and which provides it with momentum possess similar or identical properties then the question of identifying the entity but at the same time seeing it as a process, that is, dynamically, is vital for the analysis. The task cannot be done phenomenologically for only the entity is observed and, even then not the properties themselves but some visible social manifestations of them. The task can be helped, however, by raising some questions. First, what properties do organizations have in common with their environments? Second, in what way are organizations distinguished from both their environments in general and other arrangements of social relationships in particular? Third, what is the meaning of organizational autonomy in this context? And, lastly, what is the source of movement in organizations and the mechanism through which it passes? The answers to these questions constitute a theoretical approach to organizations which is both wholly distinct from and preferable to that of systems analysis.

Middle-range theories

It must be made clear that the theory which follows is not an organization theory. That is, it has no peculiarities which make it especially relevant for organizations rather than other social phenomena. It is not a middle-range theory, nor can it be. A middle-range theory according to Merton,

is intermediate to general theories of social systems which are too remote from particular classes of social behaviour, organization and change to account for what is observed and to those detailed orderly descriptions of particulars that are not generalized at all. . . . Middle-range theories deal with delimited aspects of social phenomena, as is indicated by their labels. One speaks of a theory of reference groups, of social mobility, of role-conflict and of the formation of social norms just as one speaks of a theory of prices, a germ theory of disease or a kinetic theory of gases.[10]

A middle-range theory implies that social behaviour can be compartmentalized in such a sociologically meaningful way as to warrant the use of a distinctive set of analytical tools for each compartment. In other words, it involves the use of systems and all that this implies for methodology. Indeed middle-range theories constitute models, marginally distinguished from each other, within the general theory of social systems.[11]

An assumption underlying middle-range theories is that there are no structural determinants of movement which are common to different aspects of social behaviour. Such an assumption is inconsistent with the basis of a dynamic theory which is that social reality is a continually moving phenomenon. It is possible, of course, to conceive of movement creating forces arising from each and every system without the forces in one system necessarily having anything structurally and causally in common with those in any other system, but it would involve making the highly unrealistic assumption about social reality that somehow, somewhere, in some form, every situation invariably has its own peculiar, specific, source of momentum. This assumption would lead straight back to empiricism, for nothing could be said about a situation until it had been examined.

The theory outlined here is based on the assumption that social reality is a dynamic phenomenon in the sense described earlier. This assumption requires that there should be structural connections between parts of the whole irrespective of any superstructural differences which may exist within it. It would be illogical to assume that social reality in general is dynamic without making the supporting assumption that the source of movement is a common one. In other words, a dynamic analysis cannot proceed unless it is recognized that social behaviour in general has common basic structural determinants. There are, of course, empirically verifiable differences between aspects of social behaviour, but, for the reason given above, these differences do not and cannot contain the sources of movement. An analysis which concentrates on observable differences, as do middle-range theories, is classificatory and not causal. It follows that a dynamic analysis must be a general one, capable of application in any social situation. There is a world of methodological difference between a middle-range theory and a theory capable of analysing middle-range situations. The difference represents two opposite and irreconcilable world views of social reality.

Notes

1. I debated with myself and with Dan Muir for some time before deciding to use the term Movement rather than Motion. 'Motion' is strictly more appropriate because it is unambiguous and refers to process, which I want to emphasize, but it is used mainly in physics and is not a term which figures commonly in everyday usage. Movement is more generally recognized though it can mean other things too, and it is used in a social context. So, despite its more ambiguous nature I chose to discuss Movement. I did not, moreover, want to borrow a term from physics and perhaps give the impression that I was thereby introducing precision into my analysis. 'Movement' as it is used here means the process of moving as it affects social situations and as ordinary people conceive of it through their experiences.

2. W. H. Starbuck, ed., *Organizational Growth and Development*, Penguin Modern Management Readings, Penguin Books, 1971.

3. See chapter 8 for an examination of structure.

4. Mason Haire, ed., *Modern Organization Theory*, Wiley, 1964, p. 13.

5. See *The Dictionary of Social Sciences*, ed. Julius Gould and W. L.

Kolb, Tavistock, 1964, pp. 647–8, for definitions of social change by Tom Burns.

6. Peter M. Blau, *Dynamics of Bureaucracy*, Cambridge University Press, 1955.

7. Etzioni, *Complex Organizations*, pp. 14, 297ff.

8. Talcott Parsons was meticulous in his definitions and, whatever his methodological failings, was not in this group.

9. See the argument of E. H. Carr in *What is History?*, Macmillan, 1961.

10. R. K. Merton, *On Theoretical Sociology*, The Free Press, New York, 1967, pp. 39–40.

11. On this Merton says: '. . . middle-range theories have not been logically *derived* from a single all-embracing theory, of social systems, though once developed they may be consistent with one', *ibid.*, p. 41.

8

The concept of structure

Types of dogmatism

It will be recalled that there are four main objections to using systems analysis for the study of organizations. It is unable to analyse movement, hence qualitative change in organizations. Because of this it gives misleading priority to equilibrating factors even in its categorization and description of organizational behaviour. It gives 'immutable' qualities to existing organizational forms such as the distribution of power and, therefore, provides them with a metaphysical basis. And, lastly, it introduces simplifying but distorting assumptions into the analysis, such as rational behaviour, perfect knowledge and a perfect mobility of resources which are never subsequently removed and which take on idealized characteristics. Organizations are assumed to have a pyramidal shape, a hierarchical distribution of power and unimpeded qualities for achieving rationality before any analysis of them is commenced. Like the economist's model of perfect competition this constitutes an idealized form of reality into which empirical data is compressed. In so far as the data does not fit, an examination is made to discover the impediments, the factors causing imperfections, frictions, tensions and suchlike qualities. For this reason attention is always directed to decision-making and communications and because these become the main areas of analysis it is assumed that they contain the basic problems. In other words, the attempts to fit empirical data into a preconceived idealized form leads inevitably to the conclusion that the source of all major difficulties for organizations lies in decision-making and communications. It is only one step from this to conceive of organizations as communication networks and to represent them on charts.

Built-in assumptions about reality appear in all variants of systems analysis from the extreme of empiricism to that of abstract structural functionalism. In all cases the data can tell only as much as the framework into which it is fitted permits. There are many illustrations of the procrustean methods of conventional sociologists; of unscientific dogmatism which allows the social scientist complete latitude over the use of empirical evidence so long as the form of reality he initially postulates is left intact.

Dialectical materialism is not dogmatic in this sense. It is based on the notion that reality is dynamic therefore it assumes nothing in reality as given; boundaries are not fixed, forms are not predetermined, and it neither makes stipulations about the distribution of power nor requires simplifying assumptions concerning the rationality of behaviour and the mobility of resources. Dialectical materialism is dogmatic about method and not form. Given the method, it is strictly empirical and from an analytical point of view this is greatly preferable to the dogmatism of systems analysis. It does not distort and manipulate reality and allows empirical data to represent itself largely as it is in situations.

Dialectical materialism does not, of course, lead to the truth. It consists of a set of working hypotheses which, given the present state of scientific method in the social sciences, assist in understanding social reality more effectively than any known alternative method. This point was put by Lenin in 1894 when he discussed the meaning of Marxism:

Now, since the appearance of Capital *— the materialist conception of history is no longer a hypothesis, but a scientifically proven proposition. And until we get some other attempt to give a scientific explanation of the functioning and development of some formation of society — formation of society, mind you, and not the way of life of some country or people, or even class, etc. — another attempt just as capable of introducing order into 'pertinent facts' as materialism is, that is just as capable of presenting a living picture of a definite formation while giving it a strictly scientific explanation — until then the materialist conception of history will be a synonym for social science.*[1]

On strictly methodological grounds there is no reason why this method should not be preferred to systems analysis. There are, however, strong political grounds for its rejection.

The political implications of theories

Dialectical materialism presupposes that forms change and that the present, therefore, is in all respects a passing phase. Those who regard the present with all its institutional arrangements, its property and wealth distribution and its grossly unequal allocation of power, as permanent, do not wish to analyse it as if it were temporary. They do not wish it to be seen by others as a temporary, historically transient phenomenon. Those who hold power in the present regard the conception of the present as a passing phase, as a challenge to their position, as an exposure of their inability to hold power permanently, and as a question, therefore, of the legitimacy of their claim to hold power at all. They demand a conceptual approach which rationalizes the notion that the present is permanent. Conventional sociological theory satisfies this demand. It is still as Karl Marx stated in volume I of *Capital* when he wrote that political economy remains within the bounds of the bourgeois horizon in that 'the capitalist regime is looked upon as the absolutely final form of social production, instead of as a passing historical phase of its evolution'.[2] Organizations are faithful reflections of the power system; they are microcosms of the total capitalist situation and they are regarded by those who are in control, the owners of the means of production, as having the same quality of immutability as capitalism itself. That part of conventional sociological theory, therefore, which is devoted to organizations and treats the distribution of power in organization as immutable contributes to the theoretical rationalization of the present. For this reason it is politically acceptable in general.

The political implications of social theories are important in explaining their acceptance or rejection, but they are rarely made explicit in discussions about the relative merits of one theory compared with another. When anyone criticizes dialectical materialism it is for its alleged dogmatism, its attributed unreality, its mysticism or its lack of logic. This may be done in all sincerity. Social scientists may believe that they are being scrupulously objective when they attack dialectical materialism for one reason or another, or when they ignore it for being irrelevant. They would consider it to be an affront to their academic integrity to be accused of subordinating scientific accuracy to political considerations. But if it can be shown that dialectical materialism is a superior method of explaining social reality, then this is precisely what they are doing. In order then to expose the political factors which buttress conventional sociological theory the scientific superiority of dialectical materialism has to be demonstrated.

This is not an easy task for two reasons. First, the sheer weight of intellectual opposition to dialectical materialism is enormous. In 1908, Lenin, wrote that

Anyone in the least acquainted with philosophical literature must know that scarcely a single contemporary professor of philosophy (or of theology) can be found who is not directly or indirectly engaged in refuting materialism. They have declared materialism refuted a thousand times, yet are continuing to refute it for the thousand and first time.[3]

The refutations have continued and have been taken up by economists, sociologists and political scientists. Major works such as K. R. Popper's *The Open Society*, and many lesser ones, have been devoted to the task. In

England alone there is a long list of illustrious academic names involved in the defence of conventional social analysis. The need for this defence, however, has arisen more from the inadequacy of conventional analysis than from the challenge of dialectical materialism. The second reason follows from this point. Dialectical materialism has not been developed to deal with micro-situations. It has not been refined to enable it to compete with systems analysis over the range of issues dealt with by middle-range models. Dialectical materialism has been left much as Lenin left it, conceptually sound but equipped mainly to explain macro-level structural change.

Materialism and dialectics

Dialectical materialism is about the source of social movement and the manner of its transmission. The twin hypotheses are indispensable for a dynamic theory. The use of materialism by itself does not make a theory dynamic as some sociologists would have us believe. It is not enough to state that economic factors must be taken into account or even given priority. It is possible to substitute 'materialist oriented action' for 'value oriented action' within the framework of systems analysis without affecting its static qualities at all. Indeed, this is what is sometimes done by empiricists. The result is mechanical materialism. Those who accept the causal significance of materialism but reject dialectics as 'Hegelian nonsense' are simply paying lip-service to causal analysis. On the other hand, the dialectical process without its materialist basis is pure Hegelianism. It is metaphysical. It is at its best idealism and at its worst mysticism.

Engels succinctly exposed the essential defects of Hegelian dialectics in *Anti-Duhring*:

Hegel was an idealist, that is to say, the thoughts within his mind were to him not the more or less abstract images of real things and processes, but, on the contrary, things and their development were to him only the images made real of the 'Idea' existing somewhere or other already before the world existed. This mode of thought placed everything on its head and completely reversed the real connections of things in the world. . . . The Hegelian system as such was a colossal miscarriage. . . . It suffered, in fact, from an internal and insoluble contradiction. On the one hand, its basic assumption was the historical outlook, that human history is a process of evolution, which by its very nature cannot find intellectual finality in the discovery of any so-called absolute truth; but on the other hand, it laid claim to being the very sum-total of precisely this absolute truth. A system of natural and historical knowledge which is all-embracing and final for all time is in contradiction to the fundamental laws of dialectical thinking.[4]

In his preface to the second edition of *Anti-Duhring*, Engels wrote that 'Marx and I were pretty well the only people to rescue conscious dialectics from German idealist philosophy and apply it in the materialist conception of nature and history'.[5] And so they were.

The rescue operation was not a straightforward one. The Hegelian dialectic was not applied in its original form for the application to materialism changed its character, or, as Garaudy stated, reversed it:

Marx broke with Hegelian dogmatism in passing from idealism to material-ism by the path of practice. Because of the very fact that practice applies to the real world, that it starts from the real world and tries to account for it — and not to superimpose itself a priori *on the world — dialectics is necessarily always wide open and incompleted. . . . To reverse 'the cage of the Hegelian idea' as Marx said, was not enough. To reverse it was still to remain inside it. Materialism made it possible to get out of it, i.e. not only to reverse it, but to smash it and emerge into the real world where reality is continuously generated.*[6]

The application of materialism to dialectics was essential for the utility of both.

Dialectical materialism provides the conceptual framework for a dynamic sociological theory. In the process of its formulation the two concepts have to be separated and each has to be elaborated, but it should be remembered that the separation is purely for explanatory convenience. Neither concept has any use without the other in the context of a dynamic theory.

Materialism

Every sociological theory starts from an explicit or implicit assumption about causality. Structural functionalists assume that the primary source of action is values; Etzioni gives an *a priori* ranking of equality to 'coercion, economic assets and normative values'; Weber located the source of action in 'systems of domination' which he described as charismatic, traditional and legal, while empiricists refrain from specifying any order of priority in a similar manner to Etzioni. Empiricists prefer to wait until they have seen the situation. The lack or denial of a specification is no less an assumption about causality than an expressly stated assumption. Every attempt at social explanation inevitably rests on a belief about causality.

The source of action in dialectical materialism is located in materialism. This, as in structural functionalism, is primarily a monocausal explanation, but it is a complete rejection of the structural functionalist priority. Materialism means that social action is primarily determined by economic factors, but it is not plain, straightforward mechanistic economic

determinism. The classical approach to organizations, described in chapter
3, rests on a simple mechanistic economic determinism in that it assumes
that participants are motivated by the desire to maximize their economic
returns measured in either profit or income. Economic determinism in this
sense is a simplifying assumption with an ideological basis. It makes
possible the construction of an analytical model which is consistent with
the preservation of capitalist societies. This is not the way in which
materialism is used here.

Materialism locates the source of all movement. Its classical definition
was given by Karl Marx in his 1859 preface to *A Contribution to the
Critique of Political Economy.* Both Friedrich Engels and Rosa Luxemburg made subsequent clarifying statements but without modifying Marx's
definition. The intention here is to refine the classical definition and then
to categorize it for analytical purposes.

The following statement by Marx explains the meaning of materialism.

*In the social production which men carry on they enter into definite rela-
tions that are indispensable and independent of their will; these relations
of production correspond to a definite stage of development of their
material forces of production. The sum total of these relations of production constitutes the economic structure of society — the real foundation,
on which rises a legal and political superstructure and to which correspond
definite forms of social consciousness. The mode of production in material
life determines the social, political and intellectual life processes in general.
It is not the consciousness of men that determines their being, but, on the
contrary, their social being that determines their consciousness.* [7]

Causal priority is given here to the economic structure which determines
the superstructure. The structure and superstructure comprise the social
being of people and determine their consciousness.

There should really have been no need for clarification. Marx's statement in no sense implies economic determinism nor does it involve a
mechanistic process. Nevertheless Engels felt impelled to counter misinterpretations. In a letter to Joseph Bloch in 1890 he wrote:

*According to the materialist conception of history the determining
element in history is* ultimately *the production and reproduction in real
life. More than this neither Marx nor I have ever asserted. Hence if somebody twists this into the statement that the economic element is the* only
*determining one, he transforms it into a meaningless, abstract and absurd
phrase. The economic situation is the basis, but the various elements of the
superstructure — political forms of the class struggle and its consequences,
constitutions established by the victorious class after a successful battle,*

etc. — forms of law — and then even the reflexes of all these actual struggles in the brains of the combatants: political, legal, philosophical theories, religious ideas and their further development into systems of dogma — also exercise their influence upon the course of the historical struggles and in many cases preponderate in determining their form. . . . We make our own history, but in the first place under very definite presuppositions and conditions. Among these the economic ones are finally decisive. But the political, etc., ones and indeed even the traditions which haunt human minds, also play a part, although not the decisive one.[8]

Rosa Luxemburg contributed to the debate by stating that 'even if there is undoubtedly a continuous reciprocal influence between political and economic factors in social development, the economic factor is still the determining and decisive one in the last analysis'. But, she added, those materialists who affirm that economic development goes along the tracks of history like a locomotive dragging politics and ideology, etc., behind it like so many passive railway carriages, are mistaken in their conception of the method.[9]

The meaning Marx, Engels and Luxemburg gave to materialism enabled it to serve as a broad basis for analysis in preference to idealism, mystification and superstition. It rooted analysis in concrete reality. It enabled analyses of social phenomena to be empirical in the sense that they concerned practice as it was happening and not practice which was modified, abstracted or mystified to fit a preconceived theoretical framework. This constituted an enormous improvement. However, materialism as it has been stated so far is only a basis for social analysis. It is too imprecise for many analytical purposes. It has suffered from earlier attempts at clarification without accompanying specification. For instance, although there may have been a need for a clarification of Marx's definition when both Engels and Luxemburg wrote, the way in which it was done led to further misinterpretation. The emphasis in Engels's letter to Bloch on the causal significance of economic factors led to a variety of interpretations of the word 'ultimately'. The word was seen to cover any time span and provided a justification for neglecting economic factors altogether in what might be described as short-run and superstructural situations. In other words, economic factors were seen to have causal priority only in the ultimate. Rosa Luxemburg's analogy with the train was intended to show that there was not a simple mechanical relationship between structural and superstructural phenomena but it gave no guidance about the complexity of the relationship. When, for instance, does the motive force come from a 'non-economic' source? In what situations do 'non-economic' factors have autonomy in causal terms? What degrees of autonomy may these factors have and in what sense can they be evaluated? Can the term 'ultimately' be used in an empiricist fashion to refer to any time span or does it have some other meaning such as 'eventually in any situation'? These questions raise the whole issue concerning the causal relationship between economic, sociological and psychological phenomena and it would have been most unlikely that Engels and Luxemburg could have provided the answers before separate social science disciplines had developed. But they did enough with the tools they had and it should not be necessary to provide excuses for what they did not do because they could not.

The discussion about materialism has too often been conducted by philosophers, as has also been the case with dialectics. Consequently there have been few attempts to improve its utility as an analytical tool, to break it down into recognizable, manageable components. It was an enormous step to locate the source of behaviour in materialism, but it was only a first step. Without further explanation it is as amorphous a term as environment. To say, for example, that behaviour is environmentally determined is to say no more than that a whole range of disparate variables located in environments is the source. The discussion which showed that the variables are not of equal causal weight took the analytical potential further. This was also the case with the debate about the mechanical application of the economic variable.

The principle hypothesis in materialism is that economic factors are the *primary*, not just ultimate, determinants of social behaviour and that this variable is the independent one in the equation. In other words, in any situation which might be examined the first question to ask is 'what is the economic context?' The economic context, of course, may be a vastly complex one which may need to be simplified before it can assist analysis. In any event its main causal elements need to be identified. The second question concerns the identity of the non-economic context of the situation. It is necessary to be able to describe its substance. Lastly, a number of questions arise about the causal relationship between the two contexts. The non-economic context is derived from the economic one. This follows from the initial premise in materialism. But it is not a mechanical one-way relationship; it may in fact appear to be vague, or it may cover such a long time span that the relationship cannot be identified. When can autonomy be given to non-economic factors, if at all? The questions investigators into organizations need to answer are what are the economic and non-economic elements in organizations and their contexts and what relationships do they have? Help in this matter has been given by the use of the concepts structure and superstructure as analytical devices.

Global structuralism

The term *structure* is used frequently without being given a clear meaning.

In the context of sociological analysis it has been given two main meanings. Jean Piaget described it first as 'Global' structuralism.[10] This, Piaget stated, 'holds to systems of observable relations and interactions, which are regarded as sufficient unto themselves.[11] The observable social phenomena, to which global structuralism refers, possess a form which is specified in the meaning which he gives to structure itself.

As a first approximation we may say that a structure is a system of transformations. In as much as it is a system and not a mere collection of elements and their properties, these transformations involve laws: the structure is preserved or enriched by the interplay of its transformation laws, which never yield results external to the system nor employ elements that are external to it. In short, the notion of structure is comprised of three key ideas: the idea of wholeness, the idea of transformation, and the idea of self-regulation.[12]

Shorter still, Piaget was describing a system and the whole of his examination of structuralism was related to systems analysis. He observed that in Anglo-Saxon countries structure tended 'to be reserved for observable relations and interactions'[13] and showed by his scant treatment of this meaning that it held no interest for him.

Raymond Boudon explained in some detail why global structuralism should be passed over so quickly by the analysts of structuralism.[14] For Boudon, global structuralism was described as 'an intentional definition' of structure. It was purely terminological concerned with phenomenal descriptions and as such it held no special significance because the word structure could be replaced by another word without any ill effect. There is no necessity to use the term structure for groups or groupings or any form of social relationships in order to denote their internal, mutually inter-dependent characteristics. The words organization or form could equally well be used except that there may be a convenience in using a term which 'in its most common meaning . . . normally implies the associations of "structure-system of relationships", "structure-totality", etc.'. The fact that organisms, situations or behaviour patterns are described as structures proves only 'that these elements and entities are, as has long been known, interdependent, that the organism is a whole and that this whole is more than the sum of its parts. . . . Whoever says "structure" means "whole, irreducible to the sum of its parts".'[15]

In its global meaning structure does not refer to any specific social phenomena. The range of items to which it is applied is left to the analyst, without, by and large, guidance even from its 'systems' connotation. It is thus a loosely used descriptive term without any analytical value. Piaget's obvious dismissal of global structuralism is fully justified. In most sociological works the term does not warrant a definition; it has an implied meaning, perhaps with commonsense attributes. Structure was used in this sense by Tom Burns and G. M. Stalker in *The Management of Innovation*.[16] The authors wrote about 'status structure', 'internal structure' and 'management structure' without defining the term but implying that it meant, say, framework. The term structure cropped up frequently in *The Theory of Organizations* by David Silverman. There are bureaucratic structures, organization structures, formal and informal structures. Organization structure appeared to refer to observable phenomena in organizations such as technology, nature of authority and promotion opportunities.[17] Here it could mean form or characteristics. Even Sherman Krupp in *Pattern in Organization Analysis* seemed to regard the structure of an organization as comprising tangible things such as technology, aimed at practical objectives such as efficiency and control.[18] When he came to explain 'the structure of a theory' he referred to its technology: 'Structure will be used as a catch-all term for analogies, assumptions, behaviour equations, conceptual devices, constants, final goals, fixed points, givens, inductive framework, intermediate goals, laws, limits, parameters, philosophic preferences' and suchlike.[19] The term obviously had no analytical significance for Krupp. For the editors of *A Dictionary of the Social Sciences* it had no relevance at all for it received no mention. But why bother with a term which is simply one of a number of alternatives?

Analytic structuralism
The second meaning of the term structure preoccupied Piaget and Boudon in their examinations of structuralism. This was described by Piaget as 'analytic' structuralism and was put by Boudon in the context of an 'operative' definition. Boudon stated that the structural description (meaning analytic structuralism) of an object contrasts 'with its phenomenal description, as *essence* does with *appearance*. Structural analysis does show as *coherent* the facts which appear incoherent to the outside observer'.[20] Piaget gave a similar meaning when he stated that

the peculiarity of authentic (analytic) structuralism is that it seeks to explain . . . empirical systems by postulating 'deep' structures from which the former are in some manner derivable. Since structures in this sense of the word are ultimately logicomathematical models of the observed social relations, they do not themselves belong to the realm of fact. This means, among other things, as Lévi-Strauss points out repeatedly, that the individual members of the group under study are unaware of the structural model in terms of which the anthropologist interprets constellations of social relations.[21]

Both Boudon and Piaget conceive of analytic structuralism as a form of causal analysis. The latter stated that 'the search for "deep" structures is a direct consequence of the interest in the details of transformation laws'.[22] However, in each case the ability of structuralism to explain is contained within the rigid limits imposed by the initial qualities attributed to structure. Piaget is much more explicit on this point than is Boudon. As was stated earlier a structure for Piaget was a self-regulating system and this led him to regard the structuralism in Parsonsian structural-functionalism as analytic. Boudon attempted to avoid defining structure; he was critical of Piaget's approach on the grounds that 'the concept of structure cannot be inductively defined'[23] and he relied on Lévi-Strauss to explain why. He added that when analysing the *content* of structure, as Piaget did:

It is in some ways indistinguishable from its associations. *However this is no longer the case when reference is made to the* contexts *in which it occurs. Finally then, rather than analysing the content of the concept of structure − a content which is rather banal and crude − it is necessary to investigate the role played by this concept in the contexts in which it appears. . . . Thus it becomes a question not of determining the elements common to all definitions of the word 'structure' which have been pro-pounded − such a procedure would not take one much further than the definitions by Piaget or Flament quoted earlier − but of analysing the function of the concept of structure in the scientific vocabulary of the authors who use it.*[24]

However, what Boudon ignores is that the authors who use analytic structuralism themselves attribute qualities to structure and these happen to be those which Piaget defines.

The consequence is that both Piaget and Boudon deal with the same authors, principally Claude Lévi-Strauss and Noam Chomsky, and exclude a serious consideration of authors, such as Marx and Engels and others since who have treated structure in different conceptual terms. Piaget devoted a chapter to 'Structuralism and philosophy' in which he briefly discussed the dialectic through the work of Jean Paul Sartre, Louis Althusser and Maurice Godelier, but this was peripheral to his main analysis and was included only because structuralism as he defined it 'devalues genesis, history, and function or even the very activity of the subject itself'. He was interested in the conflict between structuralism and 'the central tenets of dialectical modes of thought'. There is no mention at all in Boudon's work of Marx or any subsequent Marxist, despite the fact that, as Maurice Godelier stated,

When Marx assumes that structure is not to be confused with visible

relations and explains their hidden logic, he inaugurates the modern struc-
turalist tradition. And he is fully in accord with this tradition when he
proposes the priority of the study of structures over that of their genesis
and evolution. [27]

Boudon was correct to reject Piaget's inductive definition but the limitations of his own perception led him right back to Piaget's position, namely
that structure is conceived in static terms – in the terms set by systems
analysis which has been the subject of criticism throughout this book and
in terms, therefore, which prevent analyses of the transformation of
structures themselves.

Hidden structures

The identification of hidden factors with causal consequences for visible
social relations, which was highlighted by the work of Levi-Strauss, was a
commonplace feature in the works of Marx and Engels. Structure was
treated as the *basis* which gave rise to the superstructure. Causal analysis
was dependent on an understanding of the dialectical relationship between
structure or basis and superstructure. An analysis which treated the two as
separate entities, which focused its exclusive attention on one or the other,
was bound to be static and ahistorical in conception. The structuralists
who were the concern of Piaget and Boudon were static structuralists
while those concerned with visible social relations, superstructures, were
also static analysts, irrespective of their use of the word structure. R. K.
Merton fell squarely in this second category for he used structure to refer
to superstructural phenomena. He stated that 'the description of the participants (and on-lookers) is in *structural* terms, that is, in terms of
locating these people in their inter-connected social statuses'. [28] Thus a
structural description was one made in terms of statuses and group
affiliations.

There is very little in the works of Marx which is strictly methodological
in the sense that it explains the conceptual approach which he used.
The famous *Preface to a Contribution to the Critique of Political
Economy* is his most important single theoretical explanation. A number
of theoretical asides appear in his work but in the main Marx's methodology has to be identified through his work on particular subjects. Much
the same could be said about Engels, except that as he lived so much
longer than Marx he was sometimes called on to explain the latter's
methodology. However Marx's practical use of theory neither disguised it
nor made it difficult to identify. To say that the absence of any analysis of
Marx's treatment of 'hidden' structures by Piaget and Boudon is an omis-
sion is a gross understatement. It constitutes an inexcusable distortion of
the examination of structuralism.

Because Marx illustrated his method through analyses of actual situations he never separately examined structure and superstructure. Even in the *Preface to a Contribution to the Critique of Political Economy* he wrote:

Just as our opinion of an individual is not based on what he thinks of himself, so can we not judge of . . . a period of transformation by its own consciousness; on the contrary, this consciousness must be explained rather from the contradictions of material life, from the existing conflict between the social productive forces and the relations of production.[29]

In *The Eighteen Brumaire of Louis Bonaparte* Marx described the visible political relations in France and then added: 'If one looks at the situation and the parties more closely, however, this superficial appearance, which veils the *class struggle* and the peculiar physiognomy of this period, disappears.' Then he proceeded to examine the basis of the situation.[30] In *Capital*, however, he was more explicit about 'hidden' structures. During a detailed examination of the value of labour power and wages, Marx stated that 'All labour appears as paid labour', though the value which labour created was in excess of the value of that labour. Some part of labour, therefore, must have been unpaid but this was concealed by the fact that labour had a price, was paid a wage: 'the money-relation conceals the unrequited labour of the wage-labourer'.[31] He went on:

Hence, we may understand the decisive importance of the transformation of value and price of labour itself. This phenomenal form, which makes the actual relation invisible, and, indeed, shows the direct opposite of that relation, forms the basis of all the juridical notions of both labourer and capitalist, of all the mystifications of the capitalistic mode of production, of all its illusions as to liberty, of all the apologetic shifts of the vulgar economists . . . history took a long time to get at the bottom of the mystery of wages.

He concluded the section by stating:

For the rest, in respect to the phenomenal form . . . as contrasted with the essential relations manifested therein . . . the same difference holds that holds in respect to all phenomena and their hidden substratum. The former appear directly and spontaneously as current modes of thought: the latter must first be discovered by science.[32]

This is a clear articulation of 'analytic' structuralism but, of course, with particular conceptual implications. In chapter 1 of *The German Ideology*, Marx and Engels outlined some of these implications. There they used the philosophy of Feuerbach to illustrate the material basis of ideology and in doing so stated that

The social structure and the State are continually evolving out of the life process of definite individuals, but of individuals, not as they may appear in their own or other people's imagination, but as they really are; i.e., as they operate, produce materially, and hence as they work under definite material limits, presuppositions and conditions independent of their will. [33]

The structure of individuals consists of those conditions which exist independent of their will and which are hidden from their observation.

The inability of Piaget, Boudon and others who concerned themselves with structuralism to identify and understand the methodological significance of Marx's use of structure did not afflict Georg Lukács, Antonio Gramschi and Louis Althusser. [34] The works of each of these writers have been constructed around the structure-superstructure relationship as employed by Marx and Engels. Gramschi in particular, followed by Lukács, used the method implicitly in the examination of immediate issues concerning organization, policy formulation and political action. However it is not necessary to quote from Marx in order to establish a dynamic version of structure. There is nothing of a biblical or quasibiblical status about Marx's work. The quotations, and the works from which they are derived, are important because they illustrate the use of a method. The method is prior to a particular use of it. Structure, therefore, does not get its meaning from Marx but from the conceptual approach he used. The rejection of inductive definitions, which Boudon proudly claims to have discovered and based his book on, is a basic tenet in dialectical materialism, was already discovered and had been much used. The analytical tools must assist the identification of variables through empirical investigations and they must help their categorization in terms of their causal significance. So an early step in the construction of a model for the analysis of any social situation is to ask, what is necessary for its existence? In other words, what are the factors without which the situation could not exist? The identification of these factors and their separation from others would be an obvious advantage because any change in them must have an impact on the situation under examination. The issue concerns that of introducing the criterion of distinction into causal analysis.

The factors which comprise the necessary conditions for a social situation are its basis and are, therefore, its structure. Thus the structure of anything consists of the necessary conditions for that thing. This meaning stipulates nothing about the phenomenology of a situation, for this can only be discovered by empirical investigation, though of course this in turn is guided by the basic conceptual approach. The necessary conditions have a core economic element. This meaning, moreover, conveys the notion of process; the necessary conditions cannot be understood, indeed have no meaning, apart from the thing itself. It is not necessary to resort to a search for the hidden elements, though the necessary conditions will be hidden in that they are not visible social phenomena. Thus the necessary conditions cannot be discovered by empirical investigations conducted like research projects and using customary methods of social investigation. They lie in concrete situations, but they are there by definition; that is, their identity depends on the manner in which a situation or phenomenon is perceived, and this in turn is determined by the conceptual approach used. Put differently, the necessary conditions are stipulated by the definition of whatever is under examination.

This point can be seen more clearly by looking at an example. Trade unionism is collective action by the sellers of labour power in order to protect and improve their living standards. The core of this definition is the selling of labour power. Others, such as consumers, slaves or peasants may protest and take action, but it is qualitatively different from that taken by employees because employees are in a unique objective economic situation which produces equally unique reactions. The selling of labour power implies the existence of a freedom to sell, a mechanism by which it can be priced and the presence of potential buyers. The necessary condition for trade unionism, therefore, is a free labour market. Wherever this condition is satisfied trade unionism can be expected to occur, but if it is not satisfied then trade unionism can *never* occur. It follows that the structure of trade unionism is the free labour market situation.

The free labour market situation, however, is not a homogeneous phenomenon. In reality there are many markets and where there are distinctive distinguishing characteristics it is possible to talk of different structures. With this type of analysis one proceeds from the visible to the invisible social relationships and the analysis starts with the visible ones. So if a particular form of trade unionism is under examination then it must be defined in more detail, thus leading to a more particular structure. The structure of a skilled manual workers' union would be the market for skilled manual workers. Each skilled manual workers' union may have special characteristics in that each one may organize a particular type of skilled worker, say printing compositors, silver engravers, panel beaters and so on. The necessary condition for trade unionism among printing compositors is a free market for the labour of printing compositors. These necessary conditions have their contexts, as the demand for and supply of types of labour power do not occur in abstraction. Thus the structure of printing trade unionism contains the production and sale of newspapers, books and all forms of printed matter, a level of technology and all the factors which make print as a saleable commodity possible. What is being stated, in effect, is that the necessary conditions for printing trade unionism themselves possess necessary conditions or that the structure of printing trade unionism possesses its own structure.

The structure of business organizations can be identified in a similar manner to that of trade union organizations. Business activity in a capitalist country is the production and sale of goods and services for private, as against public or general, financial profit. Thus the necessary conditions for business organizations are those which enable such activity to take place and are the private ownership and control of the means of production and the facilities, such as a price mechanism, for utilizing and transforming the means of production for private ends. The structure of a particular business organization is the private exploitation of the means of production in a particular commodity market. In other words, the structure of a particular business organization consists of that part of the commodity market in which it operates, for that is the environment which gives the organization its form. If that environment has special characteristics the organization will also possess them.

It is the case that the structure of any phenomenon is wider than the phenomenon itself for the necessary conditions for any thing must extend beyond it. The structure of a department or section of an organization must involve the organization itself along with aspects of its own environment. There are, therefore, causal connections between structures which are hierarchically placed. Moreover, a structure will contain elements of the one preceding it.

Economic and non-economic variables

This discussion raises important methodological questions. One is the relation between structure and superstructure. Gramschi emphasized the point when he wrote: 'It is the problem of the relations between structure and superstructure which must be accurately posed and resolved if the forces which are active in the history of a particular period are to be correctly analysed.' The matter is vital for the construction of a causal analytical model.

Superstructure is related to structure as a thing is related to its origins. A superstructure consists of the visible social relations to which a structure gives rise. Actual trade unions consisting of members, officials, regulating procedures, customs and practices, are superstructural phenomena which are causally connected to the structure of a free labour market. Actual, visible organizations with men, machines, regulations and everything else visibly identifiable, are also superstructural phenomena with their own structures. As every situation has its structure so every structure has its superstructure. Each structure comprises the necessary conditions for something and that something is superstructural.

In analytical terms the distinction between structure and superstructure is clear. In general in sociological research the subject of investigation is superstructural while the structure is only identifiable through the investigation. In objective terms, however, the distinction is clear only at the most macro of levels. Structure is only separate from superstructure in a completely objective way at the level of the mode of production. It is at this level that the foundation of a society exists. It constitutes the economic basis which determines a society's institutions and ideology and, in consequence, the ways of life of its people.[36] The mode of production, therefore, is primarily responsible for the main features of a society; it comprises the necessary conditions for the particular way in which that society is organized and is, therefore, its structure. For a society, then, the mode of production is the structure while everything else is superstructural. This is what is meant when it is said that all societies have an economic basis. The mode of production is an economic phenomenon.

The discussion and arguments among Marxists about the causal relationship between economic and non-economic factors have arisen because the distinction which can be made between structure and superstructure at the primary, macro level has been used for all other levels of activity. In other words, it has been assumed that structure is always economic in content and superstructure is not. This has led to the belief that materialism stipulates that economic factors determine social behaviour at all levels of activity while empirically it often appears that they do not have that priority. The recognition of this observable appearance led such people as Engels and Luxemburg to deny that there was a simple mechanical relationship between economic and non-economic factors. But, as stated earlier, such denials without detailed elaboration have led to confusion.

The plain fact is that it is only at the mode of production level that structure is economic and superstructure is non-economic or sociological. At every other level of social activity, structure, meaning remember the necessary conditions for whatever is under investigation, contains elements of the superstructure of a prior level of analysis. The laws relating to the organization of profit-making production activities are clearly derived from the capitalist mode of production and are, therefore, superstructural. But when a particular business organization is under investigation then clearly those laws form part of the necessary conditions for its existence and, hence, of its structure. The particular organization at that level of analysis is a superstructural phenomenon. In the examination of a section of production activities within an organization then the organization itself must be amongst the necessary conditions for those activities and, therefore, be a structural phenomenon.

All structures after the mode of production consist of both economic and sociological elements in varying proportions. There is no question of the economic always standing apart from and acting on the sociological. To pose such a dichotomy would be starkly inconsistent with reality and would therefore be analytically defective. Every situation would present the intractable problem of separating economic influences from the sociological ones and assessing their causal relationships and their relative significance for the situation under review. Of course, the primary assumption in materialism is that economic factors have greatest causal significance and, therefore, as stated earlier, the first question to ask in a given situation concerns its economic context. Moreover the economic basis of a society has a pervasive influence which spreads to the most micro of social situations.

The capitalist mode of production is production based on the private ownership of the means of production and conducted and distributed through a price mechanism. This mode entails the buying and selling of labour power. The buyers are the owners of the means of production and the sellers possess nothing but their labour power which they need to sell in order to subsist. The buyers and the sellers are in different power positions in the labour market and this difference is consolidated in the authority structure in industry and in the political sphere. There is no area of social life where the repercussions from owning or not owning the means of production are not felt. The power, the status and the privileges which derive from the ownership of the means of production put the owners into a special objective economic position and constitute them into a class. The non-owners who are compelled to sell their labour power are also in a common objective economic position which constitutes them into a class. The owners and the non-owners of the means of production are in their respective class positions by virtue of their relations to the productive process and irrespective of whether they recognize the fact or not.

The interests of the two classes are irrevocably and irremediably opposed. The conflict which ensues is a permanent pervasive factor in the determination of social behaviour. It is forever present though not necessarily always visible. It is present in both the environment of business organizations and the internal relationships which make up organizations, so that the influence of conflict must always be reckoned with in the analysis of organizations. If it is neglected or assumed out of existence then the nature of organizations becomes so distorted as to make the analysis incapable of explaining reality. The point is that no matter how far removed organizational activity may appear to be from the basic mode of production, it must always form part of the necessary conditions for action. The point, when put more generally, is that there is no situation at any level of analysis where it is irrelevant to ask about the class position of the participant. Thus class enters into the necessary conditions for all aspects of social behaviour in a capitalist society.

To return to the relationship between structures and superstructures, structures will always contain prime moving economic variables but, apart from the level where the mode of production entirely comprises the structure, they will also contain elements which are superstructural in other prior situations. Thus the issue of the interaction between economic and non-economic factors does not present an analytical problem. It is resolved by the analytical method. The questions raised at the beginning of this chapter can be answered. First in every situation apart from that where the mode of production is the sole variable, the motive force for action comes from a combination of economic and non-economic sources depending on how the necessary conditions for the situation are defined and identified. Second, non-economic factors can never have causal autonomy. And third, the term 'ultimately', used to indicate when economic factors have causal dominance, confuses and distorts and should be discarded.

Sufficient conditions

The next steps in understanding structure and superstructure as analytical aids is to introduce greater clarity into the category of superstructure. The first of these steps is to introduce the concept 'sufficient conditions'. An investigator of any social situation is presented with a complexity of variables, some of which are not visibly apparent. His prime task will be to identify those which have a causal significance. Having done this he will be able to categorize them into those which are necessary for the existence of the situation and those which are not. The hidden variables will enter into the necessary conditions, along, perhaps, with some visibly identifiable ones. The remainder — those which influence a situation but which are not necessary for its existence — are the sufficient conditions. These conditions determine the form in which the situation emerges, when it emerges, and its rate of development. They are concerned all the time with the visibly identifiable phenomena which are usually described as superstructure. When the sufficient conditions alone are examined then the analysis is static and, therefore, descriptive. They have a causal significance only when examined in relation to the necessary conditions.

The necessary conditions constitute the structure of a situation but its sufficient conditions are not equivalent to its superstructure. Sufficient conditions are, of course, superstructural phenomena; they belong to visible social relations but, in so far as it is possible to separate process from the thing itself, they arise out of an environment to act on a situation in it. However, just as the necessary conditions alter in their structure/ superstructural composition as the level of analysis changes, so the sufficient conditions also change. Any set of sufficient conditions exist only in relation to a particular situation or, to put it differently, every situation has its own sufficient conditions. Some of these conditions may be shared with other situations, but the total composition differs between situations for the precise form of each superstructural phenomenon is the product of its particular environment. The sufficient conditions are simply the most significant variables in any such environment. They determine the shape or form, the rate and direction of development of situations, though always, of course, within a context of what is already in existence. If a new structure emerges the sufficient conditions have the determining effect on the outcome; if a structure already exists a change in the sufficient conditions alters the forms. They can never have a final decisive influence for that rests with the necessary conditions.

Although there is a clear analytical distinction between necessary and sufficient conditions they do not have separate objective existences. In this respect they have the same relationship qualities as structures and super-structures. As the level of analysis moves from the macro to the micro level then the sufficient conditions for a situation are likely to include variables which become necessary conditions for less macro situations. In the contrary direction, necessary conditions become sufficient conditions. There is, therefore, always a dialectical relationship between variables in different situations, decreasing in intensity with a movement from the situation under scrutiny.

The contention made earlier that dialectical materialism is essentially an empirically based methodology can be made more explicit here. The sufficient conditions have always to be identified through empirical investigations. The variables in a situation have to be examined and assessed for their causal significance. There is no scope here for guesswork, intuition or unreal assumptions about variables. The analytical tools of necessary and sufficient conditions can only be used with empirical data from concrete situations. They do not distort the data but simply categorize it for causal analytical purposes. This can be seen by looking at the relationship between trade unionism and trade unions.

Trade unionism is collective action by those who sell their labour power in order to protect and improve their living standards. Trade unionism, therefore, can take place only through sellers of labour power, or employees. The necessary condition for trade unionism is, in consequence, the existence of a market for labour power where it can be bought and sold. This condition is a vital element in capitalism so wherever capitalism is found, no matter in which country or on what scale, trade unionism may be practised. Small segments of capitalist activity in tropical Africa, Asia and Latin America possess the basic ingredient for trade unionism equally with the highly industrialized capitalist societies of Western Europe and North America. Other things being equal, one would expect to find trade unionism being practised in all the above-mentioned areas.

Other things, however, are not equal. The variables which determine the phenomenological emergence of trade unionism — its expression in organizational form — may not all be present or they may be differentially present. It can be seen from an examination of trade unionism in Western Europe that a degree of stability among the labour force, a high proportion of literacy, a level of wages sufficient to finance union organization and an element of political freedom are sufficient conditions for the actual growth of trade unions. It is not possible to specify the precise intensity of these conditions because the actual presence of union organizations is consistent with various degrees and combinations of intensity. There are positions of intensity which may vary between countries which will determine whether organizations will emerge or not. After that the differences will be reflected in different forms and rates of development. For example, the complete absence of political freedom in Nazi Germany, so far as trade unionists were concerned, prevented the emergence of union organizations. Once that freedom was restored in 1945 union organizations immediately re-emerged. In contemporary Spain trade unionism is illegal but the ability of the government to enforce illegality is limited, with the result that organizations exist but as a network of secret, subversive societies. A similar situation to that in contemporary Spain existed in Britain up till 1825 and particularly during the period of the Combination Acts from 1800 to 1825. Then trade unions were illegal, but they existed through the ineffectiveness of the government's administration of the Acts. Nonetheless the Acts had a sufficient impact to compel unions to evolve methods of secrecy such as initiation ceremonies, and to intensify disciplinary measures both to maintain secrecy and control over members in general. A significant change in any of the other sufficient conditions mentioned might not have the same impact as that of political freedom so that while a change in one of them might not affect the very existence of unions it would undoubtedly influence the manner of their existence.

As the types of sufficient conditions vary between environments it is necessary to identify them empirically in areas of tropical Africa or Asia. In general in tropical Africa a Western capitalist organizational form has been imposed which is contrary to the realities of the indigenous environments, with the consequence that unions are unsuited to the demands made on them. They are weak organizationally and industrially. It is clear that a sufficient condition for them in many cases is either external financial aid or internal governmental support. It does appear that political freedom in some degree is a universally common sufficient condition.

The pressures for collective action which arise out of labour markets have taken on different forms throughout the world because of the wide diversity in sufficient conditions. Thus an understanding of the reasons for company based unions in Japan, centralized national unions in Britain, largely locally based unions in France with strong central coordinating bodies, a small number of large, rationally delineated national unions with a powerful central agency in West Germany and so on can only be found in an examination of the conditions which are sufficient for the existence and operation of unions in those areas.

What is being stated, in effect, is that trade union organizations should be expected to be found wherever the necessary condition exists. The explanation for the fact that sometimes they cannot be found lies in the absence of one or more sufficient conditions.

The same analytical approach explains the mechanics of the spread of trade unionism between industries, occupations or other categories such as manual and non-manual. The definition of trade unionism given above does not refer to particular types of employees. It implies that anyone who sells his labour power, irrespective of the nature of his work, of his income level, social background, educational achievement or position in the authority hierarchy, is a *potential* trade unionist. It is known, however, that not all employees are trade unionists. Indeed substantial proportions remain outside union organizations. It is known also that the propensity to take collective action varies considerably between categories of employees. For example, in most countries trade unionism is less intensive among those employed in agriculture than in manufacturing industry. Here, clearly, the facility to organize is an important condition. Agricultural workers are often employed in small units widely separated from each other in contrast to workers in large factory units in manufacturing industry. They sometimes live, moreover, in feudal type environments where social obligations still play a part in determining social relationships in work situations. In all capitalist societies there are substantial areas of unorganized employees in clerical, administrative and managerial work. The environments of these employees contain strong counter pressures to those giving rise to collective action. In some countries, types of non-manual workers such as civil servants, are inhibited from taking collective action by government decrees. The actions of employers, however, have a strong causal significance. Employers have tended to react with the extremes of outright victimization or preferential treatment or they have encouraged the establishment of company sponsored associations. An ideology emphasizing the social distinctiveness of non-manual workers and the closeness of their identity with the interests of employers has been articulated through real privileges in the work and social situations, such as higher earnings, greater security in employment, more advantageous fringe benefits, preferential education and a generally higher social status. An understanding of the reasons for the absence of trade unionism among many sections of employees has to be sought in an analysis of the above visible factors. Likewise, the forms of organization and industrial methods undertaken by non-manual workers get their characteristics from the same environmental factors.

Sufficient conditions, then, have a moulding, shaping influence on superstructural phenomena. In new situations they are the forces which determine forms and methods. They can therefore be separated analytically from superstructures, as was stated earlier in this chapter. The question arises now as to what constitutes superstructures. When this is answered the equation will almost be complete.

Notes

1. V. I. Lenin, *Collected Works*, Lawrence & Wishart, 1960, i, 142.
2. Karl Marx, *Capital*, vol. i Afterword to the second German edition, p. 14.
3. V. I. Lenin, *Materialism and Empirio-criticism*, in *Collected Works*, xiv, 22.
4. Friedrich Engels, *Herr Eugus Duhring's Revolution in Science*, trans. Emile Burns, Martin Lawrence, p. 31.
5. *Ibid.*, p. 15.
6. R. Garaudy, *Karl Marx: the Evolution of His Thought*, Lawrence & Wishart, 1967, p. 90.
7. Karl Marx, Preface to *A Contribution to the Critique of Political Economy*, in Marx and Engels: *Selected Works*, Moscow, Foreign Languages Publishing House, 1951, i, 328—9.
8. Friedrich Engels, Marx and Engels: *Selected Works*, 1951, ii, 443.
9. From a letter of 15 August 1898, Lelio Basso, 'Rosa Luxemburg: the dialectical method', *International Socialist Journal*, November 1966, p. 521.
10. Jean Piaget, *Structuralism*, Routledge & Kegan Paul, 1971, ch. 6.
11. *Ibid.*, p. 98.
12. *Ibid.*, p. 5.
13. *Ibid.*, p. 102.
14. Raymond Boudon, *The Uses of Structuralism*, Heinemann, 1971.
15. *Ibid.*, pp. 19, 20.

16. Tom Burns and G. M. Stalker, *The Management of Innovation*, Tavistock Publications, 1968.
17. David Silverman, *The Theory of Organizations*, Heinemann, 1970, p. 149.
18. Sherman Krupp, *Pattern in Organization Analysis*, Holt, Rinehart & Winston, 1961, p. 15.
19. *Ibid.*, p. 56.
20. Boudon, *op. cit.*, p. 136.
21. Piaget, *Structuralism*, p. 98.
22. *Ibid.*
23. Boudon, *op. cit.*, p. 3.
24. *Ibid.*, pp. 7, 8.
25. Piaget, *Structuralism*, p. 120.
26. *Ibid.*
27. Maurice Godelier, 'System, structure and contradiction in "Capital"', in R. Miliband and John Saville, eds., *The Socialist Register 1967*, Merlin Press, London, p. 94.
28. Merton, *Social Theory and Social Structure*, p. 56.
29. Marx, Preface to *A Contribution, loc. cit.*, i, 329.
30. *Ibid.*, i, 247.
31. Karl Marx, *Capital*, Moscow, 1958, i, 540.
32. *Ibid.*, i, 542.
33. Karl Marx and F. Engels, *The German Ideology*, Moscow, 1964, pp. 36–7.
34. Antonio Gramschi, *The Prison Notebooks*, Lawrence & Wishart, 1971; Georg Lukács, *History and Class Consciousness*, Merlin Press, London, 1971; Althusser, *For Marx*, Allen Lane, The Penguin Press, 1969.
35. Gramschi, *op. cit.*, p. 177.
36. Cf. Marx, Preface to *A Contribution, loc. cit.*

9

The substance of superstructures

The questions raised in this chapter are among the most difficult to answer. Up till now the analysis of materialism has been guided by much that has already been written about it. What follows is an attempt to give a meaning to superstructure which is consistent with the general conceptual approach underlying dialectical materialism but which has not been treated satisfactorily by social scientists so far. In most Marxist writings superstructure is a term with an implied meaning. Gramschi, for example, often referred to it but never gave an explicit definition. 'Every new social organism (type of society)', he wrote, 'creates a new superstructure.' Later he referred to the historical situation which had 'not reached the level of development necessary for it to have the capacity to create new super-structures. . . .' The term obviously meant visible social relations as was indicated by his statement that 'medical advance, which has raised the average expectancy of human life . . . raises . . . complex problems of a superstructural order'. About the United States, Gramschi wrote that 'there has been a massive development, on top of an industrial base of the whole range of modern superstructures'.[1]

Althusser believed that Gramschi had made 'genial insights into the problem, basic today, of the superstructures' but he too dealt with the same unhelpful generalities. For Althusser the 'forms of superstructure' are 'the State, the dominant ideology, religion, politically organized movements, and so on . . .' or, in another context, 'the State and all legal, political and ideological forms'.[2] Althusser, however, recognized the importance of extending the analysis of superstructures.

For if Marx has given us the general principles and some concrete examples (The Eighteenth Brumaire, The Civil War in France, etc.), if all political practice in the history of Socialist and Communist movements constitutes an inexhaustible reservoir of concrete 'experimental protocol', it has to be said that the Theory of the specific effectivity of the superstructures and other 'circumstances' *largely remains to be elaborated; and before the theory of their effectivity or simultaneously (for it is by formulating their effectivity that their* essence *can be attained) there must be elaboration of the theory of the particular essence of the specific elements of the superstructure. Like the map of Africa before the great explorations, this theory remains a realm sketched in outline.* [3]

Perhaps it would help at this point to describe the problem concerning the identity of superstructures. Every situation possesses a structure and a superstructure. The structure determines the superstructure but within an historical context; the process of determination is done through the impact of variables in the environment, belonging to the category of sufficient conditions. The variables act on some part of something called a superstructure. Is that something the visible phenomena, identified by Gramschi and Althusser as business organizations, voluntary organizations, families, institutions for specific purposes such as government, worship, education, and ideology? If that something is a micro situation, say a business organization, is it employees, machines, materials, employers and management, a legal entity arranged to facilitate control and production? If this is so, how do the variables produce their results? How do they determine the actions and functions of men, machines, legal entities and ideology? Put in another way, when variables act on an organization, what is it precisely they influence?

Quite clearly the pressures eventually have to be communicated through men and women and that they do so by acting on their consciousness. Dialectical materialism is not mechanistic and it does not allocate to people the role of automatons. Karl Marx wrote in *The Eighteenth Brumaire of Louis Bonaparte* that 'man makes his own history, but he does not make it out of the whole cloth; he does not make it out of conditions chosen by himself, but out of such as he finds close at hand'. [4] The autonomy of people to act is limited, in other words, by the situations they are in. They cope as best they can within those limitations.

The question at issue is only indirectly about the scope which people have for determining their actions. It is directly about the nature of the participation of people. When this is understood the substance of superstructures will be clear.

The three components of superstructures
Just as visible social relations do not constitute their structure so the visible forms of superstructures do not indicate their substance. This substance has to be analytically identified. It is not the interaction of people with people and people with machines within the constraints of legal, written and unwritten procedures, customs and practices which make up the substance of an organization. People participate in organizations, as in

any activity, through their contribution of skills; that is through their ability and facility to contribute to the activity of organizations. Once people appear in an organization they do so as a skill element. Similarly, machines are not employed because of any particular physical quality but because of the manner in which they can improve on or contribute to the skills of people. This point will be elaborated later. Here it is sufficient to note that skills constitute the prime element in social activity and, hence, in organizations. The second factor to note is that skills themselves have two aspects: first they contribute the expertise which is necessary to produce action; second, through this, they carry an ability to control that action to some degree. The second element in social activity is that ability to control action which is derived from skills, namely power. The third and last element in social activity is the ideological setting within which the skills are used and the power is exercised. This setting includes the whole institutional context for social activity, for it is through institutions of various kinds that values are transmitted into action — that they obtain their practical significance. The substance of environments then is made up of skills, power and ideology. They reside together in different proportions and each combination of proportions represents a different situation. Organizations comprise particular proportions depending upon their activities.

A point to note at this juncture is that there is no difference in substance between organizations and their environments. This similarity permits organizations to expand, contract or to disappear altogether in their environments. The boundaries which delineate organizations from their environments and make them recognizable have by themselves no substantial sociological significance; they are of a legal, institutional character and are taken account of by the ideological element. The distinction between organizations and between organizations and their environments lies in the relationship between the three components and nothing else. This follows from the postulate that the prime determining variables lie in environments and are not peculiar to or specific to any particular social situation. The economic class divisions which result from the social relations to the means of production are not simply reflected in, say business organizations, but provide them with their source of momentum. For this reason, to cut an organization off from its environment is to isolate it from its life-blood.

In the analysis of skill, power and ideology a difficulty occurs which was raised in connection with the distinction between structure and superstructure. It is that while analytical distinctions can be clearly made between these elements, their visible relationships appear both indistinct and different. For instance, power, that most glamorous and widely used of all variables, appears in visible social relations to have priority over all other variables. Skills, as will be shown, are the basis for power but phenomenologically this is not seen. If something is significant because it gives rise to power then it must be superior to power. It is bad analysis to treat a variable which is a derivative as if it were autonomous. Power can never be fully understood so long as its origins are neglected, no matter how much they are hidden from the eyes of observers.

The relationship between skill and power is difficult to disentangle because the main significance of skill in social relationships is the power which comes from the possession or control of skills; that is, from the ability to decide how and when and for what purpose skills should be used. Nonetheless an attempt at disentangling them has to be made in order to clarify their causal positions.

Skill

The *Oxford Dictionary* defines skill as 'Practical knowledge in combination with ability', a 'knowledge or understanding of something'. This is a starting point. It must relate to practice, otherwise it can have no significance for action. It is, therefore, an applied thing, involving effort. A skill which does not involve effort is an abstraction and no consequence for anything. Effort by itself is unsatisfactory as a category because it refers only to human activity and, in any case, is simply the means whereby skill is transformed into practice. W. Baldamus preferred the term 'effort'. In his pioneering work *Efficiency and Effort* he stated:

We shall confine ourselves . . . with 'labour efficiency' the physical substance of which is human effort. The reason for selecting the human factor in efficiency lies in the fact that it alone is relevant to social science. What we are proposing, then, is that the social problems of efficiency are ultimately problems of the control of human effort. Thus the larger and more intangible question of overall efficiency can be narrowed down to the more specific problem of defining and analysing the meaning of effort. [5]

In this work, Baldamus made the mistake of assuming that technological resources could be excluded in an assessment of human efficiency. It is through men that technology attains its effectiveness, in combination with men's skills. A man's skill in killing is highly dependent on whether or not he possesses a gun, but by itself, in nobody's hand, the gun has no significance. Thus to separate that piece of technology from the 'human factor in efficiency' is to relegate it to the position of an ornament.

Skill must be seen in a wide context. It is not just something concerned with the production process, with work, or, as conventional sociology suggests, with the attainment of a common goal, but is a necessary com-

ponent in every social activity.[6] There can be no action of any kind
without a skill element. A business organization is first of all a combination of skills. The same can be said of a family, an army or a trade union.
Skill describes the element of competence which makes action possible. It
is an ability to do something, anything. Nothing would occur unless skills
were present.

Clearly in an analysis of action skill is not contributed by labour alone.
The history of changes in men's competence in doing things, subsisting,
preserving, altering, has been dominated by the acquisition by men of
technical means of doing things. What was stated above about a gun
applies to any machine. A machine is a technologically contrived means of
improving men's skills. This is so even where action appears to be fully
automated.

Skill is the key dependent variable in the equation which describes
superstructure as a function of structure. Changes in a structure, or rather
pressures which are generated in a structure make their first impact on
skills. If the pressures are unable to alter the nature of a skill or skills and,
therefore, the distribution of skills – the relationships between them –
nothing changes. If the pressures succeed in changing a skill or skills then
things will inevitably happen. In a narrower sense Baldamus gave a similar
quality to 'effort' when he stated that the purpose of his work was

*to show that the organization of industry, with all its complexities and
diversities, ultimately revolves on a single process: the administrative
process through which the employee's effort is controlled by the
employer. This means that the entire system of industrial production (is)
viewed as a system of administrative controls which regulate quantity,
quality, and distribution of human effort.*[7]

Skill in the first instance must have its basis in competence or expertise.
That is, it must relate initially to the ability to do things. A typology of
skills cannot, however, be usefully constructed by considering this element
alone because there is no criterion which can be used to rank or distinguish
between skills on the basis of competence by itself. In contemporary
industrial societies most activity is interrelated and interdependent. The
division of labour has proceeded to a point where action is made up from
and dependent on innumerable simplified tasks so that no single task can
be examined on its own technical merits. How can all the skills which comprise business organizational activity be ranked and compared in any single
organization by taking into account only the objective physical element?
Or, taking a wider perspective, how can the physical skill of a carpenter be
compared with that of an administrator in a business organization or a
police constable or a politician or an army commander? These physical

skills are ranked, of course, in all societies where labour power is given a price, but the ranking is done by attributing qualities to the skills which lie outside their physical content. In order to assess skills, therefore, these attributes have to be identified and understood. This is so whatever typology of skills is constructed. The qualities which are derived from or are attached to the physical element of competence have to be identified and analysed.

It must be made clear, however, before examining the social reality of skills that their physical element is their core. Whatever is said about skills, whatever qualities are attributed to them, must relate at some point to their physical characteristics. The attributes are dependent on the physical contribution a skill makes so that if this contribution changes then so will the attributes themselves eventually change.

The pre-eminence of the physical element can be seen when examining the relationship between skill and subsistence. All activity in a society has an economic basis which provides the prime determining factors for it. Those skills which relate most closely to that basis form that part of the superstructure which has the most significance for effectiveness of the society. The skills directly involved in the subsistence activities of the society are the most crucial for it. This point does not need to be elaborated. If these skills cease the society loses its means of subsistence and will disintegrate. This is saying that the skills relating to concrete productive activities, belonging to men and women who make subsistence possible, must constitute the basis of any typology which may be drawn up. Skills may be given different attributes but it remains as a hard, indisputable fact that at some point it is what and how they contribute to subsistence which matters most.

Power

It was mentioned above that the elements of superstructures make their impact through men and women. Skills, even those of machines, of organizations, are skills in the hands of men and women. They become determinants of social action through people. The physical qualities of skills, therefore, achieve their significance in the hands of people. Whatever other attributes they have are conveyed through people. Every skill is possessed or controlled in part or in whole by some person or persons, and its possession conveys some ability to control what is being made or done, depending on its relation to subsistence in the first place and its indispensability in the process of making or doing in the second place. The skill of a master-craftsman may give him control over the production of the whole process of production because it may encompass the whole process. This point may be put differently. The degree of control may be assessed by the impact which a withdrawal of a skill has on the process in which it is involved. What is being said is that skills carry with them power. Power is the ability to exercise control over the factors which determine the visible social relations and changes in these relations in a social situation. It is in essence the ability to control and alter structures, but it is expressed through the control of skills. A typology of skills would necessarily have to take into account the power to which they give rise.

The relationship between skills and power can be explained empirically. The power to which a skill gives rise depends on its relationship with other skills. A change in skill in relation to that possessed by others for similar purposes enhances its power element. A relative improvement in the skill of production gives a business organization greater control, therefore more power, in its market. A relative improvement in the skill of management in an organization, results in greater managerial control over those who are managed. The power of management is enhanced. A change in the distribution of skills, the displacement of some by others, the introduction of new ones, alters the power structure in an organization.

It is difficult to find illustrations to support this analysis from the mass of empirical investigations about organizational activity because of their uncertain validity. This difficulty was encountered by Baldamus but, as he stated, 'now and then there are unexpected results' which 'neither confirm nor contradict preconceived notions, but appear to assert themselves just because they are inexplicable in relation to established assumptions'.[8] Morris Janowitz employed conventional sociological techniques in his work on military organization.[9] Yet, because of dramatic changes in the techniques of warfare in recent history he was compelled to examine the causal significance of skills. He gave many illustrations of the impact on organizations of relative changes in skills in his book *Sociology and the Military Establishment* which, though published before his treatise on the professional soldier, was based on its conclusions. 'One approach to understanding the sources of organizational authority', he stated, 'is to analyze the division of labour — the skill structure — in the military establishment.'[10]

Historical research highlights the evolution of the military profession as middle-class technicians during the nineteenth century took over the specialized artillery and engineering services while the infantry and to an even greater extent the cavalry remained the domain of the aristocracy. As the simple division of labor gave way to a complex pattern of specialization, the number of ranks increased and the staff officer emerged as a specialist in planning and co-ordination. . . . All of these transformations implied that positions of authority would have to be allocated to persons with demonstrated competence, that is, on the basis of achievement.

And he went on: 'There exists a deep source of organizational strain in all three services — ground, air, and naval — because the military staff-command structure does not articulate with its skill structure.'[11]

He showed quite clearly how skills modified military discipline and status and determined the relationship between the military and civilian organizations because there 'has been a narrowing of the skill differential between military and civilian occupations'.[12] In general terms, and apart from Janowitz's survey, it can be said that increases in the skill of destruction through the acquisition of more potent weapons have inevitably altered control situations. Innumerable illustrations from colonial and neocolonial history support this contention. A common factor in colonial situations has always been the attempt to deny subjugated peoples access to skills of any kind. Neither slaves in any society nor indigenous Africans in colonized Africa were normally permitted to acquire the skills associated with their masters or colonizers because of the possible effects acquisition would have on the distribution of power. Where a prerequisition for skill was education then educational opportunities were denied.[13] The ability of white settlers in South Africa and Rhodesia to dominate indigenous black Africans is derived both from their possession of a superior skill in physical oppression and the denial of occupational skills to Africans.

In a capitalist society the major class division is between those who are compelled to sell their labour power in order to subsist and those who own capital and buy labour power to combine with it. The means of production are privately owned and ownership carries with it the right of control. Those who are compelled to sell their labour power, comprising the vast majority, are in effect selling their skills and relinquishing day to day control over them. This factor, that they possess control over the distribution and use of skills provides the owners of the means of production with their power. Whenever anyone talks of the power of capital or of property they are talking of power which is derived from the ability to purchase and control skills. It can readily be seen why strikes of wage-earners assume proportions way above their immediate economic significance. Strikes are a retrieval of the control over the skills of labour and without these skills capital, no matter what form is takes, is as useless as the gun in no one's hands. In general it can be stated that the possession of skills, no matter how exclusive or specific they are, is subordinate to the control of skills. In other words there is a power which is based on skills but not derived from them. This power has nothing to do with expertise; entrepreneurial ability is simply a rationalization of it. It is derived from the social relations to the means of production, from the hidden structure.

It is possible to add a further comment on the relationship between

skills and power in a capitalist society. Their causal relationship is reinforced by the operation of the market mechanism, whereby prices are
given to skills according to their scarcity value. Scarcity here is an ideologically based term, contrived to satisfy the ideological needs of the
society. But it has a measurable quality, with the consequence that the
prices accorded to some skills are determined, within a given range, by the
ability of their practitioners to restrict their distribution. The legal and
medical professions in many countries have for long endeavoured to
maintain a market exclusiveness through a strictly regulated control over
the acquisition of their skills. Craft unions in nineteenth-century Britain
and the United States recognized that their power in relation to employers
depended on the control of both the quality and distribution of craft
skills. It is for this reason that unions sought to impose apprenticeship
regulations, encourage emigration and resist the spread of skill-diluting
mechanized methods. The power to regulate wages is generally least among
those with the least demanded skills. As in a market economy there is a
premium on scarcity, the bargaining power derived from skills is distributed in pyramidal fashion. Other things being equal the commonest skills
are at the base and the least common are at the apex. There are, of course,
many skills other than occupational or industrial ones. In a capitalist
society as a whole, skills, and the power they give rise to, are also distributed in a pyramidal fashion with that of the owners of the means of
production at the apex and that of employees distributed hierarchically
below.

In any situation the distribution of power will match that of skills
which give rise to power by virtue of their technical competence and by
the extent to which they support or reflect the dominant ideology. This
means that power itself has an ideological basis within superstructures.
Technical competence and ideological components exist in skills in varying
proportions. The power associated with some skills has little to do with
technical competence and a lot to do with ideology while in others it has
most to do with technical competence. In order to understand the nature
of power, then, skills have to be broken down into their components.

Ideologically based power is of two kinds. First there is the power dele-
gated by the primordial power holders. Some skills, usually described as
management ones, are given mandatory power to control the distribution
and use of other skills within specified limits from those who own the
means of production. Management skills may in fact involve little technical
competence though in recent years in Western capitalist countries
desperate efforts have been made through management education to create
such a component. This would undoubtedly be revealed if the
power to manage ceased to be underwritten by the owners of the means of

production and management was required to operate on the basis of its technical competence. It would be discovered then that the power derived from management skills would be radically distributed. In conventional organization theory and in management texts this derived power is described as a formal management system and it is assumed that because management is given power to control that it does in fact possess it. A whole range of literature about the management of organizations, however, is devoted to trying to account for situations where designated decision-making power does not appear to work as it was intended to work without ever questioning this assumption. It is believed in consequence that once a 'formal management' decision is made, it can only be thwarted or frustrated by such matters as defective communications or insubordination. The question is never asked to what extent it is possible to accredit skills with power which for technical and possibly market reasons they do not possess. This question may be particularly significant where complex management structures are devised.

Secondly, there are skills which do not have deliberately designated power, such as management ones do, nor do they have any because of a particularly significant technical competence. They have it because of their association with particular social backgrounds or types of work which reflect the dominant values about work. Non-manual work in general and administration in particular are areas of activity where these skills may be found. Skills have a social grading which may have little bearing on their functional significance and there may be a relationship between the social status of a skill and the power attributed to it. The skills in this category are even more problematical than in the case of 'formal management' ones. Their identity needs to be empirically determined. What can be said, however, is that whatever power such skills are accorded is relatively easily disturbed. It does not have a basis in concrete reality. Changes in that reality can erode it or displace it altogether.

Analytically it is possible to construct three typologies of power, each one having a different pattern of distribution. The first typology would concern power derived from technical competence and would reveal degrees of indispensibility in making and doing things. The second would concern power derived from the mandates of the owners of the means of production and would reveal the pre-eminence of the primary source of power. The third would concern power with a predominant ideological basis and would reveal the pervasiveness of the dominant ideology. In reality the three typologies are superimposed on each other producing a complex picture. The apparent complexity should not be allowed to confuse the issue. Skills are the element in superstructures through which structural pressures communicate their impact on social behaviour. The technical competence component is the one which first receives the impact and through its responses affects the other components. If an impact on a skill is of sufficient intensity then it will alter its form and hence the power which is derived from it. Skills in contemporary society have dependent relationships with each other so that a change in one will affect other related ones and so on, producing a repercussion effect of some complexity. The extent and implications of this are considered in the last chapter. Here it is sufficient to note that while in micro situations mandatory power may be the dominant element in the short run, in the longer run it has to readjust itself in response to the impact from relative changes in the technical competence element of skills. There cannot for long exist two inconsistent patterns of power distribution in an organization. Mandatory power always acts in response to situations, it can never act as an initiator of them. It is the sheer ability to make and do things which, at the superstructural level, is the catalyst for change. Of course, so long as the social relations of production remain unchanged then so will the basic distribution of power also remain unchanged. The changes in mandatory power as a result of alterations in the types and nature of skills will be reflected in changes in its precise pattern within a given distribution.

Power is, by one means or another, the ability to control the use, distribution and combination of skills. It is a derived phenomenon and, except in the short-term situations mentioned above, has no autonomy. This conception of power, based on an understanding of its causes, stands in marked contrast to its conventional treatment which accords it a grand, autonomous status.

Virtually every analyst of organizations since Michels has treated power as the prime, independent variable. Its use has become so common, in academic treatises as well as in everyday usage, that its meaning is taken for granted. Analysts rarely define it and authors feel no obligation to readers to list it in their indexes. But it should be clear that the term 'power' is not simply a word. It is a word with a meaning derived from the conceptual approach of the analysts. The term, in its general usage usually refers to one version or another of Weber's view that power consists of the possibility of imposing one's will on the behaviour of other persons.[14] It is seen to operate on an interpersonal or intergroup basis, hence the use of such derived terms as compliance, subordination, sanctions, coercion, manipulation and domination. Weber's own use of power is seen in his theory of domination. Although in common usage power is used to refer to any kind of domination there is an implicit recognition that there are different kinds of power, some more important and more acceptable than others, such as legal as against illegal, legitimate as against illegitimate, for example. These and other categories get their meaning, along with the central term itself, from the conventional conceptual approach. They constitute an integral part of the dominant paradigm and, as such, act to legitimize the prevalent social relations to the means of production.

Although power is a generic term there is, in conventional usage, power which is synonymous with authority and power which is not. Authority refers to legitimized power. The question is then, what is legitimate? Authority and legitimate power are used in all models within the framework of systems analysis and their meanings are roughly the same. It is possible to take one model, namely the structural functionalist one, and from it get a good idea of the general meaning.

Within the structural functionalist frame of reference the prime motive for action, therefore the basis for all action, is the pursuit of goals. Because the underlying assumption of this approach is consensus there must in every situation (or system) be a single unifying goal, commonly acceptable. Each organization, for example, must have a formally designated goal in order to maintain its unity. The prime goal in business organizations is profit-making, and it is assumed that all action is primarily oriented towards it. This means that power, too, is oriented towards it. Action, including power, which is oriented towards the prime goal is legitimate; that which is not is illegitimate. Legitimate power, then, is that which is directed towards the maximization of profits.

The task of exercising control in the pursuit of profits is the prerogative of the owners of the means of production and their designated representatives. Thus their control is legitimate and what they exercise is authority. Authority, then, is power in the hands of those who, in terms of the dominant ideology, can claim to possess it. Power which is used for other than the prime goals and which, therefore, is potentially disruptive of the consensus must, by the above reasoning be illegitimate and contrary to the exercise of authority. Strikers can exercise power in an industry but never authority according to the structural functionalist model. It must always be assumed that illegitimate power is inferior and subordinate to authority and is, in fact, controllable by authority, otherwise not only would the consensus assumption be destroyed but the way would be open for illegitimate power to overcome authority and if this were accepted both the basis and the purpose of the theory would be destroyed.

There is no doubt that within the general framework of systems analysis, the main form of power is legitimate power or authority and this is control exercised over individuals or groups of individuals in the interests of the dominant ideology. This concentration on authority has led to a rather desperate concern about the means of enforcing decisions, that is with the ability of authority to maintain its superiority. Nothing is said about the sources of power; everything is said about *how* power of a type is exercised. The consequences can be seen in the dreary repetition of descriptions of decision-making and communications; in the almost exclusive preoccupation, in all fields of social activity, with the exercise of ideologically legitimate power and the responses to it.

Phenomenologically power is seen as control by persons over persons, and persons quite plausibly are examined for qualities which make this possible. Attributes are unearthed, like charisma or qualities making for greatness, which are consistent with the belief that power lies in people. Thus people with such attributes will rise to power. Phenomenological studies recognize that individuals can only exercise power within a context. Charismatic leaders create their own context; others, through their attributes, move into *offices* which are vested with power exercising rights. The nearest these studies get to an examination of causes is to acknowledge that the power of an individual may be derived from his office or role. But this is simply to beg the question. A discussion about power must deal with the 'thing-in-itself' and not simply with its obvious manifestation. And it must get away from the question-begging exercise which characterizes most of modern sociology from structural functionalism through to ethnomethodology.

It would be a falsification of reality, of course, to analyse power as if it did not possess a social context which impinged on it. And it would be absurd to ignore within that context, the 'actors', and their 'values' and the 'meaning they give to reality'. These factors constitute part of visible social relations. Equally, it would be a falsification to ignore the part played by ideas in influencing social behaviour. It is for this reason that ideology is identified as the third major constituent element in superstructures.

Ideology

This is, as will be shown, the institutional context through which skill and power become action. It is the context within which men and women assume whatever causal significance they have in the sphere of social action. Skills either belong to people or are handled by them. The question is, what influences do people bring to bear on their use, distribution and combination? Power is exercised in the last analysis by people. Men and women, not guns, bombs or machines, make decisions about it. The question is, in what ways do people influence its nature, its intensity, its range? Obviously criteria are used in all cases. What then are the sources, the determinants of the criteria? Both skills and power achieve their reality through the actions of people, are transformed and given their social significance by them. This, in part, accounts for the preoccupation by conventional sociologists with people. It would obviously be turning the analysis of this book on its head to deal with people as if they were autonomous. On the other hand, it would be an affront to concrete reality to treat people as if they were automatons, to adopt a purely mechanistic approach to social behaviour.

The main factors involved in the ideology element are ideas, values and consciousness. These have figured prominently in sociological discussions and cannot be treated fully here. Some related questions do not have to be raised because they are covered by the assumption underlying materialism itself which stipulates that all the above factors must have material origins, that they cannot have autonomous identities. Thus the Parsonsian position which gives values action determining qualities raises no questions here; it would be illogical and irrelevant to examine it. The logical and relevant questions are those which concern the meaning of ideas and values and the context in which they act to produce consciousness, within the framework of materialism.

Ideology is the process by which ideas, values and purposes act to influence behaviour. In part this process involves the development of consciousness and, for the rest, an imposition of standards or norms of behaviour through institutional means, irrespective of the level of consciousness. In so far as it works through consciousness it is an ever-present phenomenon because consciousness must always precede action. There can be no action in a situation until men or women are conscious of it in one way or another.

Consciousness [Marx wrote in Feuerbach*] is . . . from the very beginning a social product, and remains so as long as men exist at all. Consciousness is at first, of course, merely consciousness concerning the* immediate *sensuous environment and consciousness of the limited connection with other persons and things outside the individual who is growing self-conscious.*[15]

It is then, at first, an awareness of visible social reality. But it is also an understanding of that reality. In other words consciousness involves a perception of the nature of social reality; it is about the theory of reality. The two stages mentioned by Marx can only be separated analytically. Consciousness of a situation involves an instantaneous ordering of it according to criteria which the observer may or may not be aware that he holds, so that the theory is an inseparable part of the observation. If someone in an organization makes a decision about its activities, it is based on some understanding of them. The vital questions about consciousness, then, are where does the theory come from, on what is the understanding based? Moreover, how can a person have such a theory and not know about it? How can a theory enter into the consciousness of man, determine his perception of reality and remain hidden from his own cognizance? It has been quoted above (p. 192) but is worth repeating that 'it is not the consciousness of men that determines their being, but, on the contrary, their social being that determines their consciousness'. Where, then, in the social being of men is the source of the theory which shapes their consciousness?

Consciousness of social relations in its totality always concerns, and must always concern reality. It does not follow, however, that reality can be explained through consciousness. This is because the theoretical ingredient of consciousness can reflect reality or distort it in varying degrees. This is one reason why consciousness must be approached from its material basis and not vice versa as is the case in phenomenological studies. The distortion, if it occurs, results from the conceptual basis of the theoretical ingredient that in some way misrepresents the reality it is purportedly representing. This ground has already been covered adequately in this book. An illustration will be sufficient at this point. If the theory through which an employee sees his situation is based on the assumption that social reality is dominated by consensus then he will perceive consensus in his reality. He may see himself as having a basic common interest with his employer and may attribute disruptions in this unity to conspiratorial elements among his fellow employees; he may, in consequence, view strikes as damaging to his own interests. If reality is dominated by a permanent conflict between the owners of the means of production, namely employers, and the non-owners, namely employees, the perceived reality will be a distortion and the employee's action will stem from a consciousness which misrepresents his structural position. In this sense it may be possible to talk of 'false-consciousness'. This term, however, needs to be handled very carefully.

The need for care arises because if, as it is accepted here, consciousness is determined by social being then it can never be a false representation of that being. It would be inconsistent and illogical to believe otherwise. A consciousness which had no basis in social being would be a fantasy which could have comic, but perhaps disastrous results for action. An extreme example would be if an employee perceived the world as if he were an employer, and acted accordingly. Consciousness contributes to social action and may have practical implications. It is for this reason that a man who perceived his world upsidedown would experience comic, perhaps disastrous results. Very quickly, as a matter of urgency, he would have to reappraise his assessment of his situation and reorient it to be consistent with his social being. 'Consciousness', Marx stated, 'can never be anything else than conscious existence, and the existence of men in their actual life process.'[16]

Consciousness then is related to social action, to material conditions, in two ways. It arises from it then leads to it. A consciousness which does not arise from reality is equivalent to a free-floating value, existing without an origin except in the mind, which, it would have to be assumed, is an autonomous phenomenon. The question, 'what determines consciousness?' must be answered in a question-begging way by saying 'ideas or values'. The question, 'what determines ideas or values?' cannot be satisfactorily answered. The same difficulty in analysis arises if any part of consciousness is said to be autonomous. Those who, in the interest of humanism, feel that they are forsaking moral responsibility if they relate consciousness completely to material activity and who resolve their dilemma by stating that consciousness is partly autonomous, have to answer in a question-begging manner about the parts which are supposedly autonomous. There is no halfway house in this matter. The position can best be stated in Marx's own words when describing the contrast to German philosophy in the 1840s:

In direct contrast to German philosophy which descends from heaven to earth, here we ascend from earth to heaven. That is to say, we do not set out from what men say, imagine, conceive, nor from men as narrated, thought of, imagined, conceived, in order to arrive at men in the flesh. We set out from real, active men, and on the basis of their real life-process we demonstrate the development of the ideological reflexes and echoes of this life-process. The phantoms formed in the human brain are also, necessarily, sublimates of their material life-process, which is empirically verifiable and bound to material premises. Morality, religion, metaphysics, all the rest of ideology and their corresponding forms of consciousness thus no longer retain the semblance of independence. They have no history, no development; but men developing their material production and their material intercourse, alter, along with this their real existence, their thinking and the products of their thinking. Life is not determined by consciousness, but consciousness by life. In the first method of approach the starting point is consciousness taken as the living individual; in the second method, which conforms to real life, it is the real living individuals themselves, and consciousness is considered solely as their consciousness.[17]

If the position is as clear and unambiguous as Marx stated, in what ways can consciousness be false? To what extent can it be distorted? Strictly there can be no consciousness which falsely represents the immediate environment, namely superstructure, in which a person operates. If a non-manual worker responds to his position as an employee differently from a manual worker by refusing to act collectively it is not because he is not aware of his position but because the superstructural details of that position are different from those of a manual worker. These differences may be expressed in terms of income, social status, authority, in terms of real material privileges conferred by employers. Such factors may be reinforced by ideological pressures. It should be remembered that ideology is a real, concrete element in the superstructure of an environment.

Non-manual workers who identify themselves with employers and repudiate collective action as crass and crude, while being faithful to the superstructure of their environment, are falsely representing their objective class position as employees. This means that they do not see themselves being used as commodities, selling themselves as best as they can, subject to manipulation to satisfy cost considerations; they do not see the social character of labour and do not recognize that they belong to a common situation with common interests. They are not conscious of their own structural reality though they are undoubtedly aware of their immediate empirical reality as individuals.[18] Thus *false* has a rather special meaning. It means simply that employees are not aware of the 'hidden', structural part of their social existence while being fully aware of their immediate empirical position. If the dominant ideology correctly represents the hidden part then there can be no false consciousness. An employer, for example, for whose interests the dominant ideology serves, can never be falsely conscious of his social reality.

The discussion about the distortion of consciousness has generally been conducted in terms of the emergence of class consciousness. Indeed the discussion about consciousness itself has been largely confined by Marxists to this question. The determination of class consciousness is undoubtedly a vital, perhaps the most vital political issue in capitalist societies. The analysis in this chapter, however, is aimed at providing tools within a Marxist framework for understanding micro situations, so that the need here is to discover the moulding, perhaps distorting capacity of ideology in a whole range of social situations. For this to be done, ideology as a component of superstructure has to be examined in more detail.

The consciousness of any situation is the manner in which it is comprehended, the way in which its details are assessed and the whole assemblage given meaning. The task of providing comprehension is fulfilled by theory. The part played by theory and its relation to practice has been gone through in earlier chapters. The construction and formulation of theories is a specialist function, undertaken by small elites of intelligentsia. These elites give expression to ideas about social phenomena through the formulation of concepts which are logically related to each other. They are concerned, therefore, with ideology. But there is much more to ideology than this. Ideology is not, as Julius Gould would have one believe, just 'a pattern of beliefs and concepts (both factual and normative) which purport to explain complex social phenomena with a view to directing and simplifying socio-political choices facing individuals and groups'.[19] It involves the dissemination, application, enforcement and reinforcement of a pattern of beliefs and concepts. This pattern, moreover, does not neces-sarily enter into the consciousness of individuals. Sometimes it may be forced on to individuals contrary to their consciousness because a rejection of it carries with it sanctions of one kind or another. To put the matter more explicitly, for 'beliefs and concepts' to have any relevance they must have a means of expression, such as institutions, business organizations, legal framework, religious bodies. They must be capable of having a bearing on the lives of individuals and this can only occur if they act through the way in which individuals live − that is by being embodied in kinship organizations, educational systems, work situations, social relation-ships in general and the legal contexts for kinship, education, work and social activity. An idea about anything which is not expressed in this way is an irrelevance and can be disregarded and dismissed.

The meaning given to ideology here is similar in part to that stated by Althusser and resembles Gramschi's 'social hegemonic apparatus':

An ideology is a system (with its own logic and rigour) of representations (images, myths, ideas or concepts, depending on the case) endowed with an historical existence and role within a given society. . . . So ideology is as such an organic part of every social totality. It is as if human societies could not survive without these specific formations, *these systems of representations (at various levels), their ideologies.*[20]

Gramschi saw intellectuals as functionaries in the exercise of social hegemony, in obtaining ' "spontaneous" consent given by the great masses of the population to the general direction imposed on social life by the dominant fundamental group'.[21] Hegemonic apparatuses exist for other groups too and their total is equivalent to ideology.

Ideology, then, produces consciousness, but it can do this without the individual being aware of it. Many individuals act without knowing the reasons for their actions. They are not conscious of their consciousness. Ideology, moreover, can be imposed on people to produce responses in particular situations.

Ideology [Althusser stated] is indeed a system of representations, but in the majority of cases these representations having nothing to do with 'consciousness': they are usually images and occasionally concepts, but it is above all as structures *that they impose on the vast majority of men, not via their consciousness. They are perceived − accepted − suffered cultural objects and they act functionally on men via a process that escapes them.*[22]

Two questions arise at this point. First, is ideology a purely social phenomenon distinct from science, as Althusser suggests? [23] The position is that the use of genuine scientific inquiries, and, therefore, the development of science, is not neutral but is directed to serve and frequently to validate the dominant interests which an ideology is legitimizing and supporting. 'It is a great mistake,' Conforth stated, 'to set up science in abstract antithesis to ideology. *Under definite circumstances ideology can only be developed to satisfy its practical social function by the adoption of the methods of science.*'[24] The technology which has followed from the use of the scientific method has entered superstructures through the skill component, but its use, the significance attached to it, the purposes to which it has been directed, have been determined by the distribution of power and endorsed by the means of ideology. For the vast majority of individuals who play no part in economic or social decision-making because individually they possess no power, technology is a given factor; it is something they live with and accommodate to. Its consequences are forced on them and, even though it may harm many of them individually by putting them out of work or destroying them in war, it is generally perceived as being beneficial. This is because the meaning individuals give to progress and the part they assign to technology in the achievement of progress are ideologically determined. Thus the installation of a machine in a workshop or a computer in an office is not assessed by each individual concerned as if in a social vacuum but through the influence of ideology. A redundant worker, a craftsman whose skill is diluted, a downgraded office worker, will undoubtedly have particular views about their respective positions, but the extent to which they assign a causal significance to technology and its use will depend on general ideological factors. The outcome is not clearcut because there is no single, dominant, all-pervasive ideology but competing ones, so that the perception by individuals of their situations depends upon the relative influence of the ideologies. In micro studies, technology in particular and science in general are likely to be given factors so that the manner in which they are perceived is of particular importance.

The second question concerns these competing ideologies. Are there just one or two whose influences produce relatively uniform reactions, or are there many so that small groups, even individuals, develop their own distinctive perceptions of reality? It is worth recalling that an ideology consists not simply of a 'pattern of ideas and concepts' but also of the apparatus through which they are applied so that they either enter into the consciousness of individuals or have an enforced acceptance. The need for an apparatus which can exercise hegemony is a limiting factor. It is worth recalling, too, that the 'pattern of ideas and concepts' represents a conceptual approach to reality and basically there can be only two types: one which concerns the preservation of the existing state of affairs and one which concerns a qualitative transformation in the existing state. These two approaches have been described in earlier chapters. There it was shown that different models can exist within the framework of a single conceptual approach, but in order to understand the models the main approach has first to be understood.

It is necessary to approach this second question from both ends of the spectrum, that is from the societal level and from the point of view of the individual in society, in order to clarify what ideology means to an organization, to a small group in it, to an individual. Any and every society needs a rationalization, a theoretical justification of its existence and continuation as an essential prerequisite for its survival. Particular ideas about its primary activity must penetrate its superstructure. An ideology is essentially a mechanism for social control. It works by producing a uniformity of responses about the primary activities in a society. In other words, in various ways it imposes a conformity on a society. This is necessary for the protection of the dominant power interests. Even if it were possible for diverse ideologies to be created they would be resisted and, whenever possible, suppressed. The reality of the power situation in a society does not permit the simultaneous existence of numerous competing ideologies. Unless power is to be perpetually retained through the crude use of armed might the members of a society must be convinced of the legitimacy of the power structure. There cannot be a hierarchy of ideologies.

Each type of society, therefore, must have its own ideology. This, fortunately for existing power-holders, is not problematical. Ideologies are sometimes adapted to justify extreme forms of social activity, such as that involved in fascism,[25] but, in the main, the ideology necessary for the perpetuation of particular existing distribution of power is an integral part of the superstructure. It is there just as sure as skills and power are there. So long as people are thinking beings there must be ideas about their behaviour. There can never be an ideologically free situation.

The distinguishing characteristics of a capitalist society are, as has been stated already, the private ownership of the means of production and the use of the market mechanism. The private individual can own the means of production, through ownership he can control, and through control he can accumulate material wealth for his own ends. The market mechanism is the means whereby this activity is carried out and is the first and major ideological expression of that activity. The market imposes on every one it encompasses the need to behave as individuals seeking private accumulation. The sad fact is, of course, that the very condition necessary for private accumulation, namely private ownership of the means of production, prohibits accumulation for the vast majority of people. In all capitalist countries, wealth is concentrated in the hands of tiny minorities, so that most people start with nothing on which to base accumulation. The market mechanism, faithful to the protecting, preserving, maintaining aspect of its ideological role ensures that this inequitable situation persists. In other words while there can be a redistribution between people through the market mechanism there can never be a major redistribution between classes through it so that the shape of the distribution of wealth alters. The vast majority of people are imprisoned in relative impoverishment by the maintenance of the market mechanism. Yet, through the influence of the dominant ideology they have been influenced to see virtue in necessity. Individualism has been presented as a prime virtue; private property has been sanctified; the accumulation of capital has been projected as an ideal objective; the receipt of profit has been given superiority over the manner of its making. The dominant ideology has other facets which also satisfy the needs of the system of capitalism. Virtue is attributed to inequality; only allocation by the market mechanism is described as free while only free enterprise activities are regarded as independent; success is synonymous with the ability to accumulate while poverty is failure.

   This is not a complete list of the guidelines for thought which are provided by the dominant ideology. Nothing is left to chance. These guidelines have their expression in institutions to ensure their impact. Children and young people have to be individualists in the educational system because it is devised to test individual attainment, to compete individuals one with another, to grade them individually. Business organizations also impose on individuals behaviour consistent with the preservation of individualism. The rights of the possessors of private property are institutionalized in the law of the land. The role of institutionalized religion is important here because it emphasizes individual responsibility by putting the cause of evil in man himself, by causally relating the exigencies an individual experiences to his own personal actions, by emphasizing that the relevant actions relate to God, thus implying, often explicitly, that a removal of the exigencies depends not on altering social relationship but on concentrating on matters of the spirit. In this sense religion plays a diversionary role. It leads individuals to accept their existing material situations, no matter how oppressive these may be. The religious nonconformist ethic of nineteenth-century Britain, that people should accept their stations in life, is a version of such a diversionary function. There is no better prescription for maintaining the *status quo* and giving credence to other aspects of the dominant ideology, than advocacy of religion. In a variety of ways, then, an escape from individualism is either impossible or painful even though its acceptance may carry no rewards.

In so far as individuals are concerned, the dominant ideology provides a logically consistent framework for perception right down to the last detail. What an individual experiences is a complex of interlocking situations to which he is forced to react, negatively, neutrally or positively. In all the situations there are common aspects concerning identity, allegiance, commitment, responsibility. Each aspect involves different social relations so that there is always a question to be resolved. An individual may be a citizen, an employee, a consumer, a wife or husband, a mother or father, a trade unionist, all at the same time in a situation where the question of identity has to be resolved one way or the other. The aspects are related to each other so that the resolution of the identity question both hinges on and has consequences for the other aspects. The emphasis which may be placed on one interpretation of the identity rather than another will depend on the nature of the situation such as whether it predominantly concerns work or kinship. But the resolution of the interrelated aspects will be made through ideological factors. How an individual conceives, say, allegiance, will depend in the first instance on how the primary social relationships are identified, then ordered, in the dominant ideology. He will take account of this particular presentation of social relationships in the resolution of questions he is posed through the use of the 'instant explanations' which the dominant paradigm provides. The dominant paradigm, it will be recalled, provides 'commonsense' answers to social questions consistent with the genesis of the dominant ideology. By definition it is pervasive and comprises readymade thought categories. Its terms belong to everyday speech. An individual, without being aware of it, speaks the language of a paradigm and utilizes its 'commonsense' approach for his own use. Individuality, therefore, means the use by a single person of a generalized, therefore simplified, approach to everyday problems. The single person interprets and refines the generalized approach in the light of his own particular and specific experiences, but he does not alter it qualitatively. Thus in phenomenological terms a paradigm has many variants but they all produce common answers because their basic analytical equipment is the same. It is not that people do not think; it is that they do not think independently as individuals.

It is only in the above sense that an individual has influence over the criteria he uses in the disposition of skills and power. He cannot escape from the grip of ideology. It is possible, then, to talk, as Gramschi does, about a man being an 'ensemble of social relations'.[26] Gramschi stated that 'one must conceive of man as a series of active relationships (a process) in which individuality, though perhaps the most important, is not, however, the only element to be taken into account'. He then went on to give meaning to individuality:

The humanity which is reflected in each individuality is composed of various elements: (1) the individual; (2) other men; (3) the natural world. But the latter two elements are not as simple as they might appear. The individual does not enter into relations with other men by juxtaposition, but organically, in as much, that is, as he belongs to organic entities which range from the simplest to the most complex. Thus Man does not enter into relations with the natural world just by being himself part of the natural world, but actively, by means of work and technique. Further: these relations are not mechanical. They are active and conscious. They correspond to the greater or lesser degree of understanding that each man has of them. So one could say that each one of us changes himself, modifies himself to the extent that he changes and modifies the complex relations of which he is the hub. In this sense the real philosopher is, and cannot be other than, the politician, the active man who modifies the environment, understanding by environment the ensemble *of relations which each of us enters to take part in. If one's own individuality is the* ensemble *of these relations, to create one's personality means to acquire consciousness of them and to modify one's own personality means to modify the* ensemble *of these relations.*[27]

Gramschi's statement ends with the most important questions, ones which he does not satisfactorily answer. Why should an individual want to modify the *ensemble* of relations he has entered into? And if he does then how does he set about doing it? The answers take us back to the issue of competing ideologies, or to put the matter more accurately, of an *alternative dominant ideology*.

The alternative dominant ideology

So far in this chapter no mention has been seriously made of dialectics. At the beginning of chapter 8 it was decided purely for explanatory reasons to separate materialism from dialectics. In consequence materialism has been treated in this chapter as if it were a static phenomenon. In parts, however, as with the relationship between structure and superstructure it was not possible to avoid discussing the dialectical process. This is the case, too, with ideology. The alternative dominant ideology arises from the prime contradiction in capitalist society and makes its presence felt through secondary and internal contradictions which flow from the primary one. The completion of the discussion about ideology assumes that movement is a dialectical process. This assumption is examined in detail in chapter 10.

The ideas and beliefs projected in the dominant ideology stem from a paramount idea, namely individual attainment, and make an impact at every level of activity. They are dominant because they represent the dominant interests in a power situation. And because they are dominant they are legitimized by laws and within institutions. The fact of their dominance and legitimacy results in their acceptance or enforcement in general. In other words, the power which follows from a particular distribution of skills is reflected in ideas which suggest that what is, ought to be, and ought to continue to be. The acceptance of these ideas and beliefs is not left to chance. They are not free floating values but are embodied in institutions and are backed by the power which they reflect. Thus the dominant ideology has, at first sight, a seemingly unbreakable hold as the main determinant of consciousness. For this hold to be complete, however, the ideas and beliefs must represent an equally logically consistent reality. The lasting strength of an ideology depends on its non-coercive impact, namely its facility to enter into men's consciousness. An ideology which does not have this facility must depend entirely upon coercion for its acceptance and this is a very precarious basis with a relatively short-term life span. The extent to which an ideology influences action through consciousness depends on its affinity with the experiences of men. If these experiences persistently contradict the image of reality which the ideology portrays then the ideology will be rejected. It follows then that an ideology can only perform an integrative function for the whole of a society provided it can fairly consistently adapt itself to changes in men's experiences.

The question which arises here is, to what extent do men's experiences themselves form a pattern to which a single ideology can correspond? If men have basically common experiences a single ideology can dominate and persist, only having to adapt itself to changes in levels of experiences as the occasions arise. This, of course, is the state of affairs which the dominant capitalist ideology endeavours to portray — namely that capitalist societies comprise large numbers of individuals with basically common interests. If such a situation existed then there could be only one ideology. A competitive ideology can only exist alongside the dominant one if it has an equally firm basis in the structure of the society. There is absolutely no possibility of a dominant ideology being challenged, let alone displaced, by one which represents only superstructural changes. It would not, for one thing, have the power basis to give it the coercive apparatus necessary for its spread and acceptance. In other words unless there is a power conflict arising out of the structure of the society the conditions for competitive ideologies do not exist.

The nature of capitalist societies has already been described. There are two primary economic classes, the buyers and the sellers of labour power, whose interests are in direct and permanent conflict. There is no common ground between them. Their objective, visible experiences do not coincide. They are qualitatively different from each other. In the concrete reality of capitalism there are not just levels of experiences but wholly different categories. The dominant ideology represents one and only one category. It may, of course, coincide with some interests from the other one. Indeed it is necessary for its own sake that it should. During the period of the most rapid development of the material productive forces of society and before their conflict with the existing relations of production had become obviously manifest, it might be possible to project an acceptable image of society with basic common interests. This would be a period when material living standards in general were rising. But it would be a false representation of the 'hidden' structural situation and only a temporary representation of the visible superstructural one.

The prime contradiction in capitalism between the forces of production and the social relations of production is inherent in it. It does not appear at a particular stage, though, as Marx has suggested, the conflict it generates may become manifest at a particular stage. 'From forms of development', he wrote, 'of the productive forces these (social or property) relations turn into their fetters. Then begins an epoc of social revolution.'[28] The contradiction produces a dynamism which expresses itself through the class divisions. The forces of production develop and expand through the operation of the market mechanism. Employers compete to survive. Even to remain as they are they must continually examine their cost structures and their pricing policies. This entails reducing the relatively variable labour costs, improving the efficiency of labour through the division of labour, replacing labour power with machine power and always, eventually, increasing their productive capacity, thus making it necessary for each employer to increase his share of the market or to find new markets altogether. In the absence of new markets, an increase in the capacity to produce results in larger and subsequently fewer production units, hence there is a perpetual tendency towards increasing the degree of monopoly. This process begins with capitalism and never ceases, though it experiences alternations in the degree of its intensity. So at every stage the sellers of labour power, individually helpless because they possess nothing but their labour power which they have to sell to subsist, are manipulated to satisfy the cause of more technically efficient production. The life experiences of individual

employees are dominated by the need to subsist, the possibility of unemployment, the dilution of their skills, the imposition of managerial
authority. Their rewards, their work times, their work pace, their promotion possibilities, the utilization of their skills, lie largely outside of their
own individual control. They are pitted against each other as individuals,
divided as occupational or industrial groups. They always have to react to
situations not of their own making. Of course the sellers of labour power
are not a homogeneous class. The demands of production create a complexity of interest groups within the class, with different levels of rewards,
positions of authority and statuses. The impact of the prime contradiction
is felt differentially. But the common experience in this market of many
sellers and few buyers is individual helplessness. This experience is not a
fortuitous consequence nor, on an individual basis, a remediable one. It is
an inevitable outcome of the operation of capitalism; as inevitable as the
superior power position of employers. It has always been present.

No sooner did individual sellers of labour power experience the consequences of industrialism than they acted to protect themselves against
them. The early stages of capitalism in Britain in the late seventeenth and
early eighteenth centuries were marked by the growth and spread of
friendly societies and benefit clubs to protect the emerging class from
those periods when they were unable to sell their labour power, such as
when they were sick or old, and when they received no payment and had
no kinship network to fall back on for social support because it had been
disrupted or even destroyed by the impact of industrialism. Combinations
of workers were formed, sometimes from reorganized friendly societies,
sometimes completely afresh, to protect craftsmen from an excessive use
of apprentices, or to press for improved wages and working conditions.[29] Tramping clubs were formed to assist craftsmen to obtain
work, and, therefore, to alleviate the impact of unemployment. Some idea
of the extent of the growth of trade unionism in the eighteenth century in
Britain can be gathered from the fact that by 1750 there were Acts of
Parliament specifically prohibiting workers' combinations in all important
branches of the woollen industry, and also in the silk, mohair, furs, hemp,
flax, linen, cotton, fustian, iron and leather industries.[30] There were at
least forty special Acts on the Statue Book by 1799 prohibiting
combinations in specific trades.

The characteristics of incipient trade unionism were described by a
contemporary observer who stated that in 1741 the woolcombers had
for a number of years past erected themselves into a sort of corporation
(though without a charter); their first pretence was to take care of their
poor brethren that should fall sick, or be out of work; and this was done
by meeting once or twice a week, and each of them contributing 2d. or 3d.

[1—1½p] towards the box to make a bank, and when they became a little formidable they gave laws to their masters, as also to themselves — viz., That no man should comb wool under 2s. [10p] per dozen; that no master should employ any comber that was not of their club: if he did they agreed one and all not to work for him; and if he had employed twenty they all of them turned out, and oftentimes were not satisfied with that, but would abuse the honest man that would labour, and in a riotous manner beat him, break his comb-pots, and destroy his working tools; they further support one another in so much that they are become one society throughout the kingdom. And that they may keep up their price to encourage idleness rather than labour, if any one of their club is out of work, they give him a ticket and money to seek for work at the next town where a box club is, where he is also subsisted, suffered to live a certain time with them, and then used as before; by which means he can travel the kingdom round, be caressed at each club, and not spend a farthing of his own or strike one stroke of work. This hath been imitated by the weavers also, though not carried through the kingdom, but confined to the places where they work.[31]

The meaning of this was that workers acted collectively in order to protect themselves as individuals. In every free market work situation the spontaneous response was to act collectively, to combine as a means of redressing the balance of power. The workers did not seek individual solutions to their individual problems but recognized their common basis and united to seek a solution.

The evolution of trade unionism from friendly societies, trade clubs and tramping societies occurred in the nineteenth-century development of capitalism in the USA, Germany and France, though the process was speeded up in those countries by the fact that trade unions already existed in Britain. When capitalism spread to the colonized areas of the world it was not necessary for the workers' response to it to work its way through the same empirical process. The experiences of the Western capitalist nations did not have to be repeated. Trade unionism was an acknowledged and established reaction. It was not necessary for workers in tropical Africa to realize through experience that their subsistence was determined by their relations of production, as had been the case in Britain. In so far as employers were concerned, no matter where they were, they knew that their prosperity and power depended on their particular relations to the means of production. Consequently, collective action was seen as a challenge to the employers' position, as a threat to the power and privilege it conferred.

The idea which represents collective action is collectivism. It forms the basis of the alternative dominant ideology. Its strength lies in the fact that it arose as the antithesis of individualism out of the same structural conditions. It cannot therefore be suppressed, controlled or diverted by superstructural action, such as legislation or managerial decisions. Collective action was never an *ad hoc* contingency device or a passing phenomenon. It was and is a consolidating and expanding phenomenon. In its various forms it provides the institutional apparatus through which the alternative dominant ideology enters the consciousness of individuals. It is always illegitimate in relation to the dominant ideology, and therefore the state, but it derives its own legitimacy for workers from its relevance to their conditions. And while it can never be supported by the coercive power of the state, it does, nonetheless, have a coercive basis.

Collective action by the sellers of labour power possesses its own integral ethics. These are ethics which have not been projected on it by intellectuals or reasoned from the act or seen to be implicit in the act. They are overtly expressed in the act itself. Collective action against employers depends for its effectiveness on the unity of the workers involved, that is, on solidarity. Because the workers do not possess legal means to impose unity they can only act if the majority of them are agreed, voluntarily, to act. The ethic of solidarity does not entail 100 per cent voluntary support but the acceptance of majority decisions by the minority. Because collective action occurs within the context of class conflict, those who do not support it are often punished by whatever measures are at hand.

Historically the most important requirement has been continuing solidarity within a section of the class. Thus non-membership of a combination in eighteenth-century England was an offence against the ethic of solidarity. When cloth weavers in Lancashire formed a combination in 1757 they insulted and threatened to deny the means of employment to those who did not support it. The journeymen tailors of Liverpool went on strike in 1768 because their employer 'had employed a strange journeyman that did not belong to their club'.[32] Journeymen tailors described those who would not join their combinations as 'dung'. The efforts of tailors to achieve solidarity during the middle years of the eighteenth century attracted so much attention that in 1767 a play was produced at the Theatre Royal in the Haymarket, London, called *The Tailors; A Tragedy for Warm Weather*. It was a burlesque, dealing with a strike of tailors. The strikers met in one of their normal meeting places described as a House of Call and there one of them said:

'Tis well known to all Some timid Dungs (unworthy of the name Alike of

tailor or of man; from whom opprobrious proverbs rise to hurt our fame
Meanly descend to work for half-a-crown. [33]

The terms such as blackleg and scab which later came to refer to strike breakers, at first referred to non-unionists. It came to be regarded as a crime to threaten or break the solidarity of workers in their collective action against employers. The United Society of Cordwainers went so far, in 1792, to describe a man guilty of such an act as a traitor. 'And what is a scab?' ran the preface to their rules

He is to his trade what a traitor is to his country; though both may be
useful to one party in troublesome times, when peace returns they are
detested alike by all. When help is wanted, he is the last to contribute
assistance, and the first to grasp a benefit he never laboured to procure. He
cares but for himself, but he sees not beyond the extent of a day, and for a
momentary and worthless approbation, would destroy friends, family and
country. In short, he is a traitor on a small scale. He first sells the journey-
men and is himself afterwards sold in his turn by the masters. [34]

In the middle years of the nineteenth century, in the Manchester and Sheffield engineering trades physical violence was used against men who refused to pay their union dues or who infringed union regulations. Such men were subjected at first to rattening involving the removal of bands and tools, then to gunpowder attacks. [35]

The enforcement of the ethic of solidarity was to provide assistance to individuals in common situations of adversary on the basis of equality. Many of the unions had originally started as benefit societies and had derived a permanent involvement in social security from them. Helping each other, helping those in need, became characteristic features of trade unionism. There is a poem written by a bricklayer about a Dublin society of journeymen tailors in 1725:

> . . . A task so noble suits the brightest pen
> To write the merits of these journeymen;
> Wrapt in close Union by the Laws they've made,
> Superior be to any other trade, . . .
> Who Age supports and orphans young maintain,
> Their sick relieve, likewise their dead inter,
> What action greater can the world prefer? [36]

When the Oldham cloth weavers formed their combination in 1757 they maintained a charity box for the relief of poor weavers. They went on strike in 1758, their leaders were arrested and the existence of their union was threatened. The weavers, however, refused to leave their union, arguing that, 'if weavers sign to withdraw their subscriptions from the boxes they will at the same time withdraw their charity from one another'.[37] This sentiment of charity which arose out of conditions of gross inequality of treatment, even among wage-earners themselves, was enlarged to include the removal of the conditions of inequality as the horizons of the workers were widened through the growth of the labour markets and the linking of societies in different towns. Attempts were made to equalize wages for similar tasks and to prevent wage-payment methods based on piecework which produced differential earnings.

The concrete attempts to remove economic inequality in their work situations was made against a background of ideas about equality in a wider sense, stemming from the seventeenth century. It was a background of discussions about the rights of man initiated by the Levellers and Diggers. To quote Christopher Hill:

So although the Puritan revolution was defeated, the revolution in thought could not be unmade. . . . Even the ideas of men who would not compromise in 1660, of Milton and the Levellers, these ideas were driven underground but could not be killed. . . . The Levellers came nearer to oblivion, but their ideas continued to circulate underground. A century after the Restoration, Goldsmith's Vicar of Wakefield cried, 'I would have all men kings. I would be a king myself. We have all naturally an equal right to the throne; we are all originally equal.' This, he added, 'was once the opinion of a set of honest men who were called Levellers'. Through the writings of Catherine Macauley and others the ideas of the Levellers passed into the radical tradition of the seventeen-sixties.[38]

When wage-earners came to set up their organizations they had before them the example of seventeenth-century Dissenters from the established Church who in their endeavours to survive oppression had run their organizations on the basis of common commitment and equality. The earliest trade union organizations were based on the principle of common commitment with a strong anti-authoritarian bias. Equality within the organizations was achieved through regulated and uniform membership participation on a rotating basis. In Britain for sure, the principle of equality was embodied in trade union organizations as firmly as that of inequality was expressed in business organizations. From the outset then trade unions became expressions of an ideology of which solidarity and equality, the antithesis of all that was important in the capitalist ideology, were basic principles. Solidarity for wage-earners became a means to greater liberty.

The question of liberty in a wider, more general sense was central in the American and French Revolutions. Both events were surrounded by discourses about the ideas of liberty and democracy. In Britain, Dr Richard Price, a nonconformist radical, publicized the freedom he considered should be guaranteed while Edmund Burke, in *Reflections on the Revolution in France* wrote what amounted to a reply. Mary Wollstonecraft and others replied to Burke but the most influential answer came from Tom Paine in *The Rights of Man*, the first part of which appeared in 1791. The ideas associated with trade unionism were given an explicit political connotation by the events of the last three decades of the eighteenth century. Thereafter they were developed and refined out of and to match the life experiences of wage-earners. The poet Shelley, in his 'Song to the Men of England', gave expression to the notion of class which was emerging in the discourses. In Britain, others such as William Thompson and Thomas Hodgskin developed and expounded the notion of 'Utopian socialism' as the alternative to capitalism. The institutional expressions of these particular ideas were cooperative communities, first established by Robert Owen in Scotland. Experiments in cooperation were made in Britain and the USA, and later in other capitalist countries. Retail cooperative societies were further institutional expressions of the emerging alternative ideology.

The belief that the source of the poverty and oppression of workers lay in the capitalist system had many threads, but it was not until the second half of the nineteenth century that they became the cloth of an ideology. The work of transformation was done by Karl Marx and Friedrich Engels. Through their work and for the first time a coherent, logically constructed ideology existed as an expression of the prime dominating contradiction in capitalist societies. It did not represent an idealist or utopian alternative to capitalism but one rising from the changing reality of capitalism. It was the fact that it had roots in reality that gave it its strength and, indeed, its claim to be an ideology. The alternative ideology has become more elaborate and pervasive as the contradiction in capitalism has become itensified. It challenges the dominant ideology in all its details in that it presents an alternative perception, therefore, interpretation of reality. Because it constitutes a conceptual approach to reality it possesses paradigmatic qualities and can provide commonsense answers to the whole range of questions concerning social behaviour. Its institutional expressions are trade unions and other bodies such as strike committees or, in Britain, shop stewards' organizations which practise trade unionism, political organizations committed to achieving qualitative change, such as Communist parties and splinter revolutionary groups, and, to a lesser extent, cooperative societies. These institutions possess their own media for propagating the ideas belonging to the ideology, while trade unions have the means to enforce them. The alternative ideology has, therefore, hegemonic qualities. It will achieve complete hegemony when the prime contradiction is resolved and the alternative ideology becomes the dominant one, but this would be only a temporary phase for the new situation possesses its own contradiction and would therefore produce ideas which were the antithesis of the dominant ones.

It has been necessary to spell out the alternative dominant ideology because most social scientists do not even recognize its existence. And even those who do generally fail to see it as a coherent and logically consistent challenge to the dominant prevailing ideas in a society. For this reason many apparent inconsistencies in social behaviour are inexplicable to them. The point is that all people are subjected to ideological influences which determine their understanding of situations. Some people, because of their class positions, are subjected to qualitatively different competing influences. In capitalist societies these competitive influences are experienced only by those who suffer the exigencies of selling their labour power. Of course within each ideology there are variations corresponding to different situations within classes. The variations are equivalent to models within a conceptual framework; they have a common basis with distinguishing frills. Everyone, therefore, irrespective of his class position, is exposed to marginally competitive ideas about his reality. Ideologies, moreover, change over time to accommodate alternations in the distribution of skills and power. For instance, ideas about monopoly, the position of government, the planning of resources, the liberty of individuals within capitalist societies, have altered because the reality of capitalism has made it necessary that they should alter. No ideas can persist for long which do not correspond to some degree to reality. The state under *laissez-faire* capitalism must be viewed differently from that under monopoly capitalism. As state power becomes necessary as an instrument to buttress ailing capitalist societies, as it does in the corporate state phase of capitalism, then the state must be perceived as a desirable instrument of intervention.

The extent to which those who sell their labour power are subjected to the revolutionary influences of a competitive ideology depends on the extent to which it has been developed in its fullest sense. The alternative ideology develops with the prime contradiction. It can and does project views about the organization of future societies which do not contain the self-destroying ingredients of capitalism. These views are not utopian; they are based on the main ideas in the ideology and start from the situation where the social relations of production have changed. An image of society without economic class divisions, without the exploitation of labour and without marked relative deprivation, has attractions, and when propagated may draw the attention of people in deprived and exploited positions to their state. But it can never determine consciousness, because this depends not on images but on the manner in which ideas interpret reality: on the relevance of the alternative ideology for understanding reality and the irrelevance of the dominant ideology, and these in turn depend on the intensity of the contradiction. The alternative ideology may fall short of explaining concrete conditions, but it can never surpass them.

The two ideologies, as stated above, potentially compete with each other in all aspects of social behaviour. The actual competition is mostly much less than this. It is a situation where the dominant ideology with all the answers faces an encroaching challenge which may be patchy and intermittent, with areas where the dominant ideology may be transparently irrelevant but with nothing to take its place. In the areas where the ideologies do confront each other it is a case of individuals seeing through some explanations and seeing sense in others. Through the new explanations the individuals become able to punctuate the façade of visible social relations and to detect the 'hidden' structure of their situations so that the visible social relations take on a new and different meaning. Old questions, concerning, say, profit-making, managerial control, social status and general relationships with employers demand and get new answers. The white-collar worker, unorganized and dependent on the goodwill of his employer, feels threatened by the erosion of his economic and social privileges and suddenly sees himself as an *employee*. This, for him, is equivalent to taking on a new identity. He is still a citizen, perhaps a husband or a father as before, but he is no longer an individual worker as before. He has become conscious of his identity with a group. The employee, organized, conscious of his dependence on collective action in his work situation through a perpetual struggle to keep where he is may see for the first time the dependence of his identity as a citizen on that as an employee and recognize that his struggle is not against employers but against a form of distribution. He then becomes conscious of class relations. He may still be the dominant, chauvinistic male but he has taken on a new political identity. In all cases, areas of individual activity remain untouched by the new means of perception hence the continuation of paradoxical inconsistent forms of behaviour. The woman who realizes that she is in an exploited position may take on a new consciousness as a woman without this affecting all other identities. She may alter as a wife and mother but not necessarily as a worker or citizen. But once in that new position her consciousness about other identities will alter as she feels the need for a reappraisal. Black people may similarly have to pass through many stages before they experience a convergence of new identities and see the need to alter, in Gramschi's terms, the whole ensemble of social relations to which they belong.

The criteria for the use of skills and the exercise of power, at all levels of social activity, are provided by the competing ideologies. The decisions embodying the criteria are made by individuals but they are not characterized significantly by individuality. The ideologies, through consciousness and compulsion, provide criteria which are interpreted through the life experiences of individual persons and become a part of individual personalities. The outstanding feature of life experiences, however, is their basic uniformity and commonality within groups and classes and not their uniqueness. In the things that matter there is very little that is unique. The important questions about individuals concern the membership of economic classes and economic and social groups within classes, whether male or female, black or white, indigenous or foreign. When answers to these questions have been given, not much needs to be added to achieve an understanding of behaviour. Add class and sex positions to an American white Anglo-Saxon protestant (WASP) and the story is adequately full. It achieves completeness when the ideologies are interpreted through the minutiae of individual, family and small group environments. In other words, at this level of analysis, the meanings which individuals attach to situations are meanings reached through ideologies. In order to understand the causes of social behaviour it is more important to know the ideologies than the meanings which individuals give to situations. By recognizing the competitive existence of dual ideologies the reason for qualitative changes in meanings can be readily identified.

Broadly the meanings which individual persons attach to social situations of all dimensions relate either to maintaining them as they are or changing them. As meanings are obtained through the use of conceptual frameworks this categorization is consistent with what has been stated frequently in this book, namely that there are only static and dynamic frameworks. The dominant ideology is for the maintenance of things and employs the relatively static conceptual approach while the alternative dominant ideology is for change and rests on the dynamic conceptual approach. It is easy to see how those who adopt a phenomenological view of reality find evidence of homeostasis or self-equilibrating mechanisms, for the dominant ideological influences direct attention to the present as a permanent phenomenon and, therefore, encourage a search for such evidence. The institutions which embody the dominant ideology operate to perpetuate its existence and, therefore, the power relationships for which it stands. These institutions act to maintain the present power relationships either by making action outside or contrary to them difficult, as with the market mechanism, or by propagating ideas which are at the core of the ideology, as does the family.

The process of expressing and communicating these ideas reinforces them. Just as it is not men but skills which matter in substance, so it is not the media through which language is expressed which matter but the meanings the linguistic symbols convey. Words are a means of interpreting the world of reality and are not, and never can be, neutral. The rules of language, its visible form, are transmitted from one generation to another and have an historical continuity which, while reflecting the complexity of societies do not necessarily alter with ideologies. As Piaget has said, however, 'every word in a language designates a concept, which constitutes its signification'.[39] Words derive their meanings from the general prevalent conceptualization of reality and this, in capitalist societies, is the dominant static one. So it is easy to express ideas about the present existing social relationships, but relatively difficult to describe and analyse their transformation. For this latter purpose words have to be redefined or new ones invented to facilitate dissociation from static meanings. Where words and meanings from the dominant paradigm have entered into everyday usage, as role has for example, then it may be cumbersome to have to redefine them continually and it might be more expedient to dispense with them altogether. It is because words inhibit the expression of ideas outside and contrary to the dominant ideology that language acts as a *status quo* reinforcing element.

The belief that societies are systems with self-equilibrating mechanisms is made more plausible because of the equilibrating activities of institutions which embody the alternative dominant ideology. No institution can survive in a situation for long without taking on some of its characteristics. This is stipulated by the assumption of materialism. Trade unions and political parties which arise out of the contradiction in capitalism are not left with pure unsullied ideas and notions. They have to operate in situations dominated by the continual presence of the contradiction and, therefore, the competitive existence of the two ideologies. In some of their activities they inevitably become influenced by the dominant ideology and this puts them in the paradoxical position where they are operating to preserve and change their environments at one and the same time. Trade unionism, namely the phenomenon of collective action by employees' embodies the alternative dominant ideology as to a lesser extent, do the institutionalized expressions of trade unionism, trade unions. But trade unions have formal relations with employers which involve them in accepting capitalist situations. They engage in collective bargaining activities which imply and involve compromising with employers in order to preserve unions as organizations. They are involved with employers and governments in attempting to overcome economic and social problems as defined by the dominant power interests. The current concern of unions in most Western capitalist countries in tackling the question of inflation is a case in point. Trade unions in Britain are continually involved in advisory and consultation relationships with governments committed to preserving the main fabric of capitalism.

A good example of the paradoxical situation of unions and most related political parties in Britain concerns their attitude to industrial and political action. Trade unions use industrial action such as strikes, overtime bans, working to rule and go-slow campaigns, in order to force their demands on employers. They do not normally use industrial action to achieve political objectives, that is to force their demands on governments as governments and not as employers. This dichotomy is consistent with the dominant ideology through which industrial action for industrial ends is deprecated but accepted, whereas industrial action for political ends is totally un-acceptable. According to the dominant ideology, political decisions must be made within the rule of law through the parliamentary process. Govern-ments, however, are increasingly intervening in industrial relations and in economic and social affairs in such a way as to influence the industrial objectives of unions. Trade unions thus find themselves unable to ignore governments yet largely incapable of influencing them except through traditional political channels. The short-term consequence is that the economic system of which the parliamentary process is a part is protected from transforming pressures for at the point where trade unions should recognize the political significance of their demands they become disarmed of their power. In a variety of ways trade unions reveal the influence of competing ideologies in their behaviour through inconsistencies and para-doxes. An increasingly consistent form of behaviour occurs as one ideology, in the case of unions the alternative one, extends its influence. The extent to which this happens, with organizations as with individuals, depends on the relevance of the two ideologies for explaining reality. As unions become aware through their own experiences of either the irrele-vance of parliamentary decision-making as a determinant of living standards or the futility of controlling governments through electoral procedures, the ideas which buttress the political decision-making process will become discredited and a barrier to qualitative change will be removed. To the conformist observer this would appear as a breakdown in the equilibrating mechanism.

The political parties which have arisen from the prime contradiction in capitalism and which embody the alternative dominant ideology are notoriously and equally susceptible to the influences of the dominant ideology. In order to survive as continuing institutions these parties take on some of the characteristics and attitudes of the environment they are endeavouring to alter. As with trade unions, their achilles heel seems to be their acceptance of the predominant political decision-making process, but unlike trade unions they are not directly subjected to the pressures from the prime contradiction which produce a rejection of the process.

The point is that the ideological pressures in support of maintaining the *status quo* permeate those organizations which stand for its rejection and become institutionalized in them. These organizations, therefore, tend to reinforce the obstacles to change and give the appearance of a built-in resistance to change. The proliferation of obstacles to change in a society, however, means nothing more than that there is much institutional support for the *status quo*. It gives no indication of the means by which change is achieved or obstructed. It tells nothing about the relationships between variables in a social situation. Indeed in this respect, as in many others, appearances are deceptive. In order to understand how the pressures which emanate from economic sources are transmitted through to social action, and to identify and assess their impact, it is necessary again to examine the 'hidden' structure of reality.

Notes

1. Gramschi, *The Prison Notebooks*, pp. 452, 453, 296, 20.
2. Althusser, *For Marx*, pp. 114n, 106, 111.
3. *Ibid.*, pp. 113—14.
4. Karl Marx, *The Eighteenth Brumaire of Louis Bonaparte*, p. 9.
5. W. Baldamus, *Efficiency and Effort*, Tavistock Publications, 1961, p. 5.
6. In this connection it is worth noting that the term 'skill' is rarely used to describe the competence of, say, strikers, or trade unions, or revolutionary political groups whose actions are contrary to the common-goal oriented ones.
7. Baldamus, *op. cit.*, p. 1.
8. *Ibid.*, p. 8.
9. Morris Janowitz, see in particular, *Sociology and the Military Establishment*, New York, Russell Sage Foundation, 1959; *The Professional Soldier*, Illinois, Free Press of Glencoe, 1960.
10. Janowitz, *Sociology and the Military Establishment*, p. 26.
11. *Ibid.*, p. 28.
12. *Ibid.*, p. 98.
13. Cf. Adam Curle, *Educational Strategy for Developing Countries*, Tavistock Publications, 1963, p. 45.
14. Max Weber, *The Theory of Social and Economic Organization*, trans. A. Henderson and Talcott Parsons, p. 159.
15. K. Marx and F. Engels, *The German Ideology*, Lawrence & Wishart, 1965, pp. 42—3.
16. *Ibid.*, p. 37.

17.   *Ibid.*, pp. 37—8.
18.   Georg Lukács, *History and Class Consciousness*, Merlin Press, London, 1971, pp. 159ff.
19.   *A Dictionary of the Social Sciences*, ed. Gould and Kolb, p. 315.
20.   Althusser, *op. cit.*, pp. 231—2.
21.   Gramschi, *op. cit.*, p. 12.
22.   Althusser, *op. cit.*, p. 233.
23.   *Ibid.*, p. 231.
24.   Maurice Cornforth, *The Open Philosophy and the Open Society*, Lawrence & Wishart, 1968, p. 387.
25.   See the comments on this by George H. Sabine in his chapter on Fascism in *A History of Political Theory*, Harrap, 1963, p. 626ff.
26.   Gramschi, *op. cit.*, p. 359.
27.   *Ibid.*, p. 352.
28.   Marx, Preface to *A Contribution to the Critique of Political Economy*, *loc. cit.*, i, 329.
29.   This is not the place to reproduce the history of seventeenth- and eighteenth-century trade unionism in Britain. Such a history has not yet been written, but those who wish to see the empirical evidence can consult the many studies of industries during that period. There are, for example:
      J. V. Nef, *The Rise of the British Coal Industry*, Routledge, 1932.
      G. W. Daniels, *The Early English Cotton Industry*, Manchester University Press, 1920.
      A. P. Wadsworth and Julia de L. Mann, *The Cotton Trade and Industrial Lancashire 1600—1780*, Manchester University Press, 1965.
      F. W. Galton, *The Tailoring Trade*, Longmans, 1896.
      G. I. H. Lloyd, *The Cutlery Trades*, Longmans, Green, 1913.
      E. Lipson, *Woollen and Worsted Industries*, Cass, 1965.
      E. Welbourne, *The Miners' Unions of Northumberland and Durham*, Cambridge University Press, 1923.
      This is but a sample of the works which contain evidence of early examples of collective action. Sidney and Beatrice Webb in chapter 1, 'The Origins of Trade Unionism', of their *History of Trade Unionism*, Longmans, Green, 1920, discuss the significance and extent of the growth of friendly societies. Sir Frederick Eden's *State of the Poor*, Routledge, 1928, contains empirical evidence about trade clubs in the late eighteenth century.
30.   Cf. Lloyd, *The Cutlery Trades*, p. 238.
31.   Quoted in Webb and Webb, *History of Trade Unionism*, pp. 36—7.
32.   Wadsworth and Mann, *op. cit.*, pp. 362, 379.

33. Galton, *The Tailoring Trade*, pp. xli–xlii.
34. A. Aspinall, ed., *The Early English Trade Unions*, Batchworth Press, London, 1949, p. 84.
35. See *Sheffield Trades and Labour Council, 1858–1958*, Sheffield Trades & Labour Council, Yorkshire, pp. 26ff.
36. Galton, *op. cit.*, p. 27.
37. Wadsworth and Mann, *op. cit.*, p. 362.
38. Christopher Hill, *The Century of Revolution 1603–1714*, Nelson, 1967, p. 190.
39. Piaget, *Structuralism*, p. 74.

The dialectical process

The main issue facing organization theorists and, *ipso facto*, sociologists at large, was stated at the beginning of chapter 7 as being the analysis of movement. The last two chapters have been concerned with the location of its sources. This one deals with its process. Much of the earlier chapters would be acceptable to conventional sociologists. The act of criticizing does not involve a commitment to an alternative approach. The recent works of A. W. Gouldner and of R. W. Friedrichs,[1] for example, contain trenchant criticisms of contemporary sociology but stop there. Even sections of the chapters on materialism might be palatable to many critics of conventional theory. Materialism by itself could be described as structuralism, which is an increasingly popular designation for 'progressive' sociologists. For some, as has already been stated, materialism simply means considering economic factors and this is not too demanding. There are other conventional sociologists, who, while they would recoil from the description 'historical materialism', would agree that economic factors must be considered and treated historically. It is only when the word dialectics is mentioned that the real and absolute recoil takes place, for dialectics is seen to imply not simply a rejection of conventional analysis but a commitment to a genuine alternative, a rejection of a whole ideology for another and with it an acceptance that the *status quo*, with all it implies, is a temporary phenomenon. At the moment, the political implications of this are too much for the vast majority of Western sociologists to stomach.

Perhaps at this point it should be mentioned why the term dialectical materialism is used rather than historical materialism. It is not simply a question of nomenclature. Gramschi reverses their usage when he refers to 'historical materialism' in his *Prison Notebooks* as a term which involves the area of dialectics. In a section on 'Historical materialism and sociology', for example, he criticized sociology by stating that 'vulgar evolutionism is at the root of sociology, and sociology cannot know the dialectical principle with its passage from quantity to quality'.[2] For non-Marxist writers the two terms are often treated as synonymous but they can only be so if they are actually defined in that way. Without definitions to the contrary the terms have different meanings. The position can but be put like this: dialectical materialism must inevitably be historical but historical materialism need not be dialectical. Dialectical materialism involves recognizing that historical development proceeds in a manner which ensures that the pressures for movement are continuous and inexorable. Historical materialism might simply mean taking history into account in some way and for that reason it would be an inaccurate description of the method employed here.

The most important thing to recognize about the dialectical method is that it provides an understanding of a simple process in concrete social reality. It is not a philosophical concept, and in attempting to understand it, it would be best to forget Hegel's triad, thesis, antithesis and synthesis, and to ignore the discussion about the manner in which Marx originally conceived of the method. This is not to suggest that Hegel did not use a dialectical method, that Marx was not influenced by Hegel's work and that Marx's use of it was not in a sense an inversion of Hegel's. It is only suggested that an examination of the dialectics in terms of philosophical origins is misleading and confusing and endless. Engels emphasized this point in *Anti-Duhring*. There he reproduced a quotation from *Capital* to illustrate the way 'the negation of the negation' was used. He then added:

And now I ask the reader: where are the dialectical frills and mazes and conceptual arabesques; where the mixed and misconceived ideas according to which everything is all one and the same thing in the end: where the dialectical miracle for his faithful followers . . . Marx merely shows from history . . . that . . . the capitalist mode of production has . . . created the material conditions from which it must perish. The process is a historical one, and if it is at the same time a dialectical process, this is not Marx's fault. [3]

According to Engels the dialectical method was not a 'mere proof-producing instrument' but primarily 'a method of arriving at new results, of advancing from the known to the unknown'.[4] And for this the method had to be based in reality. Lenin wrote that:

What Marx and Engels called the dialectical method — as against the metaphysical — is nothing else than the scientific method in sociology, which consists in regarding society as a living organism in a state of constant development (and not as something mechanically concatenated and therefore permitting all sorts of arbitrary combinations of separate social elements). [5]

And he commented on Engels's defence of the dialectical method in *Anti-Duhring* as follows:

It is clear to everybody that the main weight of Engels argument is that materialists must correctly and accurately depict the actual historical process, and that insistence on dialectics, the selection of examples to demonstrate the correctness of the triad, is nothing but a relic of the Hegelianism out of which scientific socialism has grown. [6]

A difference between Marx and subsequent users of the dialectical method is that while Marx simply used the method in his analysis those who followed could not do likewise without first making Marx's own use of it explicit. In other words the method has had to be elicited from his work, formulated and examined. Unfortunately, the comments of Engels and Lenin have frequently been ignored in the process of Marxist theory construction and elaboration and the Hegelian triad has been given undue prominence. One of the difficulties has been that so long as the dialectic has been described in philosophical terms it has been extremely difficult to break with Hegel. In a relatively recent book, *The Sociology of Marx*, [7] Henri Lefebvre continually referred back to Hegel and constantly contrasted Marxism with Hegelianism. It is not intended to do that here and the discussion will not be conducted in philosophical terms. It should be emphasized, however, that the rejection of philosophy is not intended as a denigration of it but is necessary in order to present dialectical materialism as an analytical tool.

The quality of totality

The dialectical process relates to a particular relationship between variables in real social situations. The reality to which it relates possesses the pervasive quality of totality. It is only through an understanding of this quality that dialectics can be comprehended, for without it there would be and could be no dialectical relationships. Lukács emphasized the importance of totality, or what he called 'concrete totality' in his use of dialectics:

It is not the predominance of economic motives in the interpretation of society which is the decisive difference between Marxism and bourgeois science but rather the point of view *of totality. The category of totality, the all-round determining* domination of the whole over the parts *is the essence of the method.* [8]

Lukács was correct to make this point, but it should be made clear that the predominance of economic factors and the quality of totality are not separate categories which may or may not be accepted. The view of reality as a totality follows logically from accepting the causal predominance of economic factors. The case of totality has in fact already been made out in the two previous chapters on structure and superstructure. Those chapters must be seen as the context for the discussion here.

Totality is a perceived quality resting and depending on particular assumptions about causality. The totality which gives rise to dialectical relationships is one where its parts are always seen in relation to and through an analysis of itself. This contrasts with the totality which is made up of any number of parts and which has no causal significance for them. This distinction marks a crucial difference between dynamic and static theories. The static totality is a basically unmediated one in that it contains nothing which binds or holds it together. It is sociologically indeterminate for its boundaries or limits are set by non-sociological criteria – anything the analyst cares to use. Whatever it is, it can be divided and subdivided into any number of parts, all of which possess similar largely unmediated qualities. Thus a totality may be a particular ethnic society, or an area of it, or an organization within it, or a family unit. Each totality could be described as a system or a subsystem in a wider system, depending on how the analyst wishes to describe the situation he is examining. Each system or subsystem possesses the common quality of consensus or organic unity and it is for this reason that it can be subdivided or added to indiscriminately. If the greatest possible totality possesses consensus qualities then so must every part of it.

This description applies also to totalities which are regarded as having pluralistic qualities. Pluralism recognizes disrupted consensus and therefore acknowledges conflict, tensions and frictions. But it treats the divisive factors with equal priority and gives none, at any level, structural qualities. The disrupting elements, however, can be removed so the possibility of attaining consensus always exists. In conceptual terms there is no distinction between a totality with consensus and one with pluralistic qualities. Each possesses a common value system with basically commonly accepted goals. The only difference is that in the one case there is no possibility of alternative, contrasting, mediating goals, whereas in the other case this possibility does exist but only in short-run terms. It is for this reason that these totalities are described as 'basically unmediated' ones.

It is well to remember that although totality needs to be explained as a conceptualization of reality in order to identify the assumptions about reality which underlie it, it refers to all situations in which men and women find themselves. It concerns the relationship between subsisting, work and leisure. It is about the development of mankind in all its aspects, about every level of social activity and all degrees of technical intensity.

The simplification, abstraction and level of generalization necessary to equip the concept for analytical use should not be allowed to obscure that it is about the down-to-earth, day-to-day tasks of living. The basically unmediated totality implies that these tasks may be hampered by ignorance, malevolence or greed but are in no way obstructed by forces which arise out of the structure of the totality itself. The totality implicit in dialectical materialism implies that all aspects of the tasks of living are causally interrelated, that it is not possible to break the tasks into autonomous systems. The origin of this notion of totality lay with Marx. Lefebvre commented correctly that Marx's 'originality was to conceive, as a totality, the production of man by his own efforts, his own labour, starting from nature and from need in order to achieve enjoyment'.[9] Thus totality refers to very complex social relationships.

A totality which is causally superior to its parts can only be so if it possesses a structural unity. That is, there must be something about its structure which gives it a pervasive and continuing influence. In the light of the previous paragraph this amounts to stating that the business of living must possess common basic determinants of action. If every social situation possessed its own stimuli or none at all then there could be no unifying causal determinant. The basic determinants, moreover, must have continuity over time otherwise a rather odd form of empiricism would have to be practised, namely, that of discovering a succession of basic determinants. Empiricism as described in an earlier chapter, in which every situation possesses its own source of movement, is inconsistent with a dynamic reality. A totality which is causally superior to its parts, then, is one which has historically determined structural determinants.

Lukács took this explanation a stage further when he wrote in 1947:

The materialist-dialectical conception of totality means first of all the concrete unity of interacting contradictions . . .; secondly, the systematic relativity of all totality both upwards and downwards (which means that all totality is made of totalities subordinated to it, and also that the totality in question is, at the same time, overdetermined by totalities of a higher complexity . . .) and thirdly, the historical relativity of all totality, namely that the totality – character of all totality is changing, disintegrating, confined to a determinate, concrete historical period.[10]

The question 'what does a totality really mean in this context?' remains to be answered. The answer has two parts. Firstly a meaning has to be given to the dialectical character of totality. Lukács referred to 'the concrete unity of interacting contradictions'. This statement has to be given some practical significance for, after all, it purports to relate to 'concrete reality'. At first sight the totality here has no boundaries and no historical limits, though Lukács, without specifying what he means, does refer to a 'concrete historical period'. Strictly this is the case. What sense then is there in talking about a structural unity?

The prime contradiction

The reality under discussion, as was shown in chapter 7, is a constantly changing one. It is dominated by conflict, schism and tensions. It is characterized by irreconcilable economic classes which have their basis in the structure of the society. Somewhere in this structure lies the source of the movement which maintains the pressures for change. This source is not the origin of movement in the sense that it gives rise to it. There can be no beginning in a constantly changing situation, only a transitory point in its progression from one state to another. It is always necessary, therefore, to take account of what Althusser describes as an 'ever-pre-givenness':

There is no longer any original essence, only an ever-pre-givenness, however far knowledge delves into its past. . . . There is no longer any original simple unity (in any form whatsoever), but instead, the ever-pre-givenness of a structured complex unity. [11]

This should always be borne in mind in the following discussion. The source of movement as described here has its own pre-givenness, or, in the terminology of the last two chapters, its own structure.

All movement originates in material conditions of which the most important factors are the relations of production. In all societies the relations of production can be identified through the manner in which labour power is obtained and controlled. A situation in which labour power is obtained and controlled through the free market mechanism presupposes the private ownership of the means of production and the rational use of economic resources for private gain. It presupposes, in other words, production within a market and, therefore, competitive system, for sale within a society where severe production limitations are imposed on expenditure by the distribution of income and wealth which the private ownership of the means of production creates and the market mechanism perpetuates. The relationship between the distribution system set by the social relations of production and the forces of production, were identified by Marx as the prime contradiction in capitalist societies. Some bare details of the contradiction have been mentioned a number of times already in earlier chapters. It is worth adding to them, however, in order to show how the contradictory elements originate from the same set of circumstances and to reveal the true nature of contradictions.

Capitalist societies are acquisitive. The prime motive for production is the accumulation of wealth through greater profits but, in case the motive is ever likely to be forgotten, the market mechanism ensures that attention has always to be given to profit levels. It is a case of a basic idea being institutionalized and acting on people despite what they think or intend. In order to make profits entrepreneurs have to produce goods and services; in order to maintain profits they have to compete with each other within commodity markets; their profit levels therefore depend on their competitive effectiveness. All entrepreneurs have to engage in some form of competition, either in commodity markets on a local, national or international scale or, in the extreme cases of relatively effective monopoly, for larger shares of people's expendable income. Even the most apparently impregnable monopolist has to guard against the rise of potential competitors and the development of alternative products. In a dynamic market situation his impregnability can only be temporary. The forces of competition act as a continual threat to profit levels and although entrepreneurs have resorted to many devices to protect themselves from the exigencies of competition, they have eventually been forced to engage in it with greater intensity. Their formal and informal price agreements, cartels, trade associations and the like have at the best been short-term expedients. Entrepreneurs have been forced to search for new markets and for methods of production which would enable them to compete for existing markets more effectively. The discovery and opening up of new markets is, from the point of view of most entrepreneurs, something they read about but rarely witness and participate in. Even those who are fortunate enough to tap new markets, such as motor manufacturers during the last three decades, frequently live to see them saturated. The entrepreneurial function is concerned, in the main, with seeking to survive in existing markets. It is concerned at one and the same time with problems of production and distribution. These give rise to a prime structural contradiction.

There is an inherent tendency in free market economies for excess productive capacity to develop. The tendency is expressed through the actions of the multiplicity of business organizations which comprise the various commodity markets. The precise responses of business organizations to economic pressures vary as the characteristics of their particular market situations vary, but all markets have common features which produce the generalized reactions which result in excess capacity.

Every business organization is compelled to expand its production capacity simply in order to retain its existing share of the market. Put differently, any firm which is satisfied with the *status quo* market situation, which wants a quiet, stable existence, and which assumes that it needs to take no special action to maintain its position, is vulnerable and in a state of potential decline. The reality of market situations is some degree of imperfection and, therefore, unpredictability. A firm does not and cannot know what action its competitors are contemplating in order to protect their market shares. Even if no action is contemplated a firm must assume that it is and must act accordingly. The consequence is that all firms in a market have to act on the assumption that their market positions are threatened. Each firm, therefore, must at the very least hedge itself in with protective measures. It must be capable of anticipating price reductions, or improvements in the quality of competing products, or the introduction of new alternative products. Even if it is convinced that its product will not be displaced because of its monopolistic position, a firm has first to ensure that it does not price itself out of consumers' expenditure, and second to take steps to maintain its monopoly In other words, every business organization has to be cost conscious if it is to survive. This is merely an empirical expression of the logic of a situation in which there are unbroken pressures for movement. In a market situation there can never be an equilibrium position nor one of stability, only positions of frustrated movement achieved either by the temporary connivance of competing organizations or by an organization's ability to anticipate market changes.

Cost consciousness entails a constant scrutiny of production costs with a view to their reduction. All business organizations have costs with varying degrees of variability. In the long run all costs are variable but in the short run it is possible to categorize variable and fixed costs. The variable costs mainly relate to the prices of labour power while fixed costs are the prices of capital invested in land, buildings and machines.

Labour costs comprise the earnings of labour and the cost of organizing the skills and intensity of efforts of labour. These can be manipulated to varying extents depending on the resistance of workers' organizations. It is becoming increasingly difficult for employers to depress wage rates, though through their control over overtime working they can often depress earnings. Economies may be achieved by pruning work situations but they are likely to be slight. Action of this sort in order to safeguard the market position of a firm could be hampered by the ability of trade unions to make the matter public through their opposition as well as through their ability to resist unilateral action. A much more practical step for a firm would be to extend control over the skill and intensity of work. This could take the form of increased supervision, a change in the method of wage payment, an intensification of work through speeding up machines or an alteration in the division of labour. These tend to be unreliable ways of obtaining long-term cost benefits because their effects can be dissipated by uncooperative employees either collectively or as individuals. All business organizations are forced eventually, therefore, to endeavour to reduce costs by increasing productivity through the use of more technically effective machines. This method, while reducing costs, increases productive capacity. A business organization which aims to stand still, therefore, finds itself needing a larger share of its market in order to do so.

In reality business organizations both struggle to survive and plan to expand but the net effect in all cases is similar — an increase in productive capacity and a consequent need for larger market shares. As was suggested above, for most business organizations this results in a struggle for existing markets. The overall result is a constant tendency for the degree of monopoly to increase with the further consequence of increased productive capacity. Some firms inevitably lose their market shares to others, who are thus able, temporarily, to utilize their productive capacities. But virtually simultaneously with the acquisition of new markets firms have to act to consolidate their hold over them, and they go through the same process, resulting in excess capacity, but this time the excess may be greater for a particular firm than before because the scale of production is larger and the additional units of production, due to indivisibilities, may also be larger. Much depends on the nature of the production process, though in all cases some excess capacity will be generated. Even where production is increased through an acquisition of similar production units, or a duplication of existing methods, there is likely to be an economy of scale somewhere, resulting in increased efficiency. The point being made here is that the simple need to maintain production levels results in the use of more capital intensive methods which, through greater technical and administrative efficiency, increase productive capacities beyond existing requirements. Thus a byproduct of the struggle to survive is the need to sell even more products. The greater the tensions of competition and consequently the more acute the question of survival, the quicker is the rate of change.

The above analysis is not affected in any way by the diverse ways in which business organizations expand and grow. It does not matter whether a firm grows through technological efficiency, through financial takeovers or mergers, whether an expansion is in an existing market or through diversification, whether an expansion is vertical or horizontal. What matters is that a firm engages in one or more markets. Its involvement in each market, no matter how small its share, will have the effect of producing excess capacity.

The process described above occurs because of the character of free enterprise economies. This character gives rise to contradictory elements in business organizations which they can never effectively control. They may endeavour to equate their production with distribution, that is, selling possibilities, but the forces of production proceed independently of their will. Factors beyond the control of entrepreneurial ability ensure the continuing expansion of production irrespective of whether there are market outlets for the products or not. It so happens that the free market mechanism which gives rise to this phenomenon also restricts the market possibilities by ensuring that the distribution of income stipulated by the social relations to the means of production is protected and perpetuated. The expansion of production occurs, therefore, within a relatively rigid distribution system. Marx expressed the position as follows:

The periods in which capitalist production exerts all its forces regularly turn out to be periods of overproduction, because production potentials can never be utilized to such an extent that more value may not only be produced but also realized; but the sale of commodities, the realization of commodity-capital and thus of surplus value, is limited, not by the consumer requirements of society in general, but by the consumer requirements of a society in which the vast majority are always poor and must always remain poor. [12]

Herein lies the prime contradiction of capitalism. The gross effect of the contradictions which each business organization in a market economy faces is production in excess of what the markets can absorb.

It might be assumed from what has been stated above that there would be no contradiction if capitalist societies could distribute goods and services as freely as they can produce them abundantly. An implication of this assumption is that the obstructing factor, the one causing the contradiction, is the distribution system determined by the relations of production. It is often believed that provided the distribution system is changed, the forces of production will be freed from their constraints, to be utilized for the benefit of all. This is because it appears that within capitalist societies the distribution mechanism acts as a brake on the forces of production. But appearance is not the whole of reality. The forces of production do not have an autonomous existence which enable them, as they are in capitalist societies, to be adapted to any form of relations of production. To believe otherwise is to misunderstand the nature of contradictions. A contradiction is not simply an incompatibility between any two variables. It is one arising out of a situation and therefore determined in all respects by it. This means that the forces of production are as much a part of a capitalist situation as the distributive mechanism, so that a change in the structure of that situation would alter both elements qualitatively.

The above formulation is simply a restatement of the relationship between structure and superstructure. It is the structure which contains the contradiction but it is manifested, made visible, in the superstructure which serves the structure. At the core of the structure is the mode of production which comprises the private ownership of the means of production and the free market mechanism geared by the profit motive to ensure an economically rational means of private accumulation. The free market determines how and in what quantities economic resources are combined. In other words it creates everything one recognizes as the forces of production. The complete process of the division of labour — occupations and their respective rewards, their hierarchical distribution and its elitist character — the use of technology, the scale of production, the location of production, and in consequence the whole purpose of production, exist to satisfy the need for private accumulation. The inequalities and relative deprivation which the differential distribution of resources produces are essential requirements of the structure. There is no sense in which even the methods of production in manufacturing industry have an independence of the capitalist nature of society.

The manner of production and the tendency to produce are related to the inability of capitalist societies to exploit their full productive potential so that it is impossible to conceive of a qualitative change in the distribution system which does not at the same time alter the forces of production to the same extent. Distribution is achieved through the price mechanism and satisfies the requirements of the structure in the same manner as the forces of production. Goods and services go only where there is an effective demand for them. Thus their allocation is determined by the ability of those who want them, to pay for them and this, in turn, depends on the distribution of income and wealth. The shape, and therefore consumption potential, of the distribution system is determined in the first instance by the social relations to the means of production — by the fact that in capitalist societies the means of production are owned and controlled by a tiny proportion of the total population while the bulk of the remainder subsist by selling their labour power. The sellers of labour power have different earning capacities, depending upon the market value of their skills. Many factors enter into the determination of relative incomes but because of the way in which the market mechanism works the level of income is closely correlated to the scarcity value of skills which gives the distribution of income among employees a hierarchical and pyramidal shape. The owners of the means of production stand at the apex of this pyramid. As Marx pointed out, the vast majority are at the base and are poor. His contention that they must always remain so can be shown *a priori* but it has been illustrated historically and empirically.[13] What this amounts to is that the shape of the distribution of income and personal wealth remains largely unchanged over time. More than this, because of the market mechanism the shape is also largely unalterable. Two pyramids are involved here. One involves income distribution and over time its composition and to some extent its shape have been altered though it has remained pyramidal. The other, concerning personal wealth, has hardly received a dent since statistics started being collected almost ninety years ago, despite the activities of numerous governments since the introduction of progressive taxation to effect some transfer of wealth from the rich to the poor.[14] In 1968, 75 per cent of the total personal wealth in the United Kingdom was in the hands of only 10 per cent of the population. A comparable situation existed in 1911—13 when 10 per cent of the population possessed 92 per cent of the total personal wealth.[15] The concentration of personal wealth in other capitalist countries resembles that of the United Kingdom, though is reputedly not so great.[16] There are arguments about changes in the distribution of wealth and in particular, income. It is argued that the ratio of income to profits in the national income is rising. In so far as this is correct the income beneficiaries are those who receive salaries and lie in the upper regions of the pyramid. In any case this does not affect the argument. What is clear is that the mass of the population receive incomes so low that they are always consuming at the limit of those incomes — and that this will always be the case so long as the structure of society remains unaltered.

The market mechanism operates to perpetuate the long-run inequitable distribution of income and personal wealth by providing the means for simple adjustments whenever the relative share of income in the total increases. When individual wage and salary earners, either as individuals or collectively, press for increases in income, the immediate response they get depends upon the labour/capital cost ratio and the market situation of employers. Employees in highly capital intensive industries will more easily get increases than others because the increase in labour costs may have only a marginal impact on total costs. In general, however, the ability of the employer to absorb higher costs through higher prices will be the dominant factor. If an employer is in a tight or declining commodity market then he will, in all probability, resist income demands. It is only in this situation, when an employer cannot pass on increases in incomes through higher prices, that employees have the possibility of raising the share of incomes in relation to profits. It happens to be the situation where the conflict is the most intense because the employers' resistance is greatest. For this reason the possibility of employees' demands being met are usually limited to cases where they are able to display exceptional collective strength. For example, during the British dock strike of 1889 there was an unprecedented extension of militant trade unionism among semi-skilled and unskilled workers so that many employers, though in a tight market situation, were compelled to give wage increases. Encroachments on profits in this way are only, and can only be, temporary, for as soon as the market situation eases for employers they can raise their prices not only sufficiently to take account of new income demands but also to absorb earlier ones. There is no problem for employers when prices are rising for they can simply add income increases to total costs and pass them on to the consumers through higher prices in such a way as to maintain the ratio between incomes and profits.

This self-regulating mechanism works all the time in a free market economy and defies all efforts to frustrate it through intervention by governments. The mechanism, however, cannot withstand changes in the economy which the contradictions in it are producing. The effectiveness of its operation depends on the quality of operation of the market economy. As the prime contradiction intensifies and price rises take on the dimensions of inflation so that they create international currency problems, as in Britain, then there may be a resistance to price rises. If at the same time there are no factors inhibiting substantial collective demands by employees outside the formal framework of trade unions, also as in Britain, then the income/profit ratio may alter in favour of income. This was a brief phenomenon between 1968 and 1974 in Britain. The ratio is also likely to alter if as a consequence of the crisis the rate of profit declines. This, as Glyn and Sutcliffe illustrated, is characteristic of the British economy in the 1960s and 70s.[17]

Such changes as may occur in the ratio of incomes to profits do not invalidate the argument that the free market economy gives rise to a contradiction dominating from which it cannot escape and which has a transforming effect on it. The changes are not part of a long-term trend which would relieve the system of its strain for they are short-term, relatively infrequent, oscillations. Nor can the system relieve itself permanently by securing substantial new markets through either imperialism or credit systems such as the method of hire purchase. Imperialism is becoming more difficult to exercise as the world oil crisis indicates. In any event new markets have the habit of exhausting themselves. It is not possible to ease the contradiction by controlling the forces of production for the only substantial means available are large-scale unemployment and war production and both carry with them their own intense problems. Indeed the manner in which the forces of production carry on relentlessly through technological improvements produces its own contribution to the distribution aspect of the contradiction by creating technological unemployment which can become so great that the unemployed manpower cannot be relocated in jobs and becomes part of the permanently unemployed workforce. This type of unemployment, unlike the others, reduces the level of effective demand to the accompaniment of increasing total production and intensifies the problem of excess capacity.

Contradictions and the concept of process

An examination of the prime contradiction in free market economies both raises and illustrates important issues in dialectical materialism. The contradiction which has been described is the prime one in that in its inter-action it generates movement at the only level which might warrant the description of system, that is at the level of social relations to the means of production. Its identification and analysis enables the character of the system, or preferably, the totality, to be understood. But put like this it might be thought that the examination of reality in terms of contradic-tions is an analysis of cause and effect. The impression that change should be analysed in this mechanistic way might be derived from the previous chapters about structure and superstructure. Here, it might be said, is a structure, the cause, which gives rise to a superstructure, the effect. The impression need not be amended simply because there are innumerable structures and superstructures. But if such an impression is created it is misleading. The analysis of situations in terms of contradictions is essentially the analysis of processes.

Every situation is the superstructural expression of a structure. Every structure, in turn, belongs to a situation which has its own structure. There is no end to this process, and no beginning. The prime contradiction arises out of a particular structure which is itself the product of forces prior to it. The social relations to the means of production in free enterprise societies arose out of a contradiction in the relations of production prior to it and gives rise to one which produces a situation with its own and so on. Movement does not proceed in jumps, however, in the sense that the contradiction in a structure resolves itself and produces a qualitatively different situation with its own unique contradictions. No contradiction can be straightforwardly resolved because in the process of its resolution it produces further contradictions. Nor does movement proceed through a line of prime contradictions succeeding each other, such as one in feudal societies giving rise to one in capitalist societies and so on. A contradiction is prime if it arises out of the dominant social relations to the means of production. But any particular relations of production are transitory. When they are moving towards a position of dominance they accompany and are subordinate to prior relations of production with their own contra-diction. And as soon as a contradiction appears, it gives rise to new relations of production with their own contradiction which eventually becomes dominant. Thus at any one time there may be three, but at the least two, major contradictions operating in a linear fashion and reacting on each other. The position, therefore, is complex.

The contradiction apparent in a particular relation of production belongs to it from its inception. It is inevitably present. It is not as Maurice

Godelier suggested when he wrote: 'Thus the basic contradiction of the capitalist mode of production is *born* during the development of the mode of production, and *is not present* from the beginning of the system.'[18] This implies that the contradiction belongs to a particular phase of particular relations of production, namely capitalist ones, and that it is not derived from a structure which is itself a product of a contradiction. It implies, in other words, that contradictions are not related in a process, and leaves open the possibility of achieving a 'higher mode of production', namely a socialist one, from which no contradiction arises and which, therefore, has the quality of stability and permanence. Mao Tse Tung criticized the use of contradiction as expressed by Godelier, by stating that it amounted to a reversion 'to the metaphysical theories of external causality and of mechanism'.[19] It is, moreover a method of expediency to show that capitalism suffers from structural inconsistencies which do not necessarily exist in other types of societies. But, as Mao Tse Tung explains in his essay 'On Contradiction', 'Contradiction exists in the process of development of all things'.[20] This can be seen by looking again at the prime contradiction in capitalist societies.

A contradiction occurs when a solution to a problem gives rise to difficulties which negate the solution to the problem. This means, in terms of the prime contradiction in capitalist societies, that within a free market economy attempts to solve problems of distribution simply intensify it. The prime contradiction produces struggles for increased shares within existing markets, searches for new markets, a transference of resources from production to selling, attempts to reduce variable production costs, searches for cheaper materials, the introduction of new methods of production, the accumulation of unused resources such as labour power, an increase in the size of production units, the elimination of inefficient firms, and a growth in the degree of monopoly. These are all related consequences. Some of them are alternatives while others occur inevitably and inexorably.

The analytical nature of prime, secondary and internal contradictions

The generality of the prime contradiction is expressed through the activities of innumerable business organizations so that the reality of the contradiction is these organizations of differing sizes in different markets attempting to make profits, faced with problems which are shaped by the peculiarities of their particular environments. The immediate expression of the prime contradiction then is numerous different contradictions which may be described as secondary to it. These secondary contradictions get their character from the heterogeneity of the market mechanism. They vary according to such matters as the nature of the commodity being produced and the market for which it is being produced. The contradictions in expanding markets, for example, differ from those in declining markets. In each case, however, the general quality of contradictions is evident. That is, within each particular market, attempts to escape from the problem thwart the escape.

Contradictions always occur in structures. That structure which comprises the social relations to the means of production is a pure economic phenomenon so that the prime contradiction has the same quality. All other structures, however, are likely to contain non-economic phenomena so that the secondary contradictions may not be pure either. A structure of a situation, as defined earlier, consists of the necessary conditions for that situation and its economic and non-economic content cannot be specified *a priori*. What can be said with certainty is that structures at all levels reflect the complexity of the social situations at those levels and that contradictions do likewise. It can be added that this complexity increases the more it involves institutionalized activity in visible social relations.

The secondary contradictions influence social behaviour through internal contradictions. That is, they create irresolvable tensions within institutionalized activity which produce changes in social relationships. The activities of a business organization in a particular market situation may cause it to introduce new machinery in one of its departments or in a section relating to its production process. In the area where the change takes place a contradiction between new production possibilities and existing labour power provisions will occur. The new machinery will alter the labour skill requirements in that it may operate at a different level of skills than in the previous situation, or may require less labour power of a particular kind. It may in addition affect wages or conditions of work. The disposition of labour power where the machinery is introduced will in some way be altered, as will the relationship between that department and others within the firm.

The prime, secondary and internal contradictions are analytical categories. They help to clarify the manner in which contradictions operate and assist with their identification. They indicate the stages through which pressures travel from the general to the particular. But they exist only in analysis. The prime contradiction has no existence in concrete reality except in the experiences of men and women. Mao Tse Tung expressed this point by stating that 'it is precisely in the particularity of contradiction that the universality of contradiction resides'.[21] The meaning of the prime contradiction for a business organization may be the reorganization of its management structure which is necessary to cope with a changed market situation while for workers of a particular skill it may be redundancy or diluted standards or a speeded up work pace. The reality might be being forced into liquidation or a strike against depressed conditions. In the same way it can be said that economic forces have no autonomous existence but exist through mediating factors which comprise visible social relations. Contradictions at different levels and their economic content need to be identified in order to assist the analysis of situations. They introduce added specification into analyses by the use of structure and superstructure. Both structures and superstructures cease to be static conceptions through the analytical use of contradictions. In addition, their dialectical relationship can be better understood.

The interdependence of variables

It is necessary, however, to extend the discussion about contradictions before the nature of totalities is effectively exposed. First the interconnection between contradictions has to be examined. Concrete reality consists of a differential distribution of interdependent elements. The unequal distribution of resources is a visibly verifiable phenomenon. Land differs in quality and utility throughout the world; climates vary; mineral resources are placed in different locations; capital of all kinds, both fixed and variable, durable and perishable varies in its usages and distribution; labour, even of the most homogeneous kind, is unequally distributed between areas. No matter how resources are viewed the same picture is obtained. People hold material possessions unequally. An examination of variables such as income, personal wealth, educational opportunities, authority, social status and the like shows unequal concentrations. Some people possess more or less than others. If the visible social relations are identified through their mediating elements, skill, power and ideology, then the same qualities are perceived. Each element is differentially distributed. The possession of skills is not synonymous with their control over its use and distribution. The highest ranking skill is that which involves control over the skills of others through ownership. After that skills are ranked according to various criteria in a pyramidal fashion. The most numerous skills are the least important. The distribution of skills and power are roughly correlated. As for ideology its impact depends upon its relevance for explaining reality and the existence of an alternative. Its impact, therefore, varies in different situations and over time.

The three basic elements, skill, power and ideology, are interdependent, as are the visible social relations which they comprise. The character of this interdependence was shown in the previous two chapters. The elements are mediating factors which are common to all situations. Economic pressures act on social behaviour first through skills and then, in consequence, through power. Skills, and therefore power, get their meaning from ideology. As ideology is the institutionalized expression of ideas which concern either preserving the present or changing it, it acts either by dampening or stimulating changes in the distribution of power. No pressure or element can influence social behaviour without first passing through an ideological barrier.

Underlying observable reality, then, is a complex pattern of skills, power and ideology. Each actual situation represents a particular combination of these elements so that every situation has something in common with every other. This is of the greatest causal significance where situations approximate closely to each other. For instance, business organizations are comparable because they comprise similar combinations of the elements. Their immediate environments are the situations which approximate most closely to them so that without any difficulty organizations can encroach on those environments and vice versa. Where skills combine to do the same or related activities they are most dependent on each other. Every production process for example, depends at any one time on a specific combination of skills so that if one skill is taken away and nothing else changed the process must be affected. As each skill reflects power there is a comparable dependency in the relationship between power from different sources.

The interdependency in and between social situations was explained in chapter 8 in terms of the existence of a common structure. This is the factor which gives the whole or totality predominance over its parts. This structure, identified as the mode of production, contains a contradiction which, as had been explained earlier in this chapter, is as pervasive as the structure itself. The pervasiveness occurs not because there is a single prime contradiction radiating its pressures but because the reality of the contradiction is a multiple of contradictions at the phenomenological level. This is what is meant when it is stated that there is a common source of movement.

The position can be explained briefly as follows. Concrete social reality consists of differentially distributed resources. These resources are used for purposes which are dependent on each other. The interdependence is greatest when the purposes are most closely related. The interdependence can be viewed as occurring through related dependent variables. The independent variable in the equation comprises the mode of production which contains a contradiction that generates economic pressures throughout the system. This contradiction is a phase in an historical process and is not, therefore, the starting point, or the cause of movement. It is not the only contradiction, as was pointed out earlier, but it is the dominant one so long as the mode of production which gives rise to it is dominant. Its observable identity is a multiple of contradictions which make their impact at and through the point of production. These contradictions are the principal ones in any analysis; they are purely economic with their basis in the structure of the society. Their operation produces the complex of contradictions which analytically can be regarded as secondary and internal.

Repercussion effects

In order to illustrate the quality of continuity, of movement, it is useful to assume that there is a principal contradiction radiating pressures. This gives the impression of a mechanistic, cause and effect relationship, and reveals the motion transmitting qualities in totalities. It is like using the device of taking a still photograph to enable the details in a complex picture to be examined with some clarity and at leisure.

A still picture of a segment of a capitalist society would show a complex set of relationships between markets, between firms, between categories of employees, between employers and employees, between trade unions and between unions and employers. It would also show markets being shared between firms, each producing specific outputs and with resources of given qualities and quantities distributed to achieve those outputs. The rewards to the factors would be coordinated. Each type of labour power would receive a rate of payment which ensured that the quality and quantity of its type was forthcoming. The same could be said about capital. In other words, the picture would show a complete set of differentials between incomes, incomes and profit, and rates of return on capital. It would show a pattern in the distribution of authority, in living standards and in social status. In total this static picture would show complete balance and co-ordination.

Now create for one firm a principal contradiction. In order to maintain itself as a profit-making institution the firm has to improve its efficiency and in order to do so it mechanizes a process previously done by a combination of manual skills. The machinery will not have the same impact on all the skills. Some skills will be diluted and their rewards will be adjusted; the relationships between occupations will be altered to put some in a new position of comparative disadvantage; the machinery will raise the productive capacity of one part of the production process so as to create bottlenecks in other parts; the bottlenecks will act as a stimulus to change in those parts; the improvement in technical efficiency will inevitably increase productive capacity which will increase the distributive, that is, selling problems of the firm; this in turn will intensify the demands on the firm's administration. The firm will try to encroach further into its market thus affecting its relationship with other firms and stimulating a reaction from them.

As a result of the initial action of the firm a *repercussion* effect producing uneven development is created. A movement is generated which spreads out from its source and stimulates other contradictions which in turn create their own repercussion effects and hence contradictions. The steps to maintain the profitability of the firm may have repercussions in a variety of directions. It may create a demarcation dispute through reducing the job jurisdiction of a particular union. In order to survive, the union must take defensive action but this step may in fact worsen its situation by speeding up the displacement of the jobs it controls. If the dispute results in a strike it may worsen the competitiveness of the firm and evoke further action to remain as a viable profit-making institution. It may affect interunion relationships and encourage moves towards a federation or amalgamation. If an amalgamation results then the balance of power between unions in the industry may be altered, as may that in the trade union movement as a whole. This may produce defensive steps from other unions. What can be said with some assurance is that whenever a position of comparative disadvantage results then a reaction will occur which will generate fresh pressures, and these in turn will produce further positions of comparative disadvantage. The initial action may alter the relationship of skilled to semiskilled workers in the firm by appearing as a threat to skilled workers. If it makes departmental reorganization necessary it may have a direct impact on management by causing a redistribution of formal duties. If the pressures, as they are likely to, spread to other firms in the market then the whole process starts for each firm affected. And so it goes on.

It is possible now to give a meaning to the term 'totality'. It is an analytical category and as such consists of interconnections. It has no boundaries and no particular shape. Its extent depends on the scope and quality of the interconnections. These radiate unevenly from the situation under examination and become progressively weaker and less relevant the further they are from that situation. In other words the extent of a totality can be gauged by the spread of repercussion effects.

There is a twofold difficulty in identifying the spread of repercussion effects. Firstly, once movement has been activated by a principal contradiction it has a self-perpetuating and internal quality through repercussion effects and secondary contradictions which have a regenerating and diversifying effect on movement. These subordinate contradictions may react back on the principal contradiction and so intensify it. They may act on other principal contradictions as for instance where the actions of a firm produce reactions from other firms in the same market. Where contradictions feed on each other it may be very difficult to identify a totality through repercussion effects. The second difficulty is a related one. Each situation has its own totality but as every micro-situation is a part of another so each totality must belong to a more pervasive one. Moreover totalities overlap horizontally as well as vertically because of the relationship between adjacent situations. Movement in one situation must act on others so that repercussion effects spread over situations in all directions. This is a very rough and inadequate attempt to describe a dynamic phenomenon in static terms and to point out the difficulties involved in identifying usefully analytical areas.

The position is more complex than has been indicated so far because the picture contains not one firm experiencing a principal contradiction but many. It shows a variety of environments containing markets with various numbers of units of various sizes all attempting to cope with an irresolvable problem. They react on each other thus intensifying each other's position. If the picture is seen as an interruption in a continuous movement then it will be recognized that concrete reality consists of already activated principal contradictions with repercussion effects causing an infinite variety of further contradictions, reacting backwards and forwards, carrying the pressures for movement on and intensifying the conflicts, tensions and frictions in visible social relations.

This complex interaction of contradictions and repercussion effects does *not* create pluralistic situations in which there are multifarious pressure group activities of fairly equal causal significance, with no *a priori* causal ranking. The interaction is visibly expressed through what may be called tensions, frictions, conflicts and similar terms to describe group differences in social relationships, but these in no sense represent pluralism for they are dominated by a central class conflict determined by the social relations of production. In a capitalist society the main relationship is between the buyers and sellers of labour power. All other relationships are subordinate to this one. The conflict generated by the main relationship is visibly present in situations in which buyers and sellers directly confront each other, that is, at the point of production. All other situations are influenced by the context of conflict. In other words, conflict is part of their 'hidden' structures. Conflict is not simply a market phenomenon or a case of employees confronting employers at the workplace. It is a product of a particular kind of social relations of production and therefore enters in some degree into all aspects of the superstructure of a society with such relations. It is reflected in the distribution of skills and power and the nature and types of ideologies. It influences the character of social relationships and the manner in which they are institutionalized. The preoccupation of pluralists with conflict as a phenomenon to be found *within* organizations or *between* them results from the influence of systems analysis and carries with it the defects of that analysis. Class conflict can never be controlled and balanced as the pluralism implies.[22] It is the means of eventual societal transformation.

Ideology as a mediating factor

At every point of time in the existence of contradictions there are pressures for shifts in the distribution of factors of production. The pressures act in the multiplicity of micro-situations which make up economic activity. They never cease and their presence must be assumed in any and every analysis. Whether they alter anything, however, depends on their impact upon the mediating elements in superstructures. Pressures which are so weak that they have no impact on the distribution of skills can be safely ignored. If they alter the distribution of skills then some consequences must follow. At least the distribution of rewards is likely to change. In many instances this is likely to be the initial consequence. Nothing will happen, however, unless the distribution of power is altered and whether this happens depends not only on the extent in the changes in the skill differential but also on the mediating influence of ideology. Skills are differentiated, it will be remembered, not simply according to their technical competence but according to the manner in which this component is ranked socially. In other words ideas about the worthwhileness of skills influence the power derived from them. Contradiction generated pressures influence and alter the power differential through the impact which changes in the technical competence have on ideology. Thus ideology is continually under pressure.

The part ideology plays in determining how contradictions mould visible social behaviour has already been described in the previous chapter. It is enough here to repeat that ideology makes its impact via consciousness and institutions and that its precise consequence depends on the relative strengths of competing ideologies. The reality of any ideology is the exercise of ideas in and about the multiplicity of situations referred to above. The ideas which are dominant rationalize and justify maintaining basic relationships. They are not necessarily opposed to change as such so long as it is necessary to maintain those basic relationships. For example, the dominant ideology in capitalist societies is concerned with maintaining the relations of production but this is not only consistent with the acceptance of technological change and its consequent impact on social relations, it is dependent on it. In other words, any amount of movement within the system is acceptable so long as it is needed to maintain its structure and thus to protect the private ownership of the means of production. The dominant ideology on its societal form works to gain acceptance of limited movement as an inevitable feature of life — to accept craft dilution, unemployment, depressed living standards, limited educational achievements and so on. The dominant ideology in its fractured, diffused form in multifarious micro-situations operates to protect the structures of those situations. It creates a resistance to movement which the dominant ideology at another level sanctions and encourages.

The dominant ideology when viewed dialectically is itself a contradiction. Its main ideas concern the desirability of proceeding with caution, being moderate in making demands, changing things slowly in an evolutionary manner, thinking twice to avoid haste, making virtue out of necessity. When seen at the level of visible social relations these ideas concern such matters as the preservation of the family and its traditional allocation of positions, the wage differentials between related groups of workers, the allocation of privileges between groups, the relative social positions of groups and, indeed, every other differentially distributed variable of any significance. The ideas encourage a general antipathy towards movement. But at this level they are forever being challenged by the ideologically sanctioned movement. Women are drawn into the labour force and acquire skills which provide them with degrees of economic independence which alters their power position within families. Kinship organizations which experience alterations in the distribution of skills and power change their form. A management skill which becomes more important in a production process as a result of the introduction of a new method of production acquires added power which upsets the existing social relationships and involves management reorganization. Each time the dominant ideas have to be repudiated the more they appear inappropriate and the more likely are the people involved to look for an alternative expression of ideas more appropriate to what appears to be happening.

In order to understand the part ideology plays as a mediating factor it is necessary to look at the relevance of its core ideas for explaining reality and the manner and extent of its institutionalization. The strength of the dominant ideology, however, lies not so much in its relation to reality as in its widespread and intense expression in institutions. The market mechanism actually works to maintain things essentially as they are; business organizations have a power distribution which operates always to maintain its existing shape. All institutions comprise social relationships which are contained within rules and regulations, protected by sanctions and rewards and underscored by vested interests. It is these qualities which give institutions their apparent self-regulating mechanisms. When pressures for change are brought to bear on them these qualities have a filtering, and therefore weakening, effect. Sometimes the resistance is greater than the pressures and nothing ensues. When the institutions are the embodiment of ideas which themselves protect existing relationships then the resistance to change is reinforced. As all social relationships are institutionalized to some extent then they inevitably possess the quality of survival. The ideas which support survival, which are about the preferences for what exists, which rationalize and even glorify no change, work on social relationships through their institutional context.

When the ideas are about the changing nature of reality and are consistent with the pressures from contradictions then their institutional expression may still act as a filter and an obstruction, though obviously with much less effect than if the ideas were in support of the *status quo*. This is simply because the very fact of channelling movement through procedures slows it down, may divert it or even alter its character. Having stated this it is necessary to add a word of caution about the influence of organization on movement. Organizations are generally attributed with autonomous qualities by sociologists. That is they are regarded as administrative forms which are transferable between different ideological situations, in much the same way as technology is considered to be transferable. They are generally seen as ideologically free devices for transforming goals into action. The argument posed earlier in this chapter, about the lack of autonomy of the forces of production, applies here. Organizations are constructed to satisfy particular needs arising out of their environments. They have structures and these determine their shape, their precise hierarchical and authority character, their occupational distribution with its reward and status attributes, their procedures and regulations, and their methods of control over the use and distribution of resources in general. All the detail about control mechanisms, communications, line-staff divisions, decision-making procedures and the like which appear in contemporary management studies are functional in relation to the structure of organizations. The so-called negative attributes of bureaucracies, such as procedural delays and distortion, are in fact necessary organization features for the performance of their servile function in relation to their environments. Of course, the details of organizations are not and cannot be completely consistent and uniform in their purpose because the contradictions in their structures produce contradictory superstructural elements which tend to frustrate and perhaps eventually defeat this servile function. Every organization, indeed every social situation, possesses visible evidence of structural contradictions though it may be slight and on contemporary sociological terms is usually interpreted as inconsistencies, paradoxes, strains or tensions, without any structural significance.

An outstanding example of self-defeating organizational growths and where, in consequence, bureaucratic elements appear to have a negative obstruction function, is that of trade unions. Trade unions arise out of the prime contradiction in capitalism: they embody the alternative dominant ideology and they get their impulses from pressures communicated through the point of production. Their *raison d'être* is to protect and promote the interests of their members. In an unadulterated form unions should be capable of immediate responses to changes in work situations of employees and their organization should facilitate this. It should give an institutional expression to the ideas of solidarity and equality which lie at the basis of the alternative dominant ideology. Hierarchy and authority differentiation are contrary to the basic ideas; while procedural, distorting delays are inconsistent with the requirement to facilitate immediate responses. The situation, however, which creates the need for workers' organizations cannot control the development of their form because it is not the dominant feature in its own environment. The prevalent idea of organization and how it should be expressed are derived through the dominant ideology from the relations of production. They have a paradigmic quality and cannot be ignored or sidestepped by trade unionists. It may not be possible to create permanent organizations which are qualitatively different from the prevalent forms, because resources in general, and labour power in particular, are arranged, combined and distributed in a capitalist society to facilitate the prevalent forms. The very term efficiency gets its conventional meaning from the personal profit-making and accumulating nature of the society, that is from the relations of production. How trade unionists conceive of an efficient use of their resources to protect their own interests is largely formulated by forces which support the dominant ideology and have a contrary purpose to that of trade unionism. It is in this sense that organizational activity by unions may be self-defeating. When these self-defeating qualities obviously frustrate the needs of trade unionists alternative organizational forms arise, for the pressures for immediate and effective collective action at the point of production continue and build up and seek outlets. The shop stewards' organizations, rank-and-file committees and the like have arisen in Britain because of the defects of permanent institutionalized trade unionism. This development is of ephemeral bodies, with the minimum of procedures, the simplest and most direct form of representation, the fullest possible rank-and-file involvement. In effect they are not bureaucratized. They typify organization which is regarded as inefficient within the conventional meaning of the term. In terms of the alternative dominant ideology they are highly efficient.

   The point of this particular discussion is to emphasize that the bureaucratic attributes of organizations can only be analysed dynamically through an examination of ideology as a mediating factor. Bureaucracies are not, and cannot be, value-free organizations, because they are in essence organizational expressions of an ideology. Their precise details, therefore, have a functional significance and should not be treated as if they were autonomous phenomena freely transferable between types of societies. The effect of organization on movement hinges on the extent to which it embodies and gives effect to ideology.

Organizations, of course, have a dialectical relationship with ideology. Ideology, as has been seen, is basically determined by the relations of production and in so far as those relations remain unchanged so does its ideological representation. However, the actual expression of an ideology in visible social relations is heterogeneous, consisting of many diverse, sometimes contradictory parts, reflecting the equally diverse and contradictory parts of the superstructure of the relations of production. Ideology at this level is a changing phenomenon, continually seeking but not always getting accurate institutional expressions because of the resiliance of organized activity. This situation constitutes a contradiction in the dominant ideology which is the same as that described earlier but in a different context. The main ideas in the dominant ideology which are institutionalized are resistant to pressures for change. The manner of their institutionalization or their organizational form supports these ideas by channelling the pressures through a complex of procedures which are frequently provided with institutional means of maintaining themselves in the short run. For example organizational alterations frequently have to be pursued through procedures designed to obstruct them. Moreover the distribution of skills and power at any one time represent a distribution of interests which invariably acts to preserve itself. Yet in its phenomenological form the ideology is changing and in order to be fully effective it is necessary that the changes should be given an organizational expression. Thus the organization reacts on ideology by inhibiting or preventing its most effective implementation and perpetuating, in consequence, the ideological expression of a visible social reality which has been superseded.

This phenomenon is commonly described, in conventional sociological terms, as the existence of customs or traditions or habits, for this is how they appear. Althusser mentioned it when he wrote that:

Marxist political practice is constantly coming up against that reality known as 'survivals'. There can be no doubt that these survivals exist — they cling tenaciously to life. Lenin struggled with them inside the Russian Party even before the Revolution. We do not need to be reminded that after the Revolution and from then till now they have been the source of constant difficulties, battles and commentaries. [23]

Survivals, it can now be seen, are an inevitable consequence of the contradiction in an ideology which concerns the preservation of the *status quo* in situations of changing visible social reality. They are present at all levels of all organized activity where such an ideology is dominant and they occur where organized activity such as trade unionism or revolutionary politics, though based on an alternative ideology, is influenced in its form by the dominant one. In other words, the ideology which conceptualizes structural reality as unchanging carries its contradictions wherever it goes.

It is important that not all so-called traditions, customs or habits should be indiscriminately described as survivals. Some practices are described as traditions as a way of stating that they are out of date, obstruct movement and prevent change. They are practices which are said to have had relevance at one time but not now. This description is frequently applied to trade union practices such as strikes and rules to regulate work-place behaviour. Such practices are not survivals but arise from an unchanging structural situation, the recognition of which is inconsistent with the dominant ideology. The changes they are considered to obstruct are those which occur in visible social relations. For example, trade union practices which aim to regulate the ratio of workmen to machines, or the quantity of work per hour or shift, or the use of unskilled helpers by skilled workers, are frequently attacked by employers for obstructing techno-logical change, by which is meant the introduction of new machinery or other cost reduction measures intended to increase profitability. These particular practices arise from the exigencies of selling labour power and remain relevant so long as people are compelled to do this no matter what readjustments take place in the manner in which labour power is utilized. Indeed the manner of its utilization is a determinant of the exigencies which give rise to the practices in the first place.

The distinction between practices which are and those which are not survivals is made through an analysis of the mediating qualities of com-peting ideologies. Practices which are treated as survivals, but which are not, are those which are consistent with the alternative ideology and not with the dominant one. Practices which are survivals are consistent with the dominant ideology but get into difficulty because of its contradictions. These practices, though they may be described as ideas, attitudes or values, can only be survivals if they are institutionalized. In other words ideas, attitudes or values which do not relate to concrete reality because they arose out of situations which have altered can influence social behaviour in the altered situations only in so far as they are institutionalized. If they are not institutionalized they have no relevance as determinants of behaviour; they are merely descriptions of opinions.

The fact of institutionalization is not easy to establish because it is not always apparent in the immediate environment. It is necessary to investi-gate much further than organizations and to look for evidence in the way in which environments are arranged, the interests they serve, the attitudes they sanction or penalize and the manner in which this is done. Attitudes, in other words, become significant variables in so far as they are capable of being expressed in practices. The significance of attitudes about, say, racial discrimination in Britain, is derived from the fact that they receive institutional support through the need of the economy for cheap labour supplies and the consequent operation of labour markets, in which coloured labour is marketed. The attitudes are, in effect, a legitimation of the economic need to discriminate. This dialectical relationship between attitudes and reality exists in other cases too.

Social change

It is possible now to return to the question of the analysis of social change which was raised in chapter 7, with a reasonable chance of clarifying it. There the consequences of movement on social relationships were described in four main categories. The general assumption about reality which has already been clarified is that it is pervaded by pressures for continuous movement. The four categories get their meaning from this assumption. They are analytical and intended to simplify the complexities of movement in concrete reality and to assist in understanding them. They may not have direct empirical relevance in any particular situation but this in no way invalidates them.

The assumption that concrete reality is pervaded by pressures for continuous movement presupposes that reality is not an accidental fortuitous agglomeration of unconnected phenomena but comprises a totality in which there is a logic of interconnection and interdependence between its parts. The interconnection proceeds through contradictions within phenomena and the repercussion effects they generate. It is assumed, therefore, that social phenomena possess contradictory qualities in that they always pose a clash of opposite variables which are integral to them and which only resolve their incompatibility through structural changes. The sum total of these assumptions represents the dialectical method.

This can be approached in the reverse manner. If the starting point is the dialectical method then it must follow that nothing is determinate, that nothing is durable and that, in consequence, everything is emerging, developing and being transformed or displaced in the process.

The dialectical method, therefore, is inevitably historical. However, it provides for more than historical studies or for the study of the present through history. Through the approach to social reality as a process, dialectical materialism assists in a broad understanding of the future of whatever situation is under examination but it can do no more than this without becoming speculative. Those social scientists who wish to predict and engage in the expanding field of speculative sociology, now sometimes described as futurology, have a simplified and distorted view of the events they are concerned with. They often, moreover, have an accompanying desire to assist in the manipulation of social events through prediction. C. Wright Mills described the issue as he saw it in the 1950s in terms of 'the bureaucratization of social study' and the consequent growth of 'human engineering'.

Among the slogans used by a variety of schools of social science, none is so frequent as, 'The purpose of social science, is the prediction and control of human behaviour'. Nowadays, in some circles we also hear much about 'human engineering' — an undefined phrase often mistaken for a clear and obvious goal. It is believed to be clear and obvious because it rests upon an unquestioned analogy between 'the mastery of nature' and 'the mastery of society'. Those who habitually use such phrases are very likely to be among those who are most passionately concerned to 'make the social studies into real science', and conceive of their own work as politically neutral and morally irrelevant. [24]

Mills was essentially concerned about American social scientists. Since he wrote *The Sociological Imagination*, 'the bureaucratic ethos' for social scientists has become generalized and consolidated. The search for predictive qualities of the natural and pure sciences has led to mathematical sociology and away from the real situations which sociology should be about.

There is no question of being able to predict the future course of social events. Prediction implies a degree of analytical precision which is impossible in the social sciences. Mills's view was that the claims for predictive qualities

reveals a rationalistic and empty optimism which rests upon an ignorance of the several possible roles of reason in human affairs, the nature of power and its relation to knowledge, the meaning of moral action and the place of knowledge within it, the nature of history and the fact that men are not only creatures of history but on occasion creators within it and even of it. [25]

It is impossible to predict the course of complex situations where it is difficult to distinguish between variables and impossible to control them for experimental purposes. The intensity of contradictions and the direction, extent and pervasiveness of repercussion effects cannot be generally anticipated without a prior knowledge of the structures within which contradictions occur and of the mediating elements through which the repercussion effects make their impact. This knowledge can only be obtained through empirical research.

Nonetheless, while being incapable of prediction, dialectical materialism can assist in comprehending developments in a manner which is closed to static theories. Some general points can be made which are implicit in what has been stated about the method so far, but the limitations and therefore the extent of the assistance which dialectic materialism can give will become clearer as the categories of change are outlined.

First, there are continuous inexorable pressures for change, resulting from contradictions and their repercussion effects. It is known, therefore, that the present is temporary and that the future must differ in some way from the present. Because the present results from preceding pressures for change and the future will be determined in the same way, history cannot repeat itself. In other words, the future cannot be exactly like anything that preceded it. Second, as the future is derived from the present a correct analysis of the present is necessary for its understanding. The theme of much of this book has been that conventional theories are incapable of providing satisfactory analyses of contemporary situations because of their conceptual limitations. The portrayal of the present as relatively static, giving the *status quo* a character of permanence, prevents sociologists from making even the vaguest speculation about the emergence of qualitative social change. What is described as futurology in conventional sociology must either consist of specifications of modifications or comprise *ad hoc* guesses or fantasies. Third, because of the empirical nature of dialectical materialism firm and confident analyses of future developments cannot go beyond known structures. Every structure and contradiction in it has to be empirically identified before its superstructure can be understood. As the contradiction intensifies, alterations in the superstructure occur and these can be anticipated. A lot can be said, therefore, about any situation so long as its structure remains unchanged. It so happens that structures do not readily alter. Prime structures embodying social relations of production may remain basically unchanged for centuries so that their superstructures and changes in them can be analysed not only historically but as contemporary phenomena with a relatively long-term significance. Given a knowledge about the structure of a capitalist society, the broad lines of its future development may be postulated. And as the influence of a prime structure is pervasive and enters into the structures of a multiplicity of situations in the society a similar degree of continuity can be assumed for those situations. It must be emphasized, however, that only broad and tentative generalizations without a time-scale can be made, for although a structure may remain essentially unaltered it is always in the process of alteration and it is this process which produces changes in visible social relations. The development of the contradictions which alter structures, their intensity, direction and timing, is unpredictable and cannot be prescribed for analytical purposes. The extent of repercussion effects and their ability to act on secondary and internal contradictions, thus producing further repercussion effects, depends on the relative strengths and relationships of structural pressures and mediating elements. This is a matter which requires empirical analysis. The model can give no assistance in foretelling the consequences of movement in the mediating elements in particular situations. The most it can do is to indicate the possible categories of change which were mentioned at the beginning of this section. These categories it was noted, are analytical and as such may not be empirically based.

Condition of no apparent movement

This category is one in which the impression is of static conditions, where nothing moves because everything has an ordered, settled relationship with everything else. But the impression is not and cannot be the reality. The assumption about reality is that it is subject to perpetual pressures for movement. If there is no visible sign of movement this can only be explained in terms of obstructed pressures. The distribution of skills cannot have been altered either because of the relative weakness of the pressures for movement or because of the strength of the resistance to it. An analysis of this type of situation would involve a close study of the mediating influences of ideology. Where the dominant ideology is highly institutionalized, covering a wide range of social behaviour, the resistance to movement is greater than where it is not so institutionalized. The more the skills have an ideological basis the more difficult it is to change them. Similarly a change in skills influences the distribution of power but this also depends on the extent to which power itself has an institutionalized basis.

A situation of no apparent movement is in any event a temporary phenomenon. All that is necessary to accelerate the pressures for movement is an alteration in one variable. A firm with the appearance of static labour relations is one with the necessary conditions for strikes, but without all the sufficient conditions. The sufficient conditions consist of a number of variables, a change in any one of which might produce a move towards an overt conflict situation. The employer or his representatives might take arbitrary action contrary to the interests of the employees so as to expose the latent conflict situation; there might be a decline in the profitability of the firm resulting in intensified cost reduction measures; there might be an alteration in the supply situation for different types of labour used by the firm causing a change in income differentials. These are but a few of the possibilities. As the pressures for movement are perpetually present it is highly unlikely that they will be contained at all points.

The most likely static situation is one which falls into the second category, that is one involving movement which results in social adjustment.

Condition of social adjustment

In conventional terms this would be described as a condition where the essential features of a situation are static in that no alterations are taking place to forms or boundaries but where movement of a remedial kind occurs. It refers to what is often described as social change by conventional sociologists. Within a dynamic frame of reference, however, social adjustment refers to the type of movement which does not alter the distribution of skills and, therefore, effects no permanent change in social relationships. Such movement can be controlled, contained or remedied.

Movement in this second category is that initiated by contradictions in structures which is obstructed before it changes the distribution of skills and, hence, power. The pressures generated by this movement cause agitation, temporary dislocation and tension, giving rise to attempts at social manipulation and adaptation. But they produce nothing permanent because they are incapable of making irremediable impressions on the determinants of social behaviour. The analysis of this condition is similar to that for the first category, except that some movement occurs. The character of the contradictions and the mediating elements of skill and power and of ideology need to be empirically identified and analysed in detail in order to make sense of the factors giving rise to social adjustment.

Concrete reality is a configuration of movement with different degrees of intensity and ability to influence social behaviour. Pressures which can be contained exist alongside those which cannot. All make their impact on social relations through the manner in which people react to them. People make decisions either individually or through and on behalf of organizations. All decisions initiate movement of some sort. The kind of movement depends on whether the decisions are directed at structural causes or at visible, superstructural phenomena and this, in turn, depends on how the issues are conceptualized. Every policy decision which stems from conventional static analysis has an impact which results in social adjustment because it directs attention to variables which have no causal significance. Every such policy decision is invariably concerned with manipulation or adjustment within a given framework and, therefore, with the maintenance of the *status quo*. Because it is made within a context which is inevitably, inexorably, under pressure to change, it must equally lead nowhere in particular. Certainly such decisions, no matter who makes them, cannot protect situations from pressures which will eventually transform them.

The category of social adjustment is a familiar one, characterizing much

activity of everyday life, being lived out daily through the effects of multifarious decisions at all levels and stages which leave the problems they are
aimed at quite unresolved. There are mountains of examples. It is
inevitable that there should be. It is politically necessary that there should
be a belief in the effectiveness of decision-making, otherwise the basis of
most organizational activity from the level of national politics downwards
would crumble. Politicians, employers, managers of organizations of all
kinds, executives of trade unions, must always act in the belief that to
order something within the confines of their jurisdiction is enough to
ensure that it is done. And they must act on the assumption that the
analytical bases of their decisions are correct. Theories which rationalize
existing situations are dominant in almost all societies so that there is an
unending flow of confident, authoritative decisions which do little more
than cause ripples on the face of society. The consequences are familiar.
The history of Britain since the Second World War, a period in which
successive governments have tried but failed to resolve the twin problems
of the balance of payments and inflation, is an experience of painful and
frustrating examples of movement producing no real change. The present
spectacle of Western politicians struggling to cope with the issue of
inflation, using limited, constraining analytical tools from Keynesian
economies, provides the same illustration of ineffectualness. A government
which believes that legislation can eliminate strike action, an employer
who thinks he can decree an alteration in wage differentials, a trade union
which contends that wages demands can improve the proportion of the
national income going to wages, the black people who think that a
campaign for civil rights will eradicate racial discrimination, all involve
themselves in making decisions which produce social adjustment. This
form of decision-making pervades every aspect of social activity. It
dominates the field of social policy, the definition and treatment of crime,
the organization of the family, the position of women, the issue of
education, the regulation of industrial relations and so on.

Superstructural social change
The illusion of decision-making exists where social change occurs as well as
where it does not. When institutions grow and alter it is because decisions
have been made to that effect. Decisions which lead to social change, however, are always made in a context of pressures which make them possible
and determine their form and direction. It is unreal to imagine movement
which leads to social change emanating solely and independently from
decision-making, for social change depends on prior alterations in the
distribution of skills and this can only come about from the pressures of
contradictions. The illusion is encouraged by the dominant ideology

through which men, as individuals, are attributed with the power to determine their own destinies but it is facilitated by the slow, sometimes imperceptible, accretion which results in social change.

The visible evidence of contradictions, repercussion effects and further contradictions is a multiplicity of human reactions attempting to cope with, stave off, or promote, the pressures they produce. The contradictions, it will be remembered, in proceeding to their resolution, produce consequences which tend to frustrate it. The resolution only occurs through the displacement of one contradiction by another. Contradictions, it will also be remembered, occur in structures but act on superstructures. In the process of resolution many changes occur in superstructures. These changes constitute social change without effecting or accompanying a qualitative alteration in structures. Now because such changes are visible and are apparently related to decision-making they appear on the agenda of conventional social scientists and provide them with the most emphatic evidence of qualitative change that they are capable of producing within their relative static conceptual frameworks.

Those conventional social scientists who are concerned to describe superstructural alterations as qualitative changes usually take the situation in the mid-nineteenth century as their baseline and endeavour to illustrate that things have since changed beyond recognition. They are usually explicit about their intentions. What they try to show is that Marx was probably correct in his analysis of mid-Victorian capitalist Britain but that his analysis does not hold now. This, of course, is a highly political objective but it is projected as an exercise in objectivity. All the 'convergence' theorists who emphasize the causal priority of technology and bureaucracy are, in effect, saying that changes in the condition of these phenomena are capable of altering social relationships qualitatively. Both technology and bureaucracy are visible and quantifiable phenomena, so that changes in them can be positively ascertained.

James Burnham was an early and influential 'convergence' theorist. He expounded the 'theory of the managerial revolution' and stated that

we are now in a period of social transition in the sense which has been explained, a period characterized, that is, by an unusually rapid rate of change of the most important economic, social, political and cultural institutions of society which we have called capitalist or bourgeois to a type of society which we shall call managerial. . . . *At the conclusion of the transition period the managers will, in fact, have achieved social dominance, will be the ruling class in society. This drive, moreover, is world-wide in extent, already well advanced in all nations, though at different levels of development in different nations.* [26]

The control by managers over the means of production would, according to Burnham, occur 'through their control of the state which in turn will own and control the instruments of production'. He saw the ideologies expressing the social role and interests and aspirations of managers already being approximately expressed through 'Leninism—Stalinism; fascism—nazism; and, at a more primitive level, by New Dealism and such less influential ideologies as "technocracy" '.[27] The managerial society was, Burnham contended, emerging in capitalist countries through the growing intervention of the state, producing managers in the government apparatus, and through the increasing power of managers in private enterprises, occurring through the divorce of ownership from control, a consequence, in turn, of the joint stock company.

Joint stock companies, which were in an embryonic stage when Marx wrote, have been fastened on by a succession of social scientists as evidence of a qualitative change in capitalism. They have been perceived as sources of technological development, introducing, according to Peter Drucker 'the mass production revolution' and representing 'a new principle of social organization'.[28] Drucker regarded the business enterprise as 'an autonomous institution' which 'does not derive its power and function from the motives, purposes or rights of its owners, whoever they may be. . . . It has a "nature" of its own and follows the laws of its own being.'[29] A symptom of the autonomy of the enterprise, for Drucker, was the 'divorce of ownership from control'.

With but few exceptions, all the very large enterprises in America are no longer controlled by the stockholders. The stockholder is neither interested in controlling 'his' business nor able to do so. . . . Management considers (stockholders) 'outsiders' and resents any 'interference' from them.[30]

The managerial revolution so-called, was seen as necessary for the resolution of 'the basic political and social problems of an industrial society'.[31] For Drucker it transformed a class dominated capitalist society into a pluralistic one.

The divorce of ownership from control has figured as an essential ingredient of the transformation process for many who are not necessarily interested in 'convergence' but who simply want to show that capitalism has changed without the need for a revolution. Different facets of its impact have been emphasized. For example, Ralf Dahrendorf concluded that the rise of a managerial class transformed the nature of conflict from one between the owners and non-owners of the means of production to one between those with and those without authority.[32] This transformation, with changes in other variables was given as evidence that capitalism has been superseded. In a chapter entitled 'Changes in the structure of industrial societies since Marx', Dahrendorf concentrates on the 'question of fact' aspect of the definition of capitalism and lists the rise of joint stock companies, the decomposition of labour or the increased plurality of status and skill groups among employees, the growth of a 'new middle-class' and the institutionalization of class conflict, as evidence of the 'supersedence of capitalism' and the rise of 'post capitalist societies'.[33]

Ralf Dahrendorf wrote in the 1950s when the thesis of growing class-lessness was current. A crude formulation of the thesis was that due to the acquisition of material goods which had previously been denied them, the working class, meaning largely skilled and unskilled manual workers, was taking on the values of the middle-class, meaning, by and large, those employees who were not members of the working class and who identified themselves with the maintenance of the *status quo* in society. The view was that there would be a 'progressive disappearance of the working class as part of the inherent logic of industrialism' — that, in other words, a process of 'embourgeoisement' was taking place.[34] Evidence for this thesis was drawn from visible, material changes in life styles. Statistics were compiled showing changes in income levels and a narrowing of the differential between manual and non-manual workers.

Consistently with this statistics on consumption patterns could also be adduced as evidence of the blurring class differences, in economic terms at least. For example, the possession of various kinds of consumer durables — television sets, record players, vacuum cleaners, washing machines — was evidently becoming fairly general, while increasingly too manual workers were invading the hitherto almost exclusively middle-class preserves of car and house-ownership.[35]

The whole emphasis in this thesis was that visible social phenomena contained the primary determining causes of social behaviour, that their influences could be seen at work and that through them qualitative changes occurred.

The 'embourgeoisement' thesis was queried by British sociologists in the 1960s. The basis for most of the criticism was the Luton study undertaken by J. H. Goldthorpe, David Lockwood, Frank Bechhofer and Jennifer Platt in 1962 and described as the 'sociology of the affluent worker'. The criticisms were not concerned with the validity of the method. The authors still searched for causal factors in visible phenomena but they added a variable, namely the workers' perception of visible phenomena as revealed through questionnaires and interviews. In consequence they merely varied the 'embourgeoisement' thesis. They claimed that the manner in which workers perceived their new 'affluence' produced not a classlessness but a qualitative change within the existing working class. Workers, rather than being conscious of a growing identity with the middle-class were transformed into 'privatized' individuals.

Even if embourgeoisement is not occurring on any significant scale, it is still likely that within the working class the commitment to collective means of achieving economic goals — most notably, the commitment to trade unionism — is weakening, and likewise, support for 'labour' objectives and for the Labour Party in national politics. In other words, it may be envisaged that the new worker, as a man who has been able to gain a good deal for himself within the existing system, will move towards a conservative and individualistic, rather than a radical and collectivist outlook on economic and political issues.[36]

The analyses which produced theses about 'embourgeoisement' and its variant 'the privatised worker' fall into the same mould as those by Burnham and Drucker. They do for 'workers' what had already been done for 'managers', that is they used evidence of visible changes in social phenomena to show that their environments had altered qualitatively from one dominated by class conflict to one permeated by acquiescence with the existing system of social relations. The more recent analysts rested heavily on Dahrendorf's work which made it possible for them to ignore class conflict while not altogether ignoring conflict itself. Dahrendorf's work, too, gave theoretical credence to earlier contentions that a managerial revolution had taken place. The evidence of qualitative change used by Dahrendorf was drawn on for much the same purpose but with a slightly different and more exaggerated effect by J. A. Banks in 1970. In *Marxist Sociology in Action*, Banks laid emphasis on the emergence of large trade unions, centralized collective bargaining procedures, the intensified intervention of the government as well as the extended division of labour and the organization of productive workers in progressively larger viable units, in order to illustrate his thesis that British capitalism had been transformed into a state of 'voluntary collectivism'. In a rather cautious expression, Banks wrote:

To the extent that the class and power systems of contemporary society may be said to diverge significantly from those of the capitalist epoch proper, the place of trade unions and of collective bargaining procedures in such a society might be thought also to have changed from their traditional state to a new one. Indeed, only if such changes have occurred may it be legitimate to conclude that a new era has been entered, rather than that a new stage in capitalism has been reached.[37]

Banks leaves no doubt that he believes the changes have occurred. He wrote about 'the transition from capitalism' and the conversion of 'capitalist private enterprise into voluntary collectivism'.[38] Two further quotations from Banks will indicate how his mind worked.

The sequence of organizational forms — trade unions, joint industrial councils, the Trade Union Congress, the Labour Party, government committees — were seen as successive steps in the development, on the one hand, of 'revolutionary' class consciousness on the part of the union leaders and, on the other, of permanent encroachments upon the erstwhile untrammelled right of capitalist employers, leading to the eventual displacement of capitalism by another type of social system.

State interference in economic life was an important factor in this displacement process. 'The advent and development of such state policies may, indeed, be read as indicating that the final phases of transition from capitalist society have arrived.'[39]

To those who suffer in contemporary British society because of its social relations of production and who have lived through many of the changes mentioned, all these quotations probably read as a gross distortion of reality. They are indeed a distortion but they are characteristic of so much contemporary British sociology which treats social reality as a huge pot of data from which the analyst picks his facts as he thinks fit and gives them meaning to suit his fancy. It would be an attractive exercise to examine and criticize the detail in the works of Dahrendorf and Banks, but it would also be pointless and irrelevant to do it here. As has been pointed out already the detail gets its meaning from the conceptual approach of the analyst and the only sound method of criticism is to examine that approach. The quotations are presented here simply to illustrate how certain changes in social relationships are accorded the deepest causal significance. Why, it should be asked, have these changes aroused such a response? Might they not represent evidence of some form of qualitative change?

Qualitative change can be given two distinct meanings. The first follows logically from the analysis used in this book and is described below; it is that qualitative change must entail an alteration in necessary conditions. It is possible that some of the changes described as qualitative by Dahrendorf and Banks might be qualitative in these terms but if they are it is purely fortuitous and not due in any sense to their analysis, for they are not equipped with the analytical tools to enable them to identify necessary conditions. The second meaning is that the changes may be qualitative in terms of the sufficient conditions of the phenomena under examination. The sufficient conditions comprise particular combinations of the elements, skill, power and ideology. The necessary and sufficient conditions and the subject itself are inextricably and dialectically related. As the sufficient conditions alter, in so far as the subject remains unchanged so does its viability. Similarly, as the subject alters under pressure from the contradictions in its structure, so does its viability within unchanged sufficient conditions.

This can be phrased differently and illustrated. The sufficient conditions for, say, trade union organizations, are those features in an environment where the necessary conditions are present to influence the emergence, form and characteristics of unions. Trade unions as visible phenomena are products of the sufficient conditions, including political freedom, extent of literacy, level of employment, standard of living and a collective consciousness. This is an arbitrary selection of the features in an environment which in one way or another influence union forms, rate of development and the like. In the period of trade union emergence there was a fairly close match between the unions and the main features of their environments. All the features have not been of equal significance for union formation and growth. As the level of literacy altered it reacted on the manner of organization, but as the degree of political freedom has changed it has determined whether unions can operate freely or not. Now when the emergence of trade unions was politically sanctioned unions were of such a size, distribution and strength as to constitute no threat to the established holders of political power. If this had not been the case, unions, as has happened in many cases, would have been suppressed from the outset. Since that time the contradictions in the structure of unions have produced changes in their occupational composition, in their size and in their methods. The number of unions in the United Kingdom has decreased while total membership has increased. Moreover a small number of unions have grown disproportionately, with the consequence that at the end of 1972 the twenty-five largest unions, each with 100 000 or more members, together accounted for 77.6 per cent of the total membership of all unions amounting to 11 315 000.[40] There is a further unequal distribution of members among the twenty-five largest unions with two unions, the Transport and General Workers' Union and the Amalgamated Union of Engineering Workers, accounting for more than 3 million members between them. This concentration of power within a very small number of unions combined with intensified militant action by them has been seen by the dominant power-holders in British society as a threat to their tenure and inconsistent with the preservation of the instruments of political decision-making, such as the parliamentary system, which are important for the maintenance of that tenure. The response to the growth and exercise of union power was to impose new legal constraints on unions and to alter, in effect, an important sufficient condition for their existence. The 1971 Industrial Relations Act and the 1973 Counter-Inflation Act considerably reduced the political tolerance of unions in Britain. There can be no doubt that unions, largely through addition, have undergone a qualitative change in relation to the sufficient condition of political freedom. If unions continue to grow and increase their threat the level of political tolerance will be reduced further, leading, eventually, to attempts at suppression. All this has happened and is happening, it should be remembered, without a qualitative change in unions themselves.

The confrontation between the growth or change in a phenomenon and one or other of the sufficient conditions for its existence can be seen in a number of macro situations in addition to that concerning trade unions. It can be seen in the cases of the growth of monopolies from a competitive market situation and the increasing intervention of government in economic affairs within a liberal democratic environment. These confrontations all have a political significance because they represent distortions in the ideal type of capitalist system and undermine the notion that capitalism is self-perpetuating. It is ideologically important that they be explained away and the easiest and commonest way is to accept the changes and to redefine the system. This is a function which social scientists such as Dahrendorf and Banks have performed.

The main question to answer now is how does the above analysis assist the understanding of superstructural social change at all levels and in general? What has been given so far is a mechanistic view of the interaction between a subject and its environment. There is, of course, a continual interaction between these two which is made all the more complex and unpredictable because each is changing independently as well as in relation to the other. An environment comprises social situations which have their own structures and contradictions and relationships. Any particular organization has to cope with its own contradictions and the consequences of contradictions in its environment. This changing setting lays down the conditions under which the organization functions. The setting may so change as to make the continued existence of the organization untenable or impossible without serious modifications in its form or activities. If it is a voluntary organization then the increased intervention of the government could present serious problems for it. If it is a political organization the advent of a totalitarian form of government would do likewise. In other words, the sufficient conditions for its existence may alter qualitatively. The rise of nazism in Germany in 1933 did not remove the basis of trade unionism but it did result in its suppression because an important sufficient condition was removed. An organization which expands as a result of pressures from its environment may react back on it through intensifying its impact and through this create repercussions which impose further organizational changes. It moves inevitably from crisis to crisis. The organization is forced willy-nilly to accept changes; the environment is forced to impose new conditions; the changes produce further conditions and so it goes on in a never-ending, unbroken process.

Structural social change

The pressures produced by contradictions in the structures of social situations and their environments are inevitably and invariably present in social reality, and they create all the consequences which have been described as adjustment and change. The category of social change showed that these pressures could alter a social situation to such an extent that they created a qualitative change in its social relationships. Once the existence of such pressures is admitted it must also be admitted that the alterations could proceed to the point where the phenomenon is itself altered qualitatively, that is where it ceases in all essentials to be what it was previously. This possibility was referred to in chapter 7 as involving a complete transformation process, an alteration in the essential qualities and primary preconditions of social situations. Its acceptance is a matter both of simple scientific caution and of taking cognizance of the reality of social situations.

Structural social change involves qualitative change in its first meaning and, in the terminology used in previous chapters, refers to alterations in necessary conditions. It is confirmation of the belief that everything is temporary and transient. The structure of a situation comprises the necessary conditions for that situation and consists, therefore, of the factors and relationships without which the situation as it is would not exist. The structure of trade unionism, for example, is the buying and selling of labour power, and this implies the existence of a free market for labour power. Without this market there can be no trade unionism. A situation can have only one structure; if that alters the situation also must alter. If the means of distributing and controlling labour power is altered to that of age and sex categories within a kinship system or to social obligations within a feudal framework then the structural basis of trade unionism would be destroyed. Forms of protest might occur under the alternative means but they would not constitute trade unionism.

No two structures can give rise to the same situation unless they too are the same. Similarly, no two situations can be alike, no matter how closely they *appear* to resemble each other, unless they have identical structures. Take for example the case of Western capitalist and Soviet trade unions which are frequently compared. There is a close similarity between the visible organizational forms of unions in these countries. They have mass membership bases, hierarchical control mechanisms, representative policy-making bodies and similar general aims. They are called trade unions in both countries and at various times they have joined in united action. However a common view of Soviet unions in the West is that they are a perversion of the real thing because they adopt productionist policies, identify themselves with government policies and generally collaborate in the implementation of those policies. It is claimed that by these methods they cannot represent the interests of their members. This interpretation neglects the essential structural differences between the two trade union movements. The organizations are not comparable, for the social relations of production which provide their structures differ between the countries. It is as unlikely that British unions should become consistently productionist as it is that Soviet unions should adopt the consumptionist approach of British unions.

The test of whether a change has been qualitative or not can only be made through an analysis of the dialectical relationship between structure and superstructure. It cannot be made phenomenologically. Not only do similar appearances mislead, as in the case of Western and Soviet unions and bureaucratic organizations in general, but dissimilar appearances also mislead. Much of the discussion in the previous section concerned the misleading conclusions about the nature of capitalist societies which have been drawn from apparent changes in those societies. The fact that a situation looks different now compared with its appearance earlier may indicate nothing more than that there have been some superstructural adaptations. Nothing of any significance can be said about the situation until its structure has been identified; if that structure persists then the essential activities of its superstructure will continue irrespective of appearances. It is either wishful thinking or mere propaganda to talk about class conflict ceasing to exist in a society with unchanged capitalist relations of production, to intimate that trade unions have become functionless while the free market mechanism persists, or to state that control of industry can be transferred to or shared with employees while the private ownership of the means of production remains dominant. The whole of the previous two chapters has been directed at an analytical understanding of this point. But there has been an abundance of empirical evidence to support it. The persistence of capitalist relations of production has meant an equal persistence of trade unionism to survive despite innumerable employers' and governmental attempts to suppress it by the use of physical force or ideology. Indeed it is clear that the realm of political possibility depends in the first instance on an analysis of structures. What can and what cannot be achieved by decision-making can only be clarified once the structures are known.

Two main questions remain to be discussed in a clarification of structural social change. The first concerns the manner through which a change in structure is affected and the second is about the effect of structural change on visible social relationships. The first question is a highly politically charged one; it has evoked many answers which, understandably, have been formulated largely in political terms. The discussions, in other words, have been about revolutionary change. The intention here is to focus attention on the general phenomenon of structural change in a multiplicity of situations.

Given and within the conceptual framework used in this book the examination of structural change is an empirical task. It involves looking at actual situations, identifying structures and superstructures, isolating contradictions and repercussion effects which flow from them. The conceptual approach throws some light on the process of change itself but without ever allowing the process to be timed, the climax to be anticipated and its parts named.

The possibility of qualitative change occurring exists in all situations. This follows from the assumption of perpetual pressures for movement which has been made. It has to be accepted that growth through straightforward addition might alter a structure. There is, moreover, the possibility that the pressures themselves might transform structures. However, while qualitative change is a possibility, the process through which it occurs is a permanent feature of reality. Unfortunately, an examination of the process does not help much in identifying either the fact of change or the manner of its achievement because the process does not lead in a linear fashion to change. The intensity and progress varies over time and between situations and produces the kind of uncertainty which was referred to in the discussion about the prediction. This problem of identification is made more difficult because in the course of the process it is not the structure but the structure's superstructure which is being changed. Superstructural changes, or changes in visible social relations, are not reliable guides for indicating changes in structures. A close watch on what is happening to what can be seen might produce deceptive results. The two points made here are related. The process is unpredictable and in so far as it is visible it is an unreliable guide.

Qualitative change can occur, of course, only when the structure of a situation alters. As the structure comprises the necessary conditions of a situation it is not an evolving phenomenon. Once it alters, then the situation is qualitatively different from its previous state. The structure is a defined part of a situation which remains unchanged while its superstructure alters until such time as the altered superstructure is inconsistent with an unaltered structure. This arises because a structure is not a thing but the essential element of that thing. Take for example the structure of trade unionism, the buying and selling of labour power. It could be said, correctly, that a free labour market comprises the structure of trade unionism because the buying and selling takes place through it. Labour markets, however, have changed considerably over time. Crafts have become diluted or discarded; unskilled and semiskilled workers have multiplied, only to have their work encroached on or taken over by machines operated by technicians and engineers. Increases in the scale of production have brought corresponding increases in administration, and therefore in administrators. Changes in the means of acquiring and disposing of labour power have also occurred. They have become more institutionalized through the use of government employment agencies, commercial employment agencies and commercial selection bodies. A close scrutiny of labour markets would reveal remarkable and seemingly profound changes without their ever ceasing to be free labour markets. A similar picture would emerge from an examination of commodity markets over time. The composition of the markets and the means of acquiring and disposing of commodities have altered, but nonetheless they remain markets which use the price mechanism.

In order to understand this seemingly paradoxical situation where changing superstructures have apparently unchanging structures it is necessary to recall the causal relationship between structure and superstructure and remember that this relationship occurs over varied and indeterminate time spans. The structure is causally superior to its superstructure, which it moulds and alters through its contradictions. The superstructure is continually under pressure to change and as it does so it is, in effect, attempting to accommodate itself to a changing environment without altering its structure. In other words superstructural change is a means of survival in a general dynamic situation. There is no immediate reason why superstructures should affect structures.

A superstructure, however, is a visible part of a situation. It includes people in social relationships and whenever a change in it occurs, whether it be a business organization, a voluntary society, a family or a community, the social relationships are upset and have to be readjusted. The upsetting and readjusting are achieved through decisions by people who make them in the context of the dominant ideology, which supports limited and particular changes in a generally stable framework. For this reason people in the main accept upsets and the consequent readjustments in their milieux as an inevitable part of it. That is, they do not attribute causes to structural factors, and in any event generally do not wish to do much about them. This is the way the dominant ideology works in every situation, no matter how minute it is. The key to the transformation is the manner in which the situation is perceived by those in it. A structure can never destroy itself simply through the action of its own contradictions; it can only be destroyed through decisions taken to that effect. When the contradictions in the structure have such an impact on social relationships that a crisis is generated so that people involved look to the alternative ideology for an explanation, and when through that they both locate the source of what is happening to them in the structure and feel impelled to change it, then decisions to alter the structure will be made. Only at this stage can the dialectical relationship between structure and superstructure be seen in its completeness. People with different interests in the situation may feel the impact of a crisis differently and may, in consequence, have different motives in wanting the structure altered. This does not matter so long as there is a coincidence of intentions to alter the structure. Apart from the actual intensity of the crisis and its differential impact on people, the important thing is the relative pervasiveness of the competing ideologies. If there is no alternative explanation which directs attention to structural causes and thereby encourages qualitative change, then no matter how intense the crisis in social relationships the people involved will not know how to cope with it, will be able to conceive of no alternative, and will flounder in their search for a resolution, because they will always be looking at factors which are causally insignificant.

The explanation of qualitative change given above does not exclude other explanations as long as the perpetual possibility of qualitative change is accepted. A most likely other explanation is qualitative change through growth. But it is difficult to see how this comes about given the way in which structure has been defined. It has already been shown that trade unions and business organizations have remained structurally unchanged despite considerable growth. An evolutionary change in structure has to be ruled out as inconsistent with the definition of structure, so if growth can produce qualitative change it must occur at a particular stage when decisions to expand further are tantamount to decisions to alter a structure. It might be possible to see this happening in the growth from village to town. In such a case structural change would not occur imperceptibly but at some point, dramatic for the situation though unknown to the decision-makers.

The second question is equally problematical. It has been raised already in chapters 8 and 9. It is discussed here in order to clarify our understanding of the relationship between structural change and visible social relationships. It is important to know what structural change can be expected to achieve. When there is a deep dissatisfaction with a superstructure, is it enough just to alter the structure? Is it safe to assume that a new structure will give rise to a wholly new set of social relationships? It might be concluded from the chapters on structure and superstructure that that indeed is what would happen. But there the question of structural change was not raised. In those chapters the relationship between structure and superstructure was examined in a relatively static form and showed that at any given moment every structure has a superstructure which is consistent with it, and vice versa. It cannot be concluded from that analysis, however, that a new structure will produce its own super-structure. A new structure simply provides the necessary conditions for a different superstructure. Whether those necessary conditions visibly influence social behaviour will depend upon the presence of other, sufficient, conditions.

There is no doubt that a structural change must invariably be associated with some changes in the visible social relations with which it is causally identified. Except for the rather hypothetical possibility of a structural change through growth, a structure will only be altered because of intense dissatisfaction with experienced social relationships. This dissatisfaction will arise through the disruption of social situations. In other words, the contradictions in the structure will act on the superstructure in such a way and with such intensity as to make it something which people want to reject for something different. It is experience of the superstructure which produces decisions to alter the structure. When a crisis in a superstructure occurs within an ideological climate which identifies structural contradic-tions as the source of the crisis, an attempt to alter the structure is likely to be made. The presence of dissatisfaction and disillusionment with existing social relationships, and a conscious desire to change them, are important sufficient conditions for structural change. It is obvious that structural and superstructural changes go together. This merely confirms the analytical point made earlier that when the necessary conditions for a social situation alter, the situation must also alter. The question of the precise relationship between structural and superstructural change, however, remains to be discussed.

A spontaneous reaction to a structural change would mean that an im-mediate expression of the new structure was produced in visible social relationships. As there cannot be any provision for timelags in this analysis, because the determinants of a situation must always be consistent with the situation itself, structural change must possess this quality of spontaneity. It is illogical to conceive of the necessary conditions for a situation changing without reflecting comparable changes in the situation itself. If those changes do not occur it must follow that the necessary conditions have changed only to an extent consistent with changes in the situation. In other words the relationship between structure and super-structure must be viewed dialectically and not mechanically. This is what was meant above when the point was made that the fulfilment of a structural change depended on conditions in the situation which were sufficient for its fulfilment. Those conditions react on the structure and influence its transformation. Another way of putting it is that every social situation is comprised of variables in contradiction with each other and therefore causally related. Those of the variables which comprise the necessary conditions are more significant than others which make up the sufficient conditions, but none has any autonomy in that it can operate independently of the intensity and quality of the others.

The relationship between necessary and sufficient conditions in structural change can be seen clearly in the revolutionary experiences of capitalist countries in the twentieth century. The structure of a capitalist society comprises the mode of production, one vital element of which is the ownership and control of the means of production. In so far as people within the society are concerned the structural element most crucial to them is the control of the means of production. Ownership is relevant only so far as it gives access to control. When a crisis likely to lead to structural change occurs it does so because the non-owners, the sellers of labour power, regard their position as intolerable and see the concentration of control in the hands of a minority of private persons as the main cause. The primary initial concern of employees in the crisis is to acquire control over the means of production in their respective milieux. This involves taking over factories, offices, shops, and local decision-making centres. A pure transformation of a capitalist society is one where people directly control the distribution and utilization of their own labour power. It would involve a rather simple form of workers' control where no one sells and, therefore no one buys, labour power, and where workers in various kinds of collectivities make all the decisions relating to production and, in consequence, their own labour power. It would also involve the complete rejection of the superstructural expression of the old structure, namely, the hierarchical authority structure and the social division of labour; indeed all inequalities between types of labour power and between labour power in different situations, such as town and country, which have arisen to serve the capitalist mode of production.

Now a pure and complete transformation can only occur if the conditions are present to support it. Initial action in most attempts to alter the structure of capitalist societies has taken the form of uncoordinated largely spontaneous movements by workers to control their own work and social situations. This was an essential but elementary prelude to a complete superstructural expression of a structural transformation. The October 1917 revolution in Russia was characterized by workers taking over their factories and establishing Soviets to run their own immediate political affairs. This state of affairs was recognized by the Soviet government on 14 November 1917, when it passed a decree for workers' control in industry and legalized the intervention of workers in the management of the factories. Victor Serge wrote that

The liquidation of the political defence of their capitalist exploiters launched a spontaneous movement among the workers to take over the means of production. Since they were perfectly able to take control of the factories and workshops why should they abstain? If they could, they ought. The employers' sabotage of production entailed expropriation as an act of reprisal. When the boss brought work to a halt, the workers themselves, on their own responsibility, got the establishment going again.[41]

The 1905 Russian revolution had given rise to workers' committees and Soviets. The famous St Petersburg Soviet was formed at that time. The situation in Germany in November 1918 resembled the Russian experience in that numerous spontaneous and uncoordinated workers' committees and Soviets were formed throughout the country. Towns and states over a large part of Germany were controlled by workers by the end of 1918.[42] As in Russia the issue of ownership was settled through the ability of workers, aided and sometimes led by sailors and soldiers, to acquire control of the means of production in their own particular setting. Other revolutions from the Paris Commune to the Chinese one, whether eventually successful or not, have shown similar initial characteristics. Workers have endeavoured to transform the structures of their own situations by acquiring control of their own immediate environments.

In some instances, as in Germany in 1919, the sufficient conditions for the success of the revolutions themselves were absent. Nothing is to be gained by asking about the fulfilment and perpetuation of the structural transformation process in those cases. The question does arise, however, where the common ownership of the means of production was achieved and maintained. The structural changes occurred through and within the context of a revolution and its aftermath. In revolutionary situations there are common and predictable characteristics: a breakdown of central government, a disintegration of the authority of the police and armed forces, intense economic and social dislocation, attempts at counter-revolution and, possibly, foreign intervention. A common description would be general political instability in a situation of economic and social disorder. This undoubtedly fitted the situation in the Soviet Union in 1918. The attempts to maintain and carry through a structural transformation must be examined in that context. Such was the intensity of the crisis and of subsequent crises in the Soviet Union that questions concerning additional superstructural transformations involving untried forms of organizational activity were either shelved or not raised. In crises there is a tendency to resort to known methods, and in the Soviet Union this meant perpetuating the division of labour, the methods of production and organization of production — which had belonged to the capitalist mode of production.[43] The adoption of the New Economic Policy in 1921 went even further than this. As for the spontaneous growth of workers' committees and Soviets, these in the first instance filled a political vacuum caused by the disintegration of central governmental power but later revealed qualities which were inconsistent with their own survival, given the crisis conditions. Victor Serge wrote that:

This conquest of the enterprises by the factory and works committees had its risks. Each committee in the first place thought of the interests of its own enterprise (i.e. the workers it represented); from this it was an easy step to defending this interest by every means in its power, without any concern for the general economic interests of the country. Every enterprise, even though it might be backward, ill-equipped or dealing with a relatively inessential industry, demanded its own right to life, that is to re-stocking, to credit, to work. The consequence was an extraordinary mess, with the factories operating anarchically, each for its own benefit. [44]

In the interests of economic survival more authoritarian methods of control were introduced.

There were, however, other factors in the Soviet situation than political instability and economic crises which influenced the manner and extent of superstructural transformations. The crises which led to the revolution did not, and could not, destroy all institutional expressions of the old structure. The perpetuation of institutions through the revolution resulted in the preservation of attitudes which were inconsistent with it. Trade unions with consumptionist policies, for example, survived the revolution. Serge recounts that

the trade unions, even though apparently fitted to play a capital role in situations of this description, were totally overtaken by events. Too often they were run by Mensheviks, SRs or pure trade unionists. Their Central Council was paralysed by factional battles. The leaderships of the railwaymen's and post office unions were anti-Bolschevik. Other unions were often more interested in getting out of the mess than in serving the general interests of the working class. . . . The backward attitude of various sections of workers was all too evident. Sometimes it was a matter of trade unions founding co-operative shops which came all too close, inevitably, to speculating in the midst of famine. Sometimes deplorable conflicts resulted from the pursuit of immediate demands in an irrationally sectional spirit. The revolution is over, let's have double wages! Now is the time for everybody to get easy money! Similarly in the field of requisitions and expropriations, there were strong anarchistic tendencies, in which workers would exploit a factory they occupied purely for their own benefit or confiscate the first food train which went through the station nearest to them. . . . When factories closed down, the Mensheviks demanded payment of wages in advance. The Mensheviks in the chemical workers' union at Petrograd demanded exceptionally high wage rates, hinting as a bargaining ploy that they controlled large quantities of explosives. At the height of the battle of the barricades, Moscow almost ran out of bread, as the loaders in the flour mills, who cared nothing for the revolution, were out on strike for a wage increase.[45]

These were doubtless but a few of many illustrations of the existence of attitudes, which tempered and influenced the structural change. As attitudes do not exist in a vacuum but survive only in so far as they have institutional backing, it can be said that the greater the ability of institutions to survive through a process of structural change the more difficult it will be to obtain a complete superstructural reflection of that change and, in consequence, the less complete the structural change itself will be. In this respect even revolutionary organizations themselves must be suspect in so far as they were formed and matured in a pre-revolutionary society.

A further factor with modifying qualities is the ideological expression of structural change which precedes it for this determines what people expect of a structural change and what, in consequence, they will endeavour to create. There may, of course, be no ideological expression or it may be imprecisely expressed but in so far as structural change occurs through the decisions of people who have become disillusioned with an existing social situation, it is likely that at least they will have thought of an alternative. This has certainly been the case at the level of societal change. The point is that, if in the process of change events do not accord with what the participants anticipate should happen then steps may be taken to modify the events. This was obviously a factor in the Soviet Union in 1918. Members of the Bolshevik Party in 1917 entered the revolution with a broad conception of the kind of society they wanted to put in the place of Tsarist Russia and this did not correspond with what many saw emerging in the early days. As one participant noted:

We were building, not a Soviet Republic, but a republic of working-class communities based on the capitalist factories and mills. Instead of a strict ordering of production and social distribution, instead of measures towards the Socialist organization of society, the existing state of affairs reminded one of the autonomous communes of producers that the anarchists had dreamed of.[46]

Nationalization measures and central coordinating and planning institutions were much more a part of the pre-revolutionary ideological construct of a socialist society than the growth of workers' committees. As the Bolsheviks attempted to realize their conception of a socialist society, within the constraints imposed by the needs of the existing transitional situation, so the character of the structural change was influenced and altered.

The relationship between necessary and sufficient conditions in the process of structural change has so far been largely illustrated by examples from the Russian Revolution. It could equally well be illuminated by the experiences of any country where a socialist revolution has occurred. Structural change in China, for example, took place within a different historical and environmental context from that of the Soviet Union. The sufficient conditions were markedly different, therefore the superstructural outcome was also different. The emergence and consolidation of the commune both as a means of control and for organizing production is a direct consequence of the attempt to transform the quality of the relations of production within a particular and unique set of conditions.

Some of the special characteristics of the Chinese Revolution can be noted. First, in 1949 China there was not the almost total disintegration of government control and industrial production as there was in 1917 Russia. The revolution did not occur through a simultaneous overdetermination of contradictions but was the culmination of thirty years of revolutionary struggle. During that time an increasing area of land was brought under Communist control so that by 1949 virtually the whole of North China and sections of other regions had had experience of applying land reform measures and new forms of political control. The fact that a revolutionary war was being waged virtually continuously meant that a centralized authority was difficult to apply, thus leaving a large degree of autonomy to the villages and towns. This autonomy was facilitated by the near self-sufficiency of the peasants and by the fact that land reform in the first instance involved simple measures such as land and property confiscation and redistribution.

Structural change occurred within some constraints similar to those in the Soviet Union. The Communist Party was a national political institution with common rules and methods. It possessed a common ideological framework through which it perceived post-revolutionary Chinese society. It laid down some guides, therefore, for subsequent superstructural developments and in so far as it was able to influence events these guides altered the direct consequences of structural change. For example, as land reform was achieved the Communist Party endeavoured to establish the pyramid of People's Congress, starting at the village level, with three other levels and with delegates to each higher level being chosen by the delegates on the one below, thus reversing China's traditional hierarchical rule. By the end of the revolution in 1949 this type of political institution was well established in North China and in some Liberated Areas it dated back as far as 1927. Poor Peasants' Leagues and Women's Associations were formed to represent the interests of particular oppressed groups and under the guidance of the Communist Party they assisted with the task of expropriating the land and possessions of the landlords and rich peasants. Once the process of expropriation began the inclination of many poor peasants was towards complete and extreme levelling without regard to the production and military needs of the time. The intervention of the Communist Party moderated this inclination. William Hinton wrote:

Without the Communist Party the poor peasants might well have divided everything right down to the last bowls and chopsticks on the farmsteads and the last gears and shafts in the factories and in so doing would have destroyed the only productive base on which they had to build.[47]

But once a redistribution had taken place the task of reorganizing production was one for the villagers. They did it under conditions which facilitated decentralized peasant control of production. The situation in this respect was the reverse of that in the Soviet Union. The Chinese peasants moved through experimentation and adaptation from mutual aid groups designed to swap labour in production through cooperatives to communes, which tended to combine political and economic functions. The particular conditions which reacted on the process of structural change in China have been graphically described by William Hinton in his book *Fanshen*.

The process of structural change which is revealed through attempts to alter societies is a process writ large. The variables are enlarged and emphasized and the contradictions and conflicts are given prominence because the transformation concerns the dominant skills in the society and, therefore, its power relations. The issues may concern the life or death of some, and will have consequences for the manner of living for all. These factors differentiate structural transformations in the social relations of production from those in all other social situations. After that the differences cease. Structural transformations can and do occur at all levels and in all aspects of social situations. The methods of analysis are the same in all cases. Only the details of the situations themselves vary.

Notes

1. A. W. Gouldner, *The Coming Crisis of Western Sociology*, Heinemann, 1970; R. W. Friedrichs, *A Sociology of Sociology*, The Free Press of Glencoe, Illinois, 1970.

2. Gramschi, *The Prison Notebooks*, p. 426.
3. Engels, *Anti-Duhring*, pp. 159–60.
4. *Ibid.*, p. 161.
5. Lenin, *Collected Works*, i, 165.
6. *Ibid.*, i, 164.
7. Henri Lefebvre, *The Sociology of Marx*, Allen Lane, The Penguin Press, 1969.
8. Quoted by I. Meszaros in *Lukács' Concept of Dialectic*, Merlin Press Ltd., London, p. 62.
9. Lefebvre, *op. cit.*, p. 20.
10. Quoted by Meszaros in *Lukács' Concept of Dialectic*, pp. 63–4.
11. Althusser, *For Marx*, pp. 198–9.
12. Marx, *Capital* (Moscow, 1957), ii, 316.
13. See for example studies for the United Kingdom, such as: Thomas Stark, *The Distribution of Personal Income in the United Kingdom, 1949–63*, Cambridge University Press, 1972; A. B. Atkinson, *Unequal Shares: wealth in Britain*, Allen Lane, The Penguin Press, 1972; H. A. Turner, Dudley Jackson and Frank Wilkinson, *Do Trade Unions Cause Inflation?*, Univ. of Cambridge, Dept. of Applied Economics, 1972; Andrew Glyn and Bob Sutcliffe, 'Inequality today', *Labour Research*, January 1972; and *British Capitalism, Workers and the Profit Squeeze*, Penguin, 1972. A number of earlier studies make the same points.
14. See in particular, R. Titmuss, *Income Distribution and Social Change*, Allen & Unwin, 1962.
15. *Labour Research*, January 1972.
16. Atkinson, *op. cit.*
17. Glyn and Sutcliff, *British Capitalism*, ch. 3ff.
18. Maurice Godelier, 'System, structure and contradiction in Capital', *The Socialist Register*, London, 1967, p. 105.
19. Mao Tse Tung, 'On contradiction', *Selected Works*, People's Publishing House, Peking, 1960, i, 318.
20. *Ibid.*, i, 316.
21. *Ibid.*
22. On the question of pluralism see pp. 49–51.
23. Althusser, *For Marx*, p. 114.
24. Wright Mills, *The Sociological Imagination*, p. 113.
25. *Ibid.*, pp. 113–14.
26. James Burnham, *The Managerial Revolution*, Putnam, 1941, pp. 63–4.
27. *Ibid.*, pp. 64, 65.
28. Peter Drucker, *The New Society*, Heinemann, 1951, chapter 1.

29. *Ibid.*, p. 18.

30. *Ibid.*, pp. 15—16.

31. *Ibid.*, p. 17.

32. Dahrendorf, *Class and Class Conflict in an Industrial Society.*

33. *Ibid.*, pp. 41—71. See also C. A. R. Crosland, *The Future of Socialism*, Cape, 1957. Crosland considered that the salient features of capitalism — the decentralization of economic decision-making, intense and unfettered class antagonism and the like no longer existed, therefore capitalism had ceased to exist.

34. J. H. Goldthorpe, David Lockwood; Frank Bechhofer and Jennifer Platt, *The Affluent Worker in the Class Structure*, Cambridge University Press, 1969, p. 6. (This three-volume series includes also *The Affluent Worker: industrial attitudes and behaviour*, 1968, and *The Affluent Worker: political attitudes and behaviour*. The purpose of the series was to test the 'embourgeoisement' thesis.)

35. *Ibid.*, p. 8.

36. *Ibid.*, p. 165.

37. J. A. Banks, *Marxist Sociology in Action*, Faber & Faber, 1970, p. 179.

38. *Ibid.*, pp. 205, 301.

39. *Ibid.*, pp. 205, 181.

40. *Department of Employment Gazette*, November 1973, p. 1147.

41. Victor Serge, *Year One of the Russian Revolution*, Allen Lane, The Penguin Press, 1972, p. 137.

42. A. J. Ryder, *The German Revolution of 1918*, Cambridge University Press, 1967, ch. 7. Ryder lists the towns and states which came under the control of workers.

43. See E. H. Carr, *The Bolshevik Revolution, 1917—1923*, Macmillan, 1960, vol. ii, for a description of the crises and the measures devised to counter them.

44. Serge, *op. cit.*, p. 235.

45. *Ibid.*, p. 138.

46. Quoted in Serge, *op. cit.*, p. 235.

47. William Hinton, *Fanshen: a documentary of revolution in a Chinese village*, Monthly Review Press, New York, 1966, p. 605.

Index

capitalism – *continued*
  contradictions in, 233, 235–6,
    241–3, 245–7, 255–64
  and conventional sociology, 73, 189
  crisis in, 55, 56
  criticism of, 33
  dynamics of, 72–3, 180–1
  future development of, 279
  ideology of, 231, 242
  mode of production in, 204
  relations of production in, *see* social
    relations of production
  revolutionary experience of, 296
  role of religion in, 231
  supersedence of, 284–7
  theory of, 39
  and trade unionism, 206–7
capitalism, structure of, 53–4
  and liberal sociology, 26–8
case study method, 79–81
Castro, Fidel, 180
causality, causal analysis
  in problem-centred research, 78–9
  in small-group research, 97
  in sociological theory, 191
  and structure, 197, 198, 200
  and totality, 253
Chamberlin, E. H., 46, 47
change, *see* movement; social change
Chinese Revolution, 300–1
Chomsky, Noam, 197
Cicourel, Aaron, 11–13, 15
class conflict, 81, 199, 204, 238, 270,
  286
class consciousness, 227
class division, class structures, 10, 33,
  54, 204–5, 213, 218, 235–6
classlessness, thesis of emerging, 285
'clinical' approach, 77–8, 80
coercion model, 106–7
coercive compliance, 155
coercive power, 152, 156, 158
cognitive powers, limited, 136, 141, 144,
  145
cold war period, 49
collective action, *see* trade unions; trade
  unionism
collective bargaining, 286
collectivism, 237–40; *see also* trade
  unionism
  voluntary, 286–7
colonialist societies, 23
commonsense constructs, 9–10, 13, 38,
  40, 43, 44, 53
  refutation of, 54, 56
common value system, 17

communes, 300, 301
communications system, 141–2
  problems of, 187
Communist parties, 241, 300–1
compensatory mechanism, 107
competition, 22, 256–7
competitive economy, 99
compliance, 119, 151, 163
  attitudes of lower participants, 158
  control by higher participants, 152–3,
    156
  identification of lower participants,
    155–8
  responses of lower participants,
    153–4
compliance relationships, 154–5
compromise, 54
conceptual frameworks, 15–20, 42–3;
  see also dialectical frame of
  reference; static conceptual frameworks
  adaptations of, 47–51, 90
  alternative, 39, 55, 62
  dominant, 28, 40, 44
  dynamic, *see* dialectical frame of
    reference
  in empiricism, 79–80
  problems in, 51–2
  and reality, 170–2
  of sociological phenomenology, 41
conflict, 48–50, 286; *see also* class
  conflict; industrial conflict
  and change, 105–8
  and communications, 141
  in goals, 140
  and Human Relations school, 163
  in organizations, 83, 89, 94, 96,
    286
  social functions of, 163
  structuralist approach to, 162–5
conflict analysis, 106
consciousness, 224–7
  autonomy of, 226
  change of, 243
  and dominant ideology, 234, 271
  false, 225–7
consensus infringements, 19–20, 26; *see*
  also aberrations
consensus systems, 40, 50, 222; *see also*
  organic unity
  and conflict, 49
  and consciousness, 225
  and empiricism, 80–1
  impediments to, 42–3
  organizations as, 174
  and totality, 253

dominant ideology – *continued*
  and problem-centred research, 74–5
  and skills, 219
domination, 94
  forms of, 123–4
  theory of, 221
Drucker, Peter, 284, 286
dynamic conceptual approach, *see*
  dialectical frame of reference
dysfunctions, 47–8, 89, 103–5

economic factors
  in materialism, 192–4, 203, 205
  in structures, 202–5, 265
economic structure
  and materialism, 192–3
  and mode of production, 203–4
economic theory
  in Britain, 72, 73
  development of, 46–7
  free market system models, 115–16
  and functional analysis, 99
  Keynesian, 72
  and organization theory, 120
  and puzzle-solving, 51
  and sociology, 73, 116
  in Weber's milieu, 114–15
economic transactions, *see* market
  behaviour
education, and skill, 218
educational system, 24
efficiency, 78, 98, 274
  of free private enterprise, 118,
    119
  and satisfaction, 160, 162
  and skill, 214
elites, 156, 227
empirical testing, 82–3
  of sufficient conditions, 206
  of theories, 74, 146–7
empiricism, 11, 69–86
  in Britain, 69–73
  and causality, 78–81, 191, 254
  and facts, 7
  forms of, 74–8
  mathematical techniques in, 85–6
  meaning of, 73–4
  and movement, 180
  and natural sciences, 85
  and organizational analysis, 81–4,
    146–7
  and phenomenological analysis, 14
  as static in conception, 81
  theoretical approach of, 3–4, 17, 42,
    73, 80
  trends in, 84–6

Engels, Friedrich, 55, 58–60
  and dialectics, 251–2
  and materialism, 190–1, 192–3
  and structure concept, 197–9 *passim*,
    203
'engineering' approach, 77–8, 80, 278
environment
  change of, 143–4
  components of, 212–13
  and organizations, 143–5, 164,
    183–4, 213, 289–90
  and social relationships, 183
  and sufficient conditions, 206–7
equality, ideas of, 240
equilibrating mechanism, 135, 143, 173,
    244, 245
equilibrium analysis, 26, 50, 102
  and change, 17, 89, 175
  and conflict, 164
  and functional analysis, 108
equilibrium concept, 101–3, 173–4,
    176–7
'ethical neutrality', 22
ethnomethodology, 8, 9, 11, 12, 18
  in organization theory, 90
  and paradigms, 40–1
Etzioni, Amitai, 18, 31, 32–7, 42, 47,
    191
  and Marxism, 61
  and organizational analysis, 81–3
    passim, 89, 90, 95, 119, 122, 128,
    Ch. 6
  and small group research, 97
  and theory of bureaucracy, 98, 113
European Productivity Agency, 75

factors of production
  distribution of, 271
  in economic theory, 115
  mobility of, 127
  in scientific management, 92
factor theories, 106
family, 24
Feuerbach, Ludwig, 200
Follett, Mary Parker, 93–5, 98, 106
Ford, Henry, 180
Fox, Alan, 50
free labour market, 201, 208, 290
  changes in, 293
free market system, 115–16, 291
  contradictory elements in, 258–60,
    262–3
  excess productive capacity in, 256–8
  and rationality, 124–5
'free will', 6, 7
Friedrichs, R. W., 18, 32, 41, 48, 250

systems analysis, 4, 17, 41, 184
  authority and power in, 222
  and autonomy, 182
  and change, 104–5, 178, 180, 187
  dogmatism of, 187–8
  and empiricism, 73, 81–4
  and equilibrium maintenance, 103,
    174
  structure in, 195, 198
  and totality, 253

Tavistock Institute of Human Relations,
    77
Taylor, Frederick W., 91–2
technical superiority, of bureaucratic
    organization, 129–30
technological change, 276
technology
  and ideology, 229, 271
  and skill, 214–15
theory; see also social theory; syntheses
    of theories
  definition of, 89
  dominant, 39, 44, 53–5
  dynamic, 184–5
  formulation of, 227
  function of, 14–15
  in ideology, 23–5
  institutionalized, 24, 44–5
  middle-range, 184–5
  one-dimensional, 52
  political implications of, 188–90
  and practice, 4, 15, 21–2, 55, 73,
    170–1
  and reality, 27, 53–4
  rejection of dominant, 54–5
theory-building, 45–52, 227
theory displacement, 38–9, 45, 52–7
Thompson, Kenneth, 70
Thompson, William, 241
time and method study, 91
total ideology, 8
totality, 252
  and causality, 253, 254
  in dialectic materialism, 254
  and interconnections, 269–70, 277
  static, 253–4
trade unionism
  and capitalism, 291
  defects of, 273–4
  and employers, 208–9
  growth of, 236–41, 288
  and necessary conditions, 201–2, 208

  and non-manual workers, 226–7
  and political freedom, 207–8
  structure of, 290, 293
  and sufficient conditions, 206–8,
    288–9
  and trade unions, 206–7
trade unions, 74, 206, 286
  and dominant ideology, 245–6
  and environment, 288
  negative obstruction function in,
    273–4
  Soviet, 290–1, 298
  structural contradictions in, 288
  and technology, 257, 276
traditions, 275–6
training, and bureaucracy, 118, 128
Transport and General Workers' Union,
    288
typification, 13

unemployment, 26, 27, 72
  technological, 262
utilitarian compliance, 155, 159
utilitarianism, 71
utility functions, 85–6

value judgments, 7, 21, 150
voluntary collectivism, 286–7

wage-earning, 45
wage equalization, 240
wage rates, 257
Walsh, David, 40–1
wealth, transfer of, 261; see also capital
    accumulation; income and property
    distribution
Weber, Max
  authority system of, 92–3, 221
  and causality, 191
  and economics, 114–16
  theory of bureaucracy of, 72, 81, 98,
    100–1, Ch. 4, 132, 146
Wiese, L. von, 29
Wollstonecraft, Mary, 241
Woodward, Joan, 69
workers' consciousness, 69
workers' control, 296–7
workers' participation, 114, 291
work force, 92
working class, embourgeoisement of,
    285–6

Znaniecki, Florian, 7